LONGMAN STUDY GUIDE

GCSE

World History

Ed Rayner
Ron Stapley

LONGMAN

LONGMAN STUDY GUIDES

SERIES EDITORS Geoff Black and Stuart Wall

Titles available
Biology
Business Studies
Chemistry
Design and Technology
Economics
English
English Literature
French
Geography
German
Information Technology

Mathematics
Mathematics: Higher Level
Music
Physics
Psychology
Religious Studies
Science
Sociology
Spanish
World History

Addison Wesley Longman Ltd.,
Edinburgh Gate, Harlow,
Essex CM20 2JE, England
and Associated Companies throughout the World.

© **Addison Wesley Longman 1997**

First Published 1988
Second edition 1997

British Library Cataloguing-in-Publication Data
A catalogue record for this book is available from the British Library.

ISBN 0582–30545–4

Set by 35 in 9.75/12pt Sabon

Produced by Longman Singapore Publishers Pte
Printed in Singapore

CONTENTS

◢ EDITORS' PREFACE

Longman Study Guides have been written by the people who set and mark the exams – the examiners. Examiners are aware that, due to lack of practice and poor preparation, some students achieve only the lowest grades: they are not able to effectively show the examiner what they know. These books give excellent advice about exam practice and preparation, and organizing a structured revision programme, all of which are essential for examination success. Remember: the examiners are looking for opportunities to *give* you marks, not take them away!

Longman Study Guides are designed to be used throughout the course. The self-contained chapters can be read in any order appropriate to the stage you have reached in your course. The examiner guides you through the essential parts of each topic, making helpful comments throughout.

We believe that this book, and the series as a whole, will help you establish and build your basic knowledge and examination technique skills. For additional help with exam practice and revision techniques, we have published a series called **Longman Exam Kits**, which are available from all good bookshops, or direct from Addison Wesley Longman.

GEOFF BLACK AND STUART WALL

◢ ACKNOWLEDGEMENTS

We are grateful to the following for permission to reproduce copyright material:

The Associated Press for Figure 17.2; B.T. Batsford Ltd. for Figure 9.1; Collection: International Institute of Social History, Amsterdam for Figure 10.1; Les Gibbard for Figure 18.1; Heinemann Publishers for Figures 17.1 and 19.1 taken from *Map History of the Modern World* by Brian Catchpole; Hulton Getty Picture Collection Ltd. for Figure 12.1; Mirror Group Ltd. for Figures 19.2 and 20.1; Punch Ltd. for Figures 3.1 and 14.1.

Whilst every effort has been made to trace the owners of the copyright material we take this opportunity to offer our apologies to any copyright holders whose rights we may have unwittingly infringed. Unfortunately, we were unable to trace the copyright holders for Figures 6.1, 14.2, 19.3 and Table 10.1.

The GCSE in History

▷ THE AIM OF THE BOOK

This book is intended to help those studying World History for the General Certificate of Secondary Education. No book can provide you with instant success. For success you will need to devote several hours a week to concentrated study throughout the course. This book will help you to study to best advantage, but it cannot engage in discussion with you; therefore it is important to follow the guidance of your teacher and to exchange ideas with your fellow students.

If you are a private candidate studying for the examination without the benefit of contact with fellow students – even without a teacher – you will find things even more difficult. You will have no one to measure yourself against; you will have to set your own pace and you will only have books to turn to for guidance. We have therefore written this book in the hope that it will be useful to you in your self-imposed task.

WHAT YOU NEED TO KNOW

▷ **GCSE aims and requirements**

The introduction of the National Curriculum and the detailed Key Stages 1–3 in History have led all the examining boards to modify their GCSE syllabuses with effect from the examinations of 1998. The National Curriculum provides for a greater emphasis on British History and, as this is reflected in most of the new syllabuses, British History chapters have been incorporated in this book.

GCSE represented at first a move away from rote-learning and concentration on historical argument and discussion. Although this was never intended to undervalue the acquisition of knowledge, there was a danger that the new approach would encourage snap judgements and ill-informed opinion. So the National Curriculum and the revised GCSE syllabuses do stress the need for learning and understanding, with the obvious corollary that it is impossible to discuss History effectively without knowing any.

GCSE also aimed to encourage a 'feel' for the past. Students were to be encouraged to think themselves into past situations and to identify themselves with the people of the past. This 'feel' or 'empathy' can be achieved in its widest context through architecture, the arts (e.g. painting) and realistic historical reconstruction, but tended in GCSE to be confined to a narrower view in which empathy was expressed through the variety of feelings shown at the time towards some particular historical event or person. An empathetic presentation is a useful historical skill, but from 1998 it will no longer be so rigidly prescribed.

The common aims of the 1998 syllabuses are derived from the National Curriculum. They aim to give students opportunities to:

1. acquire knowledge and understanding of the human past;
2. investigate historical events, people, changes and issues;
3. develop understanding of how the past has been represented and interpreted;
4. use historical sources critically in their historical context;
5. draw conclusions and appreciate that these and other historical conclusions are liable to reassessment in the light of new or reinterpreted evidence.

Thus 1 requires students to know some History; 2 invites an empathetic approach and an understanding of cause, continuity and change; 3 (interpretations) requires a study of differing historical interpretations of the past; 4 requires a critical study of sources; and 5 requires the making of historical judgements and a recognition that such judgements cannot be infallible.

The aims of the syllabuses cannot easily be equated with how they are to be tested. So to achieve the aims, you, the student, will need to be able to develop a number of historical skills deriving from them. Thus all GCSE candidates in History will be tested under a set of assessment objectives designed to cover the precise requirements of the examinations.

> **Objective 1** To recall, select, organize and deploy historical knowledge.
> **Objective 2** To describe, explain and analyse the events, changes and issues studied, and to describe, explain and analyse the key features and characteristics of periods, societies and events.
> **Objective 3** To comprehend, interpret, evaluate and use a range of sources of information in their historical context. To comprehend, analyse and evaluate representations and interpretations of events, people and issues in their historical context.

The three objectives cannot be rigidly separated, and in particular Objective 1 will overlap both Objectives 2 and 3.

Faulty English is self-penalizing and will make it more difficult for students to express their History coherently; so a separate allocation of 5 per cent of the marks is additionally awarded for spelling, punctuation and grammar.

How candidates can develop these skills effectively will be discussed later in this chapter and, in relation to specific topics, in subsequent chapters. But before you can develop skills a syllabus has to be chosen, and this is likely to be done by your teacher or your school rather than by you. Each of the boards has one syllabus relating to the twentieth century. Two papers are normally required in which you will be tested in ways that vary between the boards. All boards use short answer questions in which the required answers may be no more than two or three sentences in length, and essay questions in which extended writing of several paragraphs is required. Essay questions are usually structured, i.e. divided up into two or more subsections. All boards require you to answer evidence-based questions, and all boards require coursework for which the mark allocation is 25 per cent of the mark for the whole examination. One board accepts a Paper 3 instead of coursework from external candidates, i.e. those studying on their own and not attending any kind of educational institution. All boards have a variety of topics with candidate choice, and do not expect you to have covered the whole of the syllabus. Some boards have Depth Studies which by definition require study in depth rather than superficial treatment. Chapter 2 gives the requirements of each board in more detail, and the table on page 10 shows how the most important topics are distributed between the boards.

▷ Preparing for the examination

Good preparation is absolutely essential to examination technique. Your preparation must be thorough in coverage, sound in depth and detail, and secure in accuracy. As the examination is largely skills based, the emphasis will be on analysis and judgement. But it would be a mistake to think that you can discuss and analyse history without using historical knowledge to substantiate and support your arguments. First you must learn what happened, and only then can you begin to tackle the basic questions of how and why it happened. No actor or musician would dare to perform in public without adequate rehearsal; similarly, no student can perform well in a public examination without adequate preparation. The commonest cause of examination nerves is going into the examination room knowing that you are ill-equipped to tackle the examination paper. To assist in your preparation, each of the requirements demanded of GCSE history candidates, as listed earlier in this chapter, will now be dealt with in turn.

The acquiring of historical knowledge

When you embark upon your course you will need a good textbook, a strong file for your notes, access to a good library and a firm commitment to study. If your teacher gives you class notes, try to become familiar with them as soon as possible afterwards while the teacher's explanation is fresh in your mind. *Understanding* what happened is vital to *learning* what happened, so seek out explanations from your teacher or your books when anything is obscure or unclear. Supplement your teacher's notes with additional material from your reading. If, as is more probable, you make your own notes under guidance, develop a good note-taking technique: use headings, subheadings and abbreviations. Make sure that you list all the main points rather than developing one or two of them in unnecessary detail. Memorable events should be listed rather than described: for example, in dealing with the circumstances of the March 1933 election in Germany, a preliminary description of the Reichstag fire would hardly be needed; an entry such as 'Reichstag fire (van der Lubbe, Nazi involvement??)' should recall for you the important facts, just as the question marks should remind you of the controversy concerning the extent both of van der Lubbe's and of the Nazis' involvement in the fire. If, when you revise, such a note makes no sense, then you should refresh your memory of it by looking it up in a textbook. But if you have developed a good note-taking technique, the incomprehensible note should be comparatively rare. Your notes will be the main source not only for factual knowledge, but also for causes, results, consequences and basic historical assessments. In the run-up to the examination, you will rely heavily on your notes. Only the genius can afford to dispense with note taking and note learning.

You should also take care not to generate too much in the way of note material, especially not multiple accounts of the same event as presented by different textbooks. Remember that the more care you take in the making of your notes, the more time and trouble you will save yourself when you come to use them. If they are pencilled in an illegible scrawl, they will be a distraction and an annoyance. Likewise it is no good supposing that, by carrying your notes about with you tucked under your arm, you will somehow absorb them. You will have to try to *learn* them. Each time you go through them, you make subsequent revisions more quickly and easily, until at your final revision you can get through them very rapidly indeed.

Once you have acquired a mastery of the facts, logic and reasoning can often help prevent the making of unnecessary errors. If, for instance, you were half-convinced that

Germany's Great Inflation began at the time of the Great Depression in 1929, a recollection that Stresemann tackled the Great Inflation effectively, and that he died in 1929 before the Great Depression began, might cause you to think again.

When you have mastered a considerable body of factual historical information, you will be able to develop all the historical skills required. Without historical knowledge, it would be like trying to make bricks without straw.

Investigating events, people, changes and issues

The process of acquiring knowledge will involve the study of events. You should make sure that in learning *what* happened, you also learn *how* and *why* an event occurred, and what were its *consequences*. Here you begin to move away from the facts into an area where ideas and arguments differ, and though you may well have lists of causes in your notes, the best way to develop the analytical skills required in this section is through the prepared essay, where the arguments based on the evidence can be brought together and presented in as convincing a manner as possible. Effective essay writing will lead naturally to effective coursework, which for most boards takes the form of extended prepared essays.

Your study of events will lead beyond mere historical narrative to the understanding of the causes and consequences of events, continuity and change, and similarity and difference. Lists of memorized *causes* can be no more than a starting point for an effective study, say, of the Russian revolutions of 1917. You will need to analyse the relative importance of the causes you select, if you are to have a real understanding of the revolutions. It would be absurd to claim (as candidates have done) that there were seventeen causes of the March revolution; someone else might produce only eight, but these might be more convincing because their relative importance has been brought out and they have been presented in a logical and coherent manner. 'Also' and 'then' are not convincing words to join your reasons together.

Consequences, too, require more than a disjointed list, haphazardly strung together with 'also'. Some consequences may well be more important than others, and, as with causes, it is important to distinguish between those that were short term and those that were long term. A short-term consequence of the German inflation of 1923 was the rise to power of Stresemann; a long-term consequence was middle-class disillusionment with the Weimar Republic, and therefore the rise of Hitler.

In studying events you will also study the personalities involved. A potted biography will make a useful start, and an effective revision framework, but will not, in itself, be enough. You will be expected to explore the motivation of the personalities you study; you will want to understand them in their historical context. Thus it is not very historical to use late-twentieth-century morality in judging the aims and interests of the key personalities of the First World War. Your judgements, too, should be reasonably balanced, with at least an attempt to look at all the facts and make a judgement based on the evidence. It may well be that you regard Hitler and Stalin as out-and-out villains, but it should be possible to find some excuses, if not justification, for some of their conduct. Thus in a question on the causes of the Second World War, some students will argue strongly that Hitler's aggressive policies were the main cause; others will shift a substantial portion of the blame on to the western powers, their policies of appeasement and their suspicion of the Soviet Union. Excellent answers should refer to both sorts of cause, attempting to strike a balance between them, but answers of similar merit may well be different in emphasis and approach so long as they do not attempt to place *all* the blame on Hitler. So absolutely one-sided arguments are to be avoided, and words such as 'entirely', 'always' and 'never' should only be used with great caution.

Understanding how the past has been represented and interpreted

Your study of the twentieth-century world and its personalities should not lead you to suppose that there are fixed judgements about them which will remain unchanged for ever. Even at the time of the Munich crisis in 1938, there were voices raised against the majority view in favour of appeasement, and since then arguments for and against Chamberlain's Munich mission have continued unabated. Similarly, Lenin, idolized by the Bolsheviks, has received varying treatment at the hands of western historians, and even now is subject to more critical scrutiny by Russian ones. Remember, therefore, that no historical verdict is ever final, and that many of those you presently accept will be revised before you are much older. George Orwell, in his novel *Nineteen Eighty-Four*, found it quite unforgivable that in future history might be rewritten so as to bear a particular interpretation – something that most totalitarian regimes attempt to do. But history is *always* being rewritten from one point of view or another. In the same way, in GCSE, the answer to the question 'Explain the importance of the German problem in international relations after 1945' must vary according to the point of view of the historian, and would certainly be answered differently by those on different sides in the Cold War. The perception of personalities and events depends on the historian's point of view, according to his or her time and place; it changes as the historian's perception changes, and has no final validity. You may well be asked to explain, for example, how and why Soviet historians writing in 1938, 1948 and 1958 differed in their judgements on Stalin. You may well find different interpretations in the sources you study, and you will need to look at the sources carefully to explain the differences.

The critical use of historical sources in their historical context

All the GCSE history syllabuses require study of historical sources, and the examiners include set questions based on source material. The sources used are most often written ones: newspapers, letters, reports, diaries, etc. But there are also maps and cartoons and, from the late nineteenth century onwards, an increasingly plentiful supply of photographs. Sources that originate from the time of the event or issue with which they are linked are referred to as *primary sources*; often the writer will have been an eyewitness of the event he or she describes. Sources written at a significantly later date – and this is true of all history textbooks – are based upon these primary sources, but because they are at one remove from the actual event they are referred to as *secondary sources*. Sometimes the classification is not quite so clear-cut. For example, newspapers are contemporary secondary sources, since they are based on reports by those who may not have been eyewitnesses. All the same, they are often regarded as primary, since they do not have the benefit of hindsight and give a contemporary view of the event as it happened.

In all sourcework careful study of the source is essential: you will need to understand exactly what a written source *means*, and you will need to grasp the *message* of a cartoon. The basic skill required is to select evidence from sources, and this usually means finding the relevant evidence and expressing it accurately in your own words. Examples of this are to be found in worked evidence questions in this book.

Students will also have to compare evidence for *reliability*; remember that what a source omits can be as important for judging reliability as what it includes. For example, if two sources deal with a riot, it will be very significant if one source states that the police were provoked by taunts and stone throwing, while the other refers to the taunts and omits the stone throwing. If there was any stone throwing, it looks from the omission as if the second source is trying to show the police action in a bad light by deliberately playing down the provocation. Or perhaps the first source invented the stone throwing in order to bolster the excuse for police intervention. You would need a third and independent source to help you decide which of the first two was more reliable.

The reliability of a source will in part depend on how far it is prejudiced or biased. There is a danger that any expression of opinion will be condemned as bias, but real bias should not be difficult to recognize. Bias arises from the deliberate or unconscious expression of some view of the author without any attempt to justify its use in the extract by reasoned argument. Take the following extract:

> The Conservatives in Britain in the years after the Second World War were
> concerned only to promote big business; they were not interested in the needs of the
> mass of the people. They paid lip-service to democracy but they did not really
> believe in it. Conservative politicians were cynical and unscrupulous, and their
> policies from 1951 to 1964 were a disaster.

This, you may think, reads like party propaganda from the Conservatives' opponents. Historians should note the lack of attempt to qualify the most sweeping of generalized condemnations; they could hardly regard this as an objective comment. If you believe the passage to be essentially true in all its details, you must none the less admit that it offers no evidence for the opinions it puts forward, relying on assertion instead of argument. Its very extremism tends to destroy the credibility of the passage.

However, bias that is more subtle can be more effective. Consider this extract:

> The settlement of 1919 saddled Germany with a crippling reparations bill, soon to be fixed at £6,600,000,000. It rendered her incapable of self-defence by depriving her of her airforce and an effective navy, and restricting her army to 100,000 men. It denied her subjects the right of self-determination, as when Alsace-Lorraine was given to France.

Here there are a number of facts: the reparations bill was £6,600,000,000, Germany did lose her air force, her army was restricted to 100,000 men, and Alsace-Lorraine was given to France. But the rest of the passage is full of opinions for none of which there is any evidence and all of which are debatable. Was the reparations bill really crippling? Was Germany's navy not effective? The implication that her subjects were denied self-determination was certainly true of Alsace-Lorraine, but it was not true of those German territories (e.g. North Schleswig) where plebiscites were in fact held. You may be asked to distinguish between fact and opinion in a passage like this, or to look for bias in it. When documents have bias, or show bias, they are said to be biased. 'To be biased' is the equivalent verb. Students often get this wrong. The same is true of the word 'prejudice': things show prejudice or are prejudiced. Once you are able to detect bias or prejudice, you will be able to point out how it is achieved; by the choice of words or the use of insinuation, or by statements that go only part of the way towards telling the truth.

Students often mistakenly assume that sources which show bias or are unreliable are of no value to historians. Of course, historians like accurate and unprejudiced sources, but these are not always easy to find. A source's value will depend on what the historian is looking for. If the historian needs to know what precisely happened, then he or she needs an unbiased and reliable source. But if the historian is interested in contemporary propaganda or contemporary attitudes, then the most unreliable source can be of great value. A speech by a dictator may be both unreliable and prejudiced, but it can tell the historian a lot about the dictator's attitude and motives, and might be invaluable in building up an accurate historical assessment of the dictator. Even an unreliable secondary source can have value: it might be very revealing, not about the event described, but about the person who wrote it, and why.

Evidence questions usually require the studying of more than one source. Single sources do not provide opportunities for the comparison of sources, but they may sometimes be used as a stimulus to trigger factual recall or argument about some event or personality. Where sources are to be used as evidence, rather than stimulus, they will be followed by a series of subquestions directly related to the evidence in the sources, and followed by more searching questions on comparison, reliability, bias and value to historians.

Historical judgements

Once you have studied the facts, and gathered the opinions of others, you will be expected to make historical judgements of your own. Even the most professional of historians will not be in possession of *all* the facts, and thus even the most learned opinion can only be provisional. There may be new evidence, or old evidence insufficiently taken into account. There may be a shift in attitude: we may not be so keen to persecute for the sake of religion as our sixteenth-century ancestors were, and so our attitude to the sixteenth century will be much different from theirs. Nineteenth-century historians judged events of the past according to how far they contributed to their ideas of 'progress'. Thus they saw, for example, King John as bad and wicked, not only for murdering his nephew, but because of his efforts to thwart the barons, and thus hinder the early growth of Parliament. We do not share the overconfidence of such historians, and are more willing to see events as contemporaries saw them, and to judge accordingly. But that does not mean that we have got it right, when nineteenth-century historians did not. You must be prepared to use the evidence you have studied to construct reasoned arguments and to make historical judgements, and you must endeavour to eliminate your own bias and try to judge objectively. But you must be aware that your judgements, like those of all historians, can never be permanent.

▷ **Coursework**   All the boards require a coursework element, for which there is an allocation of 25 per cent of the marks. The syllabuses vary between the boards: for some a local history element is compulsory, some insist that the coursework topics are directly related to the syllabus, others that the coursework topics cover related themes not directly specified in the syllabus. There is usually the option of two assignments, each about 1,000 words plus in length, or what is often described as a personal study, a single exercise of about 2,000 to 2,500 words concentrating on one theme or area of investigation. But all the coursework has common assessment objectives: Objective 1 (recall or knowledge) is obviously less important, since reference material is readily to hand, but Objective 2 (analysis and explanation) and Objective 3 (interpretations and sources) must both be covered. Students and teachers will be able to choose their own coursework assignments, and for some boards these must be submitted in advance for approval. Alternatively, students may have the option of using the coursework titles set by the boards.

The coursework will be expected to be in written form, but it may be supplemented with drawings, photographs or tape recordings. For Objective 3 it will obviously be necessary to use sources, and to make sure that the assignment covers the higher source skills of comparison and evaluation, and not merely extraction and the detection of bias. For Objective 2 students must avoid the danger of providing a narrative when they think they are analysing and explaining. The chosen title may well have this effect: 'Abyssinia, 1935–36' invites the descriptive approach, whereas 'The effect of the Abyssinian crisis on international relations, 1935–36' is more likely to trigger an analytical response. Take special care if you have a local history option. Do not become overspecialized ('The diet of the residents of the local workhouse, 1887–88') or trivial ('The history of the Bloggsville Football Club, 1897–1997'). In the case of the workhouse a comparative study over a period of years, with explanation of why the diet changed, might be more suitable, and in the latter case a hundred Bloggsville team photographs will impress the examiners far less than, say, a study of unemployment in Bloggsville, 1919–39, or the contribution of local industry to the town's development.

You will obviously discuss your choice of topic with your teacher, together with the sources you propose to consult. But do not expect precise guidance on what to write and how to write it; the coursework will have to be certified as your own work, and not that of anyone else – particularly not your teacher. It follows, too, that coursework should not be lifted in great chunks straight from your sources. There is little value in copying out paragraphs from a variety of books, stitching them together with a few phrases of introduction, and then pretending that the work is all your own. You will be expected to show skills of arrangement, analysis, assessment and argument, and you cannot do this if you simply copy what others have written. So your pieces of coursework will need to be well planned in advance; they will need to be of approximately the length asked for (*too* wide a variation could cost you marks); above all, they will need to identify and investigate a clear historical problem and offer conclusions.

Depending on the nature of the coursework set, a useful coursework method would be:

1. Choose and discuss a title.
2. Collect a list of resources.
3. Unless the theme is too specialized, read up the subject matter in your textbook(s) and make notes, so that you have a general idea of the topic.
4. In the light of the material studied, refine and modify your title so that you can be sure that your information will enable you to deal adequately with it.
5. Start tracking your selected subject in the sources; make notes and cross-references, and select a limited number of useful short extracts for quotation (if this is appropriate).
6. Select suitable visual and statistical material, if available and if relevant.
7. Read through the collected material, plan its arrangement (including visual, etc.) so as best to assist the development of your argument, and check that your conclusions are sensible.
8. Prepare a synopsis, write your first rough draft and develop your final polished version from it.
9. If the assignment consists of a series of questions on chosen sources, make sure that you are fully familiar with bias, reliability and value to historians, and that you can compare sources effectively.

Finally, remember that the work should be neatly presented, and that it should be written in as effective a style as you can manage. As your coursework carries a quarter of the marks, you must expect to spend adequate time on it. Remember that poorly prepared or hastily written coursework could well cost you a grade or even two grades in the final assessment.

▷ **Examination assessment**   As your grade will depend on what examiners think of your examination work and what your teacher (and possibly the coursework moderator) thinks of your coursework, it is useful for you to have a clear idea of what these people expect of you.

Coursework assignments and, in the examination, any written answer developed beyond a word or so will be rewarded at different *Levels* (some boards call them *bands*) according to the skills content of the answer. Let us take an example from an examination paper.

Was the intervention of the USA the *main* reason for Germany's defeat in 1918?

This is an essay-type question marked out of 12. Here you are obviously being asked not only to examine the reasons for Germany's defeat, but also to assess the relative importance of those reasons, and in particular the relative importance of the contribution of the USA. If all you can do is give a narrative account of the events of 1918, the mark scheme assesses you at Level 1.

> **Level 1.** The answer accepts the suggestion and seeks to support the opinion, e.g. by referring to American resources.
> OR an unfocused narrative of the events of 1918
> OR a simplistic rejection of the suggestion in favour of an alternative reason, e.g. huge losses on the Western Front, collapse of Germany's allies.   (1–3 marks)
> **Level 2.** An answer offering one main reason, and describing it, with passing reference to other reasons
> OR an undeveloped list of reasons with little discussion
> OR a narrative answer describing the events of 1918, but from which several reasons 'emerge'.   (4–6 marks)
> **Level 3.** An answer which develops several reasons in depth.   (7–10 marks)
> **Level 4.** A Level 3 answer which additionally considers the importance of the American contribution to Germany's defeat in relation to the other reasons
> OR considers the interrelationship of the main reasons, and thus demonstrates the relative importance of the American contribution.   (11–12 marks)

All marking, including that of coursework, is done using similar Levels. Within the Levels, marks will vary according to the depth of the knowledge, the quality of the argument, and the extent of relevant substantiation. Your grade will be determined by the overall Levels you have reached in

1. acquiring historical knowledge and being able to communicate it;
2. finding and making use of historical evidence; and
3. developing and making use of powers of historical reasoning (i.e. using knowledge and evidence to analyse and make judgements about historical problems).

Demonstrated ability in all these will earn you a high grade.

But even if you are well equipped with historical skills, marks can be lost through carelessness; and if your skills are not as strong as they might be, marks could be saved by careful attention during the examination to the following points:

1. Make sure that you know what you have to do: how many questions you have to answer, which parts are compulsory and which are the areas covering the sections for which you have been specifically prepared.
2. Read the questions, and the source material, carefully; make sure that you have properly understood the question before attempting it, that you know how many parts it contains if it is structured and what is required in each part.
3. If the marks for a part question are given on the examination paper, use that as a guide for how much you should write; if only 3 marks are on offer, a couple of sentences should be adequate. A paragraph or more would be a waste of time. But

if 8 marks are offered, you would need to make a number of supported points, and to develop the answer into a useful paragraph, to have any chance of reaching maximum.

4. Plan your time carefully; do not waste time on one question so that you run out of time on another. Make sure that you answer all the questions required within the examination time limit.

5. If you *must* make plans for the longer answers, make them brief, merely listing the pointers you intend to develop in your answer. If a plan is as long as the answer it is prepared for, you will find either that your answers are too brief or that you run out of time before you have finished. Answers which merely turn out to be a fair copy of the plan are an instance of unnecessary repetition and poor examination technique.

6. Remember that it is unlikely that full questions will call for narrative only, although a part question may do so. Skills other than merely recalling historical information are almost certain to be required, and the more skills you manage effectively to demonstrate, the higher your grade is likely to be. Where description or narrative is asked for, make sure that it is coherent and accurate. Where skills are asked for, use your historical knowledge to support your argument or analysis. Answers which try to argue without any evidence (i.e. historical facts) to support them will consist merely of unproved assertions and will not score above Level 1.

This book is not intended as a substitute for a textbook. You should use it to supplement the work done, either in class under teacher guidance or through your own reading of books. It will help you develop your skill in writing by practising the questions – of whatever type – and will provide you with a useful basis for revising the GCSE examination itself.

Each chapter is arranged in a similar way. The section 'Historical developments' gives you a brief summary of the main narrative points of the topic to be studied, and also tackles issues of cause and consequence. You should explore and develop the points given here in conjunction with notes and textbooks. The section 'Glossary' will deal with ideas, problems and vocabulary associated with the topic. 'Examination questions' give a selection of questions of different types, the answers to which are presented in three different ways: as outline answers, summarizing the content of a good answer; as tutor answers, which give you an idea of what a good answer should look like; and student answers, with examiner's comments to show you what the examiner is looking for.

At the end of the chapter is a summary of its main contents, for easy reference.

The examination boards and their requirements

There are six GCSE boards in England, Wales and Northern Ireland, and each produced a new World History syllabus to start in 1998. Full details of these syllabuses can be obtained from the boards, and it is not the purpose of this chapter to explain each syllabus in detail. What follows is a summary of each board's main features, indicating which sections are optional and which compulsory, and how far the syllabus of any board can be covered in this book is shown in the chart below.

Curriculum coverage chart

MEG	NEAB	NICCEA	SEG	LONDON	WJEC	**TOPIC**	STUDY	REVISION 1	REVISION 2
	✓		✓*	✓	✓	Ch. 3: Britain 1900–1914			
✓*	✓		✓*	✓		Ch. 4: The First World War			
	✓		✓*			Ch. 5: Economic and industrial problems between the wars			
✓	✓		✓			Ch. 6: International affairs 1919–31			
✓	✓	✓	✓	✓	✓	Ch. 7: Russia 1917–24			
✓	✓	✓	✓	✓	✓	Ch. 8: The Weimar Republic			
✓	✓	✓	✓	✓	✓	Ch. 9: The Third Reich			
✓	✓	✓	✓	✓	✓	Ch. 10: Stalin			
✓	✓		✓			Ch. 11: International affairs 1931–39			
	✓		✓*	✓		Ch. 12: The Second World War			
✓	✓	✓	✓*	✓	✓	Ch. 13: The USA 1919–41			
			✓*	✓	✓	Ch. 14: The USA 1941–80			
✓	✓	✓	✓	✓	✓	Ch. 15: The Cold War to 1963			
✓[1]				✓	✓	Ch. 16: China to 1949			
✓	✓*			✓	✓	Ch. 17: China after 1949			
✓	✓[2]	✓	✓	✓	✓	Ch. 18: The end of the Cold War			
✓*	✓*			✓	✓	Ch. 19: Palestine			
✓*	✓*		✓*	✓	✓	Ch. 20: South Africa and apartheid			

* Coursework only
[1] From 1945
[2] Paper 3

The English and Welsh boards offer candidates access to all the grades A–G, through common papers, but the Northern Ireland board (NICCEA) has two entry tiers: the higher tier and the foundation tier. The higher tier gives access to grades A*–D, and the foundation tier gives access to grades C–G only. Candidates aiming at an A or a B must obviously enter for the higher tier.

All the boards have the same assessment objectives, but they number them slightly differently. For convenience these objectives will be numbered in this chapter in the following way:

Objective 1 To recall, select, organize and deploy (set out) historical knowledge.

Objective 2 To describe, explain and analyse the events, changes and issues studied, and to describe, explain and analyse the key features and characteristics of periods, societies and events.

Objective 3 To comprehend (understand), interpret, evaluate (assess) and use a range of sources of information in their historical context. To comprehend, analyse and evaluate representations and interpretations of events, people and issues in their historical context.

▷ The Midland Examining Group (MEG)

Head Office: Syndicate Buildings, 1 Hills Road, Cambridge, CB1 2EU
Tel: 01233 553311

Syllabus content

Modern World Syllabus B.
The Core (compulsory): International Relations c.1919–c.1989
Depth Studies (optional, three must be studied, one for Paper 1 and two for coursework)

    A   Germany 1918–1945
    B   Russia 1905–1941
    C   The USA 1919–1941
    D   China 1945–c.1990
    E   Britain and the First World War 1914–1918
    F   South Africa 1945–1994
    G   Israel and the Arab–Israeli Conflict 1945–c.1994

Depth Studies E–G are not examined, but are available for coursework.

The examination

Paper 1. 2 hours. Sections A and B test the core content. Section A has two source-based questions from which candidates must choose one. Section B has four structured questions from which candidates must answer any one. Structured questions are questions divided into two or more subquestions in which the relative importance (and length of answer required) of each subquestion is usually indicated by the number of marks allocated for it. Section C tests Depth Studies A–D. Three structured questions are set on each of these, and candidates must answer two questions. Paper 1 is almost exclusively devoted to Objectives 1 and 2.

Paper 2. 1½ hours. This paper consists of a source-based investigation of an historical issue taken from the *core* content. The syllabus for each year will specify the broad area from which the specific topic for the paper will be drawn. Two-thirds of the marks in Paper 2 will be for Objective 3 and one-third for Objectives 1 and 2.

Coursework

Two assignments must be produced. These must be on two of the Depth Studies, and must differ from those chosen for Paper 1. No more than 2,000 words in total will be required. The first assignment will cover the significance of an individual or event

(Objectives 1 and 2), and the second will be a source-based investigation of an historical issue (Objective 3).

The Northern Examinations and Assessment Board (NEAB)

12 Harter Street, Manchester, M1 6HL
Tel: 0161–953 1170

Syllabus content

History Syllabus B.
Conflict in the Modern World, 1900–1963:

> Origins of conflict – the events leading to World War I, c.1900–1914
> The changing nature of warfare – World War I: The Western Front
> Civilian experience of war: the Home Front in Britain, 1914–1918
> Origins of conflict – the events leading to World War II, 1919–1939
> The changing nature of warfare – World War II, 1939–1945
> Civilian experience of war: the Home Front in Britain, 1939–1945
> Origins of conflict: the events leading to the Cold War (in effect to the mid-1950s)
> The changing nature of warfare – the nuclear age, 1945–1963

Governments in action:

> Section A: Russia/USSR, 1900–1956
>   or Germany, 1918–1939
> Section B: USA, 1919–1941
>   or Britain, 1905–1951

The examination

Paper 1. 1hr 45m. Questions will be source based (Objective 3), will usually consist of two or three subquestions, and all questions will be compulsory. The number of questions (about 4) may vary slightly from year to year. Just under 30 per cent of the marks on this paper will be for Objectives 1 and 2.

Paper 2. 1hr 45m. There will be one structured question on each topic. Candidates must choose one question from Section A and one question from Section B. Sources will be used, but only $12\frac{1}{2}$ per cent of the marks will be for Objective 3. The remainder of the marks will be for Objectives 1 and 2.

Coursework

Candidates should complete *two* assignments based on *one* of the following:

(a) Human rights: divisions in Ireland from the mid-nineteenth century to the present day; the Jews 1880 to the present day; the changing role and status of women in Britain; civil rights in the USA; apartheid in South Africa; China 1949 to the present day
(b) Colonialism: from pre-colonial times to post-independence
(c) International cooperation
(d) Modern Europe post-1945
(e) The Arab–Israeli conflict
(f) Vietnam

Between the two assignments, 60 per cent of the marks should be for Objectives 1 and 2 and 40 per cent of the marks for Objective 3.

Outline details of the planned coursework assignments must be submitted to the board for approval.

Candidates not wishing to submit coursework may substitute a written paper (Paper 3) in which questions will be set on coursework themes (c) to (f). Candidates will be expected to answer all questions on *one* of these topics.

▷ Northern Ireland Council for the Curriculum Examinations and Assessment (NICCEA)

Beechill House, 42 Beechill Road, Belfast BT8 4RS
Tel: 01232 704666

Syllabus content

Depth Studies:

Germany, *c*.1918–*c*.1939
Russia, *c*.1914–*c*.1941
USA, *c*.1918–*c*.1941

Candidates to choose one of the above.
Ireland:

Peace, war and neutrality: Britain, Northern Ireland and Ireland and the Second World War, *c*.1935–*c*.1949; or
Changing relationships: Britain, Northern Ireland and Ireland, *c*.1965–*c*.1985

Outline Study:

Superpower relations, *c*.1945–*c*.1985: superpower rivalry in Europe; flash points of the cold war; from arms rivalry to arms limitation

The examination

Paper 1. Section A: Depth Studies – Candidates will answer two questions out of four on their chosen option. Section B: Ireland – Candidates will answer two questions out of three on their chosen option. Questions will be of the short answer and structured type, and will be concerned with Objectives 1 and 2.

Paper 2: Outline Study on superpower relations. Candidates will answer three questions, one based on source material, one structured and one of extended writing (essay) type. Just under 60 per cent will be geared towards Objectives 1 and 2, the rest will be Objective 3.

Coursework

Candidates will write two assignments with a total word content of 2,500. The assignments must include the use of sources, and must extend their understanding beyond the syllabus content to periods before and after the specified syllabus dates or to contexts not specified in key issues of the syllabus. Coursework is exclusively geared to Objective 3.

Note that in this syllabus there is a two-tier entry.

▷ The Southern Examining Group (SEG)

Stag Hill House, Guildford, Surrey GU2 5XJ
Tel: 01483 506506

Syllabus content

Syllabus B: Modern World History.
Two study units from:

Peace to war, 1919–1939
The USA and the USSR as world superpowers, 1945–1963
The USA and the USSR as world superpowers, 1963–1991

Both of the following Depth Studies:

Russia, 1917–1941
Germany, 1918–1939

The examination

Paper 2. 1hr 45m. Six structured questions are set, two on each study unit. Candidates must answer three questions. This paper is 80 per cent geared to Objectives 1 and 2 and 20 per cent to Objective 3.

Paper 3. Section A – two structured questions are set, one on each Depth Study. Each question will contain a number of historical sources. Candidates must answer one question. These questions are primarily concerned with Objective 3, but also involve Objectives 1 and 2. In Section B two questions are set on Russia and in Section C two questions are set on Germany. These questions involve a single task (i.e. not structured) and candidates must answer one question from each section. These questions are geared exclusively to Objectives 1 and 2.

Coursework

This counts as Paper 1. Candidates must produce one assignment geared to Objective 2 and another assignment geared to Objective 3. The two assignments must both relate to *one only* of the following Coursework Study Units:

Social and economic developments in Britain, 1900–1939
The First World War, 1914–1918
The USA, 1918–1941
The Second World War, 1939–1945
Race relations in the USA and South Africa since 1945
The centre's own choice

It is expected that each assignment will be about 1,000–1,250 words in length.

▷ EDEXCEL Foundation (London)

Stewart House, 32 Russell Square, London WC1B 5DN
Tel: 0171–636 8000

Syllabus content

Syllabus A: Modern European and World History.
Outline Studies:

The emergence of modern Britain, 1868–1914
The road to war: Europe, 1870–1914
Nationalism and independence in India, *c.*1900–1949
The impact of war on Britain, *c.*1900–1950
The emergence of modern China, 1911–1970
The rise and fall of the communist state: the Soviet Union, 1928–1991
A divided union? The USA, 1941–1980
Britain's changing role in the world, 1945–1990
Superpower relations, 1945–1990
Conflict and quest for peace in the Middle East, 1948–1992

Depth Studies:

The Russian Revolution, *c.*1910–1924
The war to end wars, 1914–1919
Depression and the New Deal: the USA, 1929–1941
Nazi Germany, *c.*1930–1939
The world at war, 1938–1945
The end of apartheid in South Africa, 1982–1994
Conflict in Vietnam, *c.*1963–1975

The examination

Paper 1. 1¹/₂ hours. The paper will consist of 20 questions, two on each of the Outline Studies. Each question will consist of four or five short answers based on a piece of stimulus material (e.g. a brief written source) and a structured essay question. Candidates must answer two questions chosen from different topics. This paper will cover Objectives 1 and 2.

Paper 2. 1¹/₂ hours. This paper will consist of seven questions, one on each of the Depth Studies. The questions are based on a variety of sources, and will consist of a series of subquestions on one or more pieces of evidence in their historical context. Candidates must answer any two questions. Objectives 1 and 3 are covered in this paper.

Coursework

Candidates must present two assignments, each between 1,250 and 2,000 words in length. One assignment must relate to Objective 2 and the other to Objective 3. The topics chosen can be either on two topics listed in the syllabus which the candidate has *not* chosen for the Papers 1 or 2, or related to but not specified in the syllabus content. Candidates may choose assignment tasks offered by the board. Those choosing and constructing their own assignment tasks must get them approved by the board.

▷ **Welsh Joint Education Committee (WJEC)**

245 Western Avenue, Cardiff, CF5 2YX
Tel: 01222 265000

Syllabus content

Syllabus B: Aspects of Twentieth Century History.
Depth Studies:

> Lenin and the Russian Revolution, 1917–1924
> The USA, 1919–1929
> Hitler's Germany, 1933–1945
> China under Mao Zedong, 1949–1976
> South Africa, 1960–1994

Outline Studies:

> China, 1911–1990
> Germany, 1919–1990
> The Middle East, 1919–1990
> The USSR, 1924–1990
> The USA, 1929–1994

The examination

Paper 1. 2 hours. Candidates are required to answer questions on *two* Depth Studies. On each study there will be a compulsory interpretations and sources question, and two structured questions from which candidates choose one. Just over half the marks will be on Objectives 1 and 2, and just under half the marks on Objective 3.

Paper 2. 1¹/₂ hours. Candidates are required to answer questions on *one* of the Outline Studies. For each study there will be three compulsory stimulus questions focusing on a different key issue. There will also be two structured questions for each topic from which candidates will choose *one*. This paper is geared to Objectives 1 and 2.

NB Candidates must not choose topics for the two papers which would make their studies exclusively European or exclusively World; nor may they choose the same countries in both Depth and Outline Studies.

Coursework

Candidates undertake two assignments, the first of which concentrates on historical understanding and interpretations (Objectives 2 and 3), and the second substitutes source evaluation (Objective 3) for interpretations. The assignments must be based on the study of local, Welsh or Welsh/English history. Each assignment should not exceed 1,200–1,500 words in length.

Modern Britain: the progress of reform and democracy to 1914

▷ GETTING STARTED

This chapter outlines the story of British social and political reform from 1900 to the outbreak of the First World War. It deals with the fall of the Conservatives in 1905–6, after nearly 20 years of rule, and the coming to power of the Liberals in one of the most reformist governments of the twentieth century. It traces the achievements of the Liberals against the background of political crisis and social unrest.

MEG	NEAB	NICCEA	SEG	LONDON	WJEC	TOPIC	STUDY	REVISION 1	REVISION 2
	✓		✓*	✓		**The progress of democracy and reform to 1914**			
	✓		✓*	✓		The end of Conservative rule, 1901–5			
	✓		✓*	✓		The Liberals in power			
	✓		✓*	✓		The suffragette movement			
	✓		✓*	✓		The People's Budget and the Parliament Act			
	✓		✓*	✓		Continuing Liberal reform			
	✓		✓*	✓		The end of an era			

* Coursework only

▷ WHAT YOU NEED TO KNOW

The progress of democracy and reform to 1914

 The end of Conservative rule, 1901–5

In many ways, the years between the death of Queen Victoria in 1901 and the outbreak of the First World War in 1914 were years of great affluence. The Edwardian Age is sometimes called a Golden Age. This is partly because the golden sovereign was still in general use instead of paper money, but also because, after the war, people tended to look back on these years in a rosy glow, forgetting their less pleasant features. World trade was flourishing, British output and exports were high, and overseas investments were greater than they had ever been. The population of the United Kingdom, now passing 45 million, was better off than it had ever been before.

But there were serious warning signs. Much of Britain's prosperity came from the old staple trades – textiles, coal, iron and steel, and shipbuilding. These industries were starting to decline, and foreign competition from powerful world rivals like Germany and Japan was challenging Britain's position. Even the fact that there were enormous surpluses to invest abroad was itself an indication that income was badly distributed. The poor were too poor, and the rich too rich. A great deal of room still remained for social improvements in health, education and welfare; there was too much concentration on conspicuous consumption by the better-off, instead of more prudent efforts to move towards a fairer Britain.

The decline of the Conservatives

The Conservatives had been in office for about fifteen years, and their weariness was beginning to show. Lord Salisbury, who had led the government from the House of Lords almost continuously since 1886, had recently retired, and the new king, Edward VII, chose Arthur Balfour, his nephew, to succeed him as Premier in 1902. Balfour's government had achieved a number of reforms, but had at the same time given rise to serious dissatisfaction:

(a) *1902, Education Act* abolished the School Boards and made the counties and county boroughs the local education authorities. In future these authorities were to support not only the board schools, but the voluntary schools too. These were to retain their buildings and their right to appoint teachers, but otherwise their expenses were to be paid as if they belonged to the state. Religious instruction was still to be undenominational (i.e. not in accordance with the precepts of any particular sect, but based on the teaching of the Bible) in the 'provided' schools, but could continue to be sectarian in the voluntary schools. Board and voluntary schools provided only *elementary* education up to the age of thirteen; but the Act also made the local education authorities responsible for organizing and supplementing the existing provision for *secondary* education.

(b) *1904, Licensing Act* renewed the attempt to reduce the number of liquor licences, but squared this reduction with the demand by publicans for compensation for lost licences by paying such compensation out of a fund levied on the drink trade itself. This was regarded by political opponents and temperance workers as 'endowing the trade'.

(c) *1905, Aliens Act* began to check the immigration of undesirable aliens – those with a bad health record or a criminal record. Some saw this as discriminatory, others believed the law should have been more protectionist.

(d) *1905, Unemployed Workmen Act* enabled local authorities to set up Labour Exchanges to collect information, keep a register of unemployed, and even assist emigration, removal or the provision of work. No public money was to be spent on relief, but Queen Alexandra herself set up a charitable appeal for the purpose of raising funds to help.

Deep splits drove Balfour from office in December 1905 and the Liberals came to power, though it was not until January 1906 that a general election took place.

Reasons for the Liberal 'landslide'

Conservatives continued to hope until the last moment that the Liberals were too untried and inexperienced to form any kind of alternative government, but events proved this to be a vain hope. What were the reasons for the Liberals' victory?

(a) In the *imperial sphere*, there was criticism of the methods employed by the British forces in suppressing South Africa at the time of the Boer War (1899–1902), in particular of the use of concentration camps. Alarm was also felt after the war at policies which permitted the use of cheap Asian labour on the Rand – a development which was often ignorantly described as the 'Yellow Peril'. The Liberals had been split at the time of the war into anti-Boer Liberal imperialists and pro-Boer sympathizers, but they were now reunited in their criticisms of the Conservatives.

(b) There was criticism over recent *Conservative reforms*. The Education Act (1902) was widely supposed to favour the Anglicans because of the support it offered to the voluntary schools, while many Liberals were staunch non-conformists. The Licensing Act (1904) allowed the purveyors of the demon drink to claim compensation for desisting from their vile work. The Aliens Act (1905) restricted immigration, either too severely or not severely enough, according to taste. The Unemployed Workmen Act (1905) recognized at last the evil of unemployment, though not to the point of having to spend any actual money on it.

(c) Anger was felt against the *House of Lords*, long and rightly regarded as the bastion of Conservatism. Too many Liberal measures had been mauled by the Upper House, or rejected altogether (e.g. Home Rule in 1893), and the belief steadily grew that things would not be better until the power of the Upper House was limited by law.

(d) Special anger was directed against the Law Lords for their decision in the *Taff Vale case* (1901), which ruled on appeal that the Associated Society of Railway Servants had to pay damages and costs to their employers as the result of wrongful actions committed during a strike on the Taff Vale Railway in South Wales. This decision upset trade unionists, since it seemed to undermine their right to strike.

(e) Trade unionists, therefore, threw in their lot with the Liberals, encouraging the recently established Labour Representation Committee (LRC) to run candidates for Parliament to reverse the Taff Vale Judgment. Liberal and Labour parliamentary candidates got together in a number of constituencies where they might split the working-class vote between them, and worked out *Lib–Lab* pacts, which meant that in these constituencies the two would not fight against each other.

(f) The greatest weakness in the Conservative Party arose from the growth within the party of *protectionist sentiment*. Joseph Chamberlain, who in the 1880s had split the Liberals over Irish Home Rule, now threatened to split the Conservatives over a proposal to abandon that sacred dogma of British trade policy, free trade. In the last years of the century, in response to the great depression in trade and the rise of foreign competition, a movement had developed in favour of 'fair trade'. This coincided with a move towards 'imperial federation', a scheme to bind the colonies and the mother country more closely together. Chamberlain was deeply involved in both movements. As an industrialist and an imperialist, he felt that the country was getting a raw deal from the continuance of free trade. In 1903 he founded the *Tariff Reform League*, suggesting a protective tariff on foreign imports, combined with a scheme of *imperial preference*, allowing imports from the colonies to enter the country at lower rates of duty. Free traders sprang to the attack at once, arguing that tariffs would make goods dearer. Even preferential tariffs would raise prices somewhat, unless they were at zero level, in which case they would offer no protection. Chamberlain was forced into the damaging admission: 'If you are going to give a preference to the colonies . . . you must put a tax on food.'

This issue deeply divided the Conservative Party. Free traders thought that the free trade principle was too fundamental to abandon, and that policies which put up food prices would be unpopular with the voters. The protectionists argued that, though prices might go up, there would be better job security if people were buying British, and this would improve the prospects of British industry. Balfour was caught in an unenviable dilemma, and failed to give a clear lead. In 1905, he produced a policy on 'half a sheet of note paper', declaring in favour of closer ties with the empire and in favour of tariffs – but only for revenue purposes and not for general protection. This obvious fudge pleased nobody, and Balfour was forced to resign.

At the election, the Liberals swept the board, securing 377 seats, a majority over all the other parties combined of 84. Among the Liberals' supporters were 53 Labour, about half of them returned with Liberal support as 'Lib–Labs', and 83 Irish. The Conservatives were reduced to 157, and these were split into 109 Chamberlainites, 43 Free Traders and a handful who could not make up their minds. This result gave the Liberals under Campbell-Bannerman an overwhelming mandate to put through an ambitious programme of social reform.

▷ The Liberals in power

Campbell-Bannerman remained Prime Minister until 1908, and was succeeded by H.H. Asquith, who had previously been Chancellor of the Exchequer. Asquith's Chancellor was Lloyd George, who had earlier been President of the Board of Trade under Campbell-Bannerman. The new Liberal team put through sweeping, and many thought long overdue, domestic changes.

Political reforms

There was still great prejudice, even in the Liberal Party, against giving women the vote in national elections, but moves began in that direction:

(a) *1907, Qualification of Women Act* enabled women to become JPs and to sit as councillors or aldermen, mayors or chairmen of county or borough councils, in the same way that they were already entitled to sit on district and parish councils.

(b) *1907, Plural Voting Bill* tried to enforce the principle of 'one man, one vote', to prohibit a voter from voting in more than one constituency, but this was one of a number of bills that were thrown out by the Lords.

Trade union reform

The new government hastened to remedy the grievances of trade unionists over the Taff Vale Judgment.

1906, Trade Disputes Act allowed unions to strike without civil proceedings being taken against them, either for breach of contract or for damages for losses suffered as a result of the strike. Since criminal proceedings had already been forbidden in 1875, this Act meant that trade unions had become corporations almost above the law. Though some Liberals were not keen on this proposal, they passed it in the Commons, secure in the knowledge that the Conservatives in the Lords would throw it out. But the Lords dared not give the working classes more offence, and they let the bill pass. Not only were the industrial powers of the unions now secure, but also the unions were becoming politically more ambitious. They began sponsoring Labour candidates for Parliament, and also collecting from their members a *political levy* to pay salaries to their working-class MPs and to cover a number of other political expenses. This continued until it was challenged in the courts in 1909.

Labour and industrial reforms

The Liberals also embarked on remedying other working-class grievances:

(a) *1906, Workmen's Compensation Act* provided compensation for accidents arising in the course of employment (provided they were not due to the worker's own negligence), and for what were called 'industrial diseases' such as lead poisoning or silicosis. Those earning more than £250 per year were excluded from the scheme.

(b) *1906, Merchant Shipping Act* improved conditions aboard ship for British crews. It also compelled foreign shipping using British ports to conform to the same standards. This Act was the brainchild of Lloyd George at the Board of Trade.

(c) *1907, Patents Act* compelled patentees to work their patents in Britain within three years. This Act was also Lloyd George's and was accused of being protectionist in intention.

(d) *1907, first Census of Production* completed by Lloyd George, providing statistical information for government departments.

(e) *1908, Port of London Authority Act*, the most ambitious of Lloyd George's schemes at the Board of Trade, provided an umbrella authority under which the many public boards and private companies competing for work there were amalgamated. Whether the measure was based on Liberal or, as critics said, on socialist principles, it helped the development of Britain's greatest port immensely.

(f) *1908, Coal Mines Act* introduced the miners' eight-hour day – the first time a government had ever regulated the hours of adult male labourers.

(g) *1909, Trade Boards Act* harked back to earlier limited attempts in 1891 to intervene in the 'sweated industries', and introduced arbitration machinery to fix the rates of pay of those who were not generally protected by the Factory Acts. Such trades as net mending and paper-box making were often conducted in the labourers' own homes in indescribable filth and squalor, for atrociously long hours, in most cases by women workers desperately in need of protection.

(h) *1909, Labour Exchanges Act* set up Labour Exchanges under the local authorities to help the unemployed to find work. This had often been done according to curious local customs such as that described by H.G. Wells in his novel *Mr Polly*, where unemployed shop assistants used to wait in a churchyard for their likely employers to come and 'offer them a crib'. In future the country was to be divided into ten districts set up out of public money, where records of job vacancies were to be kept, and where employers looking for labour could be put in touch with workers looking for jobs.

The Liberals also tackled the land question, but without any success. In 1907 a bill passed in the Commons was mutilated by the House of Lords; two further Scottish bills were rejected by the Lords altogether. It looked as though the Upper House was determined that the rights of upper-class landowners would remain sacrosanct whatever the government might wish.

Children's reforms

The welfare of children was also something close to Liberals' hearts:

(a) *1907, School Meals Act* enabled Local Education Authorities to provide cheap, or free, school meals (lunch or sometimes breakfast) for needy children.
(b) *1907, Medical Inspection Act* required Local Education Authorities to arrange for the medical inspection of younger pupils.
(c) *1908, 'Children's Charter'* was set up in two Acts:
  (i) *Prevention of Crimes Act* was intended to safeguard the interests of young offenders. It started the Borstal system (so-called after the name of the first such institution in Kent) instead of putting children into ordinary gaols. There were to be special juvenile courts with suitable anonymity for young offenders; the Act also brought in the probation system.
  (ii) *Children's Act* forbade children to beg in the streets, or to go into public houses, or to buy liquor or tobacco.

The Liberals also tried to satisfy non-conformist grievances by amending the Education Act of 1902. The first attempt, in 1906, passed the Commons but was defeated in the Lords; two others were defeated in the Commons in 1907 and 1908. The fourth, in 1908, was in many ways the best, but the Church declared against it, and the bill was finally abandoned.

Social reforms

This aspect of the government's policies was impressive, though its general spirit was interventionist rather than truly Liberal:

(a) *1907, Deceased Wife's Sister's Act* allowed a widower to marry his dead wife's sister, rather than bring her to his house to look after small children and afterwards live with her outside marriage.
(b) *1909, Housing and Town Planning Act* empowered the Local Government Board to order local authorities which neglected their duties to carry out their obligations. It required them to demolish back-to-back housing, and allowed them to buy land for future housing development and to restrict development in the interests of amenity.
(c) *1909, Old Age Pensions Act* was very modest in its scope. It gave only 5s (25p) a week to old people over 70, and even this was hedged about with conditions. They should not previously have been in receipt of poor relief, they should not have a criminal record, and their income from savings should not exceed about £30 a year if they were to qualify. The thought of elderly citizens tottering to the Post Office for their weekly handout moved the comfortably-off to paroxysms of furious rage, but Lloyd George, now himself Chancellor, persisted.
(d) *1909, Poor Law Report* fell into two halves: a majority report, which recommended the replacement of Poor Law Guardians by local authorities, and the more ambitious minority report, which suggested the complete abolition of poor relief, and the substitution of a minimum standard of welfare services below which no one was to be permitted to fall. This idea appealed to a young Liberal called William Beveridge, but it was nearly half a century before he was able to implement it.
(e) The Liberals had least success with their *Licensing Bill*, which, like so many others, was rejected by the House of Lords.

These social reforms were very controversial, and added to the financial problems involved in providing the cash for the old age pensions law. It was these that touched off a new stage in the struggle between the Commons and the Lords. However, the programme of reform was not abandoned; it continued after 1910–11.

▷ The suffragette movement

Background

'Votes for Women' was an issue that made only limited progress in the nineteenth century. At the time of the Second Reform Act of 1867, there was little interest in it. A motion tabled on that occasion by the MP for Westminster, J.S. Mill, for female suffrage was defeated by 196 votes to 73. In the following year he wrote a book on the *Subjection of Women*, but the idea still remained that politics was man's work.

There were a number of limited advances in the years before 1914:

(a) *1870, Forster's Education Act* allowed women who paid school rates to vote in the election of the School Boards, and permitted them to become members of the boards.
(b) *1888, County Councils Act* allowed unmarried female ratepayers to vote in county and county borough elections, but not to sit on the councils elected.
(c) *1894, Parish Councils Act* allowed both unmarried and married women ratepayers to vote in parish elections, and permitted them to sit on such councils.
(d) *1906, Qualification of Women Act* allowed women to sit on County and Borough Councils, and permitted them to become chairmen or mayors of such councils, or to become JPs.

The main work for parliamentary votes, however, was done early in the twentieth century by the suffragette movement.

The suffrage movement

In view of their lack of success in Parliament, and the indifference in the subject shown in the country at large, an effort was now made to secure parliamentary votes for women by bringing pressure to bear on the government through organized public campaigns and demonstrations.

The development of the suffrage movement

In October 1903, the *Women's Social and Political Union* was founded by Mrs Emmeline Pankhurst. She was introduced by one of her staunch supporters, Keir Hardie, to the 'second Emmeline', Mrs Emmeline Pethick-Lawrence, who helped her until 1912, with a brief break between them in 1908 brought about by the autocratic behaviour of Mrs Pankhurst, when Mrs Pethick-Lawrence formed the more moderate *Women's Freedom League*.

The Liberal victory in 1906 raised the hopes of the suffragists that the new government would favour female enfranchisement, but Campbell-Bannerman, with a full programme of reforms, was not very interested, and Asquith, as Home Secretary, counselled delay. The 'suffragettes', as they were soon called, therefore resorted to direct action.

Boisterous demonstrations were organized, and women invaded the lobbies of the House of Commons. They chained themselves to the railings in Parliament Square, and embarked on a campaign of window breaking. Mrs Pankhurst said: 'The argument of the broken pane is the most valuable argument in modern politics.' A number of arrests were made as a result of these activities and, since the women refused to pay the fines imposed on them, the government faced the task of sending them to prison, where they became martyrs to the cause. In June 1909 a suffragette in prison went on hunger strike, which confronted the authorities with the unpleasant alternatives of letting her die or forcibly feeding her, by forcing a tube down her throat and pumping her full of sloppy food. When she obtained her release, her example was soon followed by others.

The culmination of the suffragists' campaign

A truce was called for the 1910 elections, but soon a new campaign was launched, chiefly of window breaking and attacks on property.

The campaign was intensified by Mrs Pankhurst's daughter, Christabel, who drove the Pethick-Lawrences from the movement by her extremism. She established herself in an office in Paris beyond the reach of the British authorities, and proceeded for two years to organize a campaign of crime.

Arson formed the main ingredient. Letters in pillar-boxes were set alight, boat-houses, a grandstand, pavilions, half a wooden railway station, empty houses and one or two private schools were torched. Attacks were made on the British Museum and the Tower of London; famous art galleries had to be closed because pictures in them were slashed and statuary mutilated. Later, bomb attacks were made on a variety of accessible targets. The orchid-houses were destroyed at Kew, and various golf greens were dug up. Telephone wires were cut, and hundreds of hoax fire-alarm calls were made. In 1913 the Derby was marred by the tragedy of the suffragette, Emily Davison, who attempted to pull up the King's horse at Tattenham Corner and died later from the trampling she received. Public opinion decided that something had to be done.

An Act, commonly known as the 'Cat and Mouse' Act, was passed in 1913, allowing the release of hunger-strikers so that they would not die on the government's hands, and then requiring them to be rearrested later to finish their sentences.

At the same time, Asquith made it known that in the new Reform Bill he was proposing, he would accept any clause on women's suffrage that the Commons would agree on. Three such amendments were put down, and the passage of one of them seemed assured, when the Speaker caused universal astonishment by ruling them all out of order. Asquith withdrew the measure, substituting a Plural Voting Bill in its place, which was duly passed. The prospects for female suffrage seemed gloomy.

▷ The People's Budget and the Parliament Act

The conflict between the Lords and the Commons had been building since the 1890s, and reached a new pitch of resentment under the Liberal government after 1906. Numerous proposals had been mutilated in debate, and a number rejected altogether by the in-built Conservative majority in the Upper House. Lloyd George in a vigorous public speech in Newcastle asked whether: 'Five hundred men, ordinary men, chosen accidentally from the unemployed, shall override the judgement of millions of people who are engaged in the industry which makes the wealth of the country.' He made fun of them by portraying them as the 'idle rich', using their station to preserve their privileges. He ridiculed the hereditary principle which gave titles and rights to the first-born, saying they were merely 'the first in the litter'. He knew he was on strong ground: if the Lords gave way, well and good; if they resisted the democratic will, he would do away with them altogether.

The People's Budget, 1909

This was the result of massive spending increases: there had been pressure for more battleships because of the supposed need to rearm against Germany; and there was also the need to finance social welfare spending, e.g. for old age pensions. The Exchequer had to find an extra £16 million (a much bigger sum than in present figures), and this was a task which Lloyd George embraced with gusto.

(a) The budget proposed:
   (i) £600,000 per year for a *Road Fund* to modernize roads, the money coming from motor licences and a tax on petrol;
   (ii) £100,000 per year for *Labour Exchanges*;
   (iii) further funding for a *Development Commission* to preserve the environment and natural resources.
(b) The tax proposals included:
   (i) an increase in the *standard rate* of income tax from 1s (5p) to 1s 2d (6p) in the pound, with reductions in tax assessments for incomes under £500 of £10 a year for each child;
   (ii) *super tax* of a further 6d (2½p) in the pound on incomes over £5,000 per year, levied on the amount by which these incomes exceeded £3,000;
   (iii) *land value duties*: an annual charge on the value of undeveloped land and minerals, plus a 20 per cent levy on the increased value of land whenever it was sold (this was known as the *unearned increment*);
   (iv) increases in *liquor and tobacco duties*.
   (v) increases in *stamp duties*, e.g. on sale of houses, plus death duties beginning on estates over £5,000 (this went up to 25 per cent on estates over £1 million).

The unwritten custom of the constitution was that the Lords did not interfere with money bills. 'Taxation by consent' meant that those who mostly paid the taxes should have the final say as to what they were. But Lloyd George was now presenting the Lords as a selfish clique of rich men trying to dodge their share of the burden. In rejecting the budget, as they did when it was presented to them, they protested in vain that they were only claiming the same rights as the Commons claimed for themselves. How could it be fair for taxes to be imposed by one section of the community and paid by another? The Lords supported the Conservative *Budget Protest League*, and Lloyd George took up their challenge in a series of derisive speeches in which he held up the Lords to ridicule, comparing them, for example, to battleships: 'A fully-equipped Duke costs as much to keep up as two Dreadnoughts; and Dukes are just as great a terror and last longer.'

The Parliament Act, 1909

In December 1909, Asquith informed the King, Edward VII, that he could not continue as Prime Minister if the Upper House persisted in denying him the supplies of money to meet the government's expenses. He asked the King to create enough peers to get the budget through. Edward agreed, but only after a *second* general election. Asquith said nothing about this at the time, but dissolved Parliament and called a general election for January 1910.

The Liberals had no mandate to alter the House of Lords before this election, and the election itself did not give them one. The Irish Nationalists were re-elected for most of their seats, 82 in number, but the Labour Party, suffering from shortage of funds, went down to 40 seats. The Liberals and Conservatives were evenly balanced, the former with 275 seats and the latter with 273. With support from the two smaller groups, the Liberals had a majority of 124. This was enough to press ahead with their plans for a *Parliament Act*, an intention which, for reasons of their own, both the other parties supported. The Liberals embarked on their bill, simultaneously passing the People's Budget a second time and again sending it up to the Lords.

This time the Lords passed it without even a division, concentrating all their attention on the coming struggle over the Parliament Act. After the requisite second general election in December 1910, with results almost identical to the one in January, the Liberals and their allies pushed through two new measures:

(a) *1911, Parliament Act* contained three main provisions:
   (i) All bills which the Speaker of the Commons declared were money bills (and this was intended to include all budgets) were to become law within one month whether or not the Lords agreed with them. This showed clearly that the Commons controlled the purse strings.
   (ii) All other bills, if passed by the Commons in three successive sessions, were to become law with the royal signature, even if the Lords rejected them, provided that two years had elapsed between the bill's introduction and its final passage.
   (iii) The maximum life of any parliament was reduced from seven years to five, making it more clearly dependent on the will of the electorate than before, but reducing the time during which the power of the Lower House was unfettered by the Upper.
(b) *Payment of MPs* was carried out not by statute, but merely by Standing Order in the House of Commons. In future, MPs were to be awarded a salary of £400 per year, about twice as much as the wages of the working man at the time. To some extent this offset the effects of the *Osborne Judgment* in 1909, when the trade union political levy was declared illegal, except on a voluntary basis. Some annoyance was expressed by the Lords that the Commons had ducked the Osborne Judgment in this way, and that they had chosen to use standing orders, which prevented the Upper House from debating the proposal. But, even if the Commons had decided to proceed by statute, the Lords would not have been able, under the terms of the Parliament Act, to block it, since it would have been certified by the Speaker as a money bill. In any case, there were good precedents for proceeding by resolution in such a matter, so the protest of the Lords did not amount to anything.

Both these measures deepened the ill-feeling which pervaded British politics at the time, springing from an unmerited triumphalism on the part of the Liberals, and sour displeasure on the part of the Conservatives. The People's Budget went into effect immediately, setting on foot a considerable redistribution of wealth. The land duties, however, were ill-conceived and never worked well, and were abandoned after the First World War. Revived after the Second World War as a bit of doctrinaire Labour baggage, they once again proved themselves unworkable and were finally dropped.

Fig. 3.1 *Punch* cartoon, 28 April 1909

RICH FARE
THE GIANT LLOYD-GORGIBUSTER:
'Fee, Fi, Fo, Fat,
I smell the blood of a plutocrat;
Be he alive or be he dead,
I'll grind his bones to make my bread.'

▷ **Continuing Liberal reform**

The period after 1911 did not produce the same flood of reforming legislation as had occurred earlier. This was due partly to the wave of exhaustion following the constitutional crisis of 1910–11, and partly to the necessity of passing the same law in all but identical terms in successive sessions, as the Parliament Act obliged the Commons to do in order to get round the Lords' veto. None the less, Parliament did pass a number of important reforms.

Political reform

1913, Plural Voting Act placed on the statute book ideas first put forward in 1907. Apart from university seats, where members continued to be elected by the graduates of the university concerned, people were prohibited from voting in more than one constituency. At the same time, the Act reduced the residence qualification for voting, so shortening the time during which voters would be left off the register if they moved house. Women, however, were still debarred from voting at the national level.

Industrial reforms

From 1911 to 1913, new laws began to regulate conditions in various industries:

(a) *1911, Shops Act* avoided the question of limiting the hours of shop assistants, but awarded them a half-day holiday.
(b) *1911, Coal Mines Act* amended the law on the subject and further improved conditions.
(c) *1911, Official Secrets Act* took the first of a series of restrictive measures against espionage, though the Act came to be used for more mundane matters.
(d) *1911, Aerial Navigation Act* was designed as a safety measure to prevent aircraft flying too low over heavily populated areas.
(e) *1911, Copyright Act* harmonized British law with continental law on the same subject, and prevented overseas pirating of copyright material.
(f) *1912, Minimum Wage Act* set up arbitration machinery by appointing joint boards of employers and workers in every district to regulate wages.

Some of the earlier land legislation was re-enacted. *1912, Smallholders (Scotland) Act* gave security to tenants of holdings of a limited size, and created a Scottish Board of Agriculture on the pattern of the English ministry. Whether they liked it or not, the Lords had to accept the passing of this Act.

Trade union reform

Since the Osborne Judgment, trade unions had found it difficult to collect political contributions from their members. This was one reason why the Labour Party did not perform well in the two elections of 1910. The remedy to this was twofold:

(a) *1911, payment of MPs* by Resolution of the Commons.
(b) *1913, Trade Union Act* permitted the creation of a political fund by unions and the imposition of a political levy, provided that it was approved by a majority of the members, was included in the rules, and objectors were allowed to 'contract out' by informing officials that they did not wish to pay. Objectors were not to be penalized by the loss of any union privileges; nor were they to be publicly named.

Social reforms

The most ambitious of these related to social insurance benefits.
1911, National Insurance Act fell into two parts:

(a) *Unemployment provisions* were chiefly designed to protect low-paid men from being out of work. This was because most of them had wives and families who would be the main ones to suffer poverty as the result of it. But even for men, insurance did not extend as far as seven 'precarious' industries (including building and engineering, where there were frequent fluctuations in prosperity). Otherwise, however, workers were to be entitled to benefits of 7s (35p) a week for the first thirteen weeks of unemployment, paid from a fund to which the worker, the employer and the state each contributed 2½d (1p) a week during normal times. Benefit would then cease until the worker was 'back in benefit' in his new job and had made a further thirteen weeks' contributions. The benefit was intended to be no more than a 'transitional' one, covering men for the transfer from one job to another. The idea that men should be unemployed in the long term was not something to which this Act addressed itself, though it became very common between the wars.
(b) *Sickness provisions* were also included in the Act. These were intended to be universal, though the better-off worker need only be a 'voluntary contributor'. The general rule was that all workers between the ages of 16 and 70, if they earned less than £160 per year, were to receive medical benefits covering illness, disablement, hospitalization and, for females, maternity grants. This scheme was also contributory: the worker paid 4d (2p) a week, the employer 3d (1p) and the state 2d (1p). This gave rise to Lloyd George's observation that the worker was getting 'ninepence for fourpence'. The scheme operated largely through the existing Friendly Societies, which achieved the status of 'approved societies' for the purpose. Workers enrolled in a system of 'panels', set up by the doctors, under which the patients had the choice of a

doctor, and this 'panel doctor' provided them with the treatment to which they were entitled.

Medical insurance aroused furious opposition. There was a large public meeting in the Albert Hall in London, where duchesses urged servant girls to cherish their independence and not become stamp-lickers. The press weighed in to stop the onslaught of bureaucracy. The British Medical Association declared against it. The trade unions were opposed to the idea of a contributory insurance scheme – if there had to be one, it ought to be free. The Friendly Societies were distinctly unfriendly, since they feared being put out of business. Employers disliked having to contribute towards the cost.

This was the sort of battle that Lloyd George relished. A number of skilful concessions eventually silenced the critics. The Friendly Societies became the linchpins of the scheme, and even the trade unions gained in influence as a result of it. Though the doctors had objected strenuously to possible 'state control', many of them did very well out of the panel system, as did the chemists. Even the workers accepted the system as being in their interests. The state was soon handing out over £6½ million a year in panel payments to doctors, and nearly £1½ million to chemists for the prescriptions they made up. By 1920, 12 million of the 14 million working population were enrolled in panels, and annually about 60 per cent of them were receiving some sort of treatment.

Welsh Disestablishment

For years there had been a strong feeling against the Anglican establishment by the mass of Welsh non-conformists, and with his Welsh background Lloyd George supported them. This produced a bill to disestablish and partly disendow the church in Wales. Passed by the Commons, the bill was rejected by the House of Lords in 1913, but was allowed to pass at its second presentation in 1914, despite stout Anglican resistance.

▷ The end of an era

By 1914, the peaceful and orderly Britain that most people took for granted in Edwardian times was already beginning to break up. George Dangerfield, in his book *The Strange Death of Liberal England*, goes so far as to say that: 'It was in 1910 that fires long smouldering in the English spirit suddenly flared up, so that by the end of 1913 Liberal England was reduced to ashes.' This could be seen in a number of ways:

(a) The vision of a peaceful *European order* was proving to be a mirage, with successive crises in foreign policy which suggested impending war. War fever, encouraged by the gutter press, was growing against Germany.

(b) The campaign for *female suffrage* was reaching its peak, with the Women's Social and Political Union pressing for changes in the electoral law. Diminishing respect for law and order could be seen in the efforts of the suffragettes to ridicule the police and challenge the ruling male order in society.

(c) *Ulster resistance* to the Irish Home Rule bill, introduced by the Liberals to reward the Irish Nationalists for their support during the recent English crisis, seemed to show that, if need be, the whole province of Northern Ireland was prepared to come out in defiance of the law.

(d) *Labour militancy* arose from the powerlessness of the trade unions and from the persistence of poor wages and conditions in a supposedly prosperous country, working hard in the cause of rearmament. Strikes threatened on the railways and in the coal mines, and socialist voices could be heard demanding the end of the whole capitalist system.

GLOSSARY

Civil and criminal law   Crimes are offences against society where a prosecution is brought against an offender by the Crown (i.e. the state) after arrest by the police. *Civil offences* are offences against individual people or groups, where the decision to prosecute is the responsibility of the individuals concerned. The former are often punished by imprisonment; the latter usually by fines and damages.

Doctrine of electoral mandate
Political leaders had always explained their views to voters at election times, but with the formation of nationally organized parties in the 1870s, the need for common agreement on policy programmes became urgent. In 1885, Joseph Chamberlain produced considerable misgiving among the Liberal leadership by issuing an *Unauthorised Programme*, thus highlighting the need for an official party manifesto. The Liberal *Newcastle Programme* in 1891 was one example of such a manifesto.

The notion that a party returned to office by a general election should be bound by promises it had made in its manifesto, and should refrain from introducing policies which were not mentioned in it, was something which the Conservatives seem to have thought of after 1906. The doctrine was used by them in order to criticize both the 1909 budget and the subsequent Liberal attack on the House of Lords. Of course, the Liberals could reply that, when there are new developments, ruling parties are compelled to bring in policies on which they have not consulted the voters. But this did not stop the idea of an *electoral mandate*, in which the voters bound the government to certain lines of policy, from gaining wide acceptance in the twentieth century.

Imperial preference
Where tariffs or duties are imposed on foreign imports, governments may choose to prefer imports from certain favoured countries, such as their own colonies. They do this by charging imports from the favoured country a lower (preferential) duty or no duty at all.

Protection
This is the economic policy of imposing tariffs on imported goods, not to raise revenue, but to protect the interests of home producers of similar goods. Thus the farmer is said to be *protected* by tariffs on farm produce, and the manufacturer by tariffs on manufactures.

Suffragists and suffragettes
The early supporters of women's suffrage were known as *suffragists*. They pursued their aim of votes for women by peaceful means – through pamphlets, public meetings, lobbying Members of Parliament, letters to the press and other legitimate forms of publicity. The increasingly law-breaking methods of the *Women's Social and Political Union* after 1906, but particularly after they intensified from about 1910, created a split in the suffragist movement. Those who believed in peaceful methods remained known as suffragists, but those who resorted to public disorder, violence and arson began to be known as *suffragettes*. For a time the distinction was blurred, and quality newspapers like *The Times* could still as late as 1911 refer to violent women demonstrators as suffragists. By 1912 the suffragettes were getting all the publicity, much of it adverse, and the public had come to believe, wrongly, that all those in favour of votes for women were potential law-breakers.

 EXAMINATION QUESTIONS

▷ **Question 1**
Study Source A and then answer the questions which follow.

Source A

The militant suffragists yesterday appeared to have lost all control of themselves. Some shrieked, some laughed hysterically, and all fought with a dogged and aimless determination. Some of the rioters appeared to be quite young girls, who must have been the victims of hysterical rather than deep conviction. A woman dressed in the uniform of a hospital nurse threw a missile through the window of the Colonial Office. Some of the suffragists carried banners, which were quickly torn down by the police, but if the bearer managed to retain the bamboo handle she used it to belabour the nearest constable. The women behaved like demented creatures, and it was evident that their conduct completely alienated the sympathy of the crowd. The police behaved with self-control and good humour under the greatest provocation. It may be mentioned that as a result of Friday's fight six policemen had to go on the sick list with bites and scratches.

(From an account of a suffragette demonstration, *The Times*, 23 November 1910)

(a) What can you learn from Source A about the attitude of *The Times* towards the suffragettes? (6 marks)

(b) Why did so many politicians oppose votes for women? (6 marks)

▷ **Question 2**   Study the sources below carefully, and then answer the questions which follow.

Source A

This is the crux of the whole problem . . . The truth is that in practice the House of Lords gives effect to the will of the House of Commons when you have a Tory majority; the House of Lords frustrates the will of the Commons when you have a Liberal majority; and in neither the one case nor the other does it consider – what indeed it has no means of ascertaining – the will of the people.

(H.H. Asquith in a speech in the House of Commons, 1907)

Source B

The House of Lords has long ceased to be the watchdog of the Constitution. It has become Mr Balfour's poodle. It barks for him. It fetches and carries for him. It bites anyone that he sets it onto. (1908)

This is a war budget. It is for raising money to wage implacable war against poverty and squalidness. (1909)

A fully-equipped Duke costs as much to keep up as two Dreadnoughts, and they are just as great a terror, and they last longer. As long as they were content to be mere idols on their pedestals . . . the average British citizen rather looked up to them.
    But then came the budget. The Dukes stepped off their perches. They have been scolding like omnibus drivers purely because the budget cart has knocked a little of the gilt off their old stage coach. Well, we cannot put them back again.
    The question will be asked whether five hundred men, chosen accidentally from among the unemployed, should override the judgement – the deliberate judgement – of millions of people who are engaged in the industry which makes the wealth of the country. (October 1909) (Lloyd George, excerpts from speeches, 1908–9)

Source C

Today will be signalled by an event of the highest constitutional and historical importance – the exercise by the House of Lords of an unquestionable and indispensable right which it has not been necessary to use for a very long time thanks to the wise moderation with which, upon the whole, our Constitution has been worked by statesmen of all parties. That traditional moderation has been abandoned by the present government. (*The Times*, 30 November 1909)

Source D

Study the cartoon of Lloyd George on page 24.

(a) Using Source A and your own knowledge, explain why Asquith was so critical of the House of Lords.   (6 marks)

(b) Source B is from several speeches; Source D is a cartoon. Which of the two sources is more useful to an historian studying the Parliament crisis of 1909–11? Explain your answer.   (8 marks)

(c) In Source C is *The Times* reporting facts or giving opinions? Explain your answer.   (5 marks)

(d) Study Sources B and C. Lloyd George and *The Times* give different interpretations of the quarrel between Lords and Commons. Why do you think their interpretations are so different?   (7 marks)

(e) 'The crisis of 1909–11 was not a minor one, but a very serious one indeed.' Using all the sources and your own knowledge, show whether you agree or disagree with this statement.   (10 marks)

▶ **EXAMINATION ANSWERS**

▷ **Question 1** *Tutor answer*

(a) *The Times* is unsympathetic. It talks of the suffragettes' hysteria and aimlessness, and repeats the hysteria accusation against young women, who, it presumes, were not capable of forming a deep conviction of their own. It hints that women deliberately dressed up as nurses to commit violence, and that they were not averse to attacking the police with bamboo handles. The women were described as demented, and their behaviour contrasted with the self-control and good humour of the police. Finally no mention is made of the probable casualties among the suffragettes in their battle with the police, but six policemen were injured – not by bamboo or missile, but by the presumably typical female weapons of tooth and nail. This is, of course, only an extract from the report, so suffragette casualties may appear elsewhere, but over-all *The Times* gives the impression that the suffragettes were behaving outrageously.

(b) The political opponents of women's suffrage believed that the woman's place was in the home. Politics and government were men's work because women behaved and thought irrationally and emotionally, as Source A 'proved'. On issues such as peace or war, women would be unable to follow the country's interests, because they would be obsessed by the horrors that war brings rather than by the prestige and power interests which would be sacrificed if the wrong decision were taken. Women were not educated for politics, and if given the vote they would meekly follow the voting instructions of their husbands, or, worse still, they would vote for the most hand-some candidate. Many politicians thought it would be a leap into the unknown to enfranchise so many women and thus more than double the number of voters. Some Liberals thought that women would be more likely to vote Conservative, but tried to justify their opposition to female suffrage on other grounds. Many Conservatives opposed change as a matter of principle. So the opposition to female suffrage was both political and sexist.

▷ **Question 2** *Tutor answer*

(a) Asquith is saying that when the Conservatives are in power the House of Lords accepts without question all parliamentary bills sent to it by the House of Commons, but when the Liberals are in power the House of Lords obstructs the legislative pro-posals of the House of Commons, even though the House of Lords is not a repre-sentative body, and has no means of discovering whether or not it is acting according to the will of the country. Asquith had justification for his assertion. The House of Lords had never obstructed Conservative legislation in recent times, but there was a long history of Lords' obstruction of Liberal legislation going back to Gladstone, in particular the Lords' defeat of Home Rule, and more recently the Lords' obstruction of parliamentary bills concerning plural voting, education and licensing. Although the Lords had accepted others, such as the Trades Disputes Bill, which its Conservative majority intensely disliked, Asquith resented a situation in which the legislation of an elected House was at the mercy of a hostile majority in an unelected House.

(b) This very much depends on what the historian wants to know. If he or she is look-ing for information, then there is certainly in Lloyd George's speeches reference to the changing function of the House of Lords, the aim of the 1909 budget, and the attitude of dukes towards the budget. Cartoons, such as Source D, on the other hand, are usually short on information and pursue a single theme. But Lloyd George is not an unbiased witness, and the information in his speeches is tainted. Source B tells the historian a good deal about Lloyd George, the brilliance of his oratory and the ruthlessness of his attack, and how a member of the government viewed the cur-rent situation. Source D gives one man's rather unflattering opinion about Lloyd George, but in so far as this is a published cartoon it must reflect the opinion of many of those who would see it at the time. Neither can be relied on for historical accuracy, but B is more useful for those who want to know about Lloyd George, and D is more useful for those interested in contemporary public opinion.

(c) There are no specifically stated facts in Source C, but some are implied, such as the House of Lords' rejection of the budget, and the fact that this has not been done for a 'very long time'. The rest is all opinion. This is not surprising in view of the fact that *The Times* was supporting the Conservative opposition. The 'unquestionable and indispensable right' was by no means either unquestionable or indispensable, and the abandonment of 'traditional moderation by the present government' would have been seen very differently by members of a government whose legislation had been mangled by the House of Lords and who would find references to the Lords' 'wise moderation' unconvincing to say the least. In this short extract no evidence is provided to support the many assertions offered.

(d) Source B consists of extracts from the speeches of a Liberal whose avowed purpose is to use the budget to wage war on poverty and whose less explicit purpose is to wage war on the House of Lords. Lloyd George was from the Radical rather than the Whig wing of the Liberal Party. He was incensed by the Lords' tactics over Liberal legislation, and lacked the caution of some of his more moderate colleagues who regarded him as a hot-head. His speeches seem almost an incitement to and a justification of class warfare.

The Times backed the Conservative Party and was widely read among the influential. It disdained to copy what it considered to be Lloyd George's gutter tactics, and sheltered behind the constitution in order to give validity to its cause. Thus not only are Sources B and C shown to be on opposite sides, but Lloyd George in his attack, and *The Times* in its defence, adopt very different tactics.

(e) The seriousness of the crisis is not immediately apparent from the sources. Asquith, in Source A, seems a model of constraint. Lloyd George, in B, is hot on rhetoric, but seems to be reserving his best ammunition for a few obscure dukes. *The Times* suggests a greater sense of urgency in its references to the constitution and an event of the highest importance, but the cartoon is more a comment on Lloyd George's financial ruthlessness than on a political crisis. Not even *The Times* is able to convey the seriousness of the political situation created by the Lords' rejection of the 1909 budget. The Lords' action meant that financial control effectively passed from Commons to Lords, that the government was deprived of revenue and the power to raise it, and that the House of Commons had to reassert its authority or sink into the role of the subordinate House. Militant trade unions and truculent suffragettes, even foreign policy, took a back seat while the parliamentary drama was played out. What made the fight more ferocious was the Conservative fear that a reduction in the power of the House of Lords would open the way to Home Rule for Ireland – this the Conservatives had always strenuously and vehemently opposed. The necessary tactics of the Liberal government – the use of general elections and of the royal power to create peers – involved the monarchy directly, adding to the constitutional dangers and party bitterness. For two years the conflict absorbed the energies and attention of the whole country; there had been no graver political crisis since 1832.

SUMMARY

In this chapter you have taken your study of British domestic history up to the First World War. The main topics you have covered are:

▷ the last years of Conservative rule, 1901–5;

▷ why there was a Liberal 'landslide' in 1906, and what it meant;

▷ the social and political reforms of the Liberals, 1906–14;

▷ the 'People's Budget', 1909;

▷ the suffragette movement;

▷ the Liberals' conflict with the House of Lords and its results;

▷ labour and trade union legislation of the period.

Material relating to other aspects of this period is to be found in other chapters:

▷ background to the First World War in chapter 4;

▷ trade unions and the Labour Party in chapter 5.

The First World War

GETTING STARTED

The culmination of 40 years of increasing friction and international tension was the outbreak of the First World War at the start of August 1914. Even so, the actual outbreak came as something of a surprise to a generation that had come to think that there was nothing that could not be solved by diplomatic effort. When a whole month passed after the Sarajevo murder without war, people began to breathe more freely, but this time the crisis did not blow over.

MEG	NEAB	NICCEA	SEG	LONDON	WJEC	TOPIC	STUDY	REVISION 1	REVISION 2
✓*	✓		✓*	✓		**The fighting in the war**			
✓*	✓		✓*	✓		The approach of war			
✓*	✓		✓*	✓		Responsibility for the war			
✓*	✓		✓*	✓		The campaigns of the war			
✓*	✓		✓*	✓		The new technology			
✓*	✓		✓*	✓		**The Home Front**			
✓*	✓		✓*	✓		The impact of the war			
✓*	✓		✓*	✓		Social consequences of the war			

* Coursework only

WHAT YOU NEED TO KNOW

The fighting in the war

▷ **The approach of war**

Historians have long asked what caused the war. This is partly because people felt that the war was so ghastly that every effort should be made to stop it happening again, and that only if the causes could be known could it be prevented in future. It is also partly because Clause 231 of the Versailles Treaty, which put the blame on Germany, came to be regarded as unjust, and led historians to search for other guilty parties. Another reason was the suddenness of the war. Though there had been crises previously, diplomacy had always resolved them; here was a conflict that was not only appalling, but also unexplained. What brought it about?

Nationalism

This had been the main motive force of European history in the previous century. To Britain, in particular, the growth of German nationalism seemed especially threatening. At the same time, many other features of the map of modern Europe were quite unfamiliar. Poland did not exist at all. Other nation groups, like the Danes and the Czechs, still lived partly under foreign domination; the map was filled up with the three autocratic empires of Russia, Germany and Austria-Hungary. The latter was a disintegrating patchwork of some fifteen nations under the rule of the Emperor Franz Josef. By 1914, too, the Turkish Empire, which had given rise to troubles for much of the previous 50 years, was almost completely in dissolution; the newly emerged Balkan states were fighting and quarrelling, and the major powers were involved there by reason of the links they had with the various states.

Economic rivalry

There was intense economic rivalry between nations and groups. Germany's recent industrialization, and its rapid advance in steel, shipbuilding and chemicals, threatened to supplant Britain in its export markets, and perhaps even in its home markets, unprotected by tariffs. Germany and Austria were also expanding in the Balkans with schemes like the Berlin–Baghdad Railway, which Britain thought might short-circuit the Suez Canal. Russia was also guilty of economic imperialism, linked with ethnic domination, in various areas of Europe and Asia.

Colonial rivalry

Linked with this there was also colonial rivalry. Britain and France already had big empires, and Germany, though a newcomer to the scene, was proving a successful rival. All these powers were driven by the prevailing wisdom that colonies were necessary sources of raw materials and outlets for manufactured exports, as well as reflecting prestige and glory on the homeland. Colonial crises, like those in the Sudan and Morocco, were examples of this European struggle for domination.

The arms race

Competition in armaments was bound to be the result. Industrial resources and technological know-how were increasingly being turned to warlike purposes, European powers, except for Britain, had adopted conscription to enlarge their armies, and the three largest were those of France and Germany, with about 600,000 men each, and Russia, with nearly 900,000. Naval rivalries also developed, especially between Britain and Germany, both sides engaging in a race to build ever heavier warships, with bigger guns, more penetrating shells, and thicker steel plate to protect them from attack. Of course, the arms race cannot be said to be a cause of war, any more than red spots can be said to be the cause of measles, but it certainly meant that when war came it would be a particularly devastating one.

The alliance system

The alliance system was also a symptom rather than a cause of conflict. Germany, Austria and Italy had formed the Triple Alliance in the 1880s, and France and Russia the Dual Alliance in the 1890s. Britain was attached to neither of them, but agreed ententes with the French and then the Russians early in the twentieth century. The entente with France, in particular, developed new significance with military and naval conversations in subsequent years, until, in spite of Britain's lingering illusions of freedom of action, it became impossible to conceive of the two countries except as allies. The war itself was a result of a quarrel between Austria and Serbia, which steadily dragged in other powers until it resulted in general war in a matter of days. The alliance system was like a rope, linking together the members of a climbing team to ensure their safety, but one which, when a climber fell, dragged the whole group to destruction. War could no longer be localized, but spread.

The nationalist popular press

Rival newspapers of the popular press were the battleground for a phantom war of words before the real war broke out. Improved technical processes meant that it was now possible to run off millions of copies of cheap papers from the 'gutter press', which exploited and inflamed the prejudices of a half-educated public. Of course, no newspaper proprietor felt any responsibility for the conduct of public affairs; he was merely trying to sell what he printed. Truth went by the board, and reporting was exaggerated and sensational. No sane government wanted war, but when there were such newspapers in circulation, it was often impossible to allay people's fears.

▷ **Responsibility for the war**

The socialist explanation

Socialists were not only looking at newspaper tycoons when they blamed the capitalist system for the outbreak of war; they thought it was capitalism itself that was to blame. In each country they saw a conspiracy of capitalist bosses to exploit and underpay their workers to get bigger profits, and to poison their minds against their fellow-workers in other countries in order that they should kill each other with appropriate enthusiasm. In the colonial empires they saw an even wider conspiracy to exploit the native peoples for the benefit of their white masters.

Rival capitalist states, too, were engaged in a cannibalistic struggle between themselves, struggling for markets and raw materials in an ever-shrinking world, while investing their treasure in armaments, and spilling the blood of their young men in order to preserve their dividends.

Marxists regarded imperialism, capitalism and war as being inseparably joined as different aspects of the same basic evil.

Which country should bear the blame?

No country in practice ever admitted responsibility for the war, and there is little doubt that none ever felt itself responsible. But the element of national obstinacy was undoubtedly present. France feared German militarism, and sought revenge for its earlier humiliation in 1870. Britain pursued a selfish policy, using the friendship of others, but unwilling to pledge firm support in return. Russian and Austrian policies dabbled with expansionist ideas, their designs diametrically opposed in the Balkans, both powers behaving recklessly in view of their internal decay. Italy, whose loyalty to the Central Powers had long been doubtful, hesitated about what to do in order to be sure of jumping on the winning bandwagon.

The Kaiser's strategic aims were clearly largely defensive. He felt he had to preserve the existence of his only reliable ally, Austria; he needed to break free of the encircling powers of the Triple Entente; he dreaded a war on two fronts; he wished to resist the military pressure of the French and the commercial competition of the British. He felt that war was eventually inescapable, and so he felt he had to make preparations for it by building up a mighty army and navy, and vesting great authority in the soldiers of his General Staff. In the end, it was not the Kaiser or the Chancellor who had the final word; it was the Chief of the General Staff, von Moltke. To the extent that these people decided, and the Kaiser allowed them, to settle their problems militarily, instead of by diplomacy, it could be said that it was Germany which caused the war.

▷ **The campaigns of the war**

The assassination of the Archduke Franz Ferdinand at Sarajevo at the end of June 1914 set in motion the train of events which led to the outbreak of war in early August, after the Austrian Emperor had successfully reassured himself of the support of his German allies. But the first real blows were struck by Germany.

The beginning of the war

Austria's attack on Serbia was the prelude to war. The immediate cause of the entry of Britain into the war was the German invasion of Belgium. This was in spite of Britain's ultimatum requesting that the powers observe Belgian neutrality, as guaranteed in the treaty of 1839. The German plan, the Schlieffen Plan, was elaborate and detailed, too complex for the Germans to modify it at a late date; hence their military leaders had to take the chance that Britain would accept their assurances that, even if they invaded Belgium, they would guarantee that the country would be re-established after the war was over.

It seems likely that Britain would have gone to war in any case, even if the Germans had abandoned the Schlieffen Plan. Although the entente between Britain and France fell short of a military alliance, Britain was already heavily committed to the side of France by the military conversations of 1907, which had closely coordinated the strategic planning of the two countries, and by the naval conversations of 1912, under which Britain was to be entrusted with the protection of the Channel, while the French concentrated on the Mediterranean. It was inconceivable that Britain should take no action while German troops poured into northern France. But by refusing to respect Belgian neutrality, Germany provided Britain with a cast-iron excuse for declaring war.

Working to a precise timetable, German troops poured through Belgium towards the French frontier. Their troop trains even carried portable wooden platforms stacked on their roofs so that when the men alighted from their carriages between stations they would not get their boots dirty, and so would look smart as they marched through captured Belgian villages. Arms, ammunition and other war materials were organized with meticulous precision to keep up with the army's advance.

Belgian forces resisted to the best of their ability, helped by as many French as could be sent in time, and by the 160,000 men of the British Expeditionary Force (BEF) on the continent – the men referred to by the Kaiser as 'this contemptible little army'; after this they referred to themselves with some pride as the 'Old Contemptibles'. At Mons, the British and the Germans clashed with each other for the first time. The rifle fire of the highly trained British troops was so rapid and accurate that the Germans thought they had run into nests of machine guns, and fell back. But in the end the British were defeated by the efficient organization and the sheer weight of numbers of the German forces.

During this campaign, there were massed cavalry charges for about the last time in modern warfare. But though the sight of them in their polished helmets manoeuvring in the late summer sunlight was impressive, they did not affect the outcome very much. Liège resisted for a week before it fell; Namur, Brussels, Malines and Louvain followed swiftly after, although Antwerp held out until the autumn. Belgium was overrun, but its gallant resistance provided a breathing space for the Allies to get their troops into position. Without this, Paris might have fallen in the first weeks of the war, which could have been over before it had started.

The French and British fell back slowly on the Marne, fighting stubbornly and suffering heavy casualties. By September the Germans had crossed the Grand Morin and the Petit Morin, and the pounding of German guns could be heard in Paris, only 30 kilometres to the west. The German divisional commander von Kluck swung his right inwards to overwhelm the Allies' left wing, but in doing so exposed his flank to counterattack. The military governor of Paris, Galliéni, rushed troops up to the front in taxicabs, causing more German soldiers to be diverted to meet them, and creating a hole in the advancing German front through which the British and French counterattacked. German lines of communication were already dangerously overstretched, their High Command nervous and their timetable breaking down; so, although they had not been seriously defeated, German commanders thought it prudent to withdraw and regroup themselves behind the River Aisne. Here both sides dug themselves in, and the front moved very little for the whole duration of the war.

The Western Front

The lines of trenches from the Swiss border to the Channel coast were the main theatre of the conflict for about 50 months, in which boredom, frostbite and typhus-carrying lice competed to destroy human life and morale, and where long stretches of inactivity were occasionally interrupted by enormously costly set battles such as the Somme (1916) and Passchendaele (1917). The trenches were subjected to artillery bombardments of unendurable ferocity; men were sent 'over the top' to such certainty of death that literally thousands of them refused the order to go, but preferred to be summarily shot for cowardice by their own men. In two days, for example, before the battle of Messines Ridge in 1917, no fewer than $4\frac{1}{4}$ million shells were fired against a short stretch of frontline, and the roar of more than 20 shells a second not only obliterated the landscape and turned it into a morass, but also unhinged the minds of the soldiers who experienced the bombardment.

Though the latest in military technology – gas, flamethrowers, tanks – was employed, neither side achieved a complete breakthrough. Any local advance proved to be no more than temporary, and then was purchased only at the cost of thousands of lives. So inhuman was the suffering that by 1917 the French army was on the verge of mutiny, and for much of the last year of the war the main brunt of the fighting fell on the British and their American allies.

Battles on the Western Front

Verdun, 1916 From February to December Gen. Falkenhayn concentrated his efforts against this major fortress, which he knew the French would make any sacrifice to defend. His idea was to draw all France's reserves into the line to be blasted by the heavy artillery he had concentrated in this sector. As foreseen, French losses were enormous, and the morale of the French troops began to crack.

The Somme, 1916 This was a belated effort to relieve the pressure on the French by staging a major attack to the north. From July to November, Gen. Haig tried to break through the German lines and advanced about 50km at a cost of 600,000 casualties – 60,000 of them on the first day. Much of the land gained was of little strategic value, and was lost again later.

Passchendaele, 1917 Futile French attacks further north near Arras led to enormous losses and a mutiny in the French ranks, when troops refused to engage in further costly and suicidal offensives. The British came to the rescue by seizing Messines Ridge, from which the Germans had overlooked Ypres. The offensive lasted from July until November, and culminated in the bloody and pointless attack on the village of Passchendaele, with losses of 300,000 men. These losses finally convinced Haig that his tactics were wrong.

Cambrai, 1917 Tanks had been useless in Flanders, where they simply sank into the mud. Firmer ground was found at Cambrai, 60km to the south, where 381 tanks went forward in November, without any preliminary bombardment. They broke through the German lines, advancing 8km and capturing 10,000 German prisoners and 200 guns. But the Germans brought up their reserves and ten days later had recovered all the lost ground and captured several tanks that had been knocked out. Thus the advantage of surprise was lost.

Ludendorff's offensive, 1918 German troops, having strengthened their position by a voluntary withdrawal to strongly fortified earthworks known as the *Hindenburg Line*, launched a counterattack in the spring of 1918.

In *March*, an attack on the Somme broke the British Fifth Army and advanced 60km, almost severing the British connections with the French.

In *April*, the land so dearly won in the Passchendaele campaign was retaken, and the British lines of communication with the Channel ports were threatened.

In *May* and *July*, the French were driven back from the Aisne to the Marne, and Paris was once again threatened. These successes exceeded even Ludendorff's expectations, and he failed to exploit his advantage.

Allied offensive, 1918 Foch and Haig counterattacked from August to November, breaching the Hindenburg Line in numerous places, advancing on Sedan and breaking the spirit of the German army.

The Eastern Front

German plans here were based on two assumptions: the first, that the western battle could be swiftly won in a *blitzkrieg* lasting no more than six weeks, and the second, that Russian mobilization would be so slow that a token force in the east could hold them at bay for long enough to end the war in the west and so avoid a war on two fronts at the same time. Both ideas failed to work out in practice. In the west, Belgian resistance saved the French from annihilation, while in the east the Russians took the field more quickly than was ever thought possible.

At the end of August, Russian troops had completely overrun East Prussia, one wing defeating the Germans at Gumbinnen and thrusting towards Königsberg, the other fanning out southwards through difficult swampy country in the general direction of the

Polish frontier. They were, however, badly trained and underequipped, and the Germans dealt them crushing blows, first at Tannenberg in 1914, and then at the Masurian Lakes. The unsuccessful invasion of East Prussia, however, meant that three divisions had to be detached from Belgium to help von Hindenburg in the east, and this came at a critical time in the campaign in the west; it also meant that Hindenburg's heavy commitments in East Prussia prevented him from helping the hard-pressed Austrians in their disastrous campaign further south in Galicia.

Here, the Austrians were heavily defeated at Lemberg, where their armies, advancing northwards into Poland, were attacked in the rear by Russian forces moving westwards into Galicia. The result was that the Austrians had to evacuate almost the entire province, leaving the Russians within a few miles of Cracow, and threatening the roads both to Vienna and to Berlin. Thousands of Slav conscripts in the Austrian armies surrendered on the spot, and the best of the Austrian artillery fell into Russian hands. Before Christmas, too, Austrian forces, which had swiftly established themselves in Serbia and captured its capital, had been driven from Belgrade and compelled to evacuate the whole of the country.

Any Russian success, however, was short-lived. German troops from the north and Austrian troops from the south operated a gigantic pincer movement, threatening to bite off what was known as the 'Polish tongue', a vast salient of territory which stretched westwards through Russian-occupied Warsaw and came within 300 kilometres of Berlin. After losing three-quarters of a million men in their efforts to stave off these attacks, Russian commanders eventually withdrew from Poland altogether, shortening their lines almost due north–south from Riga in Latvia to the Romanian frontier. After this, the Russians never seriously threatened the Central Powers again, though they sacrificed millions of men in their efforts to do so.

The Balkan Front

Gallipoli

In 1915, in a desperate attempt to end the stalemate on the Western Front, the western Allies launched an attack against the Turks, who had recently joined the war on the side of the Central Powers. The attack was on the Straits connecting the Mediterranean with the Black Sea, and on which the Turkish capital, Constantinople, stood. The immediate cause of the Gallipoli campaign was a Russian request for a diversionary attack to relieve the pressure on them on the Eastern Front. But the attack had wider possibilities: it would knock out Turkey, secure the Middle East, protect the Suez Canal, assist Serbia, persuade Romania to join the war on the Allied side, and break the economic blockade of Russia, thus making it possible to supply them with much-needed armaments.

Unfortunately the Turks were given plenty of advance notice by preliminary naval bombardments, and the invasion, when it came, was a costly failure. The Allied commander, Ian Hamilton, planned it carefully, covering his tracks with a series of ingenious bluffs:

1. The French made temporary landings on the Asiatic side, at Kum Kale.
2. A naval division staged a mock landing at Bulair, where the Turks had expected a landing and where they had concentrated their reserves.
3. The main attack was made at Cape Helles, which unfortunately proved to be too far from Constantinople.
4. A flank attack was made by the ANZACS north of Gaba Tepe.

The main landings, made on the five beaches S, V, W, X and Y, were badly coordinated. Those at S and X were almost unopposed, and yet they failed to make progress inland. W and V proved to be death-traps, swept by Turkish machine-gun fire from the surrounding heights. Y beach was the most successful and the invaders might have taken the Turks in the rear, yet they were unexpectedly re-embarked and the advantage was wasted. The failure of the initial attacks really meant the failure of the whole campaign. Turkish snipers and machine-gunners inflicted dreadful losses on troops who for the most part had little cover, and in hand-to-hand fighting inflicted gruesome injuries on them by means of their serrated bayonets. Even where they fell back they sometimes poisoned the wells so as to deprive the invaders of water supplies. Flies, dysentery, malaria and later, as winter approached, frostbite more than decimated the troops. In the end the Allied troops were forced to withdraw, the last men leaving a hastily chalked notice on equipment they had abandoned on the beach: 'You can keep your bloody peninsula!'

Salonika

Meanwhile, Serbia was invaded by Austria a second time, and simultaneously taken in the rear by the Bulgarians, cutting the Serbs off from Salonika. Troops were landed here by Britain and France to support the Serbs, but they arrived too few and too late to fulfil this purpose. Venizelos, the Greek Prime Minister who had arranged these landings, was promptly dismissed by King Constantine in an effort to keep Greece neutral.

Some of the forces who had been withdrawn from Gallipoli also went to Salonika in December 1915, and though their numbers eventually rose to about half a million they achieved very little, and proved quite incapable of keeping either Serbia or Romania (which became one of the Allies in 1916) in the war. The German commander at the Salonika bridgehead in 1918 was able to boast that it was 'the biggest prisoner-of-war camp in Europe'.

The Italian Front

In 1915 Italy joined the war – but on the side of the Triple Entente, not the Triple Alliance. It was persuaded to take this course by an agreement with the Allies at the *Pact of London* to the effect that at the end of the war they should be given those Italian-speaking areas which nationalists felt were rightly theirs, in the Tyrol, in the Adriatic, and around Trieste and Fiume.

But they did not fight with very much success. They fought their way painfully through the foothills of the Alps in Venetia during 1916, and launched almost a dozen offensives in less than eighteen months. Eventually, in October 1917, the Austrians, reinforced by six German divisions, overwhelmed the Italians at Caporetto, and the Italian position suddenly collapsed. Italy lost about 250,000 men in the battle, and there were about a further 400,000 desertions. The Italian rout ended only with the arrival of British and French reinforcements along the line of the River Piave, a few miles north of Venice. It was not until the battle of Vittorio Veneto in 1918 that the Italians were able to recapture the initiative and start to drive out the invading Austrians.

The Middle Eastern Front

Mesopotamia

British forces occupied Basra in 1914 in order to secure control of the oil wells in Mesopotamia (present-day Iraq). British and colonial troops had spectacular successes against the Turks at Amara and Kut, but pressed ahead too far towards Baghdad. The Turks counterattacked at Kut, where they trapped a large British army, forcing it to surrender in April 1916. British forces later resumed their advance, capturing Baghdad in 1917, and Mosul and its oilfields in 1918.

Palestine

At first British troops concentrated on the defence of the Suez Canal against Turkish attacks, but later aimed to liberate Palestine from Turkish control. Having built a pipeline to bring water from the Nile, British and Egyptian forces crossed the desert and reached Gaza, the gateway to Palestine, in March 1917. A new commander, Gen. Allenby, broke through the Turkish lines at Beersheba and poured troops into Palestine, capturing Jaffa and Jerusalem by the end of the year.

Meantime the Turks had to contend with an Arab revolt which broke out in Mecca in 1916. The Arabs' remarkable mobility in the desert was used and organized by T. E. Lawrence, a young British officer who won great respect from the Arab people. Under his leadership the Arabs threatened Turkish communications, especially the railways, and drew large numbers of Turkish troops from the Palestine front. In 1918 they made a great diversion in Jordan which helped British forces in Palestine.

In September 1918 the Turkish army was completely shattered at Megiddo. The Turkish right wing was smashed, and while British cavalry rode through to cut off the Turkish retreat northwards, the infantry wheeled eastwards and drove the remnants of

Fig. 4.1 The Dardanelles,
           1915

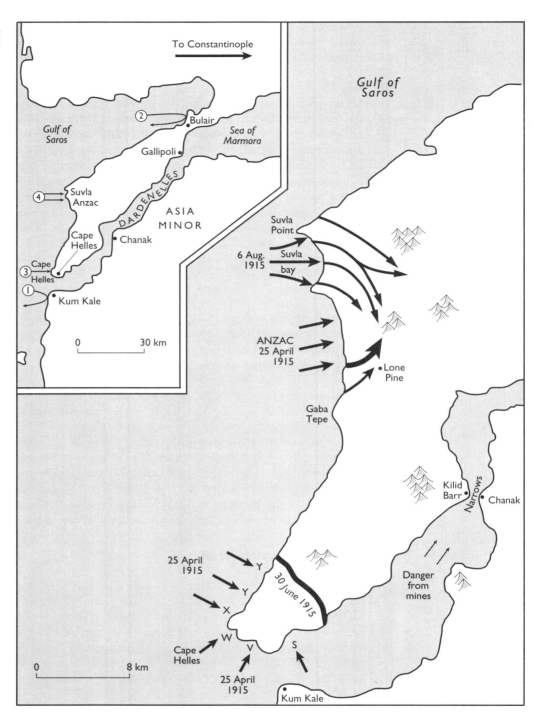

the enemy forces through the hills towards the River Jordan, and into the arms of the merciless Arabs beyond. Turkish resistance collapsed. At the same time as the Turkish armistice was being arranged at the end of 1918, Allied forces entered Aleppo and Damascus.

The war in the colonies

During the war, cut off from communication with Germany because of their loss of control of the seas, German colonies fell into the hands of the Allies:

(a) In *Africa*, *Togoland* fell to the allies by the end of 1914, and *Cameroon* was taken and divided up between the British and French in February 1916. In German *South-West Africa*, Generals Botha and Smuts, though hampered by a rebellion of Boer nationalists who did not support the war, overcame German resistance and occupied Windhoek in 1915. German *South-East Africa* offered tougher resistance. The German commander, Lettow-Vorbeck, at the head of a force including fewer than 300 Europeans, fought grimly, and when the cruiser *Königsberg* was forced to take refuge in the Rufiji River and was sunk there, he even employed its heavy guns in the defence of the colony. At the end of 1918 he was driven into Portuguese territory, but he returned to invade northern Rhodesia, where he captured Kasama. At the end of the war he was still fighting, boasting with some exaggeration that he had engaged the attention of no fewer than 137 generals and 300,000 troops, but had still survived.

(b) In the *Pacific*, New Zealand occupied *Samoa*; Australia *New Guinea* and the *Bismarck Archipelago*; the Japanese the *Marshall Islands*; and a joint Anglo-Japanese force *Kaiochao* in China, all before the end of 1914. By 1915 nothing remained of the German Empire in the Far East and Pacific area.

The war at sea

Supported by its allies the French, the British navy in the early days of the war faced daunting tasks. Not only did it have to protect the British Isles from invasion, it also had to secure the flow of foodstuffs and supplies into Britain for the war effort, and to keep open the lines of communication between Britain and the many theatres of war in which the Allies were engaged. It also had to maintain a blockade of Germany, so that the Germans could not obtain supplies from overseas, and it had to sweep German naval raiders from the seas.

In the first weeks of the war, three German cruisers were sunk off Wilhelmshaven in the Heligoland Bight; then the *Karlsruhe* after a brief career in the West Indies, the *Kaiser Wilhelm der Grosse* off West Africa, and the *Königsberg*, operating near Zanzibar. A more important victory came with the sinking of the *Gneisenau, Scharnhorst, Leipzig* and *Nüremberg* in the battle of the Falkland Islands in December 1914 – only the *Dresden* escaped, and she was later tracked down and sunk in 1915. Meanwhile, much damage was being inflicted by the cruiser *Emden*, but she was pursued across the Indian Ocean and back, and eventually was sunk off the Cocos Islands by the Australian cruiser *Sydney*.

In 1914, Scarborough, Hartlepool and Yarmouth were bombarded by German ships, but after the battle of the Dogger Bank early in 1915 these attacks ceased.

The greatest naval battle of the war did not occur until May 1916, when the German High Seas Fleet encountered the British Grand Fleet under Admiral Jellicoe off the Danish coast at *Jutland*, and 145 British ships and 110 German were engaged in a prodigious conflict of the giants. Both sides suffered grievous losses, though in many ways German tactics, ship construction and gunnery proved superior, and British losses in men and ships were marginally greater than German; but it was the German fleet which broke off the action and retired to port. British caution (Jellicoe is supposed to have said that he was the only man who could 'lose the war in an afternoon') and fear of a submarine ambush allowed the German fleet to make good its escape to port, never to emerge again until it sailed into captivity at the end of the war. All the same, even in harbour German battleships were a threat; they tied down British ships which could have been employed elsewhere, especially in keeping open the trade lanes of the Western Approaches.

In the meantime, Germany began to rely on submarines to attack Allied shipping. Already they had torpedoed the transatlantic liner *Lusitania* off the south coast of Ireland in 1915, and before long they were inflicting mounting losses on the merchant marine. In 1917 the submarine menace entered its gravest phase when Germany declared 'unrestricted' submarine warfare, its vessels sinking merchantmen, hospital ships and anything afloat, whether belligerent or neutral, without surfacing to give warning. British losses rose from 181 ships (totalling 300,000 tons) in January 1917 to 423 ships (850,000 tons) in April. Britain was on the brink of defeat. But the adoption of the convoy system and other defensive devices such as hydrophones and depth-charges enabled the supply ships to survive. By the end of 1917, 99 per cent of the merchant ships and their destroyer escorts were getting through. By 1918, the Dover Patrol was culling U-boats effectively, and attacks also took place on the U-boat pens at Zeebrugge and Ostend. More decisively, the submarine campaign led to the entry of the USA into the war in 1917, and the strengthening of the Allied side.

▷ **The new technology**

War is sometimes said to be the catalyst of economic change, speeding up technical processes that have already begun. Certainly the First World War was a scientific war in a quite unprecedented way.

The war on land

Traditional forms of combat – the manoeuvring of cavalry on open ground and the use of highly trained riflemen responding to orders with almost parade-ground precision – were now things of the past. A new style of fighting replaced it, less precise but much more intense. In the west, the armies took to the trenches in a war whose outlines smacked of science fiction: more complex and elaborate and essentially grimmer than anything that had gone before. It was a war of flesh and blood of horses and men, but increasingly it was a war of machinery. Horses were still used for haulage, but now motor vehicles were used for shifting men and materials; armoured cars and even armoured trains were introduced.

At Cambrai in 1916 the tank – perhaps the only certain way of breaking through the enemy's lines – made its appearance for the first time. Tanks, heavily armoured and armed with a machine gun or a cannon, and supplied with caterpillar traction to surmount earthwork barriers and get across trenches, were highly secret. Tanks had been found useless in soft mud, but at Cambrai the ground was hard and the tanks enabled the troops to make a local breakthrough. Unfortunately, the victory was only transitory and the advantage of surprise was lost, when a number of tanks fell into enemy hands as a result of the engagement.

Other new weapons made their appearance: flame-throwers, heavier and more accurate machine-guns, and poison gases such as chlorine and phosgene. Barbed wire, earlier used during the Boer War, was also used to make deadly entanglements to protect the lines of trenches and discourage attacks across No Man's Land.

The war at sea

Great engineering skill went into providing ever more accurate naval artillery, producing in the end great guns which could hurl shells of 16-inch diameter upwards of 25 kilometres with deadly accuracy, and a variety of more rapidly firing weapons, all equally effective. Armoured plate up to 20 centimetres thick was used to build these vessels, increasing their weight enormously and causing them to move more slowly and wallow in the water. Because of torpedoes below the water line, it became necessary to armour the ships lower down their hulls, so that in the end they became steel coffins for their crews. Smaller vessels were perfected for other specialized purposes: mine-layers, destroyers, frigates and corvettes. Later 'Q-boats' were used against U-boat attacks; these were merchantmen armed with a small-bore deck gun, and were very useful until U-boats began to torpedo ships without surfacing.

Explosive mines were laid over wide areas of sea to bar the access of ships to forbidden waters. Depth-charges and hydrophones were perfected to use against U-boats, and torpedoes were used against ships of all kinds, exploding on impact to sink them.

The war in the air

Here, too, technology made great strides. Balloons had long been used for meteorological purposes, and for observation of enemy positions, but these were at the mercy of the wind and could not be steered. Dirigibles appeared on the German side in 1915, when their civilian use was extended to include observation from the air and aerial bombardment. These airships, popularly known as Zeppelins after the name of their inventor, were able to move almost noiselessly by night, but they presented a large, slow-moving target for searchlights and anti-aircraft artillery.

Later, piston-driven propellor planes were developed both as fighters and as bomber aircraft. Fighters were equipped with machine-guns on the engine cowling, synchronized to fire between the blades as the propellor turned. The crews of the bombers at first simply heaved the bombs over the side of the cockpit when they arrived at their target, but later they were provided with quite intricate bomb-launching equipment.

Medicine and surgery

The massive casualties of the First World War brought necessary changes to medicine and surgery. The effects of these were to save thousands of young lives, but even so the deaths and injuries caused by this war far outstripped anything seen before in history. To the physical injuries are to be added the conditions of stress and shock triggered by long and violent exposure in the trenches, conditions which sometimes lasted a lifetime.

Medical and surgical services were grossly overloaded and the suffering was enormous, but doctors could – and did – work miracles in frontline hospitals, and except for their work, casualties would have been much bigger. Conscientious objectors sometimes served as medical orderlies, giving their lives to rescue injured men from exposed positions; women, too, in the Voluntary Aid Detachments (the VAD) took the same risks as men in the casualty-clearing stations, and in the hospitals gave sterling service nursing the wounded.

The Home Front

▷ **The impact of the war**   The war was perhaps the first 'total' war ever experienced in Britain, with large civilian populations being involved either directly or indirectly. After coastal bombardments at places such as Scarborough came aerial attacks, first by Zeppelins and later by aeroplanes. For British civilians this was a new experience, and though casualties were fewer than 4,000, the effects were frightening. Generally, however, Britons submitted good-humouredly enough to encroachments on their liberties which might not have been acceptable at other times.

Defence of the Realm Act, 1914

This Act, often abbreviated to its half-affectionate acronym DORA, was passed in the first month of the war, and was repeatedly strengthened thereafter in the name of national security. It brought a mass of restrictions and regulations, such as the internment of suspected spies without trial and the imposition of stiff prison sentences for food hoarding and profiteering. Some powers were not even publicly acknowledged: there was officially, for example, no press censorship until its existence was finally admitted in April 1916. There were never any restrictions on Parliament, where members usually knew how to keep their mouths shut.

Because of the war, trade union activities were seriously restricted in the name of the Act. The government spread its influence throughout the economy. Hours were lengthened, and rates of pay were controlled; new technology was introduced willy-nilly, and strikes were restricted and finally banned altogether. Wage differentials were manipulated, and unskilled men and women were introduced into the workforce after only the sketchiest of apprenticeships. At the same time, owners' profits were limited. Of course, industrial friction and even strikes still occurred, but the government was generally careful to keep labour sweet.

Finance and taxation

(a) *Income tax* was doubled in the first few days of the war, and went up to 3s 6d ($17\frac{1}{2}$p) on larger incomes and 2s 1d ($10\frac{1}{2}$p) on smaller incomes in 1915. In 1916, the standard rate became 5s (25p). Even so, the deficit increased year by year.

(b) *Loans* were used to plug the gap. Interest of $4\frac{1}{2}$ per cent was offered, and nearly £1bn was raised. Even so, this was not enough, and it had to go up to nearly 10 per cent.

(c) A whole new range of *indirect taxes* was invented:
   (i) *Excess profits tax* was levied on all profits above the usual average, at first at 50 per cent, then 60 per cent and finally, in 1918, at 80 per cent.
   (ii) *Luxuries tax* was levied on imported motor-cars and other imported luxuries, at 33 per cent; there were also heavy taxes on wines, spirits and tobacco.
   (iii) *Amusement taxes* were introduced on horse-races, theatres, etc.

But the government was still running a deficit, accumulating a debt of over £10bn, and taking over 75 per cent of gross domestic product (GDP) in public spending.

Industry

Government controls steadily spread over the economy. The government accepted responsibility for the effects of enemy action, promising to pay 80 per cent of any losses caused to shipping – a promise which later cost it very dear. It also took control of mines, railways, munitions, supplies and equipment.

A Department of Munitions was introduced in 1915. Under the Munitions Act of that year, the restrictions on trade unions were elaborated, wages and hours controlled, and owners' profits limited.

The Board of Agriculture undertook to increase the amount of foodstuffs produced in Britain to counteract the blockade, but it tried to avoid controlling prices. In the end it was forced to guarantee labourers' wages and the prices of crops. In 1917 it also took over control of flour mills.

Its powers over transport and manufacture steadily increased, guaranteeing dividends and profits on the railways until they were virtually nationalized, and phasing out the production of consumer goods in favour of wartime necessities.

Bureaucracy and government regulation

Civil controls

A National Register was introduced in 1915 for the enrolment of all persons between the ages of 15 and 65. The Military Service Act of 1916 used this register to call up men between 18 and 41 (unless they were ministers of religion, medically unfit, conscientious objectors or in reserved occupations).

New departments

Under the supreme authority of the War Office there were created departments for Munitions, Shipping Control, Scientific Research, Food Control, Liquor Control and Pensions. Late in the war there was also a Ministry of Reconstruction to superintend the transition to peace.

Civil service

In 1914, there was a grand total of 60,000 employees in all grades of the civil service, but by the end of the war this had grown to about 120,000. There was a demand to reduce this figure, but it continued to grow between the wars.

NB Two fairly new theories were now gaining a hold:

(a) *Collectivism* had increased during the war, and held sway for much of the century. State intervention in matters of employment, wages and conditions, housing, hygiene, food and even leisure became common; people increasingly looked to the state to help satisfy their needs, promote equality and improve social standards.

(b) *Nationalization* seemed sensible, to eliminate profiteering, to ensure adequate controls and to develop, in particular, heavy industries for the public good. This belief sprang from the Soviet experiments after 1917, and became the cornerstone of the Labour Party in its 1918 constitution.

▷ **Social consequences of the war**

Politically, Britain was governed at first by Asquith's Liberal government, but in May 1915 it became a coalition government enjoying the support of Conservatives as well as Liberals. A number of Labour members, however, continued to oppose the war. In December, after a crisis in the government, Lloyd George replaced Asquith as Prime Minister. All the time, the powers of the state grew, and the lives of ordinary people were greatly affected.

Military conscription

In 1916, there was an effort to keep conscription to single men and childless widowers, but the fearsome casualties of the Western Front led to its extension. By 1918, all men up to 51 might be called up; this often had a crippling effect on industry, which lost more than the army gained. Attempts were made to extend conscription to Ireland, causing discontent there (though the attempts were later abandoned).

The call-up produced a popular revulsion against conscientious objectors ('conchies'), who were often wrongly thought to be cowards anxious to 'dodge the column'. They were treated harshly by the military authorities as well as sneered at by the public at large.

Rationing

At first controls over food supplies were haphazard and piecemeal, urging economy on the housewife, encouraging home production, allotment holding and gardening, restricting meals in hotels and restaurants, and trying to stabilize prices of foodstuffs.

Queuing for basic commodities, such as bread, potatoes and sugar, became commonplace and very time consuming.

Later, in 1917, corn production and milling were controlled and a 'standard' (wholemeal) loaf was introduced to make the wheat go further.

By 1917, 85 per cent of all foodstuffs consumed came under the control of the Ministry of Agriculture, which tried to regulate 95 per cent of prices. Unfortunately, this often had the effect of driving foodstuffs 'under the counter'.

A comprehensive system of *rationing* was introduced by Lord Rhondda in 1918: it regulated distribution by requiring customers to 'register' with particular sellers, and issued *ration cards* to use for the amounts of sugar, lard, tea, butter, etc. to which people were entitled. Treasury grants enabled prices to be controlled.

Social conditions

The war ushered in a period of rapid social change:

(a) *Housing* conditions remained often poor, but wages overall tended to increase, while prices and rents were controlled.
(b) *Living standards* tended to increase, and food rationing sometimes actually improved nutritional standards. Consumption of alcohol sharply declined, and the evils caused by drunkenness diminished at the same time.
(c) *Conscription* revealed for the first time the ignorance and the poor physical condition of many conscripts, and concentrated the government's mind on remedying these evils.
(d) *Trade unions* had to accept the abandonment of restrictive practices, and the 'dilution' of labour by the introduction of female workers.
(e) *Women* came to play a more active role in the nation's life. Their style of clothing changed, became freer and less restrictive, and they began to wear trousers. It was not unusual to see them smoking, or drinking in pubs.

Attitudes towards war

These years cured romantic notions of the glory and the gallantry of war. This idea was partly due to the long period of peace which preceded the war, and which fostered glamorous and unrealistic conceptions based chiefly on lack of experience; it was due also to the unspeakably grim conditions under which the soldiers in the trenches lived.

The spirit of 1914 can be glimpsed in the words of Rupert Brooke, who wrote:

Now, God be thanked Who has matched us with His hour,
And caught our youth, and wakened us from sleeping.

This was a gallant spirit, but was soon knocked out of those who went to fight in the trenches. A later poet, Wilfred Owen, expressed his thoughts more realistically:

What passing bells for those who die as cattle?
    Only the monstrous anger of the guns.
    Only the stuttering rifles' rapid rattle
Can patter out their hasty orisons.

There was a powerful revulsion against war after 1918, prompted at least partly by the horror recollected by old soldiers, and retold in tales which lost nothing in the telling, but which nevertheless were profoundly impressive to the young. This was one powerful reason why the rising generation of the 1930s showed themselves so accommodating to Hitler's Germany.

Social reforms

War bred a sort of idealism for the future, and gave rise to a general determination to introduce reforms which had previously been neglected:

(a) *1918, Education Act*:
  (i) raised school-leaving age to fourteen;
  (ii) prohibited employment of children under twelve;
  (iii) introduced medical inspection into secondary schools;
  (iv) empowered local authorities to set up nurseries for children between the ages of two and five;
  (v) set up *Day Continuation Schools* for older pupils between fourteen and eighteen.
  NB Financial stringency after the war prevented the last two things from happening in a great many places.
(b) *1918, Parliamentary Reform Act*:
  (i) voting age for men fixed at 21; in the case of ex-servicemen, it might even be as low as 19; soldiers and sailors to vote on active service;
  (ii) residence qualification fixed at six months;
  (iii) most plural voting abolished;
  (iv) elections to take place all on one day;
  (v) votes given to women over 30 years.

NB An election directly at the end of the war (December 1918) returned Lloyd George's coalition to government with a big majority.

 # GLOSSARY

Capitalism	An economic system based on the private ownership of property, including land and industry, and operating on the profit motive. Individuals control their own money and possessions (capital), and employ them in such a way as to increase them and make themselves richer than other people. Theoretically the whole system is based on equal opportunity and on free enterprise and competition.
Central Powers	At the time of the First World War: Germany, Austria-Hungary and Italy. They were supported at first by a number of smaller powers, such as Romania. In fact, during the war, Italy and later Romania joined the Allied side, and Bulgaria and Turkey joined the Central Powers.
Coalition government	A parliamentary government in which more than one political party is represented. This may occur where no single party has a majority in Parliament (a 'hung parliament') or in the event of a national emergency such as war, when a large measure of agreement between parties is needed. A wartime coalition government was formed in Britain by Asquith in May 1915, and by Winston Churchill in 1940.
Entente	An entente (the French word means *understanding*) is a diplomatic agreement looser than an *alliance*. An alliance commits a power to an agreed line of policy when the circumstances covered by the alliance treaty come into being, but an entente does not. It merely sorts out the details of misunderstandings between the parties, particularly colonial ones in the cases of the entente between Britain and France in 1904 and Britain and Russia in 1907.
Gutter press	This describes cheap sensationalist newspapers intended for the lower end of the popular market. The expression is a term of abuse applied by those demanding a more responsible attitude from the press.

Nationalism   The desire of a people who have a number of things in common (i.e. one or more of language, religion, history, economic interest, geography and heritage) to become a state. The Czechs and the Hungarians could form separate states only if the Austro-Hungarian Empire fell apart, and the Poles could form a state only by taking territory from Austria, Germany and Russia. Nationalism is sometimes confused with patriotism: those who cared much for Prussia but little for Germany were Prussian patriots rather than German nationalists, and those Czechs and Magyars who fought loyally for the Emperor in 1914 could hardly be called nationalists; nor could those Poles who fought for Tsar Nicholas.

Total war   A war fought on land, sea and air and employing a wide variety of weapons, often of a very lethal character and indiscriminate in their effects; a war, furthermore, involving all the efforts of the populations of the states at war, and going some way towards removing the distinction between armed forces and civilians.

Ultimatum   A list of final terms, a last offer or demand. Usually applied to the final demand made by one government of another before a declaration of war.

EXAMINATION QUESTIONS

> **Question 1**   (a) 'The generals were to blame for the enormous casualties on the Western Front, 1914–18.' Do you agree? Explain your answer.   (12 marks)
>
> (b) 'Only the Western Front was really important for the outcome of the First World War.' Were the other fighting fronts of little importance? Explain your answer.   (8 marks)
>
> (c) Why, despite huge navies, were there so few surface sea battles during the First World War?   (10 marks)

> **Question 2**   (a) 'When people heard that war had been declared, the streets filled with cheering citizens, and Union Jacks could be seen everywhere' (London, August 1914). How far and for what reasons did the attitude of the British people towards the war change during the years 1914–1918?   (7 marks)
>
> (b) What was it like to be a conscientious objector during the First World War?   (6 marks)
>
> (c) 'The lives of ordinary people in Britain were little affected by the war.' Do you agree with this statement about the First World War? Explain your answer.   (12 marks)

EXAMINATION ANSWERS

> **Question 1**   *Outline answer*

(a) Answers which offer a narrative of the Western Front campaigns, however accurate, will achieve only a low Level mark. What is required is an attempt to explain the heavy casualties sustained during the fighting, and to assess how far this was the generals' responsibility. You will need to explore the early establishment of trench warfare, and how offensive operations from entrenched positions inevitably involved heavy casualties. The development of machine-guns and barbed wire, the use of heavy artillery and the use of poison gas will all need attention, and a higher Level mark will be awarded to those who explain the high death toll. But the highest Level is for those who can relate this to the generals: it has been argued that the generals did not learn from their mistakes, and that they insisted on launching hopeless attacks against impregnable positions. So Haig at the Somme and Passchendaele, Pétain at Verdun and Nivelle's offensive need some attention, and don't neglect the German generals – Ludendorff at least should be considered. However, this does not mean that exhaustive coverage of all the main campaigns and reference to all the important generals are required. Pick out some highlights, and perhaps remember that, while the generals learnt only slowly from their mistakes, alternatives to costly offensives were not necessarily available, and politicians expected results.

(b) A Western Front narrative would be of even less value here than in (a), and a description of fighting on the Russian Front, in the Balkans, at Gallipoli and on Turkey's southern flank would still only gain a low Level mark. You will need to show how Russia tied down vast German armies until 1918, and how the collapse of the German Salonika Front and Allenby's success against the Turks led to the collapse of Germany's allies Bulgaria and Turkey, and opened the way to the disintegration of Austria-Hungary. Gallipoli may have forced the Turks to concentrate, if only temporarily, on the defence of the Straits, and the Germans had to prop up the Austrians on the Italian Front. Without these other fronts, the Allies might have had to face irresistible German forces in the west, and without the fall of Germany's allies, the war might well have been prolonged beyond 1918.

(c) Those anxious to present narrative will probably have to content themselves with the Falkland Islands and Jutland, and a low mark. Risk is the key to the answer: Britain could not afford to risk highly expensive ships when they were needed to protect colonies and shipping lanes, and to guard troop movements. Jellicoe and the other admirals were well aware that, should the navy suffer a disastrous defeat, Britain would have no means of protecting itself from invasion. So believing that he could lose the war in a single day, Jellicoe was cautious, and so were both fleets at Jutland itself. The Germans, after Jutland, were not prepared to risk their fleet. They could not afford to let Britain gain absolute control of the sea, and they could prevent this by keeping their fleet in port. Moreover, they had found in submarines a much cheaper and more effective way of waging war at sea.

▷ Question 2(a)   *Tutor answer*

London's cheering crowds in 1914 were mirrored in Paris, Berlin and St Petersburg. They were spontaneous demonstrations of patriotic loyalty, and in some ways an expression of relief that the war which had been seen coming for so long had at last arrived. In London there was a sense of indignation at Austria's treatment of Serbia and even more at Germany's unprovoked hostility against Belgium. But the war was expected to be one of short duration, and one in which a quick war of movement, in which there would be few casualties, would be followed by a triumphant and deserved victory and peace. No one was prepared for the long war of attrition which 'trench warfare' made necessary. Initial idealism faded under the impact of casualty lists of unprecedented length. The horrors of the war could not be concealed, even with the most rigorous censorship. The Somme, an unspeakable slaughter-house, was probably the turning point, coinciding as it did with the introduction of conscription and the wiping out of most of the idealistic volunteers of 1914. From 1916 on, gritty determination replaced the early enthusiasm, and it was often accompanied by cynicism and despair. Not all had welcomed the war in 1914, but the new mood of 1916–18 was almost universal.

▷ Question 2(b)   *Tutor answer*

Until 1916 conscientious objectors could keep their consciences to themselves and refrain from volunteering. In this they were in company with all those who, for whatever reason, legitimate or otherwise, resisted the pressure and tolerated at worst the verbal abuse or the white feather. But with the introduction of conscription, conscientious objectors were forced into the open. Few sympathized with their moral stance. The tribunals with power to exempt them from military service adopted severe and often impossible criteria. Those who were sent as non-combatants to the front were quite often placed in unnecessary and extreme danger; those who acted as stretcher-bearers and first aid men often showed great bravery. But many conscientious objectors were refused recognition, forced into uniform and sent to gaol for refusing to obey orders. The objector, whether granted military exemption or not, was ostracized by the vast majority of his fellows, and it is not surprising that there were comparatively few of them – barely 20 per cent of the numbers who registered as conscientious objectors in the Second World War.

▷ **Question 2(c)**   *Student answer with examiner's comments*

'This could be better put: DORA needs to be explained as petrol and travel problems were not due to DORA as implied here.'

'Habit is an overstatement – it happened three times in the early years of the war.'

'This implies that the air-raids were a serious threat. Some idea of their extent and resulting civilian deaths (about 1,100) would put them in context.'

It is not true to say that British civilians were little affected by the war. Volunteers and later conscripts joined the forces in very large numbers, so that virtually every family had someone serving in France, and most families lost someone close in the terrible slaughter on the Western Front. Young women, too, saw service in nursing or the Red Cross, or worked in munitions factories or on the land. Women who before the war had been housewives were now expected to replace men in shops, offices, on the buses and on postmen's rounds and policemen's beats. For those not directly involved in war work the war still made a great impact. DORA took away many civilian liberties, petrol for cars was difficult to get, travel was difficult as buses and trains were filled with servicemen, and people suspected of German sympathies could be detained without trial. The war caused a big rise in prices, and wages were not always able to keep up, but at least there were very few unemployed. Price rises were bad enough, but there were also food shortages, and the introduction of rationing in 1918 did not entirely get rid of queues and black market. Worse still was the German habit of bombarding East coast towns from the sea, and the air-raids. These caused heavy casualties and much panic, especially in London, and even when the Zeppelin menace had been defeated air-raids were continued from German planes. On top of all this everyone had to pay much higher taxes. This was total war, and the civilian population was very much affected by it.

Examiner's decision on the student answer
This is a very sound answer, but it argues all one way with a touch of overstatement. Petrol shortages, for example, were not a universal hardship as so few people then owned cars, and most of the country was unaffected by air-raids. So this just misses the top Level and would be awarded 10/12.

SUMMARY

In this chapter you have learnt about the First World War. In particular, you have studied:

▷ the reasons for, and the events of, the outbreak of war;

▷ the campaigns on the various fronts of the war, and the main battles;

▷ developments in strategy, tactics and weapons;

▷ the circumstances of the ending of the war;

▷ the Home Front in Britain, 1914–18;

▷ the effects of the war on British society and the economy.

If you wish to study the two world wars together, or to make comparisons with the Second World War, you will find more material in chapter 12.

More information on the social and economic consequences of the First World War in Britain is included in chapter 5.

Chapter 5

Economic and industrial problems between the wars

GETTING STARTED

Britain emerged from the war with its army victorious, its navy supreme, its empire intact, and its international prestige higher than it had ever been. But there was nevertheless a high price to pay, and those who imagined that the country could now slip back into the peace and comfort of earlier days were soon disillusioned.

MEG	NEAB	NICCEA	SEG	LONDON	WJEC	TOPIC	STUDY	REVISION 1	REVISION 2
	✓		✓*			**The faltering 1920s**			
	✓		✓*			The effects of the First World War			
	✓		✓*			The growth of trade unions and the Labour Party			
	✓		✓*			The General Strike, 1926			
	✓		✓*			The economic crisis of 1929–30 and the 'National' Government, 1931			
	✓		✓*			**The stagnant thirties**			
	✓		✓*			Policies of the National Government			
	✓		✓*			Social policies			
	✓		✓*			Fascism in Britain			

* Coursework only

WHAT YOU NEED TO KNOW

The faltering 1920s

▷ **The effects of the First World War**

The cost of the war

During the war, Britain's trading exports had fallen dramatically and the government had borrowed heavily from abroad. This meant:

(a) There was an adverse balance of trade. Imports continued, but were no longer paid for by exports; such an imbalance could not continue indefinitely.

(b) During the war, Britain had left the Gold Standard and the pound was in fact devalued by wartime inflation. The weakening of the pound increased the cost of imports, and made the adverse balance of payments worse.

(c) Overseas investments had largely been liquidated to pay for imports. The gap between imports and exports had previously been financed by interest on these investments, benefiting the nation like a pension; this balance was now becoming more difficult to maintain.

(d) Loss of overseas markets. Britain's traditional exports were being replaced overseas by those of commercial rivals such as the USA.

(e) Much of British industry was old-fashioned and out-of-date, and there were difficulties in readapting production to peacetime conditions.

48

In 1918, the government still controlled services vital to the national effort, including food, transport, wages, prices and foreign exchange. While these controls continued there was prosperity, but the government found them too costly and wanted to dismantle them. Lloyd George made a 'bonfire of controls', and with their removal, economic reality had to be faced.

The decline of the staple industries

British banking, insurance, shipping and other financial services were still strong, but the basic foundations of prosperity in heavy industry were weakening. Wages and costs were too high in relation to competitors, and output was limited, old-fashioned and slow to adapt to changing conditions.

(a) The *coal industry* was burdened by heavy costs and was steadily becoming exhausted. Seams were thinner, deeper and of poorer quality.
(b) *Iron and steel trades* were hopelessly outpaced by US and later by German output and the production of the developing countries. The associated industries of engineering and shipbuilding were also starting to decline.
(c) *Textiles* were burdened with old equipment and generally unable to invest in the latest technology.
(d) *Railways* had overinvested in basic steam technology, were burdened with large loss-making areas, and were increasingly superseded by road transport.

The dissatisfaction of labour

Labour was keen to maintain the small gains made during the war, and resisted any effort to reduce industrial costs by cutting wages and lengthening hours.

The postwar years saw increasing industrial friction, with demonstrations and strikes. Employers wished to restore industrial competitiveness by cutting their labour costs, but workers were powerful and articulate, and resisted this.

Many of the Liberals in Lloyd George's coalition wanted to restore economic health by a return to free trade and to the Gold Standard, but this was a harsh deflationary discipline making the worker's position worse, and many workers felt that recovery ought to be paid for by the rich, not the poor.

▷ The growth of trade unions and the Labour Party

With a widened electorate, improved education and an influential popular press, the government felt that it could no longer ignore the workforce if it wished to avoid the fate that had befallen the ruling classes in Bolshevik Russia.

The development of trade unions

The early professionally organized trade unions, known as the 'model' unions, were based on the Amalgamated Society of Engineers (ASE). They steadily accumulated funds and strengthened their negotiating position.

(a) *1871, Trade Union Act* gave legal protection to trade union funds.
(b) *1875, Employers and Workmen's Act* made both sides of industry subject to civil contract.
(c) *1875, Conspiracy and Protection of Property Act* legalized strikes and picketing.

The model unions were looked upon enviously by other workers, and during the 1880s trade recession brought 'new model' unions for the unskilled and semi-skilled.

(a) *1888*, successful strikes by *tea operatives* and the *matchgirls*.
(b) *1889*, victory in the *London Dock Strike* for the 'Dockers' Tanner' (i.e. a rate of 6d (2½p) per hour). This encouraged other unskilled unions such as Joseph Arch's *Agricultural Labourers' Union*.

Strikes continued in the 1890s, with about 20–30 million days lost annually through strike action. In a time of weakening trade, employers grew more militant:

(a) *1893, miners' lockout*: owners forced a 10 per cent cut in wages.
(b) *1897, engineers' strike*: strikers were defeated after seven months.

Conditions improved during the miniboom caused by the Boer War, but employers did not relax their opposition to the unions. *1901, Taff Vale case* saw the Amalgamated Society of Railway Servants (ASRS) fined £23,000 in damages and £9,000 in costs for strike action on the Taff Vale Railway. Hence there was widespread labour support for the Liberal Party at the 1906 election.

Labour dissatisfaction with the slow progress of social reform after 1906 led to:

(a) an increase in 'unofficial', 'lightning' and 'sympathetic' strikes;
(b) 'direct action' strikes, e.g. in docks and railways from 1911;
(c) foundation of *Triple Industrial Alliance* in 1912 (railwaymen, miners, transport workers), with their threat of a 'general strike';
(d) 1912, foundation of a Labour newspaper – the *Daily Herald*.

Unions developed rapidly during the war: their membership topped 8 million, their leadership was vigorous, and the 'shop-steward movement' – a grass-roots organization – got well under way.

The development of the Labour Party

At first labour had no clear links with political parties, though many were Liberals.

(a) *1868, Trades Union Congress* (TUC) founded, with a secretarial staff that gave it a continuous existence.
(b) *1892, Keir Hardie* returned to Parliament for S. West Ham; he founded the *Independent Labour Party* (ILP) to give Labour a separate voice.
(c) *1900, Labour Representation Committee* (LRC) set up with Ramsay MacDonald as Secretary, incorporating the ILP, the Social Democratic Federation (founded by H.M. Hyndman in 1881), the more moderate Fabian Society (founded 1884), and the representatives of about 500,000 trade unionists. They won a few by-elections, e.g. Will Crooks at Woolwich, 1902.
(d) *1906, 'landslide' election* returned 53 Labour MPs, of whom 29 sat as representatives of the LRC, many of the rest being Lib–Labs.
(e) *1909, Osborne Judgment* outlawed the trade union political levy except on a voluntary basis, so weakening trade union funds and causing disappointing results at the two elections of 1910.
(f) *1913, Trade Union Act* reversed this judgment and legalized the levy, subject to 'contracting out' by members who disapproved; there was to be no victimization of those who chose not to pay.
(g) *1918, new Labour Party constitution* adopted, with the famous Clause 4 aiming at the 'common ownership [i.e. nationalization] of the means of production, distribution and exchange'. In the 1918 election, 10 Labour members supported Lloyd George's coalition, but there were 59 in opposition to it.
(h) *1923, Ramsay MacDonald* replaced J.M. Clynes as leader of the Labour Party.

The impact of organized labour

As the brief postwar boom collapsed, prices fell and recession set in. Widespread distress and unemployment caused strikes, especially on the part of the mineworkers.

There had already been trouble in Glasgow, where a committee of Clydeside workers, modelling themselves on the Bolsheviks, raised the red flag and called for a general strike. As a result, the government put tanks on the streets.

Later in 1919, the government ordered an inquiry into the mining industry, under Mr Justice (later Lord) Sankey. This spoke with a divided voice on the need to nationalize the industry, and provided Lloyd George with the excuse for doing nothing (most of his coalition MPs were in fact Conservatives).

The government's inaction led to a rash of further strikes, including strikes by iron-workers and cotton operatives, a nine-day rail strike which paralysed the country, and in London and Liverpool even strikes by the police. Looting and rioting followed, and troops were again called in to restore order.

The 'Council of Action'

Trade union leaders seemed to want to dictate the policies of the government on industrial and other matters. Though union membership had fallen from 8 million to 5 million as a result of their postwar difficulties, the TUC came to think of itself as a kind of rival parliament with a right to enforce its views on all sorts of subjects.

At this time, the government was trying to supply Poland with arms to fight against Soviet Russia, and was using troops to crush the republican movement in Ireland. The TUC disapproved of both these policies and tried to stop them through a *Council of Action*.

The government refused to be frightened by the Council of Action, but the episode illustrated the rebellious spirit of the times.

Strikes and unemployment

By 1920, unemployment had risen to about 2 million, and the government was forced to extend the Unemployment Insurance Act to practically all industries. But prices had started to fall and wages had to be reduced. Miners struck again, and the Triple Industrial Alliance was renewed to prevent wage reductions.

The government was forced to declare a state of emergency by the *Emergency Powers Act* (1920), opting for emergency regulations by Orders in Council and courts of summary jurisdiction to dispose of offenders quickly.

In March 1921, the miners struck again when the owners threatened wage cuts, and called on the Triple Alliance for support, but J.H. Thomas for the railwaymen let them down (this was 'Black' Friday, 15 April 1921); they fought on alone for three months before defeat. After this, they were determined not to give way again.

The miners' defeat was followed by the defeat of other strikes: engineering workers, shipyard workers, dockers, printers, builders and cotton workers. Protective machinery for workers, such as the Agricultural Wages Board and the Trade Boards, all saw their powers whittled away.

At the same time, the government was wielding the *Geddes Axe*, by which Lloyd George was trying to restore national finances by swingeing cuts in public spending.

▷ The General Strike, 1926

The fall of Lloyd George's coalition, at the end of 1922, led to the return of the Conservatives to power under Bonar Law for less than a year, and then under Baldwin until December 1923. Ramsay MacDonald was then returned to power with 191 members in a minority government with Liberal support (158 members), as against the Conservatives, with 258.

But because it was a minority government, it was hamstrung in its policies defeated in Parliament. Baldwin came back to office in October 1924. Meantime, troubles on the part of militant labour had increased rather than diminished.

Conditions in the coal industry

Strikes among German miners during the French occupation of the Ruhr brought back some prosperity to British coalfields, but goverment cutbacks and the restoration of the Gold Standard under Baldwin renewed the miners' demand for nationalization of the mines so that wages could be subsidized and prosperity guaranteed.

The miners' leader was A.J. Cook, who advocated a general strike and revolution on the Bolshevik model. He became a member of the Trades Union Council (the 'cabinet' of the TUC) and persuaded his colleagues to back the miners' claim.

In 1925 the owners gave notice of drastic wage cuts to make coal exports more competitive, and the TUC threatened to activate the Triple Alliance to resist. This was 'Red' Friday (31 July 1925).

To avert a crisis, Baldwin promised a Royal Commission to examine the problem, in the meantime agreeing to subsidize the coal industry out of public money.

The Samuel Commission, 1925

The Commission, under Liberal Sir Herbert Samuel, rejected the remedies suggested by both sides: nationalization was not recommended, but the sweeping wage cuts put forward by the owners were also rejected. It recommended:

(a) reorganization of the industry under private ownership;
(b) improved distribution, with government aid;
(c) improved relations between owners and labour, with improved housing, more pit-head baths, annual holidays with pay, etc. 'when prosperity returns';
(d) nationalization only of landowners' royalties.

The 'Nine Days' Wonder'

Neither party accepted the Commission's report, and on 1 May the miners came out on strike. Their leader Cook demanded 'not a penny off the pay, not a minute on the day'. After some last-minute hesitation, the TUC ordered the railwaymen, transport workers and printers to come out in sympathy, and a general strike began on 4 May.

(a) Docks, railways and buses all stopped and the economy came to a standstill.
(b) Police and armoured cars ensured delivery of foodstuffs from the docks.
(c) Students joined the fun as amateurs, driving buses and trains.
(d) Over 70 towns were run by 'strike committees' as local soviets.
(e) The government organized a *British Gazette* to ensure circulation of news; the TUC brought out a counterblast in the form of the *British Worker*.
(f) The BBC for the first time encouraged people to 'listen in' to the news.
(g) There were endless parades and meetings, but generally the whole thing was good-humoured and the police and strikers played football against each other.

On 12 May, trade union leaders got cold feet and called off the strike in the expectation that the question of hours and wages would be reopened. Miners once again felt they had been let down, and struggled on for several months before admitting their defeat.

Trade Disputes Act, 1927

Baldwin promised to avoid victimizing the strikers, but was forced to allow his Conservative supporters to penalize the trade unions by this Act:

(a) General or sympathetic strikes were banned (in practice very difficult).
(b) Intimidation was legally defined and made illegal (not very practical).
(c) Civil servants, e.g. police, were 'crown servants' and were not to be in unions associated with the TUC.
(d) The political levy was not banned, but 'contracting in' was substituted for 'contracting out', and many members took the opportunity not to pay.

The postwar Labour government took care to reverse this Act and bring back contracting out by the *Trade Disputes Act* (1946).

There was some effort to remedy labour grievances in the 1920s, but workers were generally looking forward to the next election to get Labour back in power.

The general election of 1929 gave Labour 287 seats, the Conservatives 261 and the Liberals 59. MacDonald formed a minority government again, but his position was much stronger than it had been in 1924.

▷ **The economic crisis of 1929–30 and the 'National' Government, 1931**

There had been some economic recovery in the later 1920s. Unemployment fell to about 1 million, there was some new investment, prices and profits recovered and trade revived. But, beginning with the Wall Street Crash in the USA in October 1929, all this came to an end with the onset of the Great Depression. Production fell, world trade shrank to one-third of what it had been, and unemployment soared to about 3 million by 1932.

Problems of the Labour government

MacDonald and most of his Labour supporters were inexperienced in economic matters and could not handle the problems created by the gravity of the slump.

(a) Exports fell from £850 million to £460 million (1929–31), and the schemes put forward by the Minister of Employment, J.H. Thomas, being largely confined to domestic projects like roads and railways, did very little to remedy the fall.

(b) Unemployment steadily rose, but the government was still bound by promises to improve welfare entitlements and ease the burdens of the unemployed. This meant that although the 'dole' was very meagre, the unemployment insurance fund was bankrupt and had to borrow heavily from the Exchequer.

(c) Receipts from taxation fell, but the government could not remedy this except by burdening taxpayers and employers further.

(d) Pressures on sterling increased as the trade balance worsened and as the Americans began to withdraw their money from Europe because of the slump.

The government's economic remedies

None of the government's measures helped much; some made the situation worse:

(a) Thomas's overseas schemes for trade came to nothing, and his left-wing critics in the ILP called on him 'to try socialism instead'.

(b) MacDonald set up a high-powered *Economic Advisory Council* to suggest radical changes, but there was systematic obstruction from the Treasury in the interests of economy, and Sir Oswald Mosley resigned in disgust.

(c) Reforming measures had little success:
   (i) *1929, Unemployment Insurance Bill* was attacked by the Conservatives for extravagance and by left-wingers in the ILP for meanness; an *Anomalies Bill* (1931) deprived some people of benefit on the grounds of 'abuses'.
   (ii) *1930, Coal Mines Act* tried to bring in the $7\frac{1}{2}$-hour day, but the reorganization of the industry it attempted was a non-starter.
   (iii) *1930, Housing Act* made a small start on slum clearance.
   (iv) *1930, Education Bill* to raise school-leaving age to fifteen was rejected by the Lords.

Attempts to reform the Trade Union Act of 1927 and to bring in proportional representation both failed. Left-wingers were getting more discontented at the government's timidity; finally the ILP was expelled from the Labour Party.

The financial crisis, 1931

The Americans, calling in their European loans, created some strain on European financial markets. The Germans, granted a year's moratorium on reparation payments, began to borrow heavily from London, which made the mistake of lending 'long', i.e. with repayment dates fixed in years rather than in weeks or months.

Austria was also borrowing from the French, but when it proposed a customs union with Germany, Paris withdrew its support, and leading banks in Germany and Austria failed in the summer of 1931. Britain had lent over £200 million to Austria and Germany, and foreign investors began to make panic withdrawals from London.

In Parliament, the opposition attacked MacDonald's extravagance, and he appointed a committee of inquiry into the financial position, called the *May Committee* after its chairman. MacDonald waited until after Parliament had risen for the summer before publishing its findings in August 1931.

May reported that the government was running increasingly into debt, and predicted a budget deficit of £120 million for the following financial year. It recommended large cuts in public spending, reduction of the insurance fund's borrowing powers (these had recently been raised again to £30 million per year), cuts in unemployment benefit and cuts in the salaries of public officials such as civil servants.

The publication of these unwelcome facts accelerated the withdrawal of funds from London, and the Bank of England began losing gold daily. MacDonald, Snowden (Chancellor of the Exchequer) and Thomas (who had been given the impossible task of 'abolishing unemployment') were all fearful and cautious, and under the thumbs of the traditional economists of the Treasury and the City.

Britain had already borrowed over £100 million from various sources, and when it approached the USA, where there was no 'dole' for the unemployed at all, US banks made it clear that they would lend to the Bank of England only 'if the budget were balanced', which meant cutting the expenditure on social services. MacDonald's only remedy was to increase taxation and cut expenditure, including a 10 per cent reduction in 'dole'. His socialist colleagues commented that he was 'putting the women and children first', not in the lifeboats, but in the workhouse.

The Labour government split, MacDonald, Snowden and Thomas for the cuts, and most of the others against. MacDonald resigned. King George V might have sent for Baldwin and the Conservatives, but instead he asked MacDonald to form a 'national' government containing leading members of all the parties, and he was flattered into agreeing ('Tomorrow every Duchess in London will be wanting to kiss me').

The formation of the National Government, 1931

When the new government met the House of Commons in early September with drastic economic proposals, it was supported by the whole of the Conservative Party, most of the Liberals (Lloyd George had been convalescing after an operation, but would have refused), and a handful of Labour supporters, the rest forming the opposition.

The remedies were open to much left-wing criticism:

(a) Snowden brought in a *supplementary budget* in September:
    (i) Income tax went up from 4s 6d (22½p) in the £ to 5s (25p).
    (ii) Exemptions and allowances were reduced.
    (iii) Indirect taxes (beer, tobacco, petrol) were sharply increased.
(b) Government *economies* were contained in a separate bill:
    (i) Salaries were reduced by 15 per cent for judges, MPs, ministers, civil servants, members of the armed forces, police, post office workers and teachers.
    (ii) Benefit rates were cut by 10 per cent, and the benefit period was limited.
    (iii) Contribution rates were increased.
(c) Britain abandoned the *Gold Standard* anyway (21 September), raising the bank rate from 4½ to 6 per cent. The pound fell from $4.86 to $3.40, but the galloping inflation which Labour leaders so much feared did not materialize.

The 'Doctor's Mandate' election, October 1931

MacDonald held a general election at the end of October, with the Conservatives hoping to 'cash in' on the crisis.

He was denounced by the bulk of his party, and later, with a handful of others, was expelled from it, but in the country at large he was acclaimed for his great act of statesmanship in saving the economy and the pound sterling. During the campaign he made great play with a German 100,000,000 mark note, frightening his hearers by suggesting it would soon cost £1 million to post a letter.

A skilfully vague manifesto – a *Doctor's Mandate* to set the country on its feet again, but without going into details – enabled each party in the National Government to make its own appeal to the voters, so that different candidates represented different things. National Labour candidates, of whom 13 were elected, denounced the policies of their own former party as 'Bolshevism gone mad'.

National candidates won 556 seats, only 55 representing the opposition (46 Labour, 5 ILP and Lloyd George's Liberals 4). The National Government soon reverted to Conservative and ruled until the wartime coalition of 1940.

The stagnant thirties

▷ **Policies of the National Government**
Labour recovered some ground at the general election of 1935, when it returned 154 members as against the 'National' party of 387 members, but as even its supporters admitted, its story was 'one long diminuendo' (i.e. a fading away).

The triumph of protection

The idea of tariff protection was not new and had conflicted for some years with Britain's nineteenth-century orthodoxy of free trade.

(a) 1903, Joseph Chamberlain formed the *Tariff Reform League* to combine protective tariffs with imperial preference, but the idea split the Conservative Party and led to its defeat in the 1906 election.
(b) 1915, a wartime tariff of 33 per cent was levied on imported luxuries; this was retained after the war, though goods of empire origin were given preference by lower tariffs.
(c) 1921, *Safeguarding of Industries Act* produced a dutiable list of 6,500 items (many from Germany) on which 33 per cent duties were imposed. Stanley Baldwin, as President of the Board of Trade, was in charge of these.
(d) 1923, Baldwin, now a convert to protection, worked with Austen Chamberlain, Joseph's son, to put the policy to the electorate in the general election, but together the Labour Party and the Liberals defeated this in the name of free trade.
(e) 1925, at the same time as he restored the Gold Standard, Churchill restored the 'safeguarding duties' at the old level, and under the *Safeguarding of Industries Act* (1926) he allowed other industries to apply to the Board of Trade for protection.
(f) 1930, the Economic Advisory Council recommended a general readoption of protection, enthusiastically supported by Mosley.
(g) 1931, *Abnormal Importations Act* gave the government powers to impose up to 100 per cent duties on articles it selected, of which about 100 became dutiable.

Snowden had deep objections to abandoning free trade and resigned from the Exchequer. In 1932, Chamberlain's younger son, Neville, as Chancellor of the Exchequer, brought the *Import Duties Act* into existence, finally abandoning free trade:

(a) A general customs duty of 10 per cent was imposed on all imports.
(b) Preferential treatment was given to empire goods; these lower duties were formulated at the Ottawa Imperial Economic Conference in August 1932, the dominions generally getting a better deal than Britain.
(c) A 'free list' contained a small number of exempted goods.
(d) An *Import Duties Advisory Committee* (IDAC) was set up to recommend imposition of any additional duties it thought fit. These duties were frequently added, so that most manufactures carried 20 per cent duties, and most 'luxury' goods 30 per cent.

All of these duties continued thereafter, until Britain's entry into the EEC, with a tendency towards greater protection rather than less.

Financial policies

Taxation policy
At first, Chamberlain maintained the harsh cuts which Snowden had proposed, and in the 1932 and 1933 budgets there was little comfort for those who were suffering. But in 1934, many of these cuts were restored, and income tax fell from 5s (25p) in the £ once again to 4s 6d (22½p).

At the same time, he made savings by converting £2,000 million of the 5 per cent War Loan to 3½ per cent. The country, he said, had left *Bleak House* and could now begin to enjoy *Great Expectations*.

Money policy

At the end of 1931, Chamberlain reduced the bank rate from 6 to 2 per cent, making it easier to borrow money. This did not affect recovery immediately, since the slump discouraged people from borrowing money, but after 1935 'cheap money' gave great encouragement to new investment, especially in housing.

The idea of planning

Political and economic planning was started as early as 1931, and a large number of books on the subject were written by distinguished economists. This move was strongly encouraged by Lloyd George's Liberals. It achieved:

(a) 1932, foundation of *British Airways* to expand air traffic;
(b) 1933, setting up of the *London Passenger Transport Board* to coordinate various kinds of transport for Londoners;
(c) large new investments in the tubes and railways, roads and bridges;
(d) subsidies for the construction of the *Queen Mary* in 1934;
(e) an expanding programme of public works – public buildings, schools, etc. *Distressed areas* of the country, like South Wales, Lancashire and the Tees–Tyne area in the north-east had high unemployment and were in a bad condition. After 1934 the *Depressed Areas Act* was passed, renaming them Special Areas, and spending limited sums (at first only £2 million a year) on them to promote economic recovery.

Industrial policy

Old industries

Ideas to improve them leaned heavily on tariff protection and on reorganization to limit competition.

(a) In the *coal industry*, the Reorganization Commission, set up under the 1930 Act, met obstruction from the owners and others; though its powers were strengthened by Acts in 1936 and 1938, it achieved very little.
(b) The *British Iron and Steel Federation* successfully had tariffs raised, and so restricted imports. It promoted combinations among existing steel works, and the closure of the less economic plants. It also began new developments like those at Corby and Consett.
(c) In *shipbuilding*, there were amalgamations of declining yards, but there was new investment at Jarrow and Gateshead and along the Clyde. Shipbuilding began to recover with government orders for naval building in 1938.

New industries

New materials and techniques played a part in the expansion of electrical goods, cars, bicycles, plastics, chemicals and new fabrics like rayon. Here the annual rate of increase sometimes topped 20 per cent, and exports grew.

▷ **Social policies**   MacDonald retired from the premiership in 1935, to be succeeded by the Lord President, Baldwin, until 1937. Then Neville Chamberlain, who had been Chancellor of the Exchequer for most of the 1930s, became Prime Minister until he retired in 1940, early in the Second World War. Chamberlain gave most of his attention to domestic problems, which helps to explain his lack of success in foreign policy.

Housing

Housing conditions, especially in towns, were still often appalling up to 1918; the spread of democracy, however, meant that this could not be allowed to continue. Even before the war ended, Lloyd George was promising 'homes fit for heroes to live in'.

(a) *1919, Addison Act* helped to create 200,000 new 'council' houses whose dimensions were often cramped and whose cost frightened respectable ratepayers.
(b) *1923, Chamberlain Act*, passed by Neville Chamberlain while he was Minister of Health, leaned more heavily on private enterprise. Addison's Act worked within the

rent restrictions of 1915, so new building gradually dried up; but new houses were built until 1929 under subsidies permitted by the Act (about 500,000 in number, 350,000 of them built by private builders).

(c) *1924, Wheatley Housing Act* raised state subsidy for rent-controlled houses and was widely taken up by local authorities. Under the Act, well over 500,000 council houses were built until the subsidy was withdrawn in 1933.

(d) *1930, Greenwood Housing Act* made a start with urban slum clearance, dealing with substandard houses and with overcrowding, which was equally common. The Act was followed by others in 1933 and 1935, building about 300,000 houses, until an Act in 1938 enforced financial economies in the programme.

After 1935, there was something of a boom in private house building and about 350,000 were built annually until the war; new private 'estates' and 'ribbon development' became common, especially in the suburbs. On the eve of the war, detached houses could be bought new for £600 and new 'semis' for £350. This still put them beyond the reach of most working people, although some borrowed from 'building societies' at a rate of about £2 15s (£2.75) per £100 per month.

Rich and poor

There was still an increasing number of *rich* people, some of them extremely rich, though the general effect of taxation was to reduce their wealth. There were bitter protests against punitive taxes, especially supertax and death duties, but those who were better-off led comfortable and sheltered lives, buttressed by privilege and cushioned by the deference of the lower orders.

The vast bulk of the nation was composed of *poor* people, many of whom earned around £2 a week if they were lucky enough to be in a job, and brought up their families on it. But even their living conditions were steadily improving.

(a) People were *healthier*. Outside the state scheme, which covered about 4 million, about 20 million people were covered by health insurance, e.g. through the trade unions and the friendly societies.

(b) Few children now avoided *schooling*, and though education in the elementary and senior schools was uninspired, it was careful and thorough; about 20 per cent of children won places at grammar schools at the age of eleven, where the door was narrowly open to higher or university education. The scheme of 'state scholarships' for university was one of the victims of the 'Geddes Axe'. Better education for the ruling classes was still confined to public schools such as Eton.

(c) *Social conditions* were generally better:
   (i) There was less *crime*, and there was a higher detection rate for crimes committed. Public opinion was strongly against crime, and penalties were often severe. There was some increase in juvenile crime, but offenders were treated more kindly and sympathetically by the courts.
   (ii) *Drunkenness* also continued to decline; after the war, it ran at the rate of about 650 cases a year per 100,000 of the population, but fell in the 1930s to 125. On the other hand, *gambling* rapidly increased, encouraged by the new 'football pools'.
   (iii) *Leisure habits* were changing. Working people took seaside holidays, e.g. during Wakes Week in Lancashire, going to places such as Blackpool and Skegness. The cinema was taking the place of the public house, audiences being fed a diet of escapist entertainment, largely provided by Hollywood. Dancing was popular at the weekly 'hop', and league football could command large 'gates' of spectators. Mass circulation newspapers were widely read, and radio broadcasts provided entertainment and instruction from the BBC.

Unemployment and its treatment

The cost of unemployment benefits by 1934 had risen to £400 million per year, and this was thought to be the main problem confronting the government. Much of the cost was defrayed by the poor themselves, through local taxation by the 'rates', and indirect taxes on things such as tobacco, beer and other taxable items (the working classes, of course, did not earn enough to pay income tax).

In Welsh mining areas and villages in County Durham, as well as in many formerly brisk industrial towns such as Jarrow, Wallsend, Stockton, Wigan and Barnsley, there was deep depression, and sometimes as many as one man in three was out of work, eking out a miserable existence on the pittance (about 30 shillings (£1.50)) which the state provided for those 'on the dole'. Some, with time on their hands, read their local library's entire stock of books.

Shops were often closed and boarded up, with aimless groups of men standing about on street corners, a few trying to sell bundles of firewood or matches.

Only the pawnshops and the cinemas flourished. There were no betting shops: betting was technically illegal and bets had to be placed through 'bookies' runners'. There was usually a shabby crowd at the Labour Exchange, some of them young, who had never had a job, but most of them long-term unemployed, who had long since run out of the benefit for which they had contributed, and who were forced back on non-contributory benefits. There were also older men, many of whom would never work again.

Originally insurance was intended to cover short periods of time, or to cushion the switch from one job to another, but this had slowly changed:

(a) *1921, Unemployment Insurance Act* created *uncovenanted benefit*, i.e. an allowance for which workers had not contributed (generally known as the 'dole' because it was handed out in small helpings); for this end, the *Unemployment Fund* was empowered to borrow up to £30 million from the Treasury.

(b) *1927, Unemployment Insurance Act* lowered some benefits and abolished extended benefits, but gave the unemployed a statutory right to benefit, provided that applicants could prove they were 'genuinely seeking work'. The trade unions and the Labour Party felt deep resentment at this provision, which was motivated by meanness.

(c) *1929, Unemployment Insurance Act* reversed the 'genuinely seeking work' provision, but was attacked by the Conservatives for extravagance. On the basis of these criticisms, an *Anomalies Act* was forced through in 1931, which had the effect of drastically tightening the grant of benefits. All the same, the Unemployment Fund was borrowing ever more heavily from the Treasury.

(d) *1934, Unemployment Act* created the Unemployment Assistance Board (UAB), taking over responsibility for administering uncovenanted and transitional benefits from the Public Assistance Committees (PACs). These payments were now largely financed by the Treasury instead of the local authorities, which were left with little more responsibility than caring for the sick, the aged and the transients of the workhouse 'casual wards'.

(e) *1934, economic cuts* were largely restored, the 'dole' going up from 30s (£1.50) to 36s (£1.80), but this was administered according to the hated *Means Test*.

The sums saved by the Means Test were piffling, but it generated deep resentment among the poorest sections of the community:

(a) It involved searching and often embarrassing interviews with insolent minor bureaucrats at the 'Labour', who had been instructed to save every penny they could.

(b) It discouraged thrift, since any assets the applicant had accumulated were taken into account when the benefit was 'doled' out.

(c) It discouraged marriage, since working women, if married, were expected to help to keep their unemployed husbands.

(d) It damaged family relations, since sons and daughters who tried to help out by earning a little (e.g. by delivering newspapers) found their earnings, too, deducted from the benefit.

(e) It encouraged 'snooping' by local busybodies or even official informers: if his underpants were hanging alongside her knickers on the washing-line in the backyard, this was proof that the couple were in effect married, and not entitled to receive separate benefits.

The social effects of the Means Test were shrewdly observed by Walter Greenwood, in his novel *Love on the Dole*.

Origins of the welfare state

The welfare state is like a safety net in a circus: it aims to save those afflicted by misfortune from perishing in the absence of basic rescue measures.

Only a sketchy outline of the welfare state existed in the 1930s, with many serious gaps in the framework, such as in unemployment insurance, where the self-employed were not insured, and where farm workers and domestic servants were not covered until the late 1930s. There were no family allowances, and health services were riddled with gaps, though basic treatment could be provided by charity.

There were a number of pension services:

(a) *Old age pensions*, introduced in 1909 for those over 70, went up from 5s (25p) to 10s (50p) under Lloyd George in 1919. A limit on private means was imposed in 1909 for eligiblility for such a pension, but this limit was raised by MacDonald in 1924.

(b) *Widows', orphans' and contributory old age pensions* were introduced by Neville Chamberlain as Minister of Health in 1925: 10s (50p) for widows, with allowances for dependent children, 7s 6d (37$\frac{1}{2}$p) for orphan children, and 10s (50p) for insured workers contributing and their wives at 65. Those drawing these pensions moved to the non-contributory scheme at 70 (but irrespective of their means). In 1940, these could be supplemented by the Assistance Board (formerly the UAB).

A small number of other benefits were provided by the Treasury, such as state scholarships for working-class children to go to university. Social service provision by both the state and the local authorities in 1934 totalled about £500 million.

Private charitable effort still carried much of the burden:

(a) In *welfare*, these concerned themselves with child welfare, maternity services, unmarried mothers, released prisoners, lifeboats, seamen, etc.

(b) In *health care*, there were over 1,000 charity hospitals in the 1930s, and there were 'public' wards in general public hospitals, where treatment was free. There were also tuberculosis sanatoria, fever hospitals, etc. provided by the local authorities.

(c) In *education*, there were nursery schools, preparatory schools and a number of special schools provided outside the state system, and a number of societies such as Dr Barnardo's which ran children's homes.

But welfare provision still tended to be piecemeal; it was only with the *Beveridge Report* of 1942 that a comprehensive system was recommended 'from the cradle to the grave'.

The royal family

The prestige of the royal family still stood very high. George V first broadcast his Christmas message in 1932 to the peoples of Britain and the empire, and this became an established institution every year following.

In May 1935, George V and Queen Mary celebrated their silver jubilee, commemorating 25 years on the throne. The King died in the following January.

In December 1936, the new King, Edward VIII, was involved in an affair with an American, Mrs Simpson, who had already divorced one husband and was about to divorce another. A deed of abdication was drawn up, and all the necessary business was put through Parliament in a single day. Edward VIII disappeared abroad with his intended wife, taking the title of Duke of Windsor. The attendant scandal was supposed at the time to have rocked the foundations of the nation.

The new King was the Duke of York, Edward's brother, who called himself George VI and had two small daughters, Elizabeth, the heir presumptive, and Margaret Rose.

The royal family's prestige increased during the Second World War, when the King and Queen refused to go safely abroad, but stayed in London throughout the Blitz.

▷ **Fascism in Britain**   Neither communism nor fascism made a very large impact on Britain between the wars. Unlike Germany, where communists held 100 seats in the Reichstag and where the Nazis actually took over power in 1933, Britain never produced more than two communist MPs, and the fascists never contested a general election.

Origins and development

Sir Oswald Mosley, a young and enterprising member of MacDonald's Economic Advisory Council, put forward ambitious plans to boost purchasing power, protect British industry by tariffs and adopt large-scale national planning, but his ideas frightened most Labour supporters. He resigned from office in May 1930, and was expelled from the party in February 1931, forming his *New Party* to tackle the problem more efficiently.

His party went under in the 1931 election, and early in 1932 he launched the *British Union of Fascists* (BUF), publishing his programme in the following September in a book called *The Greater Britain*. In it he criticized the out-of-date workings of Parliament, and put forward a programme based on vigorous action and owing much of its inspiration to Mussolini. He also admired Hitler, and married his second wife, Lady Diana Guinness, in Hitler's presence.

Mosley had a proud and confident manner, and soon attracted a wide spectrum of followers, many middle class, but including workers and unemployed. He established his headquarters in King's Road, Chelsea, where he maintained a garrison of his 'blackshirts' in barracks and gave them lectures and training.

By 1934, there were about 400 fascist branches in various parts of Britain, and the total membership of the movement was about 20,000.

Fascist agitation

Mosley organized huge meetings in large towns, sometimes out of doors and sometimes in public halls. He transported large contingents of blackshirts to them in lorries, and used every modern technique to draw attention to himself.

Anti-Semitism was not originally part of his programme, but many left-wing Jews opposed him, and there were influential anti-Semites in the movement.

His campaign led up to a meeting at Olympia, in June 1934, in which opponents were roughly man-handled and ejected with broken limbs, to be taken away by the line of ambulances waiting outside the hall. Public opinion was shocked.

There were a number of other bloody encounters, with communist and Jewish opponents, especially in the East End of London, e.g. in Cable Street, but much of the sympathy Mosley had previously enjoyed was lost.

The decline of British fascism

The movement was debated in Parliament, and two measures were passed:

(a) *1934, Incitement to Disaffection Act* took steps against the dissemination of seditious literature, and extended the powers of the police to search for it.
(b) *1936, Public Order Act* condemned the use of 'insulting words and behaviour', gave the police powers for banning meetings and processions, and forbade the wearing of political uniforms.

As sympathy for Hitler evaporated in 1938–39, so support for Mosley's BUF declined.

At the outbreak of war in 1939, Mosley was mistakenly suspected of sympathy with the enemy, and was interned in 1940 in Brixton prison under Regulation 18B.

He was released at the end of 1943, largely on health grounds, but put under house arrest and not allowed to travel. He attempted to revive his movement in 1945, but the world reaction against fascism proved to be a fatal disability.

GLOSSARY

Abdication The renunciation of (giving up) the throne by a reigning monarch, e.g. the abdication of Britain's Edward VIII in December 1936.

Dole Uncovenanted benefit. The Insurance Act of 1921 made provision for the unemployed to receive further benefit once they had used up their unemployment insurance entitlement. This additional benefit was for those 'genuinely seeking work', and like unemployment benefit was only for a limited period. As it was 'doled out' grudgingly in small amounts, it was soon nicknamed 'the dole'.

General strike A strike which is intended to paralyse a whole country rather than just one industry. Its aim could be *general* support for one section of workers (e.g. the miners in 1926), or it could have a specifically *political* purpose.

Gold Standard The system by which a country fixes the value of its currency in relation to a specific weight of gold, and is willing to buy gold at that price. Its usefulness is that it prevents fluctuations in the value of a currency. After the First World War, the currencies of countries on the Gold Standard were generally overvalued, and while this made imports cheap, it made exports dear, and thus was a major contributor to unemployment. Even so, Britain rejoined the Gold Standard in 1926, having abandoned it during the war, and remained on the Gold Standard despite increasing economic difficulties until 1931.

Inflation A fall in the value of money, hence rising prices. Its worst form, galloping inflation, is usually caused by governments printing money excessively in order to cover their expenditure, as happened in Germany in the early 1920s. The fear of such inflation as Germany had suffered tended to paralyse government actions during the economic blizzard which followed the Wall Street Crash in 1929.

Means Test Imposed as a government economy in 1931 on all those receiving uncovenanted benefits such as the dole. The Public Assistance Committees of local authorities assessed a claimant's 'means' (i.e. income and savings) before deciding whether or not the claimant was entitled to financial assistance. The Means Test was bitterly resented by those who thought it gave an advantage to the improvident.

Nationalization The takeover by the state, usually with financial compensation, of the ownership and operation of the 'means of production' (workshops, factories, banks, transport, etc.). The Labour Party believed that nationalization would end employer exploitation of the workers, and so included it as Clause 4 of the party's constitution in 1918.

Red Flag The flag adopted by the Bolsheviks, hence its use by revolutionary and left-wing groups in Britain. It is also the title of the socialist hymn sung by the Labour Party on formal occasions.

Sterling The term for British as distinct from foreign money. Originally the name derived from the quality of the silver in British coinage.

EXAMINATION QUESTIONS

▷ **Question 1** Study Source A and then answer the questions on the General Strike which follow:

Source A

> The unions are fighting in defence of the mine-workers. The responsibility for the national crisis lies with the government . . .
> The General Council of the Trade Union Congress appeals to the workers to follow the instructions that have been issued by their union leaders . . . Violence and disorder must everywhere be avoided whatever the incitement.
> (From a report in the Daily Herald, 4 May 1926)

(a) Why was there a General Strike in 1926?   (7 marks)

(b) What can you learn from Source A about the aims and methods of the strikers?
                                                                                  (5 marks)

(c) Was it the strength of the government or the weakness of the unions which caused the strike to fail? Explain your answer.   (8 marks)

▷ **Question 2** (a) Describe the events of 1929–31 which led to the formation of a National Government.   (7 marks)

(b) How successful, during the years 1931–39, was the National Government in solving Britain's economic problems?   (8 marks)

(c) Why was the Labour Party so weak during the 1930s?   (5 marks)

Question 3   'For Britain the 1930s was a terrible period in which poverty, squalor and deprivation affected the vast majority of the population.'

(a)   Do you agree with this judgement on Britain in the 1930s? Explain your answer.

(12 marks)

(b)   What progress had Britain made towards becoming a welfare state by 1939?

(12 marks)

EXAMINATION ANSWERS

Question 1   *Outline answer*

(a)   It is important to concentrate on reasons rather than description. A brief analysis of the problems in the coal industry in the 1920s – foreign competition, falling prices, underinvestment – will make a useful start. The temporary subsidy and the threat of pay cuts and longer hours led to TUC involvement, and an attempt to arrive at a solution with government help and at the national level. But the lockout, the determination of the TUC not to suffer another Black Friday, and the government's abandonment of negotiations when the printers' union prevented the *Daily Mail* from publishing a provocative article brought about a general strike that no one really wanted.

(b)   There should be no difficulty in pointing out that the *Daily Herald* thought that the aim of the strike was to support the miners, and that the TUC expected the strikers to refrain from violence. That the first was an opinion and the second an appeal means that not all strikers necessarily agreed with the *Daily Herald* and the TUC, but most strikers followed their leaders in backing away from the notion that the General Strike had any political aims, and very few indeed were prepared to resort to violence.

(c)   You will probably argue that it was a bit of both. Certainly the trade unions found themselves involved in a strike they had not expected and had not prepared for. They were alarmed that some of their more revolutionary elements wanted to use the strike as a political lever to bring down the government. Thus the TUC held back from bringing out on strike the essential services, and was, almost from the first, looking for a compromise solution. Successive governments, on the other hand, had prepared contingency plans for a general strike as far back as 'Black Friday' in 1921, and Baldwin's government had bought time with the nine-month subsidy. Its Organization for the Maintenance of Supplies, its decisive influence over radio and its propaganda through the *British Gazette* gave it a head start in the struggle for public support. Moreover, the government had some members, e.g. Churchill and Birkenhead, who were prepared for a long fight and wanted a decisive victory; the TUC lacked anyone with such commitment. In the end, the TUC shrank from tightening up the strike, was afraid of acting unconstitutionally, and was concerned about its lack of control of the miners, for whose benefit the strike had been called; it therefore ended the strike without winning any specific concessions from the government other than vague promises by Baldwin. Union weakness seems the major reason; the strength of the government was never fully challenged.

Question 2   *Outline answer*

(a)   The description has to have an effective focus; the events must relate to the formation of the National Government. So the Wall Street Crash is relevant only in so far as it affected international banking and caused a run on the pound; the coming to power of the Labour government in 1929 only in so far as it was a minority government and lacked the authority to deal with a crisis; and unemployment only in so far as it increased the government's borrowing and contributed to the financial crisis. The May Committee, cabinet divisions on the necessary cuts and George V's efforts to retain MacDonald are easier to use. This is an 'events' question, so extensive examination of the motives of MacDonald, Snowden, Baldwin, etc. is not required.

(b) How much recovery there was in the 1930s, and how much of it was due to the National Government, are both debatable. The limited nature of the recovery can be seen in the fact that unemployment fell by only just over 30 per cent during the 1930s, and that old industries like coalmining, textiles and shipbuilding hardly revived at all. The government did, indeed, solve the immediate financial problem by abandoning the Gold Standard and devaluing the £, but this became less effective as other countries, even the USA, followed suit. Government attempts to revive depressed areas had little impact except with prestige projects like the *Queen Mary*; even the introduction of protective tariffs in 1932 had only a very limited effect on slowing down imports, although, together with Marketing Boards, it was of some minimal benefit to agriculture. The government's greatest contribution was low interest rates; these helped the strongly expanding building industry and the new light industries, but did little for the declining industries of the north. Cheap borrowing therefore made some contribution, but it was consumer demand which created the prosperity of the new radio, electrical and domestic appliance industries. The cinema industry was in a state of rapid growth, but it too received little direct government encouragement. And it was not economic policy but foreign policy which led the government to begin rearmament in 1936. Overall the government provided the right economic conditions for recovery, but its efforts actively to promote it were disappointingly limited in effect.

(c) There are several issues here – the failure of the Labour government in 1931 and the Labour split which followed the formation of the National Government; the domination of MacDonald's National Government by the Conservatives; the widespread belief after 1931 that only a national government could save the country and that the Labour attack on National Labour was vindictive; the weakness of trade unions after the General Strike and the Trades Disputes Act of 1927; the weakness of the Labour Party in the 1935 general election, hampered by Lansbury's leadership and pacifism; and Baldwin's claiming credit for the National Government in 1935 for the fall in unemployment. Of course, there was, in fact, a small Labour revival in 1935, and Labour made useful progress in most of the by-elections of the late 1930s.

▷ Question 3(a) *Tutor answer*

It is usual to think of the 1930s as the period of the Depression, and there is a danger of painting a uniformly black picture. Certainly for the unemployed it was a time of great hardship: the unemployment benefit was not universal and was limited to 26 weeks, the uncovenanted 'dole' was subject to a means test and could be refused to those not 'genuinely seeking work' or to those where other income, however meagre, was coming into the household. The Public Assistance Committees were composed largely of middle- and upper-class members, and although their interpretation of the rules varied from one place to another, they were all under considerable financial restraint and did not award the dole liberally. The cuts in benefit and dole in 1931 hit hard, and the unemployed suffered disproportionately from these.

But there is another side to the picture. Even the unemployed benefited from the continuing fall in prices until 1934, and those in receipt of benefit or dole received more in real terms in 1934 than they would have received in 1929. With the return of rising prices in the mid-1930s, the unemployed were cushioned by Chamberlain's restoration of the cuts of 1931. Squalor was certainly in sharp decline in the 1930s: various Housing Acts had drastically reduced substandard housing, and councils contributed to the housing boom by building inexpensive small houses for rent. Most men had state medical insurance cover, and most children received medical and hospital cover from Friendly Societies for as little as 1d per week. Those not covered could still get free hospital attention in most parts of the country. For those in work – and this, with dependent families, amounted to more than 80 per cent of the population – falling prices until 1934 and rising wages after it brought rising living standards. Electricity, cheap new domestic products, radio, the cinema – all these added new dimensions to people's lives, even occasionally to those of the unemployed. For a minority, therefore, there was bleak despair; for the majority it was a time of slow but measurable improvement in living standards.

▷ **Question 3(b)** *Student answer with examiner's comments*

'Spelling is not strong, but "welfare state" should have been correctly copied from the question paper.'

'Labour Exchange, not Job Centre.'

'Dubious. Certainly not how the amount was determined.'

'Possibly for some. But squatting was not a 1930s problem!'

'Pensions at 65. Intended to supplement other sources, not to provide a generous living.'

'Not abolished – now run by Public Assistance Committees.'

'A modern, not a 1930s solution.'

'Not everyone. 1911 not the 1930s.'

'Overstated.'

'Elementary, not secondary.'

'Limited availability only.'

'Family allowances did not start until 1945.'

'Presumably not a spelling error, but a misplaced attempt at humour. There is no place for this sort of thing in an examination answer, especially as it was not Churchill who said it.'

> There had been a lot of progress towards a Welfair State by the 1930s. All those out of work were either found jobs by the Job Center or given enough money to live on depending on there needs. Those with nowhere to live were given one of the new council houses or allowed to squat. Those over 70 got generous old age pensions intended to keep people in cumfert in there old age, workhouses were abolished so that the local authority had to find bed and breakfast ackomodation for the homeless, and everyone was entitled to medical care and hospital treetment paid for out of there ninepence for fourpence. Slums and back-to-back houses were pulled down and new modern homes were built for everyone, children were compelled to attend school until 15, and were given free primary and secondary education. Those good enough were given free places at univercities. Free school meals were aveilable to all, and all children had there heads examined for lice by the school nurse, and there teeth attended to by the school dentist. Generous family allowances were given to parents who had children, the more they had the more money they got. So by 1939 Britain was a welfare state – as Churchill said, 'We are all shoshialists now'.

Examiner's decision on the student answer

This is a very poor and rather brief answer. There appears to be some idea of what a welfare state is, but the answer is full of inaccuracies and anachronisms. Very little idea of the 1930s in shown. This has enough understanding for Level 1, and would score at most 2/12.

SUMMARY

In this chapter you have studied the social and political history of Britain between the wars, and the economic and industrial problems facing the country during those years. In particular, the chapter refers to:

▷ the effects of the First World War;

▷ the role of the trade unions and the TUC in the 1920s;

▷ the General Strike, its causes, effects and importance;

▷ the impact of the Depression on British society and the economy;

▷ the extent of unemployment and the problems of the unemployed;

▷ the social and political problems of the 1930s.

Material relating to other aspects of this period is to be found later in this book:

▷ *Foreign and international relations*: these are dealt with more fully in chapter 11.

▷ *The Second World War* and its consequences: this is covered in chapter 12.

International affairs, 1919–31

 GETTING STARTED

The years between the wars were an extremely troubled time, a period of great tension when problem followed problem and nothing ever seemed to get settled. Many of the issues dealt with in the Second World War in fact had their origin in the First. Professor E.H. Carr refers to the period as the 'twenty years' crisis'.

MEG	NEAB	NICCEA	SEG	LONDON	WJEC	TOPIC	STUDY	REVISION 1	REVISION 2
✓	✓		✓			**Paris peace settlement, 1919–20**			
✓	✓		✓			The main personalities			
✓	✓		✓			Main features of the postwar settlement			
✓	✓		✓			**Problems of the peace**			
✓	✓		✓			Characteristics of the new Europe			
✓	✓		✓			The reparations problem			
✓	✓		✓			Dissatisfaction of the major powers			
✓	✓		✓			**The League of Nations**			
✓	✓		✓			The purposes of the League			
✓	✓		✓			The mandate system			
✓	✓		✓			Efforts to strengthen the League			
✓	✓		✓			Successes and failures in the 1920s			

 WHAT YOU NEED TO KNOW

Paris peace settlement, 1919–20

▷ **The main personalities**

All the victorious Allies were invited to the peace conference which met in Paris in January 1919, but the important decisions were taken by the *Big Four*: Woodrow Wilson, Georges Clemenceau of France, Lloyd George and President Vittorio Orlando of Italy.

President Wilson

Wilson was leader of the US Democratic Party, and had been President since 1912. He was a radical, an enemy of privilege and, like most American leaders, a tireless populist. He saw the war as an idealist crusade, proclaiming: 'The world must be made safe for democracy . . . We shall fight for democracy, for the right of those who submit to authority to have a voice in their own government, for the rights and liberties of small nations.' The peace settlement bore Wilson's mark. Coming to the conference almost as a Messiah, he achieved many of his *Fourteen Points*. He was, however, a former university academic who had limited tactical skills, and few practical plans on which his ideals of a just settlement could be built.

Self-government played a large part in the new Europe he helped to form: new states like Poland, Yugoslavia and Czechoslovakia replaced the former dynastic empires of central and eastern Europe. The League of Nations was largely his work. Because he believed the League was the only hope of permanent world peace, he was led to give way in negotiation on matters where the views of more practical statesmen conflicted with his, in order to secure their acceptance of the Covenant.

He was more popular in Europe, however, than he was at home; those Americans who upheld the traditional policy of *isolationism* were hostile, and his party was defeated in the 1920 presidential election. The US Senate refused to approve his work and would not allow the USA to become, as he wished, the main foundation stone of the League.

Georges Clemenceau

He was the most bitter of the opponents of Germany during the First World War. Mayor of Montmartre at the time of the German siege of Paris in 1870, his ruthlessness and caustic tongue won him the nickname 'the Tiger' in the 1890s, and he became Radical Prime Minister of the Third Republic in 1906 for nearly three years. He returned to the post in 1917 and was in power when the war ended.

He had no faith in Wilson's ideals. He knew exactly what he wanted – to crush Germany while he had the chance. He regarded Franco-German hostility as a fact of nature, and now that Germany was defeated, he wished to destroy the German threat to France's security. He worked for France, and for France alone: nothing else interested him. His vindictive attitude weakened the chances of a lasting peace.

Lloyd George

He had already risen to prominence in British radical politics in the years before the war, and it was in domestic politics that he was best known. In foreign affairs, however, he soon made himself at home, showing his ability to take part in peacemaking with foresight and imagination. Whereas commentators noted that the attitudes of Wilson and Clemenceau were, in their different ways, fixed, Lloyd George was extremely flexible. Indeed, his critics alleged that he had never quite mastered the difference between right and wrong. He personally favoured moderate terms, and gave only limited support to the French desire for revenge.

Though he was bound by the election promises of 1918 to deal sternly with Germany, and though he was a committed opponent of the German fleet, colonial empire and mercantile marine, he did not wish to be too harsh on Germany. He thought that it was unjust, for example, to hand over control of Danzig, so plainly a German city, to Poland. He was sometimes, therefore, suspected of being 'soft' on Germany.

Vittorio Orlando

He was another academic – a professor of law – who moved into politics to become Minister of Justice in 1916 and Prime Minister of Italy shortly afterwards. He was bent on securing for Italy territories promised under the 1915 Pact of London, which he claimed were rightfully Italian, but not yet achieved (*Italia Irredenta*). He soon came into conflict with President Wilson, who thought that Italian claims were exaggerated and contrary to his principle of self-determination. Orlando was also handicapped by not being able to speak English.

His failure in Paris to sustain Italy's point of view, and his inability at home to remedy Italy's growing unrest, led to his political eclipse. He withdrew from politics when Mussolini came to power, and did not return to office until 1946.

▷ Main features of the postwar settlement

All the treaties embodied President Wilson's desire to draw the frontiers along national lines, taking the wishes of the people into account. This was the so-called *principle of self-determination*. The treaty-makers used local plebiscites to discover what the wishes of the people were. Unfortunately, the treaties were inconsistent: the plebiscites held in 1920–21 led to German losses of territory in northern Schleswig, Upper Silesia, part of East Prussia and in Eupen and Malmédy; but no plebiscite was held, for example, in

Alsace or Lorraine, which were given to France outright, or in other areas of Germany given to Poland. Likewise, in no German colonial territory were the people consulted.

In the treaty of St Germain, furthermore, no plebiscites were held in those parts of the Tyrol given to Italy; nor were the Sudeten Germans allowed one to permit them to opt out of Czechoslovakia. The provision of the treaty forbidding the future union of Austria and Germany, even if they should wish it, ignored national self-determination and denied in advance what might have been a nationalist aspiration. There seems to be some truth in the German view that the Allies respected this principle only when it suited their interests.

Treaty of Versailles, June 1919

Germany, before 1914 the most powerful nation in Europe, was reduced to impotence by this treaty. The Germans took no part in the discussions at Versailles, and when their delegates learnt their country's fate in 1919, they signed the treaty under protest and without reading it, calling it a *diktat*.

(a) Germany lost about 13 per cent of its land area in Europe (see the map on page 68), and about the same percentage of its people. Though it lost much of its coal and iron industries, and a large part of its industrial capacity, it is perhaps worth noting that in no area was a majority population of Germans placed under a foreign government. Danzig and Memel came closest to this, but these two cities were in fact placed under the League of Nations.

(b) German colonies were entrusted as *mandates* to the victorious powers. Britain and France secured most of them, nominally in the interests of their peoples. Others were acquired by Australia, New Zealand, South Africa, Belgium and even Japan, whose colonial record was clearly inferior to that of the 'unfit' Germans.

(c) Germany was required to forfeit its fleet and mercantile marine, and was fined very heavily in the form of railway engines, machinery, lorries and cars. This was a vindictive measure designed to compensate the Allies for their losses in the war. The material was actually of little use to them, but Germany was deprived of it.

(d) Germany was savagely disarmed, its army limited to 100,000 men, its fleet restricted to a few battleships of restricted tonnage, with smaller vessels (but no submarines), no tanks or heavy artillery, and only a limited number of small aircraft. Germany also had to accept and pay for an Allied army of occupation on the left bank of the Rhine, with three bridgeheads on the German bank at Cologne, Coblenz and Mainz, and a 50 kilometre strip of demilitarized territory there.

(e) Certain key German waterways, e.g. the Kiel Canal, and the main navigable rivers, were placed under international control.

(f) Article 231 of the treaty was the famous *war guilt clause*: 'The Allied and Associated governments affirm and Germany accepts the responsibility of Germany and her allies for causing all the loss and damage to which the Allies and their subjects have been subjected as a consequence of the war ... Germany undertakes that she will make compensation for all damage done to the civilian population and to their property.'

Germany, furthermore, promised to hand over war criminals. When angry voices clamoured for the Kaiser to be tried, this was only the preliminary to hanging him; no one supposed he was going to be acquitted. In fact, at the end of the war he fled to Holland, and the Dutch refused to extradite him. As things turned out, the whole war-trial provision of the treaty was left unfulfilled.

(g) The war guilt clause provided the legal excuse for imposing heavy reparations on the Germans. The amount was left undetermined at the time of the treaty, and a special commission was set up to fix the sum demanded. The total bill, when decided in 1920, amounted to £6,000 million; at the insistence of Britain and France, and against the better judgement of President Wilson, this was increased in 1921 by the inclusion of war pensions to £6,600 million (or 136bn marks in gold at the prevailing exchange rate). By that time, the Germans were reckoned to have paid about £1,000 million to cover the upkeep of the armies of occupation; the rest was to be paid in equal instalments over a period of 42 years, including a large amount in the form of interest on sums outstanding. When the figures were published, the Germans were furious and claimed they had been cheated; this was partly because the sum was so large, and also because none of the other defeated powers was burdened so heavily.

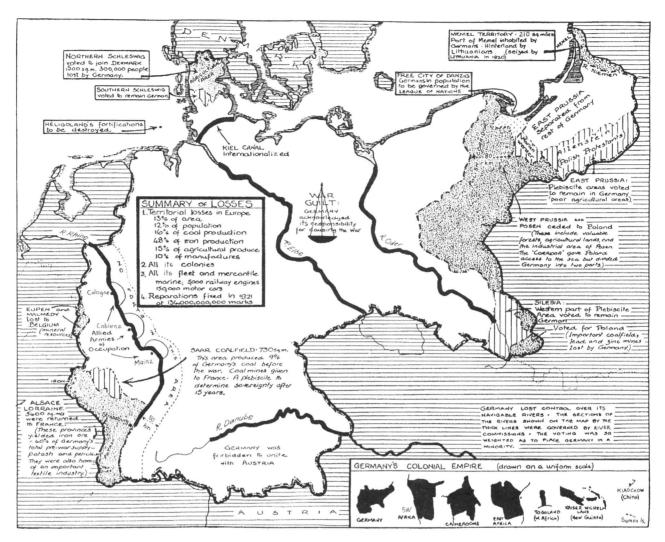

Fig. 6.1 Germany's losses

Treaty of St Germain, September 1919

The biggest alterations to the European map took place with the break-up of the Habsburg Empire, a process already well under way before the war ended. Austria and Hungary, formerly ruling nations of this autocratic, multiracial empire of 51 million, were now shorn of their dependencies to become two separate inland states. As far as Austria, the western half, went:

(a) *Czechoslovakia*, a new state already in embryo before war ended, came into existence in Bohemia-Moravia, the rich, industrially developed western portion of the state. This state controlled the German-speaking area of the Sudetenland, previously part of the Habsburg Empire. It also obtained much of Silesia – vainly claimed by Poland – and even parts of Lower Austria itself.

(b) *Poland*, a new state created at the behest of President Wilson, acquired Galicia, and the city of Cracow and its surroundings.

(c) *Italy* acquired the South Tyrol and the Trentino, Istria and the port of Trieste, together with Pola, the Habsburg Empire's only naval base, and some of the smaller islands of the Adriatic.

(d) Another new state, soon to be called *Yugoslavia*, acquired most of Carinthia and Carniola, the former occupied state of Bosnia-Herzegovina, the Dalmatian coast (eventually including Fiume) and many of the adjacent Adriatic islands.

(e) *Romania* acquired the Bukovina, claimed by Poland as part of Galicia.

(f) Austria was reduced to a small inland Germanic republic of some 6 million, a third of them living in Vienna. Most of the Austrian navy was surrendered, its air force severely restricted, and its army limited to 30,000 men. The country was supposed to pay reparations, but these were not heavy, and the powers in the end did not insist on them. Really this was quite fair, since they would have fallen disproportionately heavily on the few remaining citizens of the country.

Treaty of the Trianon, June 1920

Hungary was reduced to half its former size, and became a landlocked country whose only access to water was via the Danube.

(a) To *Czechoslovakia*, it gave up Slovakia along the Carpathian ridge with its few agricultural areas and scattered minerals.
(b) To *Yugoslavia*, it gave up Croatia and Slovenia.
(c) To *Romania*, it gave up the Banat and Transylvania, and this, together with Bessarabia from Russia, made Romania easily the biggest country in the Balkans.
(d) *Hungary* became a monarchy, ruled by a regent for a non-existent king, the regent being an admiral in its non-existent navy. There were limitations on the Hungarian armed forces similar to those on Austria, the army being limited to 35,000 men. As in the case of Austria, reparations were light and went unpaid.

Treaty of Neuilly, November 1919

Bulgaria, being one of the defeated powers, also suffered losses:

(a) To *Yugoslavia*, it gave up frontier areas known as the Strumnitza.
(b) To *Greece*, it gave up western Thrace and the whole Aegean coastline. Its only access to the sea was now along its Black Sea coast.
(c) To *Romania*, it gave up the Dobrudja.
(d) There were no changes enforced on the Bulgarian government as a result of the war, but the country was left with a number of grievances, e.g. the Bulgarian army was limited to 20,000 men, and the country had to accept liability to pay reparations.

Treaty of Sèvres, August 1920

The Turks, who had never considered themselves one of the Central Powers, were deeply upset at the severity with which they were treated.

(a) To *Greece* they lost Adrianople and nearly the whole of eastern Thrace in Europe, apart from Constantinople itself; in Asia Minor, Smyrna and the whole of western Anatolia, together with many of the Aegean islands.
(b) To *Italy*, they lost an area of Asia Minor around Adalia; they also confirmed the earlier losses in 1912 of Rhodes and the Dodecanese islands.
(c) To *France*, they lost much of the province of Cicilia, close to the border of French-occupied Syria.
(d) Most serious of all, Constantinople itself and the Straits area, together with adjacent islands such as Lemnos, went to make up the *International Zone of the Straits*, administered by the Allies on behalf of the League of Nations. Mustapha Kemal shortly afterwards moved the capital of Turkey to the inland city of Ankara.
(e) The *non-Turkish provinces* were stripped away completely, leaving Turkey confined solely to Anatolia, the peninsula of Asia Minor:
  (i) Turkey, which had penetrated deep into Armenia during the Russian civil wars, was required to provide a 'national home' for the Armenian people.
  (ii) Kurdish areas were to be given independence in the form of Kurdistan.
  (iii) Further south, Syria, the Lebanon, Iraq, Palestine and Transjordan were all mandated to Britain and France.
  (iv) Almost the whole of the Arabian peninsula became an independent kingdom under a native Saud dynasty.
(f) Turkey was to be disarmed, and was to pay reparations.

The terms of the Treaty of Sèvres proved to be impossible to enforce. Turkish nationalists, under their wartime hero Mustapha Kemal, angrily rejected them. He crushingly defeated the Greeks as they were occupying their new territory, and in 1922 threw them out of Smyrna and Anatolia altogether. Then he turned against the small Allied forces in the Straits Zone. At once, Italian and French garrisons were discreetly withdrawn; only the British General Harington was left with a handful of British troops to face him. Lloyd George briefly threatened to renew the Gallipoli campaign, but when the Australians and New Zealanders objected, he climbed down and agreed to revise the terms of the Sèvres treaty.

There followed the *Treaty of Lausanne* in 1923:

(a) Turkey regained Adrianople and eastern Thrace, and, in Asia Minor, Smyrna and the surrounding area of western Anatolia.

(b) The Straits were still to be demilitarized and neutralized, but Turkish control was restored and Constantinople was now regained, together with the islands in the Aegean covering the entrance to the Dardanelles.

(c) Turkey recovered Kurdistan and most of Armenia, and earlier requirements for local independence were quietly dropped.

(d) Turkey was excused reparations, and disarmament was abandoned. Meantime, Mustapha Kemal forced the Sultan to abdicate; the Ottoman Empire was abolished and a new republic was declared with its capital at Ankara. Mustapha Kemal became its first President.

Problems of the peace

▷ **Characteristics of the new Europe**

The dominance of France

France resumed its historical position as the dominant power in Europe, overshadowing its neighbours:

(a) Germany was heavily penalized by the peace settlement; this loss in status and prestige was damaging to the Germans and dangerous to Europe's future stability.

(b) From the remnants of the old Habsburg Empire emerged the small republic of Austria, all that was left of its traditional greatness.

(c) Italy felt weakened and neglected by its treatment after 1918; it was only with the rise of Mussolini that Italy re-emerged as a major power.

But France had not recovered its position by its own unaided efforts. It was the united strength of the Allies that had placed France on the winning side, and time was to show how dependent France had now become on external support.

The advance of nationalism

The war appeared to be a victory for democracy, as the old autocratic empires gave way to new national states, but democracy did not have very deep roots.

(a) The old ruling classes were still in existence, and soon began to recover their former control over governments. These new countries remained poor, peopled chiefly by peasants, and often influenced by rich and privileged churchmen.

(b) Smaller national groups conflicted with one another, and only in the case of Yugoslavia was leadership able to reconcile warring elements.

(c) Economic nationalism reared its head, with commercial and industrial policies aiming at supremacy, their governments jealous of their neighbours and fearful of their former rulers, especially in the Danube Basin.

The same growth of nationalism could be seen in former overseas colonies: the period before 1914 was one of European imperialism over the rest of the world, but these colonies began to seek self-government and independence after 1919, and the mandate system actually encouraged this process.

Political polarization of Europe

The two dominant political theories of the time were:

(a) *right-wing authoritarianism*: the rule by powerful dictators opposing the spread of radical reform and redistribution of property, both of which would threaten the position of rich landlords and businessmen. They played on the fears of ordinary folk, frightening them with the bogey of communism.

(b) *left-wing socialism or communism*: a populist government which claimed to act in the interests of the poorer classes against the oppression of capitalist exploiters and privileged aristocrats. It demanded a fairer, more equal society where everybody would be offered freedom from poverty.

Communism encouraged the formation of conspiratorial groups to take over power from the ruling class in the interests of a revolutionary new style of government; dictators formed military regimes to crush them and prevent this happening. As time progressed, the divisions between the two styles of government hardened.

In practice, where communists ruled (chiefly in the USSR), the methods adopted – discipline, authority, conformism, suppression of opponents – were very similar to those used by authoritarians, though they claimed quite different intentions.

▷ The reparations problem

The sum eventually agreed by the Allies for the Germans to pay – £6,600 million – was heavy, yet not outside the range of economic possibility. Perhaps the German working day would have had to be lengthened, and the economy kept working at peak efficiency under watchful management, but many were sure it could be done.

German unwillingness to pay

The real problem was not the ability of the Germans to pay, but the practicability of the Allies insisting on it. Naturally the Germans complained at the burden so as to get it reduced, but the resolve of the Allies gradually weakened. At first they took a tough line, saying: 'Justice is the only possible basis for the settlement of the account of this terrible war . . . Reparations for wrongs inflicted is of the essence of justice. Somebody must suffer for the consequences of the war. Is it to be Germany, or the countries she has wronged?' It was not until April 1921 that the final figure was announced; the Germans protested, and it was only an ultimatum from London that compelled them to agree with the Allies' decision in May.

In 1922, they once again protested, and once again the Allies insisted. Part of the money for the first payment came from the delivery of coal and timber. The non-delivery of consignments of timber in December 1922 gave the French their excuse to turn the screw, and in January 1923, in spite of British protests, French and Belgian troops were sent to occupy the Ruhr.

There were strikes in the coal and steel industries, and the factories came to a standstill. Right-wing agitators in Germany were delighted to see public opinion, at least in Germany, swinging in their favour.

The great German inflation

The paralysis of Ruhr industry, together with the German government's determination to maintain strike pay and other social benefits, led to rapid inflation. The further the German mark depreciated, the faster it was printed; and the faster it was printed, the further it depreciated. Soon barrow-loads of it were necessary to make even the simplest of purchases. Of course, it did not help Germany's reparation predicament, since the country's obligations were calculated in terms of gold.

Table 6.1 Marks to the £, 1914–23

1914	15	
1919	250	(Treaty of Versailles concluded)
Apr. 1921	500	(Amount of reparations fixed)
Nov. 1921	1,000	(Silesian plebiscite)
Aug. 1922	35,000	(Inflation out of control)
Jan. 1923	72,000	(French occupation of the Ruhr)
Nov. 1923	16,000,000,000,000	

The effect of such a massive inflation was to destroy the value of money, thus wiping out the savings, investments and pensions of millions of ordinary Germans. The public debt was also wiped out, and so funds invested in it, e.g. by insurance companies, were rendered worthless. Many were reduced to abject poverty.

Eventually a new German government under Gustav Stresemann, with Dr Hjalmar Schacht as financial adviser, was able to stabilize the currency in 1924, making 1 new Reichsmark equivalent to 1,000,000,000,000 'old' marks.

The whole operation went so smoothly that some foreign observers even suggested that the whole inflation had been planned by a few powerful Germans whose own wealth was securely locked up in land and other real property.

The solution of the reparations problem

In 1924, after a change of government in France, a committee of experts, under US Vice-President Charles Dawes, produced the *Dawes Plan* for more gradual reparations payments, with early instalments at £50 million per year, and later ones at £125 million. A gold loan of 800 million Reichsmarks was made to Germany, and over the next six years Germany received around 21,000 million marks. Foreign credit was enough to keep the exchange value of the mark stable. In effect, money was being borrowed with which to pay reparations: the Germans contributed very little. The heaviest burden imposed by the Dawes Plan never exceeded $3^1/_2$ per cent of the German national income.

Meanwhile, the Germans used the money to rebuild their railways and manufacturing plant. Some German towns even spent the money to reshape their public buildings. In 1929, however, the flow of money into Germany faltered, when the New York stock exchange offered the prospect of bigger pickings. That year, another committee under the US financier Owen Young modified the Dawes Plan, cutting Germany's total liability to £2,000 million, spread over a period of 59 years.

But the *Young Plan* in reality mattered little, for before the end of 1929 the Great Depression burst upon the world. German imports and exports fell sharply, and soon there were over 6 million unemployed. US President Herbert Hoover in June 1931 announced a one-year *moratorium* (postponement) on payments; and before this expired Germany announced its unwillingness to make further payments. A conference at Lausanne in 1932 cancelled all outstanding obligations in return for a final payment by Germany of £150 million, which the European governments insisted on receiving in order to be able to continue their own payments to the United States. In the end, the German government evaded even this last modest demand.

▷ **Dissatisfaction of the major powers**

The Paris peace settlement did not prove to satisfy quite a number of major European powers. It was not Germany alone that was angry with it.

French bitterness

The French felt cheated by Germany of a dignified and lasting peace. A former Premier of France and an old colleague of Clemenceau declared: 'France has a unique experience of Germany. No one has suffered as she has. It is useless to think of persuading France to accept close cohabitation with Germany in violation of the text of the Covenant, first of all because France will not accept it, and then because it is not just.' France's bitter mistrust of Germany had several causes:

(a) France thought that Germany had only been coerced into the treaty, and would soon break it. France thought that no help was to be expected from the USA.
(b) Germany seemed determined to avoid paying reparations, but France intended to keep these at a maximum and to insist on every jot.
(c) Germany should be kept out of the League of Nations, which the Germans only pretended to respect and which was involved in their humiliation.
(d) France suspected that Germany had no serious intention of disarming, and therefore French forces were to be kept as big as possible.

Russian isolation

After the Bolshevik revolution and the seizure of power by the Bolsheviks, Russia found itself treated like a leper, and a band of new states was created on its eastern frontier to act as a buffer against possible Russian expansion; this the Russians believed was due to the fear of communism among the capitalist powers.

Russia was denied any voice at the peace conference, was refused a share in reparations and was excluded from the League. It failed to make its voice heard in western Europe, and the only ally it could get at the *Treaty of Rapallo* (1922) was Germany – equally in disgrace.

Italian disillusionment

Italy thought that it had made big sacrifices during the war, when over 600,000 soldiers had been lost, but that its case for reward had never been considered.

(a) It had been given no colonies, and no share in the mandates distributed.
(b) It had received few lands, and its claims to Italia Irredenta had been rejected.
(c) Its finances were in ruins, but it was to receive only a derisory 15 per cent share of reparations.
(d) The economy was breaking down, and industrial relations were threatened by massive strikes and lockouts.
(e) The Italian poet d'Annunzio and a band of blackshirted nationalists seized the Adriatic port of Fiume for Italy, but Giolitti's government sent Italian troops to turn them out and crush the movement. The government's abject compliance with the Allies' wishes infuriated the Italian people.

The League of Nations

▷ **The purposes of the League**

In the nineteenth century, international problems had been dealt with by conferences of the powers. There was no machinery provided to stop governments fighting over what they felt to be their rights. To this extent, the League of Nations was a new departure – a permanent club of states to guarantee future peace.

Establishment of the League

President Wilson's *Fourteen Points* planned the creation of a League of Nations so as to outlaw war, and in April 1919 the full assembly of the peace conference accepted what became known as the *Covenant* of the League. This Covenant, later embodied as the preamble to each of the postwar treaties, comprised the 26 articles which formed the basic rules of the League.

Each member promised to refer disputes to the League before taking up arms, and if the League failed to find a solution within six months, to wait a further three months before declaring its intentions, after which it could 'legally' go to war. It was hoped that this nine-month 'cooling-off' period would provide any intending attacker with the opportunity to reflect on the seriousness of the step being taken; but equally, for the determined aggressor, the interval could be used for war preparations.

The core of the Covenant lay in Articles 10 to 17. Under Article 10 the powers promised: 'to respect and preserve against external aggression the territorial integrity and existing political independence of all members of the League'.

Article 16 went on: 'Should any member of the League resort to war in disregard of its covenants, it shall be deemed to have committed an act of war against all other members of the League, which hereby undertake immediately to subject it to the severance of all trade or financial relations . . .'

This 'severance' was called *sanctions*, and comprised a range of actions from the mere breaking off of all diplomatic relations to much more serious penalties. At the extreme, the League could impose military sanctions. This was never done, however, since it was thought that lesser sanctions would be enough. Furthermore, the League itself did not maintain any permanent armed forces; the final decision rested with member states whether or not to act on League advice.

Framework of the League

The *Assembly* was the parliament of the League, where member states met once a year to deal with problems, admit new members and control the budget.

The *Council* was the cabinet of the League, containing permanent and non-permanent members, always available in Geneva at the League's headquarters and taking day-to-day decisions, especially if the Assembly were not in session.

At first there were four permanent members (Britain, France, Italy and Japan – the USA did not join), but this number grew to five in 1926 with the admission of Germany.

There were also four non-permanent members, elected by the Assembly for three years, and re-eligible thereafter. This number had reached eleven by 1936.

However, the Council had to take all important decisions unanimously. Opposition, even abstention, would mean that nothing could be done; hence it was quite possible for one state to thwart the wishes of all the others.

The *Secretariat* was the salaried civil service of the League, handling the whole mass of paperwork that the League entailed. The Secretary-General was an Englishman, Sir Eric Drummond, whose aim was to produce an efficient professional body.

There were also various specialized bodies:

(a) *Permanent Court of International Justice* at the Hague, whose fifteen judges had the task of ruling in international cases. Since the referral of disputes to the Court was voluntary, however, the court had very little to do.

(b) Various *commissions* for specific purposes, such as the Mandates Commission and the Disarmament Commission.

(c) Various *agencies* for a wide variety of different purposes, such as refugees, slavery, drugs, postal services and communications. The most important was the *International Labour Organization* to secure economic and social justice for workers, and representing employers and workers. It sought proper entitlement to social benefits, maximum working hours, fair rates of pay, etc. Its powers, however, were purely advisory; hence the USA felt able to join without loss of dignity.

▷ **The mandate system**

The League had the job of disposing of the former territorial dependencies of Turkey and Germany. It saw itself bound by the fifth of Wilson's Fourteen Points: 'to make a free and impartial adjustment of colonial claims', and by Article 22 of the Covenant, that 'the well-being and development of such native peoples form a sacred trust of civilization'.

This produced a system of trusteeship whereby all these territories were annexed and held in trust by members of the League under the League's supervision.

The power placed in control was known as the *mandatory* and had to promise to work towards independence for the territory concerned, though in practice it did not always do this. It also made an annual report to the Mandates Commission of its work for this purpose, whose contents were sometimes optimistic.

The USA had always rejected colony building, and regarded the mandate system as empire building in disguise. Hence it refused to be associated with the scheme, and would not accept any mandates (at least until 1945).

Grade A mandates

These were granted in respect of former Turkish lands in the Middle East, where the peoples were almost ready for self-government, e.g. Iraq became independent in 1927, and a member of the League in 1932.

In practice, it proved difficult to restore independence to most of these areas. France continued to cling to the Lebanon and to Syria, and the British in Palestine soon found themselves caught up in conflicts between Arabs and Jews.

Grade B mandates

These related chiefly to Africa, where the people were thought to be backward and not able to govern themselves. In each case, the mandatory promised to ban the slave trade, native exploitation and traffic in arms and drugs. The territories were not to become armed bases, and the natives could be trained as soldiers only for defence. Other League members were to have equal rights for trade and missionary endeavour.

These did not achieve independence until after the Second World War.

Grade C mandates

These concerned isolated and undeveloped areas where there seemed to be little hope of future independence and where it seemed proper for the mandatory to assume complete control. Such territories included Papua New Guinea and German SW Africa.

In practice even these have become independent in recent years. The last to emerge was Namibia, whose hopes for independence until 1989 were persistently rejected by the South African Nationalist Party.

▷ **Efforts to strengthen the League**

After 1920, various efforts were made to water down the peacekeeping obligations of the League, especially on the part of outlying states such as Canada (which in 1920 proposed to abolish Article 10, which accepted the need to guarantee members against aggression). The same effect resulted from the 'Rules of Guidance' in 1921: these amounted to an attack on Article 16, which set out sanctions.

In the end, the efforts to strengthen the League by refining the obligations of the powers came to little.

The Draft Treaty for Mutual Assistance, 1923

Sometimes known as the 'Continent-by-continent Plan', this was a suggestion that the obligations of powers to intervene should be limited to those on the same continent as the crisis occurred. This was enthusiastically supported by powers like Canada, which were never likely to be involved in such a dispute.

The plan failed, not least because Britain objected that it held territories in every continent, and was therefore likely to be involved more than anyone else.

The Geneva Protocol, 1924

This was the brain-child of Ramsay MacDonald, and it proposed to strengthen the Covenant by making arbitration compulsory in case of disputes, and branding those who rejected arbitration as aggressors. This aimed to 'close the gaps' in the Covenant, which made possible 'legal' war, and so facilitate disarmament.

The plan failed because it left members with the same obligations for action on behalf of the League as they had had previously.

Kellogg–Briand Pact ('Pact of Paris'), 1928

France and America signed a pact renouncing war in 1928: '*Article 1* The High Contracting Parties solemnly declare . . . that they condemn recourse to war for the solution of national controversies, and renounce it as an instrument of national policy in their relations with one another.' Over 60 states adhered to the pact, which at the time seemed helpful to the cause of peace. In fact, however, nations retained the right to fight in self-defence, and the pact said nothing about punishing aggressors.

Mussolini made no attempt to hide his contempt for its principles, even though he signed it; and Hitler, too, when he came to power, agreed to it only with his tongue in his cheek. In the end its importance was more propagandist than practical.

▷ **Successes and failures in the 1920s**

Although supporters expressed idealistic hopes, the record of the League in the 1920s was a chequered one.

Disarmament

German disarmament in 1919 was intended not only as a punishment, but as a first stage towards more general disarmament later. However, this proved difficult.

A military commission was set up in 1920 to advise the Council on the subject, but it soon became obvious that it could not agree, and a *Temporary Mixed Commission* was set up in 1921. This also got bogged down in the problems rather than producing solutions, and France was not alone in becoming restive.

The *Locarno Pacts* in 1925 led to a renewal of interest and greater confidence, as did the Kellogg–Briand Pact, but before long familiar difficulties recurred:

(a) There was no agreement on what the term 'armaments' included.
(b) It was difficult to agree what classes of trained men constituted soldiers.
(c) There were problems over controlling national military budgets.
(d) Industrial armaments 'potential' was difficult to control, or even define.
(e) Even if all these things could be settled, how could infringements be penalized except by armed force, which was supposed to be controlled?

France, losing confidence in the peace settlement and in the power of the League to resolve problems, became all the more reluctant to abandon its last (and major) defence, its own enormous army.

A new Disarmament Conference met in Geneva in 1932, and here the French refused either to grant parity to the Germans by allowing them to rearm, or to disarm themselves. When Hitler came to power in 1933, French intransigence increased and before the end of the year Hitler withdrew from the conference and then from the League. Though the conference lingered on, disarmament as an issue was already dead.

Involvement in international disputes

From the start, the record of the League was patchy. Major powers tended to ignore it unless they had a cast-iron case, and it was for the minor states to be pushed about, whether by the League or in the traditional fashion.

There were a number of small successes:

(a) The League resolved a dispute between Sweden and Finland over the Aaland Islands in the Baltic; the Council successfully awarded them to Finland.
(b) The League held a number of plebiscites, e.g. in Upper Silesia to resolve the frontier between Germany and Poland.
(c) In 1924, it decided between Iraq and Turkey over the control of the Mosul oilfields, awarding them to Iraq, at that time a British mandate.
(d) In 1925, it was able to intervene to stop a war which had already begun between Greece and Bulgaria.
(e) A number of agencies did good work, including Dr Fridtjof Nansen at the head of an agency to resettle refugees, e.g. Greeks in the Aegean area in 1922.
(f) As late as 1932, the League resolved a frontier dispute in the Chaco area between Colombia and Peru.

But there were a number of failures:

(a) Polish troops seized Vilna in 1920, and the League, regarding Poland as a bulwark against Russian Bolshevism, allowed them to keep it.
(b) In 1923, Lithuania was also allowed to seize the port of Memel.
(c) In 1923, Mussolini bombarded and seized the Greek island of Corfu as the result of an outrage on the Albanian border, when an Italian general had been killed while making a survey. He went on to force the Greeks to pay 50 million lire in damages. Greece referred the matter to the League, but Mussolini persuaded the Council of Ambassadors (still in session in Paris) to back him, and the League allowed it.
(d) In 1923, France and Belgium acted unilaterally in occupying the Ruhr to enforce payment of reparations.

The main diplomatic success at this time, the signature of the *Locarno Pact*, was arranged by traditional methods between the powers and Weimar Germany, and was not due to the League of Nations at all.

But the most resounding failures of the League were in the 1930s, beginning with the Japanese seizure of Manchuria.

GLOSSARY

Arbitration A means of settling disputes by which the parties to the dispute submit their case to a third and independent party. The third party acting as arbitrator gives a ruling which may be a compromise or may favour one side more than the other. It is usual for those who agree to arbitration to agree in advance to accept the verdict of the arbitrator, otherwise arbitration will have been nothing more than time wasting.

Conference of Ambassadors A permanent conference of representatives of four of the victorious powers of the First World War, i.e. Britain, France, Italy and Japan (but not the USA), established in Paris under French chairmanship. Its task was to deal with matters arising from the Paris peace treaties. In dealing with such problems as Vilna and Corfu, it sometimes seemed to be exceeding its powers and trespassing on the work of the League of Nations, but the conference was not finally disbanded until 1931.

Demilitarization The withdrawal of all troops from an area, and the removal from it of certain specified armaments, or of all armaments.

Mandate The Covenant of the League regarded the encouragement of the development of the colonial peoples as one of the duties of the more advanced nations. The former colonial territories of Turkey and Germany were thus handed over to the League of Nations after 1918. These territories were held in 'mandate' by powers known as 'mandatories', the word 'mandate' implying a legal right granted by a superior authority. Such territories which later came under the control of the United Nations were known as trust territories and were held by a trustee.

Plebiscite A popular vote taken on some specific issue, usually relating to the state to which the area voting is in future to be attached. In the 1920s and 1930s, plebiscites were often held for this purpose in respect of certain areas, e.g. Upper Silesia, or even for whole countries, e.g. Austria in 1938. The outcome of a plebiscite is often a foregone conclusion, and confirms the wishes of the authority which arranged it. A 'referendum' is a similar reference back to the wishes of the whole people on a particular issue, occasionally provided for in the more democratic type of constitution.

Reparations A form of international compensation, generally applied to the defeated powers after the First World War. They were intended to compensate for death and injury to armed forces and civilians, and for material destruction and damage. Attempts to add indirect losses to reparations (e.g. loss of business – as distinct from loss of goods – arising out of submarine warfare) were abandoned as impracticable. German reparations were assessed at £6,600,000,000 in 1921, but were reduced in 1924 and again in 1929. The payments ceased altogether in 1931, and Hitler made it clear in 1933 that Germany had no intention of resuming them. Total payments made by Germany in reparations amounted to less than £2,000,000,000, most of it in goods (e.g. coal) rather than money. The USA lent Germany money to help with reparation payments, money which for the most part was never repaid. Reparations from devastated Germany after 1945 would have been unrealistic, but Russia did remove from Germany a great deal of Germany's surviving heavy machinery in order to re-equip its own devastated industry.

EXAMINATION QUESTIONS

▷ **Question 1**

The European powers and their membership of the League of Nations in the 1920s and 1930s

Britain	1919 ──────────────────→	still a member in 1939
France	1919 ──────────────────→	still a member in 1939
Japan	1919 ──────────→ 1933	
Italy	1919 ──────────────→ 1935	
Germany	1926 ──────→ 1933	
USSR	1934 ──────────→ expelled December 1939	

(a) For what reasons was the League of Nations formed in 1919?   (5 marks)
(b) Why did Germany not join the League until 1926?   (5 marks)
(c) Why did the Soviet Union not join the League until 1934?   (5 marks)

(d) The diagram shows that Japan left the League in 1933 and Italy left in 1935. How similar were the circumstances in which they left the League? (8 marks)

(e) Describe the circumstances in which Germany left the League in 1933 and those in which the USSR left in 1939. How do you explain the fact that Germany left of its own accord, but that the USSR was expelled? (7 marks)

 Question 2 (a) 'Germany had good reason to complain about the severity of the Treaty of Versailles.' Do you agree with this statement? Explain your answer. (12 marks)

(b) 'By the end of 1938 little was left of the Versailles Treaty.' Do you agree? Explain your answer. (12 marks)

EXAMINATION ANSWERS

▷ **Question 1** *Outline answer*

(a) The creation of the League should be linked with the First World War and the Paris settlement, as well as the determination to construct a framework for permanent peace and to avoid a repetition of the horrors of war.

(b) Germany's original exclusion as a defeated power was followed by repeated German efforts to gain admission. The continued opposition to Germany's membership by countries such as Spain and Brazil delayed its joining the League much longer than most defeated powers.

(c) The Soviet exclusion is partly the result of widespread world hostility to Bolshevism, but is also partly due to the self-inflicted isolation of Soviet Russia.

(d) Elementary answers will see the common element in the aggression of the two powers, but better answers will point out how the League reaction to the aggression differed, and that the Italians, while following the Japanese lead, had an even weaker case in Abyssinia than did the Japanese in Manchuria.

(e) Description will focus on Hitler's walking out of the Disarmament Conference and the League, and on the League's last gasp expulsion of the Soviet Union because of its invasion of Finland. While aggression may have been the root cause for both of them, Germany was only preparing for it, whereas the Soviet Union was actually committing it. German rearmament might seem a lesser crime than the Soviet attack on Finland. But it could be argued that German rearmament threatened the Soviet Union and that the Soviet attack on Finland was defensive rather than expansionist.

▷ **Question 2(a)** *Tutor answer*

In 1918 Germany had been defeated in the most costly war in history. It was not surprising, then, that Germany could expect peace terms which would be difficult to accept. The fact that the peace terms were not negotiable gave rise to Germany's view that the settlement was a 'diktat', so that by the late 1930s it was almost axiomatic that Germany had been harshly treated in 1919. Its loss of Alsace-Lorraine was hardly an unexpected blow as France was determined to recover what it considered rightly France's. Elsewhere in Europe, Germany's losses, such as Eupen and Malmédy and northern Schleswig, were confirmed by plebiscites of the local inhabitants. The loss of the Polish Corridor and Danzig, however, which separated East Prussia from the rest of Germany, was not put to plebiscite. The principle of self-determination was thus sometimes shelved when it might have benefited Germany, and the ban on the Anschluss could be regarded as a direct violation of it. Germany was deprived of all its colonies: these had contributed little to Germany's economy, and were more important for prestige, which Germany's defeat had damaged anyway. That they were to be helped to independence through the mandate system might have been more of a consolation if the victorious powers had been preparing their own colonies for independence, but they were not – so Germany had some right to feel aggrieved.

The disarmament clauses of the treaty were not inspired by a desire to humiliate Germany, but were intended as a prelude to general disarmament, and to prevent a renewal of the war. If, indeed, Germany's aims were peaceful, it did not need more than an army of 100,000 men, a much reduced navy without capital ships, and only a few aeroplanes. Germany might well be at a disadvantage in facing an aggressor, but there were no likely aggressors and it was more Germany's pride than Germany's security that was hurt by the disarmament clauses.

The Allies regarded reparations as just payment for war damages. They did not impose a punitive indemnity, but it seemed to Germany very much like one, and a very large one at that, when its figures were finally announced. So, to the Allies, reparations were a small contribution to the enormous cost of the war, while to the Germans they were a huge financial punishment for being on the losing side.

Losers are bound to complain, but the only vindictive power was France, which was held back by the idealistic USA and by the realistic Britain. The treaty could have been a lot worse for Germany, but nevertheless it did provide plenty of ammunition for Hitler and plenty of justification for the tender consciences of the appeasers.

▷ Question 2(b) *Student answer with examiner's comments*

'Good on reparations.'

'The Sudetenland had never been part of Germany and was not part of the Versailles Treaty.'

'By implication, then, these parts of the Versailles settlement had not been altered.'

'You recognize the need for argument, but this contradicts the evidence you have given.'

During the 1920s the main undermining of the Treaty was in regard to reparations. These were reduced by the Dawes Plan which extended the time for repayment, and the Young Plan which cut the total of reparations to less than one third of the original sum. In 1931 Germany was allowed to suspend payments because of the world depression, and in 1933 Hitler announced that Germany had no intention of paying any more. As Germany had paid only a very limited sum, and that by unsaleable coal or non-repayable loans from the USA, Germany had escaped from the most crushing part of the Versailles settlement almost unscathed.

The main territorial changes came in the 1930s. In 1936 Hitler moved German troops into the Rhineland in defiance of the Treaty. He had already announced that he was going to break the disarmament clauses of the Treaty. In 1938 Austria was united with Germany – the Anschluss – in direct defiance of the Treaty. Then in October 1938 Hitler seized the Sudetenland which had originally been given to Czechoslovakia.

Hitler was now poised to get back other lost territories such as Alsace-Lorraine, Eupen, North Schleswig and the Polish Corridor. He was also hoping, by creating a great navy in defiance of the Treaty, to get back all those colonies which had been taken away from Germany in 1919.

So it is quite clear that little was left of the Versailles Treaty in 1938, and that the work of the peacemakers was in ruins.

Examiners' marking scheme
Level 1: scattered and disconnected material relating to Versailles after 1919. (1–3 marks)
Level 2: a list of the main changes only OR limited changes with some development.
(4–6 marks)
Level 3: deals with both the terms that were changed and those that were unchanged with some development. (7–10 marks)
Level 4: as Level 3, but with a sharp focus on the truth of the statement. Those who argue that it is true will need to be very convincing if they are to reach this Level.
(11–12 marks)

Examiner's decision on the student answer
Overall, apart from the reference to the Sudetenland, this is very well informed and covers the main themes. But the conclusion is perverse and effective argument does not emerge. This is good Level 3, but Sudetenland deprives it of maximum, so 9/12.

SUMMARY

In this chapter you have studied changing international relations and attitudes in the years after the First World War, in particular:

▷ the Paris peace settlement of 1919–20, including:

  ▷ the main personalities,

  ▷ the main terms of the Treaty of Versailles,

  ▷ the changes made by the other treaties;

▷ the main problems associated with the peace settlement, including;

  ▷ the nationalities question,

  ▷ the attitudes of the European powers after 1920,

  ▷ the reparations problem;

▷ the League of Nations, its powers and membership:

  ▷ the peacekeeping role of the League,

  ▷ attempts to strengthen the working of the League,

  ▷ early problems and crises.

Information on the subject of *International Relations, 1931–39* is to be found in chapter 11.

Russia, 1917–24

▷ **GETTING STARTED**

Russia in the form of the Soviet Union emerged into prominence with the communist revolution, and dominated much of the history of the twentieth century. It is to this history that we now turn.

MEG	NEAB	NICCEA	SEG	LONDON	WJEC	TOPIC	STUDY	REVISION 1	REVISION 2
✓	✓	✓	✓	✓	✓	**Tsarist government of Russia**			
✓	✓	✓	✓	✓	✓	Nature and diversity of Russian society in 1917			
✓	✓	✓	✓	✓	✓	**Two revolutions in 1917**			
✓	✓	✓	✓	✓	✓	The February Revolution			
✓	✓	✓	✓	✓	✓	The October Revolution			
✓	✓	✓	✓	✓	✓	**The policies of Lenin**			
✓	✓	✓	✓	✓	✓	Features of Lenin's rule, 1918–24			
✓	✓	✓	✓	✓	✓	Character of the new Russian state			

▷ **WHAT YOU NEED TO KNOW**

Tsarist government of Russia

▷ **Nature and diversity of Russian society in 1917**

In the early years of the twentieth century, Russia was in many ways a backward country, poor, underdeveloped and badly governed by a powerful autocracy.

The Russian class system

Russia's population at this time was about 180 million people scattered over a land mass of about one-sixth of the world's surface. All but about 10 million of these lived west of the Ural mountains in European Russia, where there lived also many non-Russian peoples such as Ukrainians, Kossacks and Caucasians; the rest lived in the barren wastes of Siberia and the Eastern Provinces (all the way to Vladivostok on the rim of the Pacific), where they ruled over a variety of thinly scattered native peoples like the Yakuts, the Samoyeds, the Tartars and the Mongols.

The upper classes

A tiny fraction of the Russian people, perhaps less than 1 per cent, were *aristocrats*, dominating the army and the ruling class, some immensely rich and privileged (one among them owned estates bigger than the whole of Britain). At the head of this small clique was the Tsar himself. The aristocrats were well educated, spoke polite French and did little that was socially useful.

The *churchmen* of the established Orthodox Church were also extremely rich and powerful in Russian society. The church had vast estates in the country, and many church leaders sprang from the same aristocratic class as Russia's rulers, whose outlook and attitudes they shared. They proved a useful bulwark for Tsardom.

Next to them, and scarcely more numerous, was a class of public *functionaries and officials*, all of whom maintained the Tsarist system because it provided them with a career and a fat salary. Some of them were relatively minor officials, but they were none the less set apart from the bulk of the ordinary people.

The middle class

There were also perhaps a million *middle-class people*, often living in towns, but generally less active and enterprising than their counterparts in Britain. They were known as the *bourgeois* (or, in Russian, the *bourjui*) and were specially marked down for the scorn of Marxists as social parasites. Relatively few were in business or manufacture, which they rather considered to be beneath them, but many were professional people like lawyers, newspaper owners, teachers and academics. Many Russians had a healthy mistrust of academics, whom they dismissed as *intelligentsia*, but the more liberally minded among them were sometimes held in good esteem as potential leaders.

The peasantry

Over nine-tenths of the total population were peasants, living in primitive conditions; poor, ignorant and superstitious, they worked hard with their simple tools just to keep themselves alive. Serfdom had by this time been abolished, but most of the people were little better than serfs in their standards and attitudes. Life for all these people was very hard and bitter, and the enormous improvements in wealth and social standards taking place in the West at this time simply passed them by.

Industrial development

Industrial development was slow, and industrial towns were few and scattered. Much of the country's raw materials lay outside Europe, and hence were not developed until quite late in the nineteenth century, when the first railway network, largely constructed by French capital, was built. The largest factories, like the Putilov arms works in St Petersburg, were very large indeed, but most factories were small workshops. Russian coal production was less than 5 per cent of Britain's, and over a quarter of Russia's coal was imported; but steel production was rising and oil output in the Caucasus was beginning to develop.

Foreigners were important in this: the Swedish Nobel brothers helped to open up oil output in Baku, and the Welshman John Hughes began a coal, iron and rail works in the Dnieper Valley. Much Russian industry was foreign owned, largely in Paris; foreign investment in 1913 was running at 2,200 million roubles per year, and profits were being syphoned out of the country.

Education was also limited and backward. In 1894 there had been only eight technical schools in the whole of Russia, and, though this number had greatly increased, it still fell far short of the country's needs. Thus Russia was in need of skilled workmen and managers in practically every industry.

When *social and economic change* came, it burst on Russia like a storm. Conditions in the factories and mines were appalling, and sanitary and living conditions in working-class areas of towns were like those in England during the Industrial Revolution: safety provisions were poor, hours were long, wages were low and food was dear and scarce. Trade unions were banned, so leadership tended to fall into the hands of extremist agitators, most of them known to the Tsarist political police. Hence Russia in the early years of the twentieth century was a country in turmoil.

Tsarist autocracy

Article I of the Russian legal code confirmed that Russia was a despotism: 'The Emperor of all the Russias is an autocratic and unlimited monarch; God himself ordains that all must bow to his supreme power, not only out of fear but for reasons of conscience.' His authority was reinforced by the fact that he was titular Head of the Church, but until 1906, there was *no central Russian parliament*. The Tsar was advised by:

(a) a *Council of State* to which he could refer whenever he wished for expert advice on whatever subject;

(b) a *Committee of Ministers*, whose numbers were increased to fourteen in 1900, and all of whom were appointed; and

(c) a *Senate*, dating from 1711, but which now acted as Supreme Court.

There was some limited representation in *local government assemblies*, introduced in the reforms of Alexander II (the 'Tsar Liberator'):

(a) The *mir* was the village commune. Thousands of these were employed under the Emancipation Edict ending serfdom in 1861. These were responsible for tax collection, and collected the redemption payments made by peasants buying their land. Their powers were whittled away after the appointment of land captains to supervise their actions in 1889.

(b) The *zemstva* were provincial assemblies elected to carry out local duties. Each zemstvo, however, was elected on a complicated franchise which gave most power to the richer citizens, and these powers, too, were later whittled away.

(c) There were elected *municipal councils* in towns and cities after 1870, often with quite wide franchises, but they too had little real power and were dominated by the upper class and by appointed local officials.

After an abortive revolution in 1905, prompted by defeats in the Russo-Japanese War, Tsar Nicholas II issued the *October Manifesto*, under which a national parliament was elected for the first time.

The *State Duma* consisted of two Houses, the Lower House being elected on a democratic franchise and having theoretically wide powers. In practice, however, these were reduced in a special proclamation only a week before the Duma met in May 1906, and it found itself incapable of controlling policy or of influencing ministers. The first two Dumas (1906 and 1907) proved ineffective, and the Tsar then modified the franchise, making it much less representative than previously, so that fewer 'Cadets' (i.e. Constitutional Democrats) were elected than before.

Neither the Third Duma (1907–12) nor the Fourth (1912–17) therefore made any serious inroads into the problems of reform.

Two revolutions in 1917

▷ **The February Revolution**

The collapse of the monarchy

By 1917, the Tsar's leadership had become thoroughly discredited. Waste, corruption and incompetence were in evidence throughout the system. The bureaucracy was selfish and inefficient, the police and the courts repressive. Everywhere the aristocracy and the church discouraged change, and, while Nicholas II had inherited the high sense of moral duty which had inspired his ancestors, he showed himself a man of restricted intelligence and small imagination.

The *Liberals*, drawn chiefly from the enlightened nobility and the professional classes, wanted a democratic constitution and a form of limited monarchy. They wanted to transform the Duma into an effective parliament.

The *Anarchists*, many of them bred in the universities, wanted to use terrorism to overthrow the Tsar, and were enemies of whatever government.

The *Communists*, followers of Karl Marx, wanted to set up a new order of society in which the workers would control the distribution of wealth and the means of production. They drew their main support from the trade unions and the factory workers, organized in workers' committees or *soviets*. They grew in influence:

(a) 1898, Russian Social Democratic Workers Party founded in Russia.

(b) 1903, at a conference in London, the party split into Bolsheviks ('majority' men) and Mensheviks ('minority' men) over their preferred party aims and methods.

(c) 1906, Bolsheviks were gradually squeezed out of the Duma, and finally boycotted it, preferring to reject parliamentary methods.

(d) 1906–17, many Bolshevik leaders were driven underground, or into exile.

But it was the disasters of the First World War which hastened the coming of revolution:

(a) Serious defeats and heavy casualties highlighted the shortcomings of the system, while industrial backwardness produced desperate shortages of materials and munitions.

(b) The government and the army placed great reliance on the railways for transportation, but these broke down as the war progressed. Even horses were conscripted for transport and for fighting at the front.

(c) The occupation of some of Russia's western provinces caused population movement and economic disruption, and had bad effects on farming.

(d) There were acute food shortages, queuing in shops and high inflation. Citizens of large towns faced situations little short of famine.

(e) Taxation was crippling, large sums of public money still being spent on paying the interest on foreign loans.

(f) The Tsar was unpopular. Many believed the war was no more than a personal whim of Nicholas, and that his wife, Alexandra, had pro-German sympathies and was betraying Russia's innermost secrets. A series of disastrous advisers were appointed by Tsar Nicholas, both he and his wife being much influenced by the ruffian Rasputin. He was a coarse Siberian peasant who appeared to be able to cure the young Tsarevich Alexis of his haemophilia, and who gained a reputation of being a holy man, though he got Russia into an unholy mess. His assassination in December 1916 opened the way to events which finally led to the revolution.

Events of the February Revolution

Until 1918, the old Julian calendar was in use in Russia. It was thirteen days behind the Gregorian calendar in use in the rest of Europe. Hence the February Revolution, by western reckoning, actually took place in March, and the October Revolution in November.

(a) 8 March, strikes and looting of foodshops in Petrograd.
(b) 11 March, general strike called in factories and offices.
(c) 12 March, Tsar's Guard joined the strikers.
(d) 13 March, Petrograd Soviet sought to establish authority.
(e) 14 March, Committee of Duma took over; Prince G.E. Lvov formed a liberal ministry.
(f) 15 March, Nicholas II abdicated; his brother Grand Duke Michael refused the throne.

Policies of the Provisional Government

Until a new elected government could be formed, the Liberal ministry in the Duma governed Russia *provisionally*, under Prince Lvov, and, after July, under Alexander Kerensky, a former Minister of Justice and afterwards Minister of War.

It ignored urgent basic issues and formulated a largely political programme:

(a) an amnesty to excuse all political prisoners;
(b) freedom of speech and belief, together with a ban on discrimination;
(c) elected local government and police officials;
(d) soldiers to retain arms and to retain freedoms consistent with discipline;
(e) direct, equal, secret and universal elections to a new assembly.

The government had inherent flaws which eventually caused its failure:

(a) It stood on a narrow middle-class basis and was acceptable only to like-minded Liberals who saw largely political answers to the country's problems.

(b) It sought to continue the fight with the Kaiser, loyal to its Allies, but the disastrous failure of the summer offensive, 1917, made the war impossible.

(c) Its membership was bound by middle-class values and attitudes:

  (i) Amnestying political prisoners had the effect of letting loose agitators and terrorists who were no friends to parliamentary methods.

  (ii) It refused to muzzle public opinion by censorship of the press.

  (iii) Hesitating to act improperly or illegally, they deferred reform schemes until after elections had been held.

  (iv) It refused to nationalize land or other property until adequate compensation for existing owners could be arranged.

(v) In particular, it left the Bolsheviks at liberty, who were a good deal better organized and less scrupulous than the Liberals in their actions.

Its main enemies were the Bolsheviks, whose influence steadily grew:

(a) April, Lenin returned to Russia from Switzerland, pronouncing his *April Theses*.
(b) May, they held few seats in both Lvov's first and second cabinets, but it was only through the cooperation of the *Petrograd Soviet* that things got done.
(c) June, an *All-Russia Congress of Soviets* gave the Bolsheviks conspicuous backing.
(d) July, the Bolsheviks felt strong enough to stage a *coup*, but it failed.

In September, a former Tsarist general, Kornilov, moved to crush the more extreme elements of the revolutionary rabble, and asked for Kerensky's approval. Kerensky hesitated. If he went with Kornilov, it branded him as an enemy of the people; if he opposed him, he weakened the forces of order further and left the radicals in control. In the end he went with the Bolsheviks, and afterwards was at their mercy.

▷ The October Revolution

The carefully timed coup which followed created a ruthless Bolshevik dictatorship in Russia, which pretended to act in the best interests of the Russian people, but which created a system of autocracy and oppression lasting for more than 70 years.

The establishment of Bolshevik rule

Kerensky's Liberal regime collapsed in a few days almost bloodlessly:

(a) October, the Petrograd Soviet formed a *Revolutionary Military Committee*.
(b) November, Trotsky enrolled *Red Guards* from the Petrograd workers.
(c) 7 November, mutiny of the *Aurora* and the revolt of the forts Peter and Paul on the Neva led to the surrender of the Provisional Government.
(d) 8 November, second *All-Russia Congress of Soviets* vested leadership in Lenin.
(e) 8–15 November, attempted counter-coup by General Krasnov failed; Kerensky fled abroad.

The creation of Bolshevik control

Lenin, as chairman of the *Council of People's Commissars*, loosed a flood of reforming decrees: 193 were passed between 8 November and 31 December 1917. He offered freedom to all the subject peoples of Russia; he abolished money; he handed over the land to the peasants and the factories to the workers; he nationalized church property and abolished religion; he began to plan revolutions of a similar communist character all over Europe.

In reality, he opened up the gap between practical fact and political fiction. Some of these reforms were simply beyond the bounds of possibility; others were quite possible, but were not seriously intended. Lenin was a skilled and unscrupulous propagandist; he invented a wonderfully modern technique of making people promises he could not keep, afterwards apologizing for the changed circumstances which stopped him from carrying them out. The reality was that the country was now in the relentless grip of an authoritarian clique much smaller and less competent than that of the Tsar, and at the mercy of the Bolshevik secret police.

The policies of Lenin

▷ Features of Lenin's rule, 1918–24

Lenin took the view that 'anyone of reasonable intelligence was fit to govern a country'. There is no doubt that the six years of his rule proved not only his intelligence, but his success in practice.

Peace with Germany

One of the impossible promises was that Russia should put an immediate end to the war with 'a peace without indemnities and without annexations'. Obviously the Germans were not going to agree to such a peace.

The Bolsheviks agreed an armistice with the Germans in December 1917, and Trotsky began negotiations with them in the New Year. Trotsky found the German terms too harsh to accept, and was forced into making interminable speeches at the conference table so as to slow matters down. Lenin knew that he could not continue the war, and ordered demobilization and immediate peace as a 'breathing space' for the revolution.

Trotsky refused to sign such a crippling treaty, and it was a former Tsarist official, Count Chicherin, who initialled the *Treaty of Brest-Litovsk* in March 1918:

(a) Russia was to pay an indemnity of 300 million gold roubles to Germany.
(b) Russia gave up Kars, Ardahan and Batum to Turkey (later partly recovered).
(c) The Ukraine was to become independent, and was to hand over an annual tribute of 1 million tons of best wheat to the Central Powers.
(d) Poland was to be placed under a German-controlled government.
(e) The Baltic states – Latvia, Esthonia and Lithuania – were to be independent and also under German-controlled governments.
(f) Finland was to become independent, and ruled by a German prince.

The Russian people were relieved about the ending of the war, but less happy with the terms on which it had been ended.

'The land to the people'

Lenin's *Decree on land* abolished private ownership at a stroke, and guaranteed that the peasants should be free to work their land without compensation to the previous owner. State, church and landlords' estates were confiscated and distributed among the peasants by the mir. The richer peasants (the *kulaks*) were plundered; ordinary peasants even plundered each other.

The effect of this was to weaken the individual title to land, whose ownership in any case belonged to the state.

Peasants' fears were reinforced by compulsory requisitioning of crops, and by forced sales of 'surpluses' to the state at knock-down prices. Many peasants retaliated by growing only what crops they needed.

The 'Great Famine'

Crippling shortages occurred in Russia as a result. Normally, the countryside sold its foodstuffs to the towns in return for manufactures, but the towns now had nothing to give in return. At the same time, inflation eroded the value of money, and the Bolsheviks attempted to do away with it altogether. They substituted *commodity cards* as a form of rationing, but these had no exchange value and the peasants refused to accept them in payment.

The Bolsheviks therefore tried to introduce cooperative farming methods, but these went against peasant traditionalism, and the whole rural economy broke down.

Widespread famine lasted several years, and many thousands starved.

The Russian Civil Wars, 1918–20

Factors leading to the outbreak of civil war in Russia were:

(a) growth of anti-Bolshevik elements prompted by the unpopularity of their policies: their enemies ranged from Tsarists to Mensheviks;
(b) peasant dissatisfaction with land policies;
(c) national secession movements of non-Russian peoples, e.g. Ukrainians;
(d) growth of foreign intervention:
 (i) Denikin and Wrangel in the Ukraine and the Crimea attacked from the south.
 (ii) General Petliura held Kiev and General Yudenich advanced on Petrograd.
 (iii) Admiral Kolchak seized the Trans-Siberian Railway and attacked from the east.
 (iv) Japanese, US, British, French and Romanian expeditions were also sent.

For a time, the Bolshevik area of control shrank to the Moscow–Leningrad area; it looked as if Lenin's infant revolution might be snuffed out. But the Bolsheviks were able to win through, and Kolchak, the last of the 'Whites', was executed in Irkutsk in February 1920, his body pushed under the ice of the frozen River Angara. Bolshevik success was due to:

(a)   superior discipline and ruthlessness of the Bolshevik 'Red Army';
(b)   tactical genius of Trotsky, the Bolshevik commander;
(c)   the advantage of interior lines of communication;
(d)   divisions and friction between the various 'White' armies;
(e)   Bolsheviks could call on the patriotism of the peasantry against foreigners.

Simultaneously, the Poles occupied lands east of the *Curzon Line*, which had been drawn to divide Poland from Russia at the time of the Versailles Treaty.

Britain gave financial aid and sent arms; France sent troops under General Weygand to support the Poles. For a while they were successful and penetrated over 300 kilometres into Russian territory, threatening Kiev and almost reaching Moscow.

The Red Army counterattacked and drove the Poles back on Warsaw, but there they rallied successfully at the *Miracle of the Vistula* and once again advanced.

Treaty of Riga (1921) gave Poland large areas east of the Curzon Line, and the Allies, thoroughly afraid of Bolshevism, approved.

War Communism and the NEP

The name *War Communism* likened the campaign to introduce a communist regime in Russia in place of the existing capitalist system to the emergency of the war. Swept along by the force of its own convictions, it was inclined to make no compromises:

(a)   Land, industries and businesses were all nationalized; and banking, insurance and foreign trade were taken over by the state.
(b)   Social insurance, an eight-hour day and better wages and working conditions were decreed.
(c)   A Supreme Economic Council (*Gosplan*) was set up to plan the economy, the old market economy being replaced by thoroughgoing state planning.
(d)   Workers' organizations, like the newly legalized trade unions, cooperated in the running of factories, electing members to the local *soviet*.

Unfortunately, the removal of management control and the ineffectiveness of the new worker committees led to a deterioration in relations with the Bolshevik leadership. The result was the appointment of 'bourgeois specialists' to help to manage the factories, and a tightening of worker discipline in which the Bolsheviks paid increasingly little regard to the workers' wishes.

War casualties, starvation and the dislocation of the economy made the Bolsheviks all the more determined to override objections and make the system work. The result was a deep disillusionment that the people's revolution had not brought about the freedoms that had originally been promised.

In March 1921 the sailors of the Kronstadt garrison rose in revolt alongside the mass of the Petrograd workers, demanding 'Soviets without Communists', i.e. an end to Bolshevik dictatorship and, instead, true industrial democracy. They wanted free elections, freedom of speech and the right of all left-wing parties to participate in government.

The Bolsheviks represented the affair as a White conspiracy, but Lenin was thoroughly frightened. Trotsky ordered the Red Army across the ice to Kronstadt to crush the mutiny; for the Bolshevik leadership it was, as Lenin put it, the 'lightning flash which lit up reality'.

The *New Economic Policy* (or NEP) replaced War Communism after March 1921. Pure communism had to be set aside in order to enable the country to recover from the war and the dislocation following it; as Lenin's opponents put it, communism had to be abandoned to make it work.

The Russian people were no longer asked to work selflessly for the benefit of the state; the 'profit motive' was to be made respectable again:

(a)   In agriculture, compulsory requisitioning was to be replaced by a state tax paid in foodstuffs; surplus crops could be sold on the market for profit.

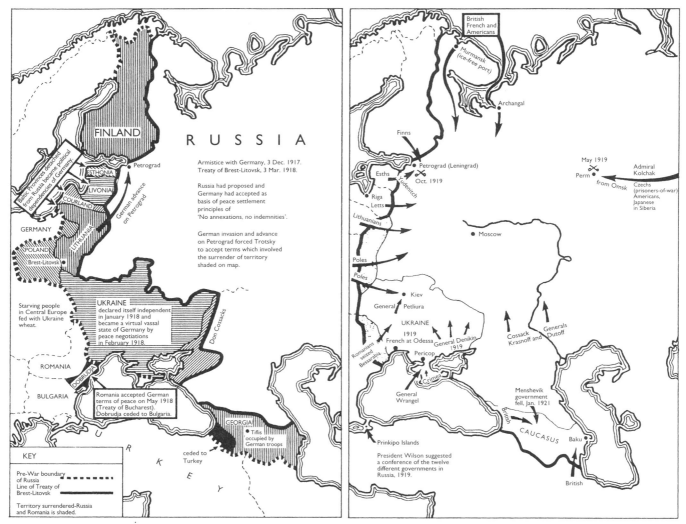

Fig. 7.1 Treaty of Brest-Litovsk   **Fig. 7.2** Invasions of Bolshevik Russia

(b) In industry, businesses employing fewer than 20 were to be returned to private owner-ship, or run as cooperative concerns. Only the 'commanding heights of the econo-my' – the coal mines, the steel mills, the oil wells, the railway system and the central planning network – were to remain in the hands of the state. For the critics of the 'NEPmen' this was a 'Brest-Litovsk on the economic front' – an attempt to secure a breathing space until the country could move towards socialism.

Building the party

There were too few loyal Bolsheviks to run the country, though Lenin valued their qual-ity (he called them 'little but good'). He had to fall back on Tsarists and ex-soldiers, and in 1919 commented: 'At the top we have, I don't know exactly how many, but a few thousand of our own people. But, at the base, hundreds of thousands of former officials whom we inherited from the Tsar, and from bourgeois society, are working, partly con-sciously and partly unconsciously, against us.'

When the newly elected Russian parliament, deferred by the Liberals, met in January 1918, the Bolsheviks were in a small minority (with their Social Revolutionary allies they held 215 out of 707 seats). They therefore refused to allow the parliament to continue and disbanded it. For the members of his party, Lenin insisted on:

(a) the importance of tight party discipline and of party unity;
(b) acceptance by all of his political police (*Cheka*) to counter deviationism;
(c) the execution or exile of all dissidents.

Character of the new Russian state

(a) It was a *one-party dictatorship*, working towards 'democratic centralism'. Bolshevism represented the true interests of the Russian people; other groups (even national groups, though these had been promised their freedom) were said to be deluded if they wished to break away. Supporters were required to 'toe the party line', and were 'purged' if they did not; opponents were suppressed.

(b) It imposed *strict controls* on the country and did not hesitate to use methods of terror. It was highly bureaucratic, even repressive. The old restrictions on people's lives continued, and many more new ones were introduced: on their movements, their rights of meeting and their membership of other bodies. Trade unions remained, but were subordinated to party purposes. There was strict censorship of the press, and other media were also controlled. Detention and forced labour were used for dealing with opponents, and the political police (first the Cheka, and afterwards similar organizations like the OGPU, the NKVD and the KGB) exercised wide, and sometimes uncontrolled, powers.

(c) It followed Marxist teachings in denouncing the Christian Church as the 'opium of the people', and *abolished religion*, especially the Orthodox Church. Priests were shot or imprisoned, churches were ransacked and looted, and buildings were employed for secular purposes; church estates were taken over by the state. There was to be no religious teaching, and church services were banned.

(d) It created the *command economy*, substituting the planning machinery of the state for the machinery of individual enterprise, governed by demand and supply in the pursuit of profit (the 'market economy'). Planning was often cumbersome, and, without the guidance of supply and demand, disastrous mistakes could be made.

(e) At the same time, however, Bolshevik government produced for the average Russian a lot of worthwhile *improvements*. Unemployment was abolished, factory conditions were improved, free medical and dental treatment was introduced, working-class flats were constructed to replace appalling slums, and education for all children was provided. This explains why, though people often grumbled, the Communist Party remained relatively popular.

GLOSSARY

Communism   This comes from the thoughts and writings of the German scholar Karl Marx (1818–83), and is sometimes referred to as Marxism. Marx believed that, in the past, aristocratic government had been replaced by the rule of the bourgeoisie – the middle-class property-owners who controlled the means of production and were the employers of the working class – the proletariat. As society evolves, the domination of the middle-class ruling group will be challenged by the emergence of powerful forces from below. History is thus composed of a series of class struggles, and political power moves to the working classes as the bourgeoisie are overcome. In capitalist society, deep tension exists between the middle class and the working class which it has exploited; the interests of these two classes cannot be reconciled and out of their conflict new political structures emerge. Marx believed that the capitalist class 'digs its own grave' by its increasing exploitation of the proletariat; eventually the injustices will become so unbearable that the workers will rise against their masters and the old order of society will be revolutionized.

In this sense, the revolution is inevitable. That is not to say that it will happen automatically without anyone having to worry about how to organize it, but eventually workers' organizations will be stung into taking action on behalf of the unfortunate masses. When this happens, the old order will be overturned, those formerly exploited will exploit the exploiters, and a new form of society will emerge, radically different from the old one in that power will now be in the hands of representatives of the underdog. Gradually, by force if necessary, the worst abuses of the old system will be destroyed, and society will edge a little closer to true justice. Eventually, Marx predicted, the need for force and compulsion will cease, a 'classless society' will follow and so the state will 'wither away'. Marx drew up no actual blueprint of this ideal form of social organization, since he saw himself as being not so much a prophet as a social analyst. Thus when the revolution did actually take place, years after Marx's death, it is hardly surprising that Lenin found himself with no guidance from Marx's writings on how to proceed.

Contribution of Lenin

Lenin's contribution to the development of Marxist communism was a significant one. He found himself called upon not only to put the ideas of Marxism into operation, but to flesh out Marx's bald statements with greater detail. From the early 1920s, therefore, the theory comes to be referred to as that of Marxist-Leninism. In those stages of the capitalist order, for example, which had largely developed after Marx's death, Lenin saw imperialism as the last, and highest, stage of monopoly capitalism, when the capitalist classes turned to colonial exploitation in their desperate attempt to disguise the increasing injustices of the system; and with colonial exploitation came arms and naval races, both of which acted as shots in the arm for the flagging vitality of capitalist production. In the end, however, Lenin believed that capitalism was bound to fail and the revolution would be all the more bloody when it came.

He had views, too, on the work of the party – a detail with which Marx had never concerned himself – in bringing about the revolution and masterminding it while it was in progress. He believed the party should be kept small and highly disciplined, working loyally towards the objectives set by the leadership. Lenin despised the bourgeois parties, where policies were trimmed and current issues fudged with a view to capturing the fleeting approval of a mass electorate; he favoured a selfless and dedicated band of leaders who would pursue the true path to progress with a single-mindedness that was almost religious in its conviction.

Lenin was also called upon to explain why the coming of the classless society which was the final goal of communists was so long delayed, and why the 'dictatorship of the proletariat' seemed to show no sign of coming to an end. His explanation was that the bourgeoisie were cunning and persistent, always lurking ready to make their come-back, and that the leadership had to continue to be vigilant if it wished to prevent a counter-revolution. Lenin believed that the post-revolution period fell into two phases: the intermediate, and socialist, phase where the tyranny of the proletariat had to be continued by maintaining the full apparatus of the state; and the final, or communist, phase in which – eventually – as Marx had predicted, the communist utopia (ideal state) would arrive. To this view, at least officially, the Russian leadership continued to subscribe throughout the period of communist rule.

 EXAMINATION QUESTIONS

▷ **Question 1**   Why were there two revolutions in Russia in 1917?   (15 marks)

▷ **Question 2**   Read the extracts below and then answer the questions which follow.

Source A

The Bolshevik Party [in the spring of 1917] was waging a determined struggle to win over the masses. The struggle was headed by Lenin . . . He frequently addressed mass rallies and meetings. Lenin's appearance on the platform invariably triggered off the acclamations and enthusiasm of the audience. Lenin's speeches, noted for their profound content and brilliant delivery, inspired the workers and soldiers to a determined struggle. The Bolshevik Party's membership began to grow rapidly.

(From Y. Kukushkin, *History of the USSR*, 1981)

Source B

When Lenin arrived in St Petersburg in April 1917, his party comrades called him mad and delirious. The experienced militants criticized him; *Pravda* [the Bolshevik newspaper] disowned him. But suddenly it became clear that he had the ear of the man in the street . . . and in three weeks he had a majority in the party.

(Adapted from V. Serge, *From Lenin to Stalin*, 1937)

Source C

No Tsar of modern times was such an autocrat as Lenin and none was more ruthless. The Tsar put people to death for crimes against Russian laws but Lenin has massacred thousands without trial. Lenin justified his actions by the same excuses tyrants have always used. The people, he said, were not yet able to tell the difference between truth and falsehood. He insisted that the government had to decide what the people might hear and what they might read.

(A British view of Lenin written about the time of his death in 1924)

Source D

Lenin was a great leader; he was a giant among statesmen but the most humble of men. His achievements in the October revolution, in defeating foreign invaders and destroying the Whites, in bringing peace and prosperity and in dealing ruthlessly with counterrevolution are well known. He has replaced Tsardom with rule by the people and we are forever in his debt.

(A Russian view of Lenin written at the time of his death in 1924)

(a) What important differences can you find between Sources A and B in their accounts of Lenin in the spring of 1917? How would you explain these differences?

(6 marks)

(b) How do Sources C and D differ in their interpretations of Lenin? Why do you think these interpretations are different? (7 marks)

(c) Using your own knowledge, do you think that Source D provides an accurate assessment of Lenin and his achievements? (12 marks)

EXAMINATION ANSWERS

▷ **Question 1** *Outline answer*

The question is unstructured, i.e. it is not divided into sections, and this is unusual but not unknown in GCSE. You therefore have freedom to develop your own explanations of the causes of the two revolutions in your own way. It is not, however, a factual recall question, and separate lists of reasons for the two revolutions will not answer at the highest Level why there were two revolutions rather than one. Answers which contain a narrative of events in Russia in 1917, memorized from your notes, will of course, be low Level, and will score relatively little unless there is some attention to causes of revolutions. An answer could be along the general lines of 'There were two revolutions because developments showed that one was not enough', dealing with the causes of the first revolution, and then going on to show how the first revolution failed, and created a situation which made a second revolution most likely. Alternatively, your answer could have as its central focus the idea that there were two very different kinds of revolution; the first a political revolution which changed the regime, but brought to power a new government which in a number of ways was reluctant to change policies; the second a more profound type of revolution which aimed to change the whole social system of the country. Such an answer would see the causes as ideologically different. Both these approaches would be far superior to an historical outline which left the examiner to infer the causes.

▷ **Question 2(a)** *Tutor answer*

The main difference is that, in Source A, Lenin has a smooth ride in leading the party and urging it on to revolution, whereas in Source B it is clear that Lenin had to fight within the party for support for his revolutionary plans, and that it was Lenin's popularity with the masses which dragged the party leadership behind him. Provided that Lenin's difficulties are not part of the omission shown in Source A, the explanation must rest with the circumstances and purpose of the writers. Kukushkin is obviously a Russian historian, and Serge could well have been. Kukushkin is writing in 1981, when the party is more important than individuals, and he is attempting to show the party in a good light. Serge, writing in 1937, at a time when Stalin was promoting himself as the natural successor to Lenin, is showing how Lenin, at a vital moment in the history of the revolution, is right and the party is wrong. All this is speculative: we are not given sufficient information about the writers to pinpoint their circumstances and motives with greater accuracy.

▷ **Question 2(b)**   *Tutor answer*

Here the differences are much more significant than in (a). Source C represents Lenin as a tyrant; Source D represents him as a hero. The British observer in Source C has freedom to tell the truth, as he sees it, about Lenin, and he concentrates on the worst features of Lenin's rule with its repression and killings. He is obviously not a Bolshevik sympathizer and is representative of the majority view in Britain which was hostile to Bolshevism. The Russian in Source D presents himself as an admirer of Lenin. Even if he was not, he had little choice about what he wrote as the police state Lenin had established was very vigilant in rooting out dissenting opinions and dissenters. So he concentrates on what he sees as Lenin's achievements, and no hint of the police state referred to in Source C appears. In 1924 it was state policy to elevate Lenin's memory with eulogistic obituaries. This is just one example.

▷ **Question 2(c)**   *Student answer with examiner's comments*

'Avoid semi-slang phrases such as this.'

'Except presumably for the NEPmen.'

'January not December.'

'A hedged conclusion.'

In source D the writer is heaping unstinted praise upon Lenin, and is likely, therefore, to go over the top. He begins by describing Lenin as a great leader, and certainly he led his party with consummate skill during the revolution and in the subsequent years, as for example, when he persuaded the party to replace war communism with the New Economic Policy, even though it meant a partial restoration of capitalism. But it is difficult to see how Lenin was a 'giant among statesmen'; he did not meet other statesmen, and had only limited dealings with them even after foreign intervention in Russia ended. Nor could he really be described as 'humble'; he had the greatest confidence in his own abilities and expected his colleagues to rubber-stamp his decisions, although he had something of a common man touch in his dealings with ordinary people. The Source is right in praising Lenin's part in the October revolution; without his determination and decision there would have been no revolution. Similarly the overthrow of 'foreign invaders and the Whites' owed much to his policy decisions and appointments of military leaders, although Trotsky and others deserve a lot of the credit. He, too, insisted on paying a high price for 'peace' in 1918, when Trotsky thought the price to pay was too high. That the Russians owed their 'prosperity' to him might well be disputed by those who starved in the 1921 famine or had their property confiscated. Prosperity remained a distant mirage for the Russians long after Lenin's death. He certainly, as the source says, dealt 'ruthlessly with counterrevolution'; the Cheka and the police state were his methods, but Source D ignores the many who were exiled or executed on the flimsiest of pretexts. 'Rule by the people' was neither Lenin's intention nor his method. He had squashed parliamentary democracy in December 1918 by getting rid of the Assembly, and the people were ruled, not by themselves, but by a party élite. Whether the Russian people were in Lenin's debt in 1924 may be debatable, but the party certainly was. If communism really was good for Russia, then in bringing it about and consolidating it Lenin did deserve the unstinting praise and gratitude of the Russian people as expressed in Source D.

Examiners' marking scheme

Level 1: isolated fragments on Lenin OR a generalized, but undeveloped assessment.

(1–2 marks)

Level 2: a description of Lenin's career with minimal reference to the source OR limited tackling of two or three points raised in the source.   (3–6 marks)

Level 3: an uncritical and in-depth agreement or disagreement with the points in the source OR a critical survey of Lenin's career with only limited reference to the source.

(7–10 marks)

Level 4: a balanced assessment covering the main themes in the source and with specific reference to the source.   (11–12 marks)

Examiner's decision on the student answer

This must be a Level 4 answer. The points in the source are tackled in turn and individually assessed. 'Over the top' and 'December 1918' are not sufficient to detract from the overall excellence of the answer. It is worth maximum, 12/12.

SUMMARY

In this chapter you have studied the two Russian revolutions of 1917 and the establishment of communist rule in the years 1917–24, in particular:

▷ the Treaty of Brest-Litovsk with Germany;

▷ the civil wars in Russia, 1918–20;

▷ the main political developments, including War Communism and the New Economic Policy;

▷ the role of Lenin;

▷ the main features of the Soviet state.

The rule of Josef Stalin in the Soviet Union is dealt with in chapter 10.

The Weimar Republic

▷ **GETTING STARTED**

The Weimar Republic did not arise out of the democratic wishes of the German people; it was the result of defeat in war and the abdication of the Emperor. The democratic institutions it set up were new, untried and, with many, unpopular; certainly they were too superficial to withstand the problems resulting from that wartime defeat.

MEG	NEAB	NICCEA	SEG	LONDON	WJEC	TOPIC	STUDY	REVISION 1	REVISION 2
✓	✓	✓	✓		✓	**The foundation of the Republic**			
✓	✓	✓	✓		✓	The end of the Hohenzollern Empire			
✓	✓	✓	✓		✓	The Weimar Constitution			
✓	✓	✓	✓		✓	**The weaknesses of the Weimar Republic**			
✓	✓	✓	✓		✓	The 'years of crisis'			
✓	✓	✓	✓		✓	The role of Stresemann			
✓	✓	✓	✓	✓	✓	The Great Depression in Germany			
✓	✓	✓	✓	✓	✓	**The growth of Nazi power, 1920–33**			
✓	✓	✓	✓	✓	✓	The rise of Hitler			
✓	✓	✓	✓	✓	✓	Nazism and the economic crisis of 1930–33			

▷ **WHAT YOU NEED TO KNOW**

The foundation of the Republic

▷ **The end of the Hohenzollern Empire**

Weimar politicians failed to retain the support of the population at large, which turned to more extreme political groups. The parties loyal to Weimar were too weak and disunited to provide acceptable alternatives to Hitler.

German attitudes at the end of the war

Germany found defeat in the First World War difficult to accept:

(a) Germans were convinced of the rightness of their cause: most of them believed the war was a defensive one against powers intent on crushing them.
(b) There was a powerful military tradition in Germany inherited from Prussia: the prestige of the army was well respected.
(c) The country was governed by an efficient bureaucracy which had no sympathy with western liberal methods of government: to be beaten by them was unimaginable.
(d) Germans were embittered by losing the 'public relations' war; they believed that the idea that the Allies represented freedom was pure propaganda.
(e) They did not accept that they had been truly defeated: they thought their government had been 'stabbed in the back' by left-wing Germans who lacked patriotism.

Germany was resentful of its treatment at the peace conference in Paris in 1919:

(a) They would have preferred the conference to have taken place on neutral ground; Paris was the capital of their bitterest enemy.
(b) They were not allowed to take part in conference business, but were presented with a treaty they had no part in making; hence they signed it unread.
(c) They believed the peace was to be made on the basis of the Fourteen Points, but they thought the Allies applied these only when it suited their interests.
(d) They thought the terms were harsh and vindictive, especially regarding the loss of resources, productive capacity, colonial empire, etc.
(e) In particular, they rejected war guilt, and felt that Germany was singled out for a reparations burden that was both unfair and cripplingly heavy.

The Weimar government

When Kaiser Wilhelm II abdicated and fled, a republic was declared, and a right-wing socialist, Friedrich Ebert, headed a new government, a coalition of several parties, including the Democrats and the Centre. Germans accepted this because they thought a republic would get a better deal from the Allies.

Elections were held in 1919 to choose a Constituent Assembly to devise a new constitution. It met in the small university town of Weimar in February 1919, chosen because the major cities of Germany, especially Berlin, were suffering outbreaks of disorder involving extremists of both the right and the left. It was not intended that Weimar should become the capital of Germany permanently, and in fact the capital was moved back to Berlin as early as 1920.

The Assembly met from February to July, and its composition was largely middle class. The constitution was the work of academic and jurist Hugo Preuss.

▷ **The Weimar Constitution**

This was a written constitution, and one of the most democratic ever devised:

(a) Rights of individuals were guaranteed: personal liberty, equality before the law, freedom of movement, expression, association, collective bargaining, etc. Plebiscites or referenda could be held if demanded by a petition of one-tenth of the population.
(b) Germany was to be a federal state of eighteen Länder; Prussia was the biggest, as big as all the others put together.
(c) The President was to be elected by everyone over 20. Normally he was a figurehead, but in an emergency he could suspend the constitution and rule by emergency decree (Article 48).
(d) There was a bicameral (two-chamber) parliament:
  (i) *Reichstag*: this was to be elected every four years on a system of proportional representation; 60,000 votes were sufficient as a 'quota' to secure a seat.
  (ii) *Reichsrat*: represented the governments of the Länder – but Prussia was not allowed to have more than two-thirds of the seats.
(e) The President chose the Chancellor (Prime Minister), but he had to command a majority. There was cabinet responsibility for all ministers.
(f) There was to be a *National Economic Council to* advise parliament on economic matters.

The weaknesses of the Weimar Republic

▷ **The 'years of crisis'**

From the beginning there were weaknesses in Germany's new system.

Problems arising from the war

These were matters for which the German Empire was responsible, but for which the 'November criminals' took the blame:

(a) They were forced to accept the 'diktat' of Versailles.
(b) They were made responsible for heavy reparations payments.
(c) They were denied equal status, and membership of the League.
(d) There were foreign armies of occupation on German soil.
(e) They suffered heavy losses of materials; there followed poverty and serious food shortages.

Internal threats

These came largely from people on the extreme right: soldiers, industrialists, Junkers, bureaucrats of the old civil service.

The radicalism of disappointed rightists could be seen in the murders of left-wing leaders such as Kurt Eisner and Matthias Erzberger.

(a) *1919, Spartacist Rising* in Berlin forced the government to meet in Weimar. Led by communist leaders, the rising was no match for the regular officers who had served the Kaiser, and was bloodily crushed.

(b) *1920, Kapp Putsch*, Dr Kapp and General von Lüttwitz deposed the Berlin government and tried to enthrone the Crown Prince. The workers called a general strike and the monarchist movement collapsed. Kapp fled, but the other ringleaders got off lightly.

(c) *1922, Rathenau murder*, Jewish Minister of Foreign Affairs, Walter Rathenau, was murdered by ex-officers of the army.

(d) *1923, Küstrin Putsch*, Major Buchrucker and his 'Black Army' tried to capture Berlin by marching on it from the fortress of Küstrin, but failed.

(e) *1923, Munich Putsch*, Hitler's Nazi Party attempted a rising in Munich, but this was easily suppressed, and Hitler and other leaders were gaoled.

Political weaknesses

(a) German people were democratically inexperienced; to them democracy seemed like a foreign import and not part of their way of life.

(b) This was a period of extremism and violence; a lot of these groups were struggling for existence, and gathering paramilitary forces.

(c) Proportional representation produced nearly 30 different political parties; there was no majority in the Reichstag, and coalitions resulted, with short-lived cabinets (there were four different Chancellors, 1920–22). The most important of these parties were:

> Communist Party (KDP)
> Social Democratic Party (SPD)
> Catholic Centre Party (Zentrum)
> National Socialist German Workers' Party (NSDAP)
> German National People's Party (DNVP)
> German People's Party (DVP)
> German Democratic Party (DDP)
> Bavarian People's Party (BVP)

German inflation and the reparations burden

The imposition of a heavy reparations settlement accelerated inflation (see chapter 6, pp. 71–2) and produced appalling consequences for Germany:

(a) The middle classes found their savings worthless and were reduced to penury. Those on war pensions found they could scarcely buy a postage stamp. In 1933 they turned to Hitler rather than let it happen again.

(b) Germany was able to write off its internal debts; payments for mortgages, etc. could be made in worthless paper. The man who had lent his government 100,000 marks during the war found this was worth only a few pence in 1923.

(c) There was a boom in trade and employment; German exports now undercut all others. Those in work found that their wages almost kept up with inflation.

(d) There was a flight from money. Aristocrats with wealth in land, and businessmen who could borrow and repay in devalued currency, grew rich. Ordinary people bought almost anything to avoid holding money – tinned food, old car tyres, celluloid shirt-collars, etc.

(e) Extremist parties grew in number and became very indignant. Various breakaway movements, e.g. in the Palatinate, sought to disrupt the Weimar Republic.

▷ The role of Stresemann

A rather dumpy, unimpressive figure, he was much underestimated in Germany.

Stresemann as Chancellor

In August 1923 Stresemann agreed to form a government to deal with the combined problems of the Ruhr and the economy:

(a) He dealt with extremist movements such as the Communist Putsch in Hamburg in October and Hitler's in Munich in November by proclaiming *martial law* in conjunction with army command. An attempt to create a separatist 'Republic of the Rhine' was also defeated.

(b) He persuaded the French to leave the Ruhr by promising to resume reparations payments in October; in November he passed an enabling law allowing Schacht to restore order to the mark at a low level.

(c) After Stresemann's resignation in November, the old worthless mark was replaced in April 1924 at a rate of 1 new Reichsmark to 1,000,000,000,000 old Rentenmarks, and a new independent Reichsbank was created to control the currency and inspire public confidence in it. At the same time, the Dawes Plan resumed the supply of foreign loans to Germany.

Stresemann as Foreign Minister

He could play the part of the international statesman convincingly, but his true aim was the recovery of Germany's European authority.

(a) 1925, *Locarno Treaties* signed by Austen Chamberlain (Britain), Aristide Briand (France) and Stresemann:
  (i) *In the West*, the demilitarization of the Rhineland was agreed, and there was a mutual guarantee of Germany's western frontiers by Belgium, France and Germany, all of which promised to resolve their differences by arbitration. Britain and Italy stood as guarantors to enforce the agreement.
  (ii) *In the East*, arbitration treaties were made between Germany and its neighbours Poland and Czechoslovakia in case of frontier problems. These were guaranteed by France in separate defensive treaties, but Britain was not party to these guarantees. This meant in effect that the Germans did not bind themselves to respect their eastern frontiers as they did their western; westwards they recognized their frontiers as permanent, but eastwards they still cherished their ambitions.

(b) The Allies had disappointed Germany in 1925 by refusing to evacuate the Cologne bridgehead and the northern third of the Rhineland when the time agreed at Versailles arrived, but Stresemann was now able to persuade the Allies to do this in 1926.

(c) September 1926, Germany was at last admitted to the League of Nations with a permanent seat on the Council.

(d) 1927, the Central Control Commission supervising German disarmament was wound up; disarmament now proceeded on German good faith.

(e) 1928, Germany was one of 65 states to sign the Kellogg–Briand Pact renouncing war as an instrument of policy.

Allied troops were withdrawn from the second zone of the Rhineland a month after the death of Stresemann, and from the third zone in June 1930. But by 1930 the international skies were once again beginning to darken: the Wall Street Crash and the Great Depression were beginning to have their effect on Europe.

▷ The Great Depression in Germany

The death of Stresemann removed the Weimar Republic's ablest politician from the scene; the onset of the Great Depression wrecked Germany's chance of economic revival. US loans were recalled, the demand for German exports dried up, and the Reichsbank got into difficulties. There were fears (unfounded, as it turned out) for the Reichsmark.

The effects of the financial crisis, 1929–30

The main problem at the time was unemployment: the number of those out of work in September 1929 was 1.3 million, and over the next three years it rose sharply to 6 million. A popular plebiscite against the Young Plan failed in December to reach the required numerical limit, but it led to the resignation of Hermann Müller as Chancellor over contributions to unemployment insurance, and the end of the parliamentary period of the Republic.

Heinrich Brüning became Chancellor, and, early in 1930, was forced to resort to presidential powers under Article 48 to pursue deflationary policies with emergency decrees to safeguard public finances, lower prices, cut back on wages, slash spending and reduce unemployment benefit.

Both the policies and the methods of enforcing them were unpopular, and provided opportunities for the extremist parties to exploit the situation. In the elections to the fifth Reichstag in September 1930, the communists and Nazis made big gains.

The spread of violence, 1930–32

Violence developed from both sides. The communists made no secret of their wish to overthrow the Republic and set up a Bolshevik state. They battled in the streets and resorted to violence to intimidate their opponents. In this they were outdone by the Nazis; their violence was better organized, and their 'storm troopers' proved more than a match in most of their street battles with the left.

An eyewitness, Kurt Ludecke, reported:

Brownshirts were everywhere in evidence . . . Private armies, equipped at the very least with jack-knives and revolvers, daggers and knuckle-dusters, were shouting in the squares and rampaging through the towns. Processions and meetings, demonstrations and protests, festivals and funerals, all wore the same face but a different uniform – except that the SS and the SA of the Nazis and the Red Front of the Communists marched more defiantly, the Social Democrat Reichsbanner more fatly, the Stahlhelmer more sedately. It was the Reichswehr who were the least in evidence.

By 1932, the respectable classes of Germany had almost given up hope of a stable government, and were beginning to turn their backs on politics altogether.

The growth of Nazi power, 1920–33

▷ **The rise of Hitler** Populist and careerist, statesman and gangster, he was a new phenomenon in politics.

Early career

(a) 1889, he was born at Braunau near the Austrian border; his father was a minor customs official. He had an undistinguished school career; later he tried art and architecture. As a young man, he drifted to Vienna, where he lived with down-and-outs in dosshouses.
(b) 1913, he crossed the Austrian border to live in Munich. He joined the army and fought 1914–18 in the war. He loved the discipline of army life, was wounded and decorated with the Iron Cross.
(c) 1918, he was in a hospital in Munich recovering from his gas injury at the end of the war. He accepted a minor job keeping an eye on extremist political meetings; he became a disgruntled member of the Freikorps.
(d) 1919, he became member no. 7 of the German Workers' Party, which became the National Socialist Party, with Hitler as chairman.

His *Party Programme* of 1920 (the *Twenty-five Points*) included:

(a) promotion of popular welfare – but the state comes before the individual;
(b) self-determination for *all* Germans;
(c) cancellation of Paris peace treaties;
(d) elimination of Jews;
(e) reduction of mortgage interest ('ending of bondage of interest payments').

Munich Putsch, November 1923

The attempted coup was provoked by:

(a) resentment at the 'betrayal' of Versailles;
(b) the harshness and injustice of the peace terms;
(c) the financial collapse of 1922–23 and the French occupation of the Ruhr;
(d) the development of Bavarian separatism. An earlier attempt in April 1923 had easily been foiled by the Bavarian police, and Hitler was humiliated by the rebuff. This time he had more powerful allies, like von Kahr, Ludendorff and Röhm.

The object of the coup was to provoke the Bavarian government into a separatist rising. SA men surrounded a beer hall where local political leaders were meeting; Hitler entered the hall, mounted a table, fired his pistol into the ceiling and declared that the national revolution had begun.

Next day, a march of 3,000 storm troopers, with Hitler, Goering and Ludendorff in the front rank, collapsed ignominiously after a burst of firing in which sixteen Nazis were killed. Hitler was slightly wounded, fled and was later arrested.

He was later tried for sedition, but contrived to turn his court appearance into a theatrical act in which he turned the tables on his accusers and justified his actions. At his trial, Hitler said:

> The army we have formed is growing from day to day ... I nourish the proud hope that one day the hour will come when these rough companies grow to battalions, the battalions to regiments, the regiments to divisions; that the old cockade will be taken from the mud and that the old flags will wave again ... For it is not you, gentlemen, who pass judgment upon us. That judgment is spoken by the eternal court of history ... The goddess of the eternal court of history will smile and tear to tatters the sentence of this court. For she acquits us!

Sent to prison for five years, he served only nine months before release. He lived in some style in the fortress of Landsberg during these months in his own room, receiving guests and able to dictate the first part of his book, *Mein Kampf*, to his secretary and deputy, Rudolf Hess.

Party beliefs and organization

For the party's *beliefs*, the main bible of Nazism was Hitler's two-volume work, *Mein Kampf*, in which he set out his plans and his ideas.

(a) He was intensely patriotic, believing in struggle and sacrifice, not in materialism. His thinking attracted ex-officers and old soldiers.
(b) He believed that Germany was not defeated, but had been betrayed by the 'November criminals', who had been perverted by liberalism.
(c) He had an intense hatred of communists and Jews.
(d) He had an idealistic hope of bettering the lives of ordinary Germans through discipline rather than comfort. Gradually the socialist element in National Socialism faded in importance because he increasingly depended on businessmen and industrialists to supply him with finance.
(e) His methods showed that he had a sensitive finger on the popular pulse:
   (i) He loved *theatricality*, e.g. his use of uniforms, brownshirts, the Swastika, and his passion for enormous mass rallies.
   (ii) He made skilled use of propaganda, blurred the distinction between truth and falsehood, and knew how to play on people's elementary fears and hates.

In *Mein Kampf* (1924) Hitler summed up his position:

> One Blood demands one Reich. Never will the German nation possess the right to engage in colonial politics until, at least, it embraces its own sons within a single state. Only when the Reich borders include the very last German, but can no longer guarantee his daily bread, will the right to acquire foreign soil arise from the distress of our people. Their sword will become our plough, and from the tears of war the daily bread of future generations shall grow ...
>
> Blood mixture and the resultant drop in the racial level is the sole cause of the dying out of old cultures. For men do not perish as the result of lost wars, but by

the loss of that force of resistance which comes only from pure blood. All who are not of good race in this world are chaff . . .

If the Jews were alone in this world, they would stifle in filth and offal; they would try to get ahead of one another in the hate-filled struggle and exterminate one another, insofar as the absolute absence of all sense of self-sacrifice, expressing itself in their cowardice, did not turn battle into comedy here, too . . .

The crown of the folkish state's entire work of education and training must be to burn racial sense and racial feeling into the instinct and the intellect, the heart and the brain of the youth entrusted to it. No boy or girl must leave school without having been led to an ultimate realization of the necessity and essence of blood purity.

In its *organization*, the party operated on the autocratic principle of personal leadership (the *Führerprinzip*), with power concentrated in Hitler's own hands, and in the hands of his deputy, Hess, and the national leadership. But in reality they had little power: he ignored them and overrode their decisions as he wanted.

There was an elaborate political *organization for the provinces*: the province (*Gau*), the county (*Kreis*), the cell (*Zelle*) and the local 'block' (*Block*) each had its own organization. This provided a good many supporters 'on the books', but it made the whole apparatus extremely expensive.

These structures were supposed to take their own decisions and act responsibly, but Hitler frequently ignored them, or called them sharply to order.

It was part of the character of Nazism that contesting groups or individuals were often left to fight things out for themselves so as to identify the 'survivor'.

There were elaborate *subordinate bodies*:

Schutzstaffel (SS), Hitler's blackshirted *corps d'élite*
Sturmabteilung (SA), the brownshirts (originally hall guards)
Hitler Youth (HJ) and the League of German Girls (BdM).

There were numerous associated bodies, such as the German Workers' Front (DAF), National Socialist People's Welfare (NSV) and professional bodies deriving from various occupations, e.g. Nazi teachers, Nazi lawyers.

None of this meant very much in practice; it was all part of Hitler's mania for giving an impression of thoroughness and efficiency when he was really rather casual.

▷ Nazism and the economic crisis of 1930–33

In the 1920s, the Nazi Party had made very little progress, and its Reichstag representation was down to twelve by 1928, but the Great Depression provided this and the other extreme parties with their big chance.

Causes of Nazi success

(a) Hitler was always harking back to the injustices of the Treaty of Versailles, and to the iniquity of the reparations settlement; he rejected even the Young Plan as being part of the Weimar conspiracy against the nation.

(b) There was rising unemployment, falling wages and poverty, and officials of the Weimar Republic left the impression that they did not know how to handle them.

(c) Many Germans found Nazism appealing; Hitler had a good speaking style and passionately believed he was right. He attracted:
  (i) ex-servicemen, who shared his experiences and grasped his style instinctively; many were down on their luck and waiting for something to turn up;
  (ii) unemployed, who thought that Hitler understood their problems; they felt frustrated with Weimar incompetence and bureaucracy;
  (iii) ill-educated drifters and ruffians, with mind-sets similar to Hitler's, who thought his remedies were excellent; they could earn a small salary if they joined one of his organizations, and were always ready for a punch-up;
  (iv) anti-Semites, who shared his obsessional hostility towards Jews.
  (v) many middle-class people, who sympathized with the patriotic and conservative elements of Nazism, and who dreaded the renewal of hyperinflation, or the possibility of a communist takeover.

Table 8.1 Reichstag elections, May 1928–March 1933

	May 1928	Sept. 1930	July 1932	Nov. 1932	March 1933
Communists (KPD)	54	77	89	100	81
Social Democrats (SDP)	153	143	133	121	120
Catholic Centre	62	68	75	70	73
Ger. Nat. Peo. P. (DNVP)	73	41	37	52	52
Nazi Party (NSDAP)	12	107	230	196	288
Ger. Peo. Party (DVP)	45	30	7	11	2
Ger. Democratic P. (DDP)	25	20	4	2	5
Bavarian Peo. P. (BVP)	16	19	22	20	19
Other parties	51	72	11	12	7
Seats in Reichstag	491	577	608	584	647

Decline of the Weimar Republic

The Great Depression brought a swift succession of governments:

(a) 1930–32, *Brüning* was Chancellor. The right-wing parties abandoned the SDP when social insurance benefits were stepped up; they feared an inflationary surge. President Hindenburg was forced to govern by emergency decrees under Article 48.

April 1932, a failing Hindenburg was re-elected President with 19.4 million votes, but Hitler ran him a close second with 13.4 million.

May 1932, Brüning proposed a settlement of unemployed workers on Junker estates ('a Bolshevik agrarian policy'), and fell because the right wing rejected this.

(b) June–December 1932, *von Papen* was Chancellor with a 'Cabinet of National Reconstruction'. Elections in July gave Hitler 230 seats, but Papen got little support for himself.

He joined with the Nationalists (DNVP) after the election in November, but this gave the Nazis 196 seats, and the KPD 100 seats.

He planned to create a 'New State' free from dependence on the Reichstag, and with army support, but the attempt failed and he resigned.

(c) December 1932–January 1933, *von Schleicher* was Chancellor. Hitler reached an agreement with Papen: Hitler was to be Chancellor and Papen Vice-Chancellor. Hitler came to power in January when Hindenburg accepted this arrangement – everyone thought Hitler would be an obedient puppet, out of his political depth.

(d) January 1933, *Hitler* became Chancellor.

Reasons for the failure of the Weimar Republic

The roots of democracy in Germany were not deep, and many Germans never accepted the regime. Hitler had great political flair and the perception of how to turn situations to his own advantage; he was not burdened with moral standards.

The Republic was saddled with the responsibility for accepting the unpopular Treaty of Versailles, the burden of reparations, and the humiliation of losing German territory, especially to inferior neighbours such as Poland.

The economic crises of 1923 and then of 1929 destroyed the Republic's credibility; it lacked the knowledge of how to deal with these economic problems.

The personalities were weak, and proportional representation made for unstable governments. The government also failed to ban paramilitary organizations.

GLOSSARY

Left wing and right wing   Generally, left-wing politicians are those committed to major and rapid change in politics and society, and right-wing politicians are those who wish to preserve existing society and institutions, with change and reform only when it is absolutely necessary. Extremists of the left want revolutionary change and are usually identified as communists or their close allies. Extremists of the right want a capitalist and authoritarian state, and are usually labelled as fascists.

In Germany during the 1920s and 1930s, the description 'right wing' was given to those who wanted authoritarian government, the restoration of the monarchy and the maintenance of the capitalist system. The right wing's main group was the nationalists, but after some wavering the national socialists committed themselves to capitalism and secured the support of a section of 'big business', so that in the early 1930s the right wing was dominated by the Nazis.

The German left wing consisted of the extreme socialists and communists who worked for the overthrow of capitalism. Left wing and right wing, during the period of Weimar, had in common that they both resorted to violent methods and that they both wanted an end to the Weimar Republic.

Nationalists   The Nationalist Party was a German right-wing party which secured 44 seats in the election of January 1919. They strongly supported capitalism. Most of them wanted the return of the monarchy; they resented Germany's defeat in 1918 and they opposed the Treaty of Versailles. While they paid lip-service to the new republic, their true beliefs were better shown by the fact that they absented themselves from the Reichstag when Ebert was sworn in as first President. The German army (Reichswehr) was largely nationalist in sympathy, and so was Hindenburg, the President elected in 1925. The Nationalists were outbid for votes by the Nazi Party in the elections of the early 1930s, and their leaders Hugenburg and von Papen, by eventually agreeing to give the Nazis Nationalist support, paved the way for the end of the Weimar Republic.

National Socialists –   This party was founded soon after the end of the First World War. Its early combination of nationalism and socialism seems somewhat contradictory, and it was soon to outdo the Nationalist Party both in right-wing extremism and in ruthless organization. It used propaganda, prejudice and violence as its principal methods of gaining support. Its socialist aims soon faded, and its early socialist background (lingering on among the leadership and membership of the SA) became something of an embarrassment during and after the successful Nazi bid for power.

Spartacists   The Spartacists were extreme left-wing revolutionaries, taking their name from a famous slave rebellion in ancient Rome. Their leaders were Rosa Luxemburg and Karl Liebnecht. They were both communists, and powerful and effective agitators, and they aimed to turn Germany into a Soviet republic – in effect, the Spartacist movement was indistinguishable from a Bolshevik movement. Right-wing action, mainly by the Freikorps in January 1919, destroyed the Spartacists, and Rosa and Karl were murdered by officers of the Guards Cavalry Division on their way to prison.

EXAMINATION QUESTIONS

▷ **Question 1**   Show to what extent the Weimar Republic was successful during the 1920s in dealing with:

(a)   inflation   (5 marks)
(b)   reparations   (5 marks)
(c)   unemployment   (5 marks)
(d)   political extremism.   (5 marks)

▷ **Question 2**   Study Sources A–E below and then answer the questions which follow:

Source A

The stage of the National Theatre was festively decorated with the new [black, red and gold] colours of the Reich and with plants and flowers . . . The House was packed with the exception of the Nationalists' and the Independent Socialists' benches which remained ostentatiously empty. After an organ prelude Ebert, short, broad-shouldered, in dark morning dress and wearing gold-rimmed glasses, appeared on the stage, followed by the Cabinet also in black.

(Contemporary report of the Inauguration of President Ebert, 21 August 1919)

Source B

Dogs and Frenchmen forbidden. (Notice in a Ruhr café, 1924)

Source C

The Weimar politicians urged passive resistance against the French because they were too weak to find a political or economic solution. It was easy for the politicians to pose as patriots, but it was the workers of the Ruhr who actually confronted the French troops. While the country faced economic ruin the politicians paid off the country's national debt by reckless printing of paper money. Germany rid itself of the internal burden of war by ruining those who had lent money to pay for it, and at the same time whined so much about the external burden of war that the allies developed a guilty conscience and the Americans came to the rescue.

(An historian's comment on 1923)

Source D

Election of a party man, representing one-sided extremist views, who would subsequently have the majority of the people against him, would expose the Fatherland to serious disturbance whose outcome would be incalculable. Duty commanded me to prevent this . . . If I am defeated, I shall at least not have incurred the reproach that of my own accord I deserted my post in an hour of crisis . . . I ask for no votes from those who do not wish to vote for me.

(Election radio broadcast by Hindenburg, 10 March 1932)

Source E

Hindenburg replied that because of the tense situation he could not in good conscience risk transferring the power of government to a new party such as the National Socialists, which did not command a majority and which was intolerant, noisy and undisciplined.

At this point Hindenburg, with a certain show of excitement, referred to several recent occurrences – clashes between the Nazis and the police, acts of violence committed by Hitler's followers against those who were of a different opinion, excesses against Jews and other illegal acts . . . After extended discussion Hindenburg proposed to Hitler that he should declare himself ready to cooperate with other parties, particularly with the Right and Centre, and that he should give up the one-sided idea that he must have complete power. In cooperating with other parties, Hindenburg declared, he would show what he could achieve and improve upon . . . Hindenburg stated that this also would be the best way to eliminate the widespread fear that a National Socialist government would make ill use of its power and would suppress all other viewpoints and gradually eliminate them.

(Report of a meeting between Hitler and Hindenburg, 13 August 1932)

(a) How far do Sources A and C appear to be biased?   (4 marks)
(b) What can we learn from Sources B and C about the reaction of the Germans to the occupation of the Ruhr?   (4 marks)
(c) How effective an appeal for votes would you regard Source D? Give reasons for your answer.   (4 marks)
(d) Hindenburg's loyalty to the Weimar Republic has sometimes been questioned. How far does the evidence of Sources D and E confirm or deny that Hindenburg was a loyal servant of Weimar?   (4 marks)
(e) What can be deduced from these sources about the strengths and weaknesses of the Weimar Republic?   (8 marks)

▷ **Question 3** (a) Why did the Weimar Republic survive throughout the 1920s?   (10 marks)
(b) Was unemployment the most important reason for the collapse of the Weimar Republic in the 1930s?   (10 marks)

EXAMINATION ANSWERS

▷ **Question 1**   *Outline answer*

A description, even with good coverage, can reach only Level 2 and gain 3 marks at maximum. You are asked to measure (i.e. to assess) Weimar's success in dealing with each of the four problems; showing *how* the problem was dealt with does not in itself involve an assessment of *how effectively* it was dealt with.

(a)   You may well criticize the almost criminal irresponsibility of the Republic for the accelerating inflation of the early 1920s, but you will need to show the effective tackling of inflation with the new Reichsmark at the end of 1923. It is important to point out, in assessing success, that inflation did not reappear in the remainder of the 1920s and that inflation was *not* a feature of the depression. Even so, the government might be able to create a strong new currency, but it could not easily repair the economic, social and political damage brought about by the collapse of the old currency.

(b)   In dealing with reparations, it is easy to be led into lengthy accounts of such events as the occupation of the Ruhr: keep to the reparations theme – the early difficulties, the Dawes Plan and the Young Plan – and show that by the end of 1929 the reparations problem had been reduced, but not eliminated.

(c)   Your main theme here will be economic recovery after the crisis of 1923, and that unemployment following the Wall Street Crash is relevant to the 1930s, but hardly to the 1920s.

(d)   The main theme is the handling of the extremists of 1919–21 and the Munich Putsch of 1923, with the success story of the later 1920s when extremism was at its lowest ebb. As with (c), you should avoid trespassing into the 1930s, although it would be worth pointing out that the rapid resurgence of extremism in the 1930s shows that the extremists of 1926–29 were not demoralized, but waiting for their opportunity.

▷ **Question 2**   *Tutor answer*

(a)   Source A is not specifically biased, but the concentration on trivia – plants and flowers, organ prelude, Ebert's gold-rimmed spectacles – gives something of a comic air to the description and might appear to belittle the importance of so historic an occasion. Source C is obviously biased in its hostility to the Weimar politicians – it describes them as weak, and it uses emotive words such as 'reckless' and 'whined'. Its comment 'pose as patriots' even casts doubt on the patriotism of the politicians, and the rest of the sentence queries their courage.

(b)   The German politicians, according to Source C, encouraged patriotic resistance to the occupation. This resistance was to be passive, and therefore violence was to be avoided. If Source B is accurate and typical, it seems that the inhabitants of the Ruhr were effectively responding to their politicians' call, for equating Frenchmen with dogs was a deliberate insult to the occupying forces.

(c)   Source D shows Hindenburg pointing out the danger of voting for a party man, and implying the need for a man above party if civil strife is to be avoided. Hindenburg poses as a man of honour committed to doing his duty, rather than a power seeker, which by implication his opponent is. Those Germans who were sick of party bickering and violence in the streets would be much attracted by Hindenburg's appeal.

(d)   In his broadcast Hindenburg certainly seems to equate extremism with a threat to the fatherland, and he feels it his duty not to surrender to extremism, but to continue in office as President. In the meeting, Source E, he shows reluctance to transfer power to a party that is irresponsible, and he seems concerned to give Hitler the opportunity to show that his party will, in effect, work within the constitution. Since there is nothing in these sources to cast doubt on Hindenburg's sincerity, he seems in both instances to be working to defend and sustain Weimar rather than to overthrow it.

(e)   Source A demonstrates that, from the start, at least two parties, the Nationalists and the Independent Socialists, were not prepared to welcome the new constitution. If they would not welcome it, they might not be prepared to work to uphold it. Source C indicates that the government's inflation policy must undermine the support of the middle classes ('ruining those who had lent money to pay for it'), but that the workers of the Ruhr did respond to the government's call. If Source C can be believed, it shows the Weimar politicians to be weak and irresponsible. Sources D and E show a serious political crisis, with violence and extremism on the streets, and the rise of the Nazi Party. Thus the sources mainly suggest Weimar's weaknesses. The only strength shown in these sources is President Hindenburg's trying (desperately in Source E) to preserve the Republic.

▷ **Question 3**   *Student answer with examiner's comments*

'Be more precise and name two or three of them.'

'An exaggeration. Only one was executed.'

'He was still quite shrewd although outwitted by Papen and Hitler.'

'This needs explanation: the Wall Street Crash was an indirect cause of German unemployment.'

'Hitler was already in power. Weimar had already virtually collapsed. The burning of the Reichstag gave Hitler the excuse to outlaw the communists and introduce the Enabling Law – things he intended to do anyway.'

(a)   The Weimar Republic was set up in 1919. It was elected on a very democratic franchise, and there were lots of political parties. In the early 1920s there was much political disorder and much street fighting. First there was the Spartacist rising led by Rosie Luxemburg and her friend Karl. It was a communist rising and was put down by the Free Corps, and Rosie and Karl were murdered. Then the Free korps led a rising called the kapp Putsch. It was stopped by a general strike. As Germany could not pay reparations the French and Belgians occupied the Ruhr. The locals resisted and the French executed many of them. Then the German currency collapsed and had to be replaced by a new currency after nearly all the middle-class had lost its life savings. Stresemann became the new Chancellor and Hindenburg succeeded Ebert as president. When Stresemann died in 1929 the Weimar Republic was still in existence.

(b)   The Weimar Republic collapsed in the 1930s because of many reasons. The middle-classes were afraid of inflation returning and wanted a strong government to stop it happening. Hindenburg, the president, was very old, and could not cope with his job. There were many unemployed caused by the Wall Street Crash and they wanted a new government. Hitler and his cronies promised to make things better, and went round beating up those who argued against the Nazis. They fought the communists in the streets, and the communists did not like the Weimar Republic either. There were too many political parties for there to be a strong government. Everyone was disgusted with the Treaty of Versailles and the Diktat, and they blamed the allies and the Jews, so wanted to get rid of Weimar. The last chance of the Weimar Republic disappeared when a mad Dutchman Van der Lubbe burned down the Reichstag and destroyed the Weimar Republic's parliament house.

Examiner's decision on the student answer

(a)   This is a factual account of Weimar in the 1920s. It makes no attempt to give reasons for the survival of Weimar, and no reasons emerge from the narrative either. So it would be firmly fixed in Level 2 (narrative) rather than top Level 4 (analysis of reasons) and would score at most 4/10.

(b)   This offers a list of reasons for the fall of Weimar. It does not discuss whether unemployment was the most important reason; in fact unemployment gets only a brief mention. It gets beyond Level 2 (narrative), but does not reach Level 4 (reasons sharply focused on unemployment). In a mark range of 6–8 for Level 3, this would score 6/10 as the reasons offered are rather disjointed and lacking in explanation.

SUMMARY

In this chapter, you have studied Germany under the Weimar Republic, dealing with the problems of the Republic and the growth of Nazi power in the years to 1933.

▷ The problems of the Weimar Republic included:

    ▷ the working of its constitution;

    ▷ German attitudes towards the Treaty of Versailles;

    ▷ the nature and results of disorder in Germany to 1924;

    ▷ recovery in the later 1920s;

    ▷ the role of Gustav Stresemann.

▷ The growth of Nazism in the period to 1933 included:

    ▷ the party's beliefs and organization;

    ▷ the Munich Putsch, 1923;

    ▷ the growth of support for the Nazi Party, 1923–33;

    ▷ the rise of Hitler to become Chancellor, 1933.

The history of Germany continues in chapter 9.

Chapter

9

The Third Reich, 1933–45

 GETTING STARTED

The weakening and collapse of the Weimar Republic provided the opportunity for Hitler to make good his claim to power, and it is to the rule of Hitler that we now turn.

MEG	NEAB	NICCEA	SEG	LONDON	WJEC	TOPIC	STUDY	REVISION 1	REVISION 2
✓	✓	✓	✓	✓	✓	**Consolidation of Hitler's power**			
✓	✓	✓	✓	✓	✓	The immediate steps			
✓	✓	✓	✓	✓	✓	Building up Nazi control			
✓	✓	✓	✓	✓	✓	**Nazi domestic policy, 1933–39**			
✓	✓	✓	✓	✓	✓	Features of Nazi policies			
✓	✓	✓	✓	✓	✓	Machine or morass?			
✓	✓	✓	✓	✓	✓	Nazi economic policy			
✓	✓	✓	✓	✓	✓	**Foreign policy, 1933–45**			
✓	✓	✓	✓	✓	✓	A policy of design or drift?			
✓	✓	✓	✓	✓	✓	A policy of recovery			
✓					✓	The Second World War and the end of Hitler			

 WHAT YOU NEED TO KNOW

Consolidation of Hitler's power

▷ **The immediate steps**

With Hitler's appointment, the Weimar Republic was virtually at an end. Though the name lingered on for some time, in reality its death-throes were short-lived.

Propaganda as a political weapon

Hitler felt the need to convince Germany and the world of his importance:

(a) The same night as he became Chancellor, he took the salute in the open Chancellery window in Berlin of a brownshirt procession which lasted four hours.

(b) He pressed Hindenburg to dissolve the Reichstag and hold yet more elections as a more accurate reflection of the new political mood in the country. Though he had repeatedly refused this, Hindenburg agreed to dissolve and hold elections on 5 March.

(c) He mobilized all his propaganda to secure a parliamentary majority, using funds from many sources to finance the attempt.

His main theme in his election speeches was that only he could save Germany from its danger; he wanted a four-year 'probationary period' to prove himself, after which he would go back to the electorate to ask for a renewal of his mandate.

Meanwhile he began to pay off old scores – to eliminate from office known opponents, and those who were suspected of being lukewarm to the Nazi cause.

The Reichstag Fire

Hitler's main henchman, Goering, carried out something like a reign of terror during February to intimidate opponents, reinforcing the civil police with 50,000 men from the SA and the SS. Goering was appointed Chief Minister of Prussia, and Frick as Minister of the Interior, so blurring the dualism between the Reich and Prussia.

After the dissolution of parliament, the Reichstag building mysteriously burned down on the night of 27 February, a crime which the Nazis were so prompt in blaming on their communist rivals that for years afterwards the suspicion was widespread that they had done it themselves.

The *Reichstag Fire Trial*, which the Nazis spent over six months preparing, took place the following autumn, and was not a conspicuous success for its authors. The pathetic Van der Lubbe, the communist stooge put up for trial, was convicted and executed, but a number of other accused defended themselves so vigorously that they reduced their prosecutor Goering to incoherence and had to be acquitted.

Meanwhile, before the election, Hitler embarked in earnest on 'safeguarding the state from internal subversion' by persuading Hindenburg to issue a series of emergency decrees under Article 48 to:

(a) 'absorb' the whole government to Nazi principles – the policy of 'coordination' (= *Gleischaltung*) was supposed to 'protect the people';
(b) suspend all guarantees of personal liberty written into the Weimar Constitution – henceforth no German was safe from arbitrary arrest, torture or even murder at the hands of Goering's police.

▷ Building up Nazi control

The Reichstag elections, March 1933

At the election, the Nazis won 288 seats, but only 44 per cent of the popular vote; with their nationalist allies, however, who had polled 8 per cent, they could lay claim to an absolute majority.

Hitler was determined to preserve Republican legality, and went to bizarre lengths to give the impression of working within the constitutional framework:

(a) He brought in the *Enabling Bill*, March 1933, under which it was said that 'parliamentary government ceased to exist in Germany':
   (i) National laws could be enacted by the cabinet as well as by the Reichstag.
   (ii) Such laws could 'deviate' from the constitution if the cabinet thought fit.
   (iii) New laws were to be drafted by the cabinet and then published; they would become law the following day.
   Hitler used this law to put through a whole raft of new laws which would not have passed in the constitutional way.
(b) For such a measure, Hitler had to have a two-thirds majority. Hitler, who with his ally Papen had just over 50 per cent of the seats, managed it by a variety of ways:
   (i) He barred communist deputies on grounds of complicity in the Reichstag Fire; those daring to appear were arrested and beaten.
   (ii) He half-promised a concordat with the Papacy as a bait to the Catholic Centre to accept the Enabling Law.
   (iii) Only the SDP voted against it, but their protest was ignored.

Centralization of the government

Germany, previously a federal state, was transformed into a unitary one as part of the policy of Coordination:

(a) Nazi powers were centralized in Berlin early in 1933:
   (i) March, the composition of state parliaments was 'adjusted' to match the national election results.
   (ii) April, Nazi *Stadthalters* were appointed to control actions of state governments.
   (iii) In January 1934, state governments were abolished altogether, and the Reichsrat was dissolved.
(b) Police powers were assumed by the Nazi Party, supplementing those of the regular police. The political police (*Gestapo*) was established in 1934.

(c) May 1933, political parties and trade unions were dissolved.
(d) December, the Nazi Party became the 'state party'.

At the same time, Hitler concentrated power in his own hands:

(a) The newly established Gestapo gave a free hand to the SA and the SS in a display of power outside the control of the courts.
(b) November 1933, a plebiscite gave Hitler 98 per cent approval of his measures.
(c) June 1934, he purged the SA; Röhm and 400 other SA officers were shot in a *Night of the Long Knives*.
(d) August 1934, Hitler became President and Commander-in-Chief as well as Chancellor on the death of Hindenburg; he was known as *Führer*. This step was followed by another plebiscite which earned him 96 per cent approval of a 90 per cent poll.

Nazi domestic policy, 1933–39

▷ **Features of Nazi policies**

Though Hitler's government, at least in the beginning, based itself on the will of the people, it was based on no clear constitutional foundation, and often operated in an arbitrary fashion. Hitler was invested with an almost God-like authority, and the SS and the Gestapo operated free from restraints. At the same time, the state extended its tentacles into areas of life where previously it had never ventured.

Totalitarianism

Hitler controlled the Nazi Party, and the party operated through the army and the police. Other parties were banned and civil rights set aside. Minorities were brutalized and opponents confined in concentration camps. Voting was compulsory at elections, but only Nazi candidates were allowed ('Ein Reich, ein Volk, ein Führer': 'One empire, one people, one leader').

This was the meaning of the word 'totalitarian': the state could regulate every aspect of the citizen's life, even in the most intimate areas, since the individual had no real significance, or even existence, outside the state. This had been implicit in Nazi thought ever since the 'Twenty-five Points'.

Racialist philosophy

At the root of Nazism, also, lay its racialist philosophy: the view that the Germans (or Aryans) were the master race, and all others to a greater or lesser degree were inferior. At the top, victors in the unrelenting struggle, were the Aryans, blond, athletic and beautiful; near neighbours such as the Swedes were a little below them in the hierarchy; then the English and then the Latin races; and finally, at the bottom, the contemptible non-people such as the gypsies and the Jews. This theory was as dangerous as it was ridiculous; though buttressed by the findings of pseudo-science, it was basically unsound.

The Jews, as Hitler repeated tirelessly in *Mein Kampf*, were to blame for most of the country's difficulties: they were bourgeois blood-suckers holding the nation to ransom; they inspired lazy liberal thinking and at the same time were the dominant force behind the communist threat; and they had treacherously stabbed the Kaiser's government in the back and were the main authors of the Weimar fiasco. Hitler denounced even the colours of Germany's flag as seditious, the black representing the Catholic International, the red the Socialist International, and the yellow the cowardice of the Jewish conspiracy. He replaced them with the swastika.

Linked with this racialism went a lust for territory. The Nazis laid claim to what they called the 'empty' lands of the east, peopled only by Slavs, which they could put to better use as living space (*Lebensraum*) for the chosen people. It was the destiny of this chosen *Volk* to conquer and to rule the world. A lot of Germans were flattered into believing this seductive nonsense; those who did not usually thought it better to keep their doubts to themselves.

Anti-Semitism

It was the Jews who bore the brunt of Nazi policies. Germany had about 600,000 Jews, many in key positions in government, universities, civil service and the professions. They were regarded as scapegoats for all Germany's ills, and driven from public life. There were many Germans who were happy to see them removed in order that they might plunder their property, or walk into their jobs.

(a) 1933, *Law to Restore the Professional Bureaucracy* dismissed non-Aryans from the medical profession, the civil service, the universities and administration.
(b) 1935, *Julius Streicher* began systematic Jew-baiting, destroying and confiscating property especially in retail business, despoiling synagogues, etc.
(c) 1935, *Nuremberg Laws* redefined citizenship to exclude Jews. Those in trade were deprived of their shops and offices; manufacturers were not allowed to employ non-Jewish labour, since it was not fitting that a Jew should be the master of a German; finally Jewish families were not even allowed to employ German girls as housemaids. In the end, thousands of Jews were rounded up and carted off to concentration camps, where they eventually died of neglect or were pitilessly exterminated.
(d) 1938, *Crystal Night* (the 'Night of the Broken Glass', 9 November) organized by the SA and the SS, set fire to synagogues, looted shops and arrested large numbers of Jews; afterwards Goering fined the Jews 1 billion marks 'for their ruthless crimes'.
(e) 1942, the *Final Solution*, i.e. complete extermination for the Jewish race, was planned with Himmler as the 'front man', and Hitler always taking care to distance himself from it in the records of discussions.

This was to most people the most inconceivable part of Nazism, one which was so monstrous that many were not able to believe it even with the evidence before them.

The churches

The churches also came into conflict with the Nazis.

The Catholics

Hitler signed a concordat with the Papacy in 1933 in the hope of appeasing opinion in Catholic parts of Germany; but his racialism upset the Pope and in 1937 Pius XI condemned Hitler's policies in his encyclical *Mit brennender Sorge* ('With Burning Anguish'). Resistance to Hitler was greatest in the Rhineland.

The Lutherans

The Lutheran Church was also alienated, part of it rallying behind the ex-submarine commander Pastor Niemöller in condemning Hitler's behaviour. Niemöller was sent to a concentration camp, and the rest of his church was cowed into silence. Hitler had at least one willing supporter, Pastor Müller, who was made evangelical bishop of the Reich in 1933, adapting the church's teachings to the Nazi philosophy, and claiming to find racialism in the scriptures. Church observance continued within the Reich, but its role was strictly subordinated to the state.

Youth

Hitler attached great importance to the young, many of whom were more fanatical than their parents. Children would join the Little Fellows at six, and the *Jungvolk* at ten, and could graduate to the Hitler Youth at fourteen. The girls joined the League of German Maidens, revering motherhood as the highest aim to which they could aspire. Formed in 1926, the Hitler Youth by 1934 numbered 6 million boys.

Great emphasis was laid on outdoor activities and physical fitness, with summer camps, drilling and learning Nazi doctrines. On leaving school, boys did six months' compulsory labour service for the good of the Reich, followed in most cases by two years in the army. Some later joined the SS or the Gestapo. In the case of girls, stress was laid on domestic things ('Kinder, Kirche, Küche': 'Children, church, kitchen').

Nazis had an instinctive revulsion against intellectuals, whose independent habits of thought they distrusted and feared. Under Hitler, education became a vehicle of state propaganda, like the radio and the newspapers.

Culture

Tight controls were also maintained on theatre, films, music and all forms of art. The standards enforced were not only politically rigid, but morally extremely conventional and puritanical – for instance, the use of lipstick was banned, and in detective stories only one murder was allowed 'for fear that the baser instincts should be encouraged'. At the same time, the top leaders did not always subscribe to these standards, but were shamelessly corrupt and cynical. Critics of the regime found themselves singled out for punishment, and publications hostile to the Reich and even works of genuine scholarship were burned on bonfires.

▷ **Machine or morass?**

Germany, however, was far from being a truly totalitarian state. It possessed a frightening apparatus of control and detection – concealed microphones, sophisticated interrogation techniques and so on – but these were only spasmodically applied. The much-vaunted state control was really rather patchy. Vast vested interests went unchallenged by the state, and there were many private empires of control from which the Nazis averted their eyes, or which they even actually encouraged.

In particular, Nazi economic controls were a hit-and-miss affair, in which favouritism and jobbery were rampant and business malpractice almost routine. With these interests and with the Gestapo and the SS free from proper civil control, Nazi government operations resembled the seedy machinations of the gangster underworld rather than any systematic tyranny. It was as much the frivolous caprice of the Nazi regime as its brutality which struck terror into the hearts of those who observed it.

▷ **Nazi economic policy**

Though Hitler had broad general aims when he came to power, he had given little sustained thought to actual policies, and had none ready to put into effect. In practice he was in the hands of civil service officials, and simply left them to get on with it. Hence his policies in 1933 were largely those that had earlier been suggested to Brüning by his civil servants, but which had been rejected by him then because of their cost.

Labour relations

From the tone of all his speeches, one of Hitler's main aims was to remedy the grave unemployment problem existing in Germany when the Nazis came to power. To a large extent his efforts were successful. Many people found jobs in the huge new Nazi bureaucracy and in organizations such as the Hitler Youth, however pointless many of these jobs may have been. Others were able to take over from displaced Jews. A number stayed in jobs where they were really redundant, kept there by government orders; yet others went into the forces or into arms factories as rearmament progressed. The Nazis drafted young people into compulsory labour service, in camps and working for a little pocket-money to show their patriotic devotion. Before the end of the 1930s, unemployment had shrunk to little more than 250,000.

Hitler had much natural sympathy with German labour, and took care to cultivate good relations with it. After the suspension of trade unions in 1933 on account of their support for his political opponents, Hitler put forward his *German Workers' Front*, and in January 1934 he produced a *Law Regulating National Labour* which brought labour organizations under state control, and appointed 'trustees of labour' to look after their interests. In the following October, all these were brought together into the *German Labour Front*, under Dr Robert Ley, Gauleiter of Cologne, a man more known for his capacity for strong drink than for his interest in workers' problems.

There is no doubt that many German workers benefited from Nazi government. They were always regularly in work, and conditions were good. Wages, though controlled, improved during the 1930s, and in any case Hitler also controlled rents and prices. Workers saved to buy the cheap sturdy cars that Hitler promised to make available; they had sports and recreational activities, and were provided with holidays with pay, so they were able to take their families to 'strength through joy' holiday camps.

Industrial policy

Though there was duplication and inefficiency, this was largely successful in restoring Germany's economic health:

(a) *Public works.* These included forestry, land reclamation, the construction of auto-bahns, town planning improvements and new public buildings.

(b) *Manufacturing.* The Nazis concentrated on heavy industrial capacity, especially for war purposes. Coal, steel, shipbuilding and chemicals all developed rapidly. There was some development of consumer manufacture, e.g. automobiles, but even this was subordinated to heavier road transport.

(c) *Rearmament.* After 1935, work began on the construction of a new *Luftwaffe* (air force); after 1936, Goering's *Four-Year Plan*, which to some extent was clearly inspired by Stalin, stimulated massive increases in arms output. In 1938–39, the Siegfried Line was built to protect Germany's western frontier.

(d) Germany aimed at economic independence (*autarky*), so avoiding waste and cutting back on imports. This involved systematic salvage campaigns, and the use of *ersatz* materials, like coffee made from acorns or dandelion roots, oil and petrol from coal, and a tough sort of synthetic rubber used for vehicle tyres. Goering's Four-Year Plan was supposed to make Germany entirely independent of imports, but in fact produced only limited results.

Financial policy

Hitler had been aware from the start that the main danger to his programme would be inflation. If the government succumbed to the temptation to print money, as it had in 1923, another flood of worthless paper might swamp the country. In order to satisfy the numerous groups which feared inflation, Hitler was obliged to keep things in check. One way was by strict controls over wages and prices. These could never be completely successful, but at least they put a brake on uncontrolled rises.

Budget deficits were avoided by raising loans from people with money to invest, relying on the confidence which such people felt in the government. Those who benefited most from flourishing trade, low tax levels and modest wage increases were the employers, who were made to pay for the privilege with rising corporation taxes, so that the companies had to help to pay for the schemes they were working on.

The Nazis also helped to finance heavy government spending by allowing the issue of special bonds (called 'Mefo' bonds, because they were based on the *Metalforschung* – a private steel-making company, whose dividends were guaranteed by the state). They were used for paying for public works projects, and could be cashed immediately at the Reichsbank, or kept for up to five years at a rate of 5 per cent, at which time the state redeemed them. Their issue postponed the evil day, but ultimately they were as inflationary as printed money: by 1938 the bonds amounted to 42,000 million RM.

Trading policy

One result of job creation was greatly increased consumer demand, producing a steep rise in imports. But since much of the work being done was for rearmament and construction work at home, Germany had little to export in exchange. Thus the country soon found itself in a balance of payments crisis. The task of dealing with this crisis fell to Dr Schacht, President of the Reichsbank.

His aim was to manage trade in such a way as to boost exports and restrict imports. One way of doing this was to pay for imports by exporting part of Germany's arms output. Customers were not always interested in buying this, but if they bought guns, they would certainly need ammunition later. Another method was to arrange deliveries of foodstuffs and raw materials, to delay paying for them as long as possible, and then in the end to pay with credits which could only be spent in Germany. Most complex of all was a fiendishly ingenious system whereby Schacht maintained over 250 different exchange rates at the same time for the German mark, blocking off all the country's external trade into a series of different compartments, each at a different rate of exchange.

By the end of the 1930s, Germany's trade was becoming more and more unbalanced. Schacht was forced to resign from the cabinet in 1937, and then from the Reichsbank in 1939, his 'system' in ruins about him. In the end, the Nazis were forced to leave their import bills unpaid; having failed to trade with their neighbours in the normal way, the Nazis were driven to cheat them; and finally, they were driven to exploit them by conquest and occupation.

Foreign policy, 1933–45

▷ **A policy of design or drift?**

Hitler's motives on coming to power were clear. He wished to remove the stigma of the Treaty of Versailles, repudiate the notion of war guilt, reject the reparations burden and set about the restoration of the country's self-esteem.

In particular, he did not intend to be bound by the disarmament clauses, which were clearly unfair if they did not lead to general disarmament, and which were in any case an affront to German honour and pride. He was also determined to recover the territories taken from Germany in 1919, and even to establish control over lands where there was a German population living, even though these lands had not previously been in German ownership. 'One blood demands one Reich' was the phrase he used to describe these foreign policy objectives.

The question is still debated whether Hitler had – as many historians have believed – some 'grand design', a carefully worked out programme of expansion and, if need be, war; or whether he was purely an opportunist with broad but flexible objectives, seizing every opportunity to exploit the weaknesses and fears of other powers. Some see him as a lucky gambler who came up on so many bets that he began to think he could not lose.

▷ **A policy of recovery**

(See also chapter 11, pp. 141–3.) From the start, Hitler aimed to reverse the Treaty of Versailles and to reunite the German people under the government of the Reich.

In 1934, however, he had little success, for Mussolini – a man whom Hitler much admired and respected at first – blocked his designs on Austria. He was forced hastily to disavow his attempted takeover of that country and to try to shift the blame on to the Austrian Nazi Party. It was a humiliating reverse, but as yet he was not strong enough to cope with opposition.

The start of rearmament

In *January 1935*, Hitler wanted to find out the inclinations of the Saarland, since he wished once again to incorporate it into the Reich. He therefore arranged a plebiscite there, and was gratified to see that nearly all of its people rejected its existing status, and 95 per cent of them wanted to be reunited with Germany. Hitler issued a special postage stamp to commemorate the reunion; the caption on it read 'The Saar Comes Home'. This did not breach the terms of the treaty, though the French feared that it might mean the start of Germany's westwards expansion.

In *March 1935*, Hitler went on to his first clear breach of the Versailles Treaty. After the collapse of the Geneva Disarmament Conference at the end of the previous year, he repudiated the treaty's disarmament clauses, and set about the building of a peacetime army of 36 divisions, or about 550,000 men. Though this number was more than five times greater than the figure allowed under the treaty, his actions passed almost unchallenged.

Hitler even persuaded Britain to sign a naval treaty in June, agreeing to the rebuilding of the German navy, provided that its total strength did not exceed 35 per cent of the British navy, and that there were no submarines. He had no intention of being bound by this for ever, but at least he was starting rearmament with consent.

Remilitarizing the Rhineland

In *March 1936*, while Italian troops were engaging the world's attention by invading Abyssinia, Hitler struck again. This time, he repudiated the Locarno agreements as well as breaking the Versailles Treaty, by marching his troops into the Rhineland to remilitarize it. It was Saturday morning, 7 March. This was an act of considerable daring, since only three battalions of troops, many on motorbikes, actually crossed the Rhine that day. If there had been resistance, Hitler would almost certainly have been compelled to withdraw again. His own position in Germany was not yet completely secure, and this might well have been the end of him. But neither Britain nor France reacted, and Hitler was allowed to get away with his defiance.

On the outbreak of civil war in Spain in the summer of 1936, Hitler used the opportunity to reassert Germany as a major power by sending help to the nationalist side. He also took advantage of circumstances to sign two alliances with sympathetic powers:

(a) In *November 1936*, Germany and Japan, both feeling themselves threatened by the Soviet Union, signed the *Anti-Comintern Pact* (the Comintern was the Communist International, set up in Moscow supposedly to supervise subversive activities in capitalist states, but was really no more than an organ of Russian propaganda). Italy had also been pencilled in as a member, but did not actually join until 1937.

(b) In *October 1937*, a vague, but rather important pact was signed with Mussolini; it was known as the *Rome–Berlin Axis*, and under it both powers sent forces to the support of Franco in Spain.

The Anschluss with Austria

Hitler's failure to secure an *Anschluss* (= Union) with Austria in 1934 still rankled in his mind, and, now that his position was stronger, Hitler determined to renew his efforts. In February, he summoned the Austrian Chancellor Schuschnigg to Berlin and berated him in the most undiplomatic terms:

> Don't think for a moment that anyone is going to thwart my decisions. Italy? I see eye-to-eye with Mussolini . . . England? England will not move one finger for Austria . . . France? It is too late for France. I give you once more, and for the last time, the opportunity to come to terms. Either we find a solution now, or else events will take their course. Think it over, Herr Schuschnigg, and think it over well.

Schuschnigg was simply browbeaten into submission. Austrian Nazis such as Seyss-Inquart were promoted to key positions, and in March, after stirring up violence by means of its suppliant Nazi groups, Hitler provided himself with an excuse to march his troops in on the pretext of restoring order, and to take over power there.

Again the western powers did very little. Hitler was left glowing with pride that his native Austria was now part of the Third Reich.

The Sudetenland crisis and the annexation of Czechoslovakia

With the annexation of Austria, Czechoslovakia was now exposed to pressure from three sides. It was against that country later in 1938 that Hitler made his next move. The German population of the Sudetenland, led by Konrad Henlein, claimed that they were being persecuted by the Czechs. They produced a list of grievances, demanding that they be investigated at once, and remedied; if not, they wanted independence from Czech control for German-speaking areas. During the investigation, the crisis cooled off somewhat, but it blew up again in September with a violently anti-Czech speech by Hitler at the Nuremberg Rally. A conference was held in Munich at the end of the month to resolve the problem, as a result of which the western powers eventually allowed Hitler to have his own way, and to take over areas where German-speaking populations lived. This action could still be represented as reuniting the German people under the Reich.

Little more than six months later, Hitler seized the rest of Czechoslovakia as well, making it into a protectorate of the Reich and responding to Slovak criticisms of its government by splitting off the eastern half of the country. For the first time, Hitler, instead of working for the reunion of German peoples with the Reich, could be accused of blatant aggression against a friendly neighbouring state.

The Polish crisis

In *March 1939*, Hitler presented an ultimatum to Lithuania and occupied Memelland, where a considerable number of Germans lived; Memelland was then added on to East Prussia.

Then it was the turn of Danzig, the other leading city on the Baltic coast denied to Germany by the Treaty of Versailles. In March, Hitler made his interest in its 600,000 citizens known. Hitler demanded not only that Albert Forster, its Nazi Gauleiter, should be left free to manage their affairs free from Polish interference, but also that Danzig should be ceded to Germany. The Germans should also be granted the right to open up a strategic road and rail route across the Polish Corridor, thus connecting Germany with

East Prussia via the city of Danzig. The Poles took this as an affront to their own national pride and angrily rejected these demands.

The western democracies also made it quite clear that they were not prepared to tolerate a Nazi attack on Poland.

In *August 1939*, however, Hitler pulled off his most brilliant coup by settling with Soviet Union, which had its own ambitions in eastern Poland. Molotov and Ribbentrop, whose officials had been negotiating in Moscow since May, produced a Russo-German *Non-Aggression Pact* – an agreement which included secret clauses arranging the partition of Poland between the two. Hitler thus successfully pulled out the rug from under the western democracies, leaving them quite incapable of aiding Poland in any practical way. On 1 September, after carefully staged frontier incidents, Nazi forces invaded Poland and the Second World War began.

▷ The Second World War and the end of Hitler

Though spectacularly successful in overrunning Norway, Denmark, the Lowlands and France, and much of the Balkans, Hitler, by invading the Soviet Union in 1941, eventually bit off more than he could chew. He seemed to think that the USSR could easily be overrun – he said at the outset of the campaign, 'You only have to kick in the door and the whole rotten structure will collapse' – but for once his 'intuition' was not infallible and his run of luck deserted him.

Reasons for Hitler's defeat

Hitler was at war with Britain and the Commonwealth, with the USA and with the Soviet Union, whose combined *populations and natural resources* far outstripped his own. Though he secured control over Romanian oil, he never quite reached the rich resources of the Caucasus, and his access to other valuable materials was also very restricted.

At sea, he was beaten by the British and Allied navies and was subject to a crippling blockade. Submarine counterattack in 1941 and 1942 was very successful for a time, but ultimately the U-boats were neither numerous nor powerful enough to influence the final outcome of the Battle of the Atlantic. By 1943, the Nazis were penned into 'Fortress Europe' and their contacts with the outside world were severed.

After the Battle of Britain and the Blitz in 1940–41, the Allies also achieved great superiority *in the air*. German towns, ports and industrial plants were mercilessly hammered. Thousand-bomber raids took place by night, and in the later stages of the war, daytime raids proceeded almost incessantly. When they re-entered France in 1944, Allied troops had invincible air cover and were able to drive the once-victorious Luftwaffe from the skies.

Fig. 9.1 Maximum expansion of Germany

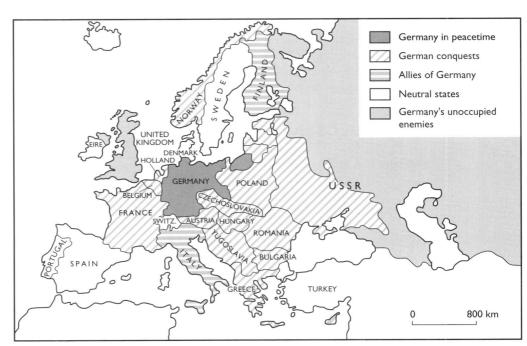

Local *resistance movements* also played their part in wearing the Germans down. In a number of countries, such as France, the local 'Maquis' (so called after the moorland brushwood where the resistance sometimes had its hideouts) sabotaged bridges, railways, local supply lines and troop movements, organized espionage and helped in the transportation of escaped prisoners-of-war and crashed airmen to safe locations. Communist sympathizers figured large in such movements, and this gave a somewhat political flavour to resistance activities.

Hitler, too, relied on some rather unsatisfactory *allies*. One of them, *Japan*, was on the other side of the world and was only of limited value; the Japanese were brilliantly successful for a time, but eventually ran out of steam in their efforts to dominate the Pacific. *Finland* was technically his ally as a result of the Soviet Union's attack during the Winter War of 1940–41, but had only a small population and few resources, and was never whole-heartedly on the Nazi side. *Italy*, of course, came closest to Hitler's outlook and ambitions, and had been his rather luckless ally during the Spanish Civil War; but Hitler was called on to go to the support of the Italians both in North Africa and in the Balkans, and in the end Mussolini's alliance was more trouble than it was worth.

The German resistance

Within Germany there was little resistance to the Führer's rule. Opposition groups took care to stay out of sight; like fugitive Jews they sometimes had to live in self-imposed imprisonment in order to survive. After 1943, furthermore, the Nazi leaders were hidden away from the public eye; no one was able assassinate them, even if they were willing to take the risk. Hitler hid himself in the Chancellery in Berlin, at Berchtesgaden in Bavaria, or at his remote military HQ in the fastnesses of East Prussia; he moved from one to another unpredictably, and hardly anybody had the least idea where he was at any given time. Few people ever came into regular contact with him, and those who did were never allowed to be armed – revolvers made the Führer nervous. Besides, every German soldier had taken a personal oath of loyalty to him, and the vast majority would rather die than betray him.

Nevertheless there were a few of the officer class who rated their loyalty to their fatherland higher than their loyalty to the Führer. Two early attempts to kill him – one by handing over a bomb which was supposed to be a gift of bottles of brandy, the other by demonstrating to him a new type of army greatcoat which happened to have explosive charges hidden in the pockets – both came to nothing in 1943. The *Stauffenberg Bomb Plot* of 1944 came the closest to success. It was carefully planned and meticulously executed, and it failed by the merest of flukes. But the hideous reprisals inflicted on the participants (which were filmed and then screened for the entertainment of Hitler and his cronies) were a sufficient deterrent to any others thinking along the same lines.

By 1945, the Russians were at the gates of Berlin, having overrun Poland and most of eastern Europe. On 30 April, with the Red Army scarcely half a mile away, Hitler shot himself in his bunker and his body was doused with petrol and burned in the garden of the Chancellery. The Third Reich, which was to have lasted a thousand years, had perished in little more than ten.

GLOSSARY

Gestapo   A secret state police, *Geheime Staatspolizei*, created when Hitler came to power in 1933. Its leadership was given to Himmler, already chief of the SS, in 1934, and by 1939 it was part of the SS organization. Its particular responsibility was the intelligence service, and it sought out opponents of the regime and could imprison and execute without recourse to law. Together with the SS it was given responsibility for the concentration camps and the mass exterminations which took place within them. It ended with the regime in 1945.

SA   An organization of the Nazi Party, *Sturm Abteilung*, founded by Hitler in Munich in 1921. Its members became known as brownshirts because of their distinctive brown uniforms, and it became the Nazi Party's unofficial militia. At first it merely helped to organize and control public meetings, but it soon began organizing and distributing party propaganda, attacking opponents and breaking up their meetings. It adopted a vigorously anti-Semitic stance, and encouraged and participated in physical attacks on Jews and the destruction of Jewish property. Some of its members clung to the early socialism of the Nazis and this made them suspect both with the new Nazi supporters among the business classes and with the army. When the army made it clear that its support of Hitler was conditional on his getting rid of the rival army, the SA, Hitler did not hesitate, and on the Night of the Long Knives the SS killed Röhm and the rest of the SA leadership, and the rank and file membership was disbanded or absorbed into the SS.

SS   Founded in 1925, originally as Hitler's personal bodyguard, the *Schutzstaffel* demanded absolute loyalty to the leader and absolute ruthlessness in carrying out its duties. Members of the SS wore black uniforms and the distinctive emblem of a lightning flash to symbolize their speed and efficiency. In 1929 Heinrich Himmler became its chief, a post he retained until 1945; he turned the SS into a militarily trained and politically indoctrinated Nazi élite. The SS was used to eliminate its larger rival, the SA, in 1934. Together with its political wing, the Gestapo, it took responsibility for the running of the Nazi concentration camps, and it was the most feared of all instruments of Nazi terror.

EXAMINATION QUESTIONS

▷ **Question 1**   Study Sources A–C below and then answer the questions which follow.

Source A

The meeting began at 7.30 and ended at 10.45. The lecturer gave a talk on Jewry. He showed that wherever one looks, one sees Jews. It is a scandal that the German workers . . . let themselves be so harassed by the Jews. Of course the Jew has money in his hands. The Jew sits in government and swindles and smuggles . . . Therefore, Germans, be united and fight against the Jews!

(A local party secretary describes one of Hitler's first speeches, 1919)

Source B

Teachers are directed to instruct their pupils in the nature, causes and effects of all racial problems, to bring home to them the importance of race . . . to awaken pride in their membership of the German race . . . and the will to cooperate in the racial purification of the German stock.

(Order from the Reich Minister of Education, Dr Rust, January 1935)

Source C

Berlin had [in 1933] 32% Jewish chemists, 48% Jewish doctors, 50% Jewish lawyers, $8\frac{1}{2}$% Jewish newspaper editors . . . No people on earth with a vestige of pride in itself could put up with such domination of many professions by members of a completely alien race.

(Dr Gross, Head of the Reich Bureau for Enlightenment on Population Policy and Racial Welfare, quoted in a book published for British readers by the German Embassy in London, 1938)

(a)   How would you demonstrate Hitler's bias in Source A?   (4 marks)
(b)   What can you learn from Source B about the nature of the Nazi regime in Germany?
                                                                      (4 marks)
(c)   How reliable is Source C as a statement of the position of Jews in Germany in 1933?   (5 marks)
(d)   How for do these sources show why there was no widespread opposition in Germany to the persecution of the Jews?   (7 marks)

▷ **Question 2**   (a)   What were the main aims of Hitler's foreign policy?   (15 marks)
              (b)   Why was there no large-scale opposition in Germany to Hitler's foreign policy?
                                                                      (10 marks)

▷ **Question 3**   The world economic depression; the Reichstag Fire; the Enabling Law; the Night of the Long Knives. Each of these played an important part in Hitler's taking control of Germany. Which do you think was the most important? Explain your answer.

EXAMINATION ANSWERS

▷ **Question 1**   *Outline answer*

(a) The bias is to be found in the emotive language – 'scandal', 'harassed', 'swindles and smuggles' – in the deliberate linking of Jews with money, and in the overall tone of the passage, which culminates in a call to fight Jews.

(b) The source shows the totalitarian nature of the regime, in that not only does it instruct teachers on racialism, it expects them to conform and to teach a state-directed view of race and racial purification. The implication is that by controlling education, the state will control the minds of the young.

(c) Because the figures in Source C originate from the German government in an attempt to defend its anti-Jewish policy, the figures may well be suspect. Even if true, they do not show how far the Jews were overrepresented in comparison with their percentage of the population. The hostile use of the figures made by Dr Gross, and the overstatement ('dominated'), suggests that the figures have been inflated.

(d) All the sources are relevant here. Source A shows that from the very beginning of Nazism it pursued a vigorous policy of anti-Semitism, and the indoctrination of adults shown in Source A was in the early 1930s extended to children (Source B). Source C shows the pseudo-statistical support the Nazis used to try to justify their policy. Anti-Semitism has tended to breed where there has been poverty, envy and ignorance. The Nazis, by deliberately fostering it, and by the totalitarian methods hinted at in Source B, tried to make sure that the silent majority would be at worst supportive of and at best indifferent to the Nazi anti-Jewish policy. The sources do not show how successful the Nazis were in spreading anti-Semitism; the lack of widespread opposition to it may well have had more to do with the difficulties encountered by any sort of opposition under a totalitarian regime.

▷ **Question 2**   *Tutor's answer*

(a) Hitler's overall aim was to make Germany a great power again. He did not consider the Weimar Republic a great power, tied as it was to the Treaty of Versailles, committed to paying reparations, compelled to disarm and shrunk in size. So although his first priority was to overthrow Versailles, this would have to take place over an extended period, because the overthrowing of Versailles required the rebuilding of Germany's military capabilities. As the German disarmament required by Versailles was not accompanied by any genuine move to worldwide disarmament, Hitler regarded the disarmament clauses as unfair and discriminatory. In 1933 he took Germany out of the Disarmament Conference and began the building up of an army greatly in excess of the 100,000 allowed by Versailles. This army was necessary if the territorial arrangements of Versailles were to be challenged. The naval agreement with Britain in 1935 was more about the recovery of prestige than naval necessity. Hitler's aims were purely continental, and he did not plan the recovery of Germany's lost colonies, for which a navy would have been essential. Nevertheless a strong navy would be needed to counter a blockade such as the Allied one of 1917–18, which had been so effective. Hitler was also determined to create a German air force. This was in part intended as a direct defiance of the disarmament clauses of Versailles, in part as a prestige issue, and in part as a necessity if Germany was to play an active and aggressive role in international relations. Hitler's intervention in the Spanish Civil War gave his forces some valuable war experience and his country some valuable prestige, and reiterated Hitler's hatred of communism.

Hitler regarded the crippling burden of reparations with contempt. It was part of the diktat by which the Allies blamed Germany for the war and extracted financial compensation. Hitler could not build his armaments or rebuild Germany's prestige if Germany was to continue to be drained of money to pay reparations. Hitler simply announced that Germany would no longer pay, and the Allies had neither the inclination nor the means to enforce payment.

Allied unwillingness to challenge Hitler made his aim to reverse the territorial provisions of Versailles easier to achieve. His first priority, to restore full German sovereignty over the Saar and the Rhineland, was achieved in 1935 and 1936. The *Anschluss* had been an ambition clearly indicated in *Mein Kampf*, and, although thwarted by Mussolini in 1934 and specifically forbidden by Versailles, it was accomplished in 1938. Hitler's policy of including all Germans within a greater German Reich moved a step closer with the absorption of the Sudetenland in 1938. Memel, lost at Versailles, was seized in 1939. The recovery of the other lost lands of 1919 had to wait until the Second World War: Danzig and the Polish Corridor in 1939; northern Schleswig, Eupen and Malmédy and Alsace-Lorraine in 1940.

War enabled Hitler to fulfil another of his *Mein Kampf* ambitions. His search for *Lebensraum*, to give the German people more living space, was not directed against Germany's western neighbours, but in 1939, following the occupation of Poland, thousands of German settlers poured into Posen and West Prussia, and part of the justification for the attack on Russia in 1941 was the plan for the eventual settlement of German populations in the Ukraine and on the Russian steppes.

There was probably no pre-conceived plan for the achievement of these various aims, but by 1941 Hitler could well claim that he had virtually achieved all of them.

(b) It is difficult to organize large-scale opposition to anything in a totalitarian state. Most people do not wish to stand up to be counted, even in a democracy, and to oppose Hitler publicly was the quickest way to summon the unwelcome notice of the Gestapo. Hitler's Reich naturally had no opposition parties to channel dissatisfaction with his policies, and those who disapproved wisely kept their opinions to themselves. Their private opinions, too, were subject to the attentions of Hitler's propaganda machine. It had been so often repeated that the Treaty of Versailles was a diktat that the vast majority of Germans had come to believe it. That Hitler intended to tear up the Versailles Treaty was to them a laudable aim if it could be done without effective international opposition. Through the 1930s Hitler's foreign policy consisted of one success after another – the Saar, the Rhineland, Spain, the *Anschluss*, Czechoslovakia – so that it seemed that Hitler could do no wrong. Germany was a great power again. And when war came in 1939, whatever their misgivings, the German people rallied patriotically behind Hitler, and his early successes consolidated that support. In the later stages of the war, when there was disaster in Russia, and German cities were being devastated by air attack, it was too late: German people could despair, but they had neither the will nor the means to oppose.

Of course, there was one group which could well have opposed Hitler's policy at an early stage. He depended on the generals and the army to carry out his plans if they met with resistance. But the army had been bought. In insisting on the removal of the SA as a condition of their support for Hitler in 1934, they became implicated in the Night of the Long Knives, and no longer retained the independence to oppose Hitler. As late as Munich in 1938, some officers were planning to use a foreign policy setback to remove Hitler and avoid the danger of a Second World War. But there were no foreign policy setbacks, and the army tamely submitted when its Commander-in-Chief was dismissed in 1938. Nor did the army make any concerted attempt to resist Hitler's rush to war in 1939. All the other organizations, the police, the judiciary, the church, the Hitler Youth, the teaching profession were under close Nazi control; their ability to organize large-scale opposition was negligible. And so, despite the disasters that Hitler's foreign policy had brought upon Germany by 1945, the regime was destroyed not by internal opposition, but by the external enemy.

▷ **Question 3** *Student answer with examiner's comments*

All these are important in Hitler's rise to power and the establishment of his dictatorship. The answer really depends on whether coming to power means taking control, or whether taking control means achieving absolute and unchallengable power. If the former, then the economic depression is most important. It brought about the massive unemployment among the working class and the fear of inflation among the middle-class that boosted the Nazi Party electrally into the largest single party. In so doing it made the Nazis indispensable in any political manoevrings within the Weimar Republic so that when Hindenburg had exhausted all the options

'The argument becomes a little tortuous at this point.'

he inevitably turned to Hitler. Without the depression Hitler's chance might never have come. His 12 seats in the Reichstag in 1929 did not provide him with a power base, and while Germany enjoyed the Stresseman boom the German electors rejected extremist parties like the Nazis.

So the deppresion brought Hitler to power, and he took control immediately. The strings of ministerial decrees, the removal of known opponents from public office, the intimidation on the streets – these did not wait for the Fire or the Enabling Law. Hitler had every intention of ruling by decree and outlawing the communists; the Reichstag Fire merely gave him the opportunity to do so with a semblance of legality. With the Enabling Law the Reichstag was reduced to impotance; but Hitler had actually taken control the moment he became Chancellor in January. After the Enabling Law the problem was not so much one of control, which by now was firmly established, but the need to eliminate any possible challenge. By offering the SA as a sacrifice to the demands of the army, Hitler had bought the support of the army and made his control even more secure. But only the World Depression was vital to his taking control; the others merely smoothed his path afterwards.

Examiner's decision on the student answer

Not all would necessarily agree with this line of argument. It could well be argued that Hitler did not really have absolute control until he had the army in his pocket. But that does not matter. For GCSE any well-substantiated argument must reach a high Level. Here top Level is for those who take all the listed points into account and argue which one was the most important. The slight hiccup in the argument referred to above is not important enough to detract from the overall quality of the answer. Some good answers will be longer, but this is admirably succinct. With a tariff for the highest Level of 18–20, it would be difficult to refuse 20 for this work, in spite of the spelling.

SUMMARY

In this chapter you have studied the main features of the Nazi regime in Germany. These include:

▷ the Nazi consolidation of power, e.g. the Reichstag Fire;

▷ the centralization of the Nazi government;

▷ Nazi methods of control and repression;

▷ Nazi racial policies, their aims and results;

▷ Nazi policies towards the churches, youth and culture;

▷ economic policies, finance and trading;

▷ labour relations under the Nazis;

▷ Nazi rearmament policies;

▷ Hitler's foreign policy;

▷ Hitler and the Second World War;

▷ the growth of resistance in Germany to Hitler's rule.

Further information relating to this subject is provided in:

▷ chapter 11 on international relations 1933–39;

▷ chapter 12 on the Second World War;

▷ chapter 15 on the treatment of Germany after the Second World War.

Chapter

10 Stalin

 GETTING STARTED

After the death of Lenin, Josef Stalin clawed his way to the top and was effectively ruler of the Soviet Union from 1926 to 1953. During this time, he dragged the Soviet Union into the twentieth century, transforming it from 'a country with wooden ploughs into one with atomic generators'.

MEG	NEAB	NICCEA	SEG	LONDON	WJEC	TOPIC	STUDY	REVISION 1	REVISION 2
✓	✓	✓	✓	✓	✓	**Stalin works his way to the top**			
✓	✓	✓	✓	✓	✓	The rise of the 'Grey Blur'			
✓	✓	✓	✓	✓	✓	Stalin and Trotsky			
✓	✓	✓	✓	✓	✓	**Stalin and the Five-Year Plans**			
✓	✓	✓	✓	✓	✓	The collectivization of Soviet agriculture			
✓	✓	✓	✓	✓	✓	The industrialization of the Soviet Union			
✓	✓	✓	✓	✓	✓	**Stalin the control-freak**			
✓	✓	✓	✓	✓	✓	The control of thoughts and actions			
✓	✓	✓	✓	✓	✓	The Great Purges			
✓	✓	✓	✓	✓	✓	**Stalin and the world**			
✓	✓	✓	✓	✓	✓	The beginnings of Soviet policies			
✓	✓	✓	✓	✓	✓	The approach of war			
	✓			✓	✓	The 'Great Patriotic War'			
	✓			✓	✓	**Later career of Stalin**			
	✓			✓	✓	Internal reconstruction, 1945–53			
	✓			✓	✓	External expansion			
	✓			✓	✓	**Assessment of Stalin**			

 WHAT YOU NEED TO KNOW

Stalin works his way to the top

▷ **The rise of the 'Grey Blur'**

Under Stalin, Soviet industry made spectacular advances; agriculture was collectivized; the Bolshevik revolution was completed and consolidated; and Stalin led his people triumphantly through the Second World War.

Yet collectivization was a near fiasco and led to widespread famine; the 'purges' of the Communist Party were a nightmare; and Stalin's clumsiness in foreign policy was compounded by strategic errors in the early stages of the war. None of Stalin's successors would have retained power in the light of such blunders, yet his ruthlessness allowed him to survive; indeed, at the time of his death his power still seemed unshakeable.

Stalin's background

Josef Djugashvili was born in 1879 in the Caucasian province of Georgia in the south of the Russian Empire. Though his parents were poor – he was one of the few Bolshevik leaders to spring from the working class – his parents sent him to a Tiflis seminary to train for the priesthood, and it was there that he fell under the influence of Marxist teachings. His political activities and his lack of religious commitment led him to expulsion from the seminary and into trouble with the Tsarist police – though he retained to the end something of the high priest's style in the devotion he accorded to the precious scriptures produced by Marx and by Lenin.

Like most of the other revolutionaries, he adopted a shorter and in his case a less non-Russian 'alias', Stalin, and spent much of his time in activities that would be difficult to reconcile with any lofty revolutionary ideals. He was frequently on the run from the police. Indeed, he spent about seven years in gaols and in labour camps before 1917. These years gave him plenty of experience as an agitator and a revolutionary, distributing propaganda, holding secret political meetings and organizing demonstrations. He even planned a remarkable bank robbery in 1907, but its success was marred by the fact that the banknotes were marked and were therefore unusable. But while Hitler was lying on his back daydreaming in a Vienna dosshouse, Stalin was learning to weigh up and to outsmart his ambitious political rivals.

Stalin and the Central Committee

By 1917, Stalin was a well-known figure in his native province of Georgia, and though he was in exile in Siberia when the February Revolution took place, he was soon released under the amnesty, and returned to European Russia along with a number of others, such as Lev Kamenev. He gained valuable experience as co-editor of *Pravda*, the Bolshevik newspaper, where he set about advocating cooperation and reunion with the Mensheviks, and support for the Provisional Government in the war. These were views of his colleagues, rather than his own. But when Lenin came back to Russia in April and found it necessary to oppose such thinking, Stalin swung round and became one of his early converts, won over by the persuasiveness of Lenin's arguments.

After the Bolshevik coup, Lenin rewarded Stalin by making him People's Commissar for the Nationalities, a post for which he was thought to be particularly suitable on account of his Georgian origin. During the civil wars which followed, he gave useful service as a military commissar, though he did not always see eye to eye with Trotsky, and Lenin was rather irritated at the way the two quarrelled. When, in 1919, he took charge of the Workers' and Peasants' Inspectorate, he acquired the right to intervene in the operation of all government departments, an activity which he really relished. But his most important appointment was in 1922 when the Politburo appointed him to the newly created post of party General Secretary. It may be that certain of the party leaders thought that in this post Stalin would be smothered in administrative detail, while they got on with the real business of policy making; but in reality Stalin took to the work enthusiastically and soon developed the post far beyond what they had anticipated. He used his control over personnel records to keep a close watch on leading figures, as well as to appoint loyal followers to key positions and weed out those he could not entirely trust.

Through the Secretariat, Stalin created a party bureaucracy, loyal to himself, providing information and drawing up agendas for the Politburo to discuss. That Stalin was building up enormous power did not go unnoticed. In December 1922, only a few months after approving Stalin's appointment, Lenin wrote of him: 'Comrade Stalin, having become General Secretary, has concentrated enormous power in his own hands, and I am not sure whether he will always be capable of using that authority with sufficient caution.' Lenin's doubts led to distrust, and only a few weeks later he criticized Stalin again, even suggesting that he should be sacked: 'Stalin is too rude, and this shortcoming, though bearable in relations among us Communists, becomes quite unbearable in a General Secretary. I therefore suggest to you that you should remove Stalin from his post, and replace him with someone who is more patient, more loyal, more polite, more considerate to the needs of the comrades.'

But Lenin suffered a severe stroke soon afterwards, and was never able to follow through his threat by getting Stalin dismissed. Trotsky, who agreed with Lenin about Stalin, seemed unwilling to attack him while Lenin lived; for the moment Trotsky seemed more anxious to avoid splitting the party.

▷ **Stalin and Trotsky**   Lenin's illness left him helpless for a year, and when he died in January 1924 it was unclear who would take over from him. The main contenders were Stalin and Trotsky.

Basic issues

From their early encounters, Stalin saw things differently from Trotsky, and Trotsky felt that Stalin was boorish and uncouth.

Trotsky, though closer in sympathy to Lenin, was on rather shaky ground: he wanted *world revolution* to take precedence over socialism in Russia, but hopes of world revolution, high in 1918, had faded by 1924. Stalin shared with many Bolsheviks the view that the world should be left to its own devices: the party should concentrate on revolution within Russia ('*Socialism in one country*') to strengthen the country's resources and prepare it for defence, even if this meant continuing with something like the NEP, which many communists found repugnant.

Stalin's strength lay in reducing to their simplest elements issues which seemed complex to others, in encouraging his enemies to make mistakes, and in controlling the votes of the Central Committee, which he filled with his own nominees.

The power struggle

On Lenin's death there was a 'collective leadership' of Kamenev, Zinoviev and Stalin; these three worked together for their limited aims. Their cooperation brought the charge from Trotsky that Stalin was undermining party democracy, but Stalin's response was to increase membership of the Central Committee, chiefly by bringing in yet more of his own supporters.

By 1926, Zinoviev and Kamenev realized that Stalin was merely using them in the power struggle. They decided to throw in their lot with Trotsky, but it was too late. Stalin controlled the press, and *Pravda*'s innuendoes could not be contradicted in public; nor could the pair of them get any other public platform to explain their case. Thus Stalin made sure not only that Trotsky and his supporters were outvoted in the Fourteenth Party Congress (1925–26), but also that neither the Central Committee nor the Congress would so much as give them a hearing.

Trotsky was stripped of his Red Army command, then he and Zinoviev were expelled first from the Central Committee, and then from the party altogether. Kamenev made a humiliating recantation of his 'errors' and was allowed to stay (for the time being), and Zinoviev was also reinstated after being made to grovel – but Trotsky was too proud and too honest to do anything of the sort.

In 1928, he was exiled to Alma Ata in central Asia in the middle of the night, wearing only his pyjamas: his unexpected and humiliating arrest was a foretaste of things to come. In 1929 he was expelled from the USSR altogether, eventually settling in Mexico, where he was murdered in 1940 by a suspected Stalinist agent.

Stalin and the Five-Year Plans

▷ **The collectivization of Soviet agriculture**   The USSR was still mainly an agricultural country; capital for industrialization was scarce and seemed likely only to come from agriculture, by paying low prices for agricultural products and charging the peasants high prices for industrial goods. How was the Soviet Union going to be able to pull itself up by its own bootstraps?

Stalin's aims in collectivization

The NEP had produced good results in helping to restore the Soviet economy, but neither Lenin nor Stalin saw this as a final solution to the problem. Stalin aimed:

(a) to replace peasant subsistence agriculture by mechanized collective farming on state-managed farms;

(b) to eliminate what remained of the landlord class, and those better-off peasants (*kulaks*) who had built up their farms through the NEP; those who resisted would lose their holdings, and would suffer death or deportation;

(c) to create efficient, productive large-scale farming, so that people would have more to eat, and there would still be a surplus for export;

(d) to encourage the migration of surplus peasantry into the towns for the new industrialization drive; this would create an urban rather than a rural economy;

(e) to enable the Soviet Union to catch up with the West. Stalin said in 1931:

> The history of the old Russia has consisted of being beaten again and again because she was backward ... If you are backward and weak, you are in the wrong and you will be beaten and enslaved. But if you are powerful, people must beware of you ... We are fifty to a hundred years behind the advanced countries. We must make up this gap in ten years. Either we do this, or they crush us!

The Soviet Five-Year Plans

First Plan, 1929–33

Until 1929 it was thought that collectivization would take place slowly. There had been a bad harvest in 1928, and this led to the reimposition of rationing. The attempt to eliminate private grain traders in 1929 led to breakdown in the purchase and storage of grain. The decision to overcome the shortages by confiscating grain led to peasant riots and non-cooperation. Though his original aim had been 55 per cent collectivization, Stalin decided to speed things up by forcing the pace and compelling farmers to join collective farms in which land, resources and profits would be pooled, and there would be no private ownership.

The peasants strenuously resisted, slaughtering their cattle and burning their crops. During the months of December 1929 to March 1930, millions were uprooted from their homes and sent to punishment camps or to Siberia. The situation became so serious that in March 1930 Stalin was forced to relax the pressure, putting it down to the over-enthusiasm of junior officials (saying they were 'dizzy with success').

By June 1930, collectivization had fallen back to a mere 24 per cent; but in 1931 it was reapplied and the peasants were starved and defeated. Some historians have reckoned that perhaps 20 million perished. No official news of this famine ever reached the outside world, and no appeal for help was made by Stalin – on the contrary, Stalin took the line that there was no famine, and that the hostile reporting was simply part of the capitalist plot against his country. His conduct contrasted sharply with that of Lenin, who had welcomed foreign aid in 1921, when a famine of similar dimensions afflicted the country.

Table 10.1 Soviet economic growth

Category	1913	1921	1928	1933	1940	1953
INDUSTRIAL GOODS						
Electricity (bn kWh)	2	0.5	5	16	48	120
Oil (m tons)	9	4	12	21	31	47
Coal (m tons)	29	9	35	76	166	301
Steel (m tons)	4	0.2	4	7	18	34
Machine tools (000 units)	2	0.8	2	21	58	75
Tractors (000s)	0	0	1	74	32	99
CONSUMER GOODS						
Cars (000s)	0	0	0.1	10	6	60
Bicycles (000s)	5	8	11	126	255	1,650
Washing machines (000s)	0	0	0	0	0	4
Radios (000s)	0	0	0	29	161	1,295
Leather shoes (m prs)	60	28	58	90	211	238
Canned food (bn cans)	0.1	0.1	0.1	0.7	1	2
AGRICULTURAL						
Grain (m tons)	86	36	73	69	96	83
Livestock cattle (m)	71	60	70	39	67	58
Pigs (m)	23	13	19	10	28	29

Source: Official Soviet statistics.

Second Plan, 1933–37

Collectivization continued under the Second Plan, but it was never 100 per cent successful. Peasants still kept their houses, gardens and orchards, and managed to water down the adverse effects of collectivization.

Sovkhozy (government-run state farms) were Stalin's preferred method, with the farm workers as state employees, but there were relatively few of these, and too often their managers were guilty of gross mistakes of planning.

Kolkhozy were really peasant cooperatives, where the peasants pooled their resources and shared out their profits. Groups of these were served by Motor Tractor Stations (MTS), which supplied and serviced modern agricultural equipment. By 1935 there were 4,500 such stations.

Artels were less close-knit than cooperatives; they were private homes, plots and livestock, but 90 per cent of their output was sold to the state at fixed prices, and the rest disposed of on the private market.

Before the outbreak of the 1941 'Great Patriotic War', 25 million peasants had moved or had been drafted to the towns, but collective agriculture was still far from efficient. Grain production was scarcely more than it had been in 1913.

▷ **The industrialization of the Soviet Union**

Industrialization was beginning before the First World War, and in places was making such rapid speed as to threaten the whole rather out-dated fabric of rural Russia. It has been argued that the Bolshevik revolution provided an interruption of the industrialization process rather than a catalyst for it.

Stalin's aims in industrialization

Stalin's objective was to force the pace of industrialization so as to bring Russia into line with western countries, an aim he shared with many reformers from Peter the Great onwards. He wanted to:

(a) concentrate on heavy producer goods so as to supply the means of further expansion: hydroelectric stations, steel mills, machine tools, etc.;
(b) produce big increases in the output of basic materials such as coal, steel and oil, with which to drive industrialization onwards;
(c) provide infrastructure: railways, canals, navigable rivers and new roads;
(d) develop distant areas – central Asia, Kazakhstan, Siberia, etc. – in inhospitable regions where labour had to be drafted for work;
(e) outstrip the West in the production of industrial and consumer goods, and develop an invincible modern defence capability.

By the outbreak of the Second World War, the USSR was well on the way to achieving these aims, but the social costs were considerable by way of regimentation, harsh conditions and shortages. Though the USSR was importing only a small proportion of its capital goods, there were still relatively few consumer goods available and many workers suffered extreme privation.

Industry and the Five-Year Plans

First Plan, 1929–33
Work had already begun in 1927 on the Dnieper Dam and hydroelectric scheme and on the Stalingrad tractor plant, and the last link on the Trans-Siberian Railway complex was completed. The plan (which in fact began in 1928), as presented to the sixteenth Party Congress, aimed to double industrial production within five years. It set production targets, rewarding success and penalizing failure; but enthusiasm proved to be a poor substitute for capital.

Its emphasis was on the production of capital goods – coal, oil, iron, steel, electricity, cement, timber, etc. – to make possible further production, rather than on consumer goods to improve the standard of living.

'Surplus' grain was to be sold abroad to pay for the purchase of machine tools and other industrial equipment.

The results were good, in spite of a good deal of human suffering; but output fell short of the targets set by about 10–15 per cent, and the plan was not an unqualified success, especially in consumer goods.

The plan produced the *Order of the Stakhanovites*, and gave honours to those workers who had done their best to follow the example of Alexei Stakhanov, the Donbass miner who had hewed over 100 tons of coal in a single shift. Those given the award enjoyed visits to the Kremlin, party membership, seaside holidays, medals and cash prizes, and the adulation of their fellow-workers.

Second Plan, 1933–37

This plan undertook an even more ambitious programme of heavy industrialization; it completed the Dnieper Dam project, created a huge new steelworks at Gorky and at Magnitogorsk and another at Kutznetsk, and embarked on a rapid expansion of electrical supplies and industrial chemicals.

Communications improved with the completion of the Baltic–White Sea Canal and the Moscow–Volga Canal, and the building of more railways. Rail freight doubled after 1932. Air and road transport also improved.

The plan still relied heavily on exploitation and compulsion, but supplemented these with improved incentives, including higher rates of pay and factory 'honours boards' for better workers, and more competition between factories.

Third Plan, 1938–41

This aimed also at the production of more consumer goods, but the deteriorating international situation brought a change in priorities, and the plan came to concentrate heavily on defence requirements. By 1939, a quarter of the national budget was being spent on defence. The plan also involved the physical moving of much of Russia's productive capacity east of the Urals for defence reasons.

Fourth and Fifth Plans, 1946–51 and 1951–56

These aimed to restore the Soviet Union's industrial capacity after the ravages of the Great Patriotic War, but there was a good deal of wishful thinking in both, and the latter was only partly complete when Stalin died in 1953.

Labour and social conditions

There was much improvement, but the system remained generally oppressive:

(a) Direction of labour remained the standard practice, with restrictions on movement and internal passports. Wages improved, but remained low.
(b) Conditions of work, especially in remote areas, remained bleak and inhospitable, and labour was worked very hard over long periods.
(c) Slave labour was common, provided from camps holding political detainees, criminals, etc.
(d) Standards of education were low, and industrial skills were generally lacking among illiterate ex-peasants.
(e) Accommodation was primitive; in Moscow in the 1930s few households had more than one room, and over a quarter shared even this. Food was monotonous and poor.
(f) Trade unions existed, but they were not independent and served the main purpose of 'selling' government policies to the masses.

But by the eve of the war in 1940, there were discernible improvements:

(a) Wages were improving, and there were additional incentives like bonuses and holidays. But misdemeanours, too, could be entered in the individual 'work-book' and the penalties for indiscipline were severe.
(b) Housing schemes were beginning, especially in the cities like Moscow; but workers' flats were dreary and shoddily built, and furniture and consumer goods were lacking. Features like the Moscow Metro were impressive, but were chiefly prestige projects.
(c) Education was regimented and a vehicle for state propaganda, but it was getting better. Illiteracy was down to about 20 per cent of the population, and there were over 100,000 graduates, men and women, in industry by 1940.
(d) Medical services and hospitals were made free, and there was an ambitious state health service. The 1936 constitution laid down the right to old age pensions, but there was not always the money to fund them.

Stalin the control-freak

Stalin exercised ever-tightening control over the Soviet Union during his career, to the point that his government developed steadily into a tyranny. This he did to preserve the purity of party doctrine and to safeguard it from the evils of deviationism; yet essentially communism was about equality and freedom.

▷ The control of thoughts and actions

The use of propaganda

Propaganda was information put out for consumption by the public without any sort of critical evaluation. It might be entirely true, or partly true and partly misrepresented, or it might be entirely false; but it was required to be believed.

Propaganda was useful to Stalin as Soviet leader for a number of reasons:

(a) It told people what he thought they ought to believe and gave them the right social attitudes.
(b) It prevented deviation from socialist teaching and avoided unnecessary debate within the party.
(c) It provided uniform belief and action by the leadership, and the obedience of the party rank and file to Stalin's interpretation of communism.
(d) It identified Stalin's opponents and gave him the excuse for dealing with them.
(e) It enabled the Soviet Union to present an acceptable face to the rest of the world and to conceal its shortcomings.
(f) It helped Stalin to give a patriotic 'spin' to communist teachings.

The use of censorship

Stalin maintained a rigid control of opinion so as to reinforce his power.

(a) He controlled the content of education, rewriting such subjects as history and biology to match with communist values, e.g. he removed Trotsky as a 'non-person' from historical accounts of the Bolshevik revolution.
(b) He reinstated traditional values where politically desirable, e.g. he encouraged marriage and families, and discouraged divorce and abortion.
(c) He doctored the content of newspapers and radio broadcasts to ensure they gave the official party line on events.
(d) He repressed freedom of speech and curtailed unauthorized meetings.
(e) He discouraged individuality in artistic endeavour, encouraging what he called 'socialist realism' from writers, painters and musicians, so as to stress the importance of the revolution's achievements. Even Stalin's daughter said, 'The leadership viewed art from the bigoted and puritanical point of view prevalent in the party.'

The use of repression

Stalin established the NKVD (the Internal Affairs Commission) to take over the work of the former OGPU. This body had wide powers and operated beyond the law, rooting out information and rumour on which thousands were deported or imprisoned – material relating to efforts to 'wreck' the economy, restore capitalism (with the help of Hitler or Trotsky!) or assassinate Stalin.

Those arrested numbered about 7 or 8 million, many of whom were sent to *labour camps*, where perhaps 2 million died. Most did mining, lumbering and general construction work, e.g. on building railways. Conditions were unendurably hard, and many perished from physical or mental disease.

▷ The Great Purges

The 'show trials'

At first, repression was directed against those outside the party so as to ensure acceptance of Stalin's policies, e.g. against the kulaks, but it was soon extended to those within the party whom Stalin thought he had reason to distrust.

Stalin had weeded out the 'left' who had wished to abandon the NEP, and after Stalin himself had begun to take this line, he weeded out the 'right' as well, saying they were too favourable to NEPmen or kulaks. Stalin filled the vacant ranks with his own nominees, though later he came to feel that even their loyalty was suspect; in some cases he eliminated them in their turn.

In 1934, it was the murder of Sergei Kirov that touched off the reign of terror. Kirov was the young, energetic and popular party leader in Leningrad, and he was known to oppose Stalin's plan to escalate political persecution. His mysterious death, and the death, supposedly in an accident, of the chief witness to the crime, led later to the belief that Stalin was himself implicated in the affair.

In 1935, leading communists and chief members of the Politburo were put on trial. There were several such *show trials*:

(a) 1936, Trial of the Sixteen, including Kamenev and Zinoviev.
(b) 1936, Trial of the Seventeen, including Radek, Muralov and Pyatakov.
(c) 1938, Trial of the Twenty-One, including Bukharin, Rykov and Krestinsky.

Stalin became obsessed with fear of opposition; unity was needed to consolidate the revolution, and divisions menaced his leadership. As he told the party: 'These comrades did not always confine themselves to criticism and passive resistance, they threatened to raise revolt in the party . . . More, they threatened some of us with bullets!'

Stalin's fears had some substance, in that Trotsky was publishing from abroad information which could only have been leaked by Stalin's closest colleagues; as a result, Stalin eyed all his associates with suspicion.

Khrushchev, however, in 1956 put a different interpretation on Stalin's actions:

Stalin originated the concept of 'enemy of the people'. This term rendered it unnecessary that the errors of the men engaged in controversy be proven; it made possible the most cruel repression, violating all norms of revolutionary legality . . . The term 'enemy of the people' eliminated all possibility of any kind of fight, or even the making of one's views known on this or that issue.

For the ordinary Soviet citizen, the false denunciation, the arrest at the dead of night, the slow death in a labour camp or the quick dispatch by firing squad was a constant nightmare. For senior party members there was physical and psychological torture – confessions were wrung from those who were confused, or those who feared for the safety of their families. Bukharin, in his last latter to his wife in 1937, confessed: 'I feel my helplessness before a hellish machine which has acquired gigantic power, and which uses the Cheka's former authority to cater to Stalin's morbid suspiciousness . . . Any member of the Central Committee, or any member of the Party, can be rubbed out, or turned into a traitor or a terrorist.'

After this, it is not surprising to hear that no attempt was made to give the accused a fair trial. The Chief State Prosecutor, Andrei Vyshinsky, dog-like in his devotion to Stalin, usually ended his denunciation of the accused with the request: 'I demand that the mad dogs be shot, every one of them!' And they usually were.

The army purges

Above all, Stalin feared the power of the army. He was convinced that it was plotting his downfall, since his influence over the army was less than it was with the party.

In January 1937 Stalin reshuffled the senior commands, removing troops from commanders to whom they might be loyal. The Red Army Chief, Marshal Tukhachevsky, implicated by documents probably forged by the Germans, was charged with treason and shot. Large numbers of others followed:

3 of the 5 Soviet marshals;
13 of the 15 army commanders;
50 of the 57 corps commanders;
154 of the 186 divisional commanders;
all 16 political commissars;
98 of the 108 members of the Supreme Military Soviet.

The damage to the senior command of the army was all too obvious in the Finnish campaign of 1939–40 and in the early months of the Nazi invasion of 1941.

In 1938 the purges seemed to be accelerating out of control, but Stalin, blaming his subordinates for their overenthusiasm, deliberately slowed down the killings and earned himself a reputation for moderation. The worst of the purges were over. But it was not until after Stalin's death that ordinary Soviet people could feel secure from the security forces and the secret police.

At the time of the purges, it was thought by many inside and outside the USSR that the accused, having confessed, must indeed have been guilty. Few believed physical and mental torture could actually persuade innocent people that they were guilty.

The killings were not part of the ideology of communism: Lenin killed because he felt he had to; Stalin killed out of fear and paranoia. Even in his final illness, Stalin believed that eminent doctors, far from treating him, were involved in a sinister conspiracy to poison him. Only his death delivered them from the danger.

Stalin and the world

▷ **The beginnings of Soviet policies**

The Bolshevik leadership as a whole were totally without experience in their conduct of foreign affairs, and, without the help of professional advisers, stumbled painfully to an understanding of how best to safeguard their country's interests.

The threat of the Comintern

At first, the Bolsheviks expected world revolution and the general collapse of capitalism, but their early successes in Germany and Hungary were short-lived.

The Comintern held conferences at regular intervals to encourage risings, but with dwindling success. A number of efforts were made to create *revolution from above* in Bulgaria, Estonia, etc., but all failed. In 1924 the policy was changed to one of *united front from below*, in cooperation with workers and trade unions, but the value of this was largely propagandist.

Trotsky's aim of world revolution was eventually replaced by Stalin's line of *socialism in one country*, making the destiny of the revolution dependent on the success of the efforts of the USSR. After this, the work of the Comintern came to be usually subversive, supplying propaganda, money and encouragement to left-wing movements – as in Britain.

Its activities were hated and feared by capitalist governments, and the International was disbanded in 1943 at the request of Stalin's wartime allies.

The problem of recognition

After the humiliating Treaty of Brest-Litovsk in 1918, Soviet Russia was completely isolated and ignored by most established states. It sought recognition.

(a) 1921, trade deal was signed with Lloyd George in Britain.
(b) 1922, Treaty of Rapallo was signed with Weimar Germany. Both were international outcasts, but Germany gave the USSR recognition and support, and in return the USSR promised raw materials, training facilities and secret armament production.
(c) 1924, British Labour government under MacDonald recognized the USSR, followed by France and then Italy.
(d) 1926, Treaty of Berlin continued Rapallo cooperation.

The USA withheld recognition of the Soviet government until 1933.

The USSR and the League of Nations

Stalin's aims were defensive rather than menacing, and he moved steadily closer to League policies, partly out of ideological conviction, and partly for reasons of weakness. In this he was supported by Maxim Litvinov, Commissar for Foreign Affairs after 1930 and a Jew, who used every means to resist the growth of fascism in Germany.

(a) 1928, he signed the Kellogg–Briand Pact against war and supported disarmament.
(b) 1934, he eventually joined the League of Nations, with a seat on the Council.

Asian policies

As part of the popular struggle against capitalism and colonialism, the USSR championed nationalist policies in China. Stalin therefore supported Jiang Jie Shi (Chiang Kai-shek), but when he ordered Mao Zedong (Mao Tse-tung) to collaborate with the nationalists, he was rebuffed when Jiang massacred communists in Shanghai in 1927.

This emphasized Soviet isolation in the East in the 1920s and 1930s, especially at a time when Japan was threatening expansion.

▷ **The approach of war**

Stalin had been of the opinion that the bourgeois threat of the Weimar Republic was more serious than that of Hitler's fascism, but as the 1930s went on it became obvious that he had underestimated the latter danger.

The Spanish Civil War, 1936–39

Stalin's caution, and his unwillingness to get involved outside the Soviet Union itself, drove him to half-hearted aid for the republican side. On the other hand, the fascist powers gave military and air support to Franco, and steadily the republican cause declined until Franco's final victory in 1939.

As early as 1936, the Anti-Comintern Pact between Germany and Japan threatened Stalin with war on two fronts, and he began to feel his isolation, with both Britain and France deeply suspicious of the growth of communism.

The Czechoslovak and Polish crises

The Soviet Union took a serious view of Hitler's threat to Czechoslovakia, and even suggested it might be willing to activate its 1935 treaty in order to assist the Czechs, but neither Britain nor France was enthusiastic over this.

Stalin found himself shouldered aside during the crisis, and was not even invited to attend the Munich Conference in September 1938. Events suggested to Stalin that the democracies were unreliable allies, and would readily leave him in the lurch as they had Czechoslovakia; he therefore had to fend for himself.

When Poland was threatened in 1939, both Germany and the West angled for Soviet assistance, but Stalin thought that the democracies were not to be trusted. In April he dismissed the pro-western Litvinov and decided on his own 'Munich' with Hitler.

His new Foreign Minister, Molotov, negotiated with both parties, but in August 1939 Stalin settled for a *Nazi–Soviet Non-Aggression Pact* (the Molotov–Ribbentrop Pact), providing a ten-year peace agreement between the two countries, and containing secret clauses to arrange the carve-up of Poland between them.

Stalin congratulated himself on his smart move, and duly recovered much of the land lost after the establishment of Poland in 1919, but Hitler had no intention of remaining bound by the agreement and in 1941 denounced it.

▷ **The 'Great Patriotic War'**

Remarkably enough for such a cynical politician, Stalin remained loyal to the Non-Aggression Pact, and fulfilled his obligations under it to supply Germany with what Hitler required. Meanwhile, he pocketed his gains in Poland and took over the Baltic states to help in the defence of Leningrad. Only Estonia posed any threat to Leningrad; the others were taken to keep them out of German hands.

The coming of war

Stalin also tried to force Finland to give up land near Leningrad in late 1939, so producing the 'Winter War' against the Finns. The 'phoney war' in the West enabled Britain and France to toy with the idea of sending help to Finland, which could only have cemented the German–Finnish alliance.

In the end, all that happened was the exposure of Soviet military incompetence, and the expulsion of the USSR from the League for its aggression.

Meanwhile Stalin's support for Germany continued with the shipment of oil, steel and other materials; Stalin ignored the warnings of the West about Hitler's intentions, and persisted in the belief that Hitler would not attack.

It was by accident rather than by design that Stalin complemented his pact with Germany by another with Japan in 1941; Japan had tangled with the Soviet Union in the Far East and wished to clear the decks for the coming struggle with the USA and Britain. This treaty was well timed, for in June 1941 the Germans invaded the Soviet Union, taking Stalin completely by surprise.

Stalin's war against Germany

Until the very day of the invasion, Stalin maintained a conciliatory attitude towards Germany, and the initial disasters of the war suggested that he was losing his grip. But in July 1941 he made a radio broadcast to the Soviet people in which the appeal was to patriotism rather than to party, and the Soviet people responded magnificently. Stalin the tyrant became Stalin the father-figure, exhorting his people to sacrifice and obscuring the memories of their suffering, while identifying himself with the 'brothers and sisters' he would previously have addressed as 'comrades'.

He turned his considerable administrative abilities to organizing the war, and the German advance was halted in 1943 at enormous cost, and then turned into a well-planned counteroffensive. By 1945 the Soviets had overrun Poland again and were at the gates of Berlin.

Stalin's war achievements, however, were as much diplomatic as military. At Yalta and especially at Potsdam in 1945, he won concessions that were to bring much of eastern Europe under his control, and so give to the Soviet Union that security in the West which it had lacked in the 1920s and 1930s.

Over 10 million Soviet civilians died in the war – 700,000 in Leningrad alone – and nearly 7 million of the armed forces. The economy was in ruins, railway lines were twisted and tangled, bridges wrecked, factories destroyed and fields uncultivated. Not all was the work of the Germans; part of the devastation was due to the Soviet 'scorched earth' policy. But what Stalin had helped to destroy it was now his task to rebuild, and it was his achievement to bequeath to his successors a superpower which Lenin might have envied and which would have been unthinkable in the dark days of the 1930s.

Later career of Stalin

▷ **Internal reconstruction, 1945–53**

Stalin squandered the respect he had created with his wartime leadership and achievements, by his reversion to harsh discipline after 1945. Many contemporaries thought the time had come for some political relaxation and material improvement; but instead Stalin's postwar rule was as oppressive as ever, and it looked in 1953 as if he was gearing up for another purge.

Industrial recovery

The privations of war were continued in peacetime. While the fourth Five-Year Plan was a step towards postwar reconstruction, Stalin promised little and delivered less by way of material rewards. The Soviet people braced themselves for the peacetime battle for the economy in the same way that they had for the wartime battle against the German invader.

Soviet industry achieved a remarkable revival within three years. Recovery was helped by reparations from East Germany and from eastern European countries, by the labour of 2 million prisoners-of-war, and by one-sided trading agreements with the satellite countries which the USSR now virtually controlled.

Good planning, and the nation's wonted submissiveness, helped to defeat almost insuperable difficulties, and both targets and actual production figures streaked ahead. There were, by the time of the Fifth Plan in the early 1950s, some expensive prestige projects such as the Volga–Don Canal, short on traffic but plentiful in statues of Stalin, and vast hydroelectric schemes which would take decades to make any contribution to the economy.

But the prewar base had largely been restored by 1953, and might well have made a significant impact in raising living standards had not so high a proportion of industrial production been set aside for armaments.

The agricultural economy

Progress in agriculture was slower. There was a poor harvest in 1946 and near famine conditions in 1947, and agricultural recovery was held back by the low priority awarded to agriculture and by shortages of labour and machines.

Some policies of the period, such as the merging of smaller collectives into larger ones, failed to improve production problems, and others, like the planting of trees in areas where trees did not normally grow, were a damaging waste of resources.

The fundamental problem was one of low agricultural productivity due to poor planning and lax management, and to the absence of incentives for farm workers to exert themselves; Soviet crop yields continued to trail far behind the production norms of even fairly inefficient western farms.

It was not until 1953 that farm output began to recover, and even then it was well behind the output of 1940. In times of crop failure, the Soviet Union was not uncommonly forced into importing thousands of tons of foodstuffs.

▷ External expansion

In 1945 the Soviet Union had an enormous army, and used it to occupy much of eastern Europe. The suspicions of Churchill and Truman were speedily aroused. But contrary to alarmist belief in the West, it seems highly unlikely that Stalin, who was well aware how exhausted his country was, had any serious intention to dominate Europe, and he certainly did not wish to conquer the world. His aim remained what it always had been – security, a security which he had failed to attain in the 1930s.

Stalin's satellite empire

Thus Stalin in 1945 undertook to extend the area of Soviet control:

(a) He incorporated the Baltic states into the Soviet Union as member republics, establishing regimes there which favoured such a union.
(b) He used the cover of the Red Army to encourage the formation of favourable communist regimes in Romania, Bulgaria and Hungary.
(c) He engineered a coup in Czechoslovakia when he feared the newly re-established state would come under US influence by accepting Marshall Aid.
(d) He used every tactic short of armed force to bring Tito to heel in Yugoslavia when he demonstrated his independence of the Moscow 'line'.

But this strategy steered clear of Trotskyism. It had strict limits and was clearly not part of a plan to dominate the world for communism:

(a) He made no attempt to impose communism on Finland.
(b) He held off from direct intervention in Greece.
(c) He withdrew his troops from Iran and recognized the Shah.
(d) He gave only grudging and lukewarm support to Mao Zedong's communists in China. For some time his prewar policies of favouring Jiang Jie Shi continued, when commonsense dictated that he change sides.

The 'Cold War' in Europe

Stalin was widely seen as an aggressor by the West after 1945, and his cautious and limited objectives were not easy to judge at the time:

(a) He squeezed East Germany very hard for reparations, and would willingly have taken a slice of West German resources too. He regarded the western inclination to protect West Germany from being plundered as secret support for the recreation of Nazi influence and military power.
(b) He suspected that western efforts to reconstruct West Germany, to give it financial aid and to promote the reunification of the currency were part of a plot to oust the USSR from its domination in the Soviet Zone.
(c) He countered western plans to revive the German economy by bringing about the Berlin crisis of 1948–49, which produced the Berlin airlift and, on its conclusion, the new western alliance, NATO.
(d) He detonated the first Soviet atom bomb in 1949, as much a triumph for Soviet science as for Soviet espionage.
(e) He toughened his attitude in international meetings and at the United Nations (UN) by appointing Vyshinsky as his Foreign Minister. He remained impervious to persuasion and pressure, and 'Niet' became the word he most often used in applying the Soviet veto to block UN action being taken in international disputes.

The Korean War, 1950–53, which was not of Stalin's making, brought East–West relations to a new low as the Cold War began to spread to other continents.

Assessment of Stalin

Soviet historians replaced praise of Stalin in the 1930s with criticism in the late 1950s. It is true that, as a mass killer of the twentieth century, Stalin was second only to Hitler, but he also was responsible for many solid achievements.

It could be argued that it was harsh to use such excesses as he visited on the USSR during the party and army purges, but he used them to stiffen the discipline of the country and to remove the dangers confronting the leadership. Possibly only he among Soviet political leaders had the ruthlessness and the determination to carry these policies through. Similarly, his policies of industrialization and collectivization were nasty medicine, but they were for the Soviet people's own good and they were forced to swallow them.

Totalitarian rulers have less need of qualms than democratic leaders, and more easily apply weapons of coercion and repression to secure themselves in power. The fact that Stalin used them should therefore cause less surprise.

Stalin can be criticized for his morbid suspicion of others, but his suspicions of the western democracies were all too justified. Western attitudes in the 1940s and the secretiveness of the West over, say, the atomic bomb, all gave adequate justification of his uncooperativeness. Stalin was taken in by assurances in 1939; perhaps now he was absolutely determined not to repeat his mistake.

But the Soviet people had some reason to be grateful to Stalin in spite of all his mistakes and excesses. His Five-Year Plans, though they fell short of their targets, transformed the Soviet Union; his leadership made possible the survival of the Soviet Union in the Second World War. His leadership was far from flawless; but he achieved order and progress and above all victory. There are not many leaders who can say more.

GLOSSARY

Comintern The name given to the Third Communist International, formed in Moscow in 1919. The first two Internationals had been concerned with the spread of socialism; the third was concerned to promote worldwide revolution. It was regarded by western leaders as subversive and dangerous, but when it became clear that worldwide revolution was neither imminent nor inevitable, Stalin concentrated on promoting socialism within the Soviet Union, and the Comintern became more of a nuisance to the West than a threat. In 1943, as a goodwill gesture to his allies, Stalin dissolved it; they believed he was being magnanimous, he knew otherwise.

Party and government The Bolshevik Party was renamed the Communist Party in 1918. It was always a minority party and membership of it was a privilege and not a right. A minimum of three members in a workshop or factory had the right to form a cell and to elect representatives to the local district committee. Through the local committees was chosen the Party Congress, meeting annually and delegating its continuous and routine administration to the Central Committee. This was normally too big to conduct business except on a formal basis, and immediate decisions were taken by the very senior members of the Central Committee. These men were known as the Politburo and could be as few as five in number. They were, in effect, a kind of Communist Party cabinet.

Side by side with the party was the government. It was headed by the Council of People's Commissars, and its chairman was the Prime Minister. As he was also a member of the Politburo, and government posts were all held by party members, the party was able to keep firm control of the government both at central levels and at the lower levels of province and district. Elected soviets (councils) were responsible for local and central government, but in practice election to these was controlled by the party. Thus even after the new constitution of 1936, it was the Central Committee of the party and its power group, the Politburo, which determined policy and ran the country.

Secret police Lenin's dreaded Cheka was less active after the successful end to the civil war made the Bolsheviks more secure. But although the Cheka was abolished in 1922, its activities were merely transferred to the NKVD – the People's Commissariat of the Interior. Its headquarters in Moscow copied that of the Cheka in combining the functions of an administrative centre for the conduct of all Soviet security, a prison, a court for secret trials and a busy execution centre. The OGPU or GPU was the secret police section of the NKVD and played a major part in conducting Stalin's purges in the 1930s.

> ## EXAMINATION QUESTIONS

▷ **Question 1**   Study Sources A, B, C and D and then answer the questions which follow.

Source A

The characteristic feature in the work of the Party during the past year is that we, as a Party, as the Soviet power, have developed an offensive along the whole front against capitalist elements in the countryside. To launch an offensive against the Kulaks means that we must smash them, eliminate them as a class ... Today we have an adequate political base for us to strike, break their resistance and replace them by the output of collective farms. (Communist Party statement, Moscow, 1929)

Source B

Will it ever be known how terrible was the disorganization of agriculture that resulted? Rather than hand over their livestock to the *kolkhoz*, the peasants slaughter their beasts, sell the meat and make boots out of the leather. Through the destruction of the live market ... trainloads of deported peasants left for the icy North ... in seven years 1929–36 over 5 million families disappeared.

(From the writings of an opponent of Stalin)

Source C

Table 10.2
Agricultural statistics

	1928	1929	1930	1931	1932	1933
Grain harvest (m tons)	73.3	71.7	83.5	69.5	68.6	68.4
Livestock cattle (m head)	70.5	67.1	52.5	47.9	40.7	38.9
Grain taken by the state (m tons)	10.8	16.1	22.1	22.5	18.5	22.6

By 1931, 56 per cent of all farms were collectivized.
By 1932, 62 per cent of all farms were collectivized.

(Adapted from official Soviet sources)

Source D

Table 10.3
Industrial statistics

	1928	1933	1940
Effective power (bn kW)	5.0	16.3	48.3
Crude oil (m tons)	11.6	21.5	31.1
Coal (m tons)	35.5	76.3	165.9
Steel (m tons)	4.2	6.9	18.3
Locomotives (units)	479	948	928

(Adapted from official Soviet statistics)

(a)   Which of Sources A and B is the more useful as evidence about the collectivization of Soviet agriculture? Explain your answer.   (8 marks)

(b)   Sources C and D are both based on Soviet official figures. Does this make them unreliable as evidence of the USSR's economic progress?   (8 marks)

(c)   From Sources A, B, C and D, is it possible to form a clear picture of agricultural and industrial change in the Soviet Union during the 1930s?   (8 marks)

▷ **Question 2** Study Source A below and then answer the questions which follow.

Source A

Fig. 10.1 Stalin with his
people

(a) What enables you to date this poster to the time of the Five-Year Plans?

(3 marks)

(b) What do you think is the main purpose of this poster? Explain your answer.

(7 marks)

▷ **Question 3** From 1928 major changes in agriculture and industry took place in the Soviet Union.

(a) Why were these changes introduced?   (10 marks)

(b) How were the ordinary people of the Soviet Union affected by these changes?

(10 marks)

▷ **Question 4** (a) How was Stalin able to achieve power?   (10 marks)

(b) 'Stalin maintained himself in power by terror alone.' Do you agree? Explain your
answer.   (15 marks)

 EXAMINATION ANSWERS

▷ **Question 1** *Outline answer*

(a) The two sources are useful for different things: Source A is an emotive statement of
policy; Source B is an emotive comment on events. Thus their usefulness will depend
on what the historian is looking for: Source A is valuable to historians of government policy and communist propaganda; Source B is valuable to historians studying opposition to Stalin and the effects of collectivization. You should point out that
both are limited in their usefulness.

(b) What is needed here is a brief comment on the general reliability of statistics and a
developed discussion of the reliability of these statistics in particular. Their reliability is closely related to the circumstances in which the sources were produced: managers anxious to achieve targets, the remoteness of some collectives and factories
with little chance of checking their figures, and the purposes of such official figures
– as propaganda and to justify such economic measures as collectivization and the

Five-Year Plans. But even official figures such as these can reveal trends and are by no means completely unreliable.

(c) It should be explained that a clear picture is unlikely from propagandist texts and statistics of doubtful accuracy. The limited nature of the statistics needs pointing out, e.g. only three agricultural products and five industrial ones, and the texts are too brief and limited to provide much detail. We learn very little about the Five-Year Plans from these sources, and consumer goods are omitted altogether. How these limited sources could be effectively supplemented by others needs to be discussed.

▷ Question 2   *Outline answer*

(a) The setting is industrial and shows Stalin marching with factory workers and miners, each of them carrying his tools. The parade appears to be in a factory yard. The emphasis at the time of the Five-Year Plans was always on industrial achievement, and the poster would have little point if it was dated before 1928.

(b) Stalin is shown here as an ordinary man, a comrade of the workers, and in step with them; a fictional Stalin very different from the recluse of reality. Everyone is smiling: an indication that everyone is pleased with the industrial achievement, and ignoring the stress and suffering that the Five-Year Plans entailed. The poster is showing Stalin as understanding and in step with the national interest, while his prominent position in the poster emphasizes his leadership. Success and solidarity are the keynotes, and the poster is intended to glorify Stalin and to rally support behind him. It is typical Soviet propaganda.

▷ Question 3   *Tutor answer*

(a) It had always been the intention of the Bolsheviks to eliminate private ownership and private profit, and the New Economic Policy had been a temporary expedient to alleviate massive shortages and to defuse peasant discontent. Although this policy had been successful within limits, the party faithful found the revival of capitalism in agriculture distasteful, and in particular they, and the poorer peasants, resented the growing numbers and increasing prosperity of the NEPmen. But apart from ideological reasons for change, there was the need to make agriculture more efficient. The poorer peasants lacked the means to mechanize their farming, and much of it was subsistence agriculture. Those who had surpluses were unwilling to sell them to the state at artificially low prices. In 1928 there was a poor harvest and state grain purchases fell by 25 per cent. Greater agricultural efficiency could only come through state intervention and would have the added advantage of releasing surplus peasant labour for work in the towns. Industry had stagnated since the rapid growth in the latter days of Tsardom. The First World War had devastated much of the industrial heart of Russia, and the Civil War wreaked further havoc. Industrial regeneration could only come through the injection of capital. Since France was no longer prepared to finance Soviet industrial growth and the Soviet Union was isolated diplomatically, investment capital had to be found from within the country. The low prices paid to peasants for their grain allowed grain to be sold abroad for profits which could be invested in industry. Thus the revival of industry depended on the prosperity of agriculture, so it was no mere coincidence that the first Five-Year Plan was announced at the same time as the first attempt to collectivize agriculture.

(b) Those poor peasants who joined the collectives benefited from security of employment and from basic housing and social welfare. They probably found it difficult to adjust to cooperative working after scratching a living on their private plots. At least they escaped the fate of the kulaks who in the main resisted collectivization, and slaughtered their livestock and burnt their grain rather than hand it over to the state farms. In their hundreds of thousands, the families of the richer peasants were uprooted and force-marched to slow death in the labour camps or the gulags, or were immediately despatched by the soldiery. Many peasants in areas of overpopulation were forced to seek work in the towns. Here the long hours, the remorseless toil and the drive to meet ever-increasing production targets made life grim. Even for those born and bred in the towns, life was austere. There was a credit side, in social welfare, education and literacy, and worker incentives, but these paled beside the squalor, the lack of decent housing and the political surveillance. Most of all, the concentration on heavy industry and the neglect of consumer needs meant that even many of the basic necessities were lacking. Lack of toothbrushes, toilet paper and soap might have been more tolerable had there been adequate basic food, but ordinary people in both town and country were hit by the famine of 1932–33, which killed more than the terrible famine in Lenin's time; and this time there was no foreign aid. Once the worst of the famine was over, things improved slowly: every material advance, however small, helped to convince the ordinary Russian that the good times lay ahead. What actually lay ahead was the Second World War.

▷ **Question 4**   *Student answer with examiner's comments*

'This is biographical, i.e. about the life of Stalin rather than an explanation of how he came to power.'

(a) Stalin was not really a Russian. He was born in Georgia of poor but religious parents who sent him to train as a priest. He soon showed more interest in politics than religion, and was expelled. He now moved among revolutionaries and gave up his Georgian name, and tried to lose his Georgian accent to try to impress the native Russians among his friends. But he was always something of an odd man out. Even so he worked very hard preparing pamphlets, arranging meetings, planning bank robberies – that is when he was not a guest of the Tsar in one of his labour camps or jails.

'This part is quite an effective explanation of Stalin's rise.'

Stalin's importance grew because of his close links with Lenin; when other Bolsheviks questioned Lenin's plans to take over in October 1917, Stalin soon gave Lenin his backing, and Lenin came to trust him. Some important posts brought Stalin valuable experience and brought him in close contact with other Bolsheviks whom he closely watched. As a military Commissar Stalin saw a good deal of Trotsky and did not always agree with him. But it was Stalin's appointment as General Secretary of the Communist Party which gave him his real opportunity: he was at the centre of politics, he knew the agenda of all the various committees, he promoted his friends, he passed over his enemies and even got them demoted or dismissed; there was no activity within the party that he was unaware of. Lenin's health never recovered from the attempt made on

'It is not necessary for the student to show lack of knowledge in this way. Careful rewording could help hide the fact that the student had read about Ida Kaplan, but had forgotten her name: for example, just take out "by ...".'

his life by . . . . . . , he had a stroke, was nursed carefully by his wife Krupskaya, but was no longer able to work hard. He suspected Stalin of being power-hungry, and although he put his reservations about Stalin in writing, these were hidden by the Politburo on Lenin's death. After all the Politburo did contain a majority of Stalin's men. Thus with the help of Kamenev and Zinoviev he was able to beat off a challenge by Trotsky, and by 1928 so dominated the Party that he was able to send Trotsky into exile.

(b) Once in power Stalin set about ruling by terror. His secret police were everywhere. No one dared oppose Stalin, they were all too frightened. First he killed off or exiled all the richer peasants, the Kulaks. Then he began the purges. He wiped out many of the party faithful. He killed off most of the higher-ranking army officers. He was threatening another purge when he died in 1953.

'Grammatical weakness here.'

Examiner's decision on the student answer

(a) A mixture of biographical narrative and explanation. It is not sharply focused enough for Level 4, but would reach Level 3 and would probably deserve 7/10.

(b) The student did not notice that 15 marks were allocated for this. It is nothing more than a limited description of Stalin's terror. A good answer would need to discuss whether there were other factors which kept Stalin in power (improved living standards and social provision, effective party management, propaganda, etc.). This is very brief, but more than just the few isolated facts of a Level 1 answer. It would just reach Level 2 (the narrative option) and is so limited that it would be at the bottom end of Level 2, probably 3/15.

SUMMARY

In this chapter you have studied the history of the Soviet Union under Stalin, and have learned about:

▷ the struggle for power in the Soviet Union in the 1920s, and the reasons for Stalin's success;

▷ the development of Stalin's dictatorship, and his use of propaganda;

▷ the policies of agricultural collectivization, and their results;

▷ the Five-Year Plans in industry and their results;

▷ the 'show trials' and the purges;

▷ the role of Stalin in foreign affairs and in the 'Great Patriotic War';

▷ the policies of Stalin in the postwar years.

The chapter concludes with an assessment of Stalin's importance in Soviet history.
  There is further information on:

▷ international relations in chapter 11;

▷ the Second World War in chapter 12;

▷ international relations after the Second World War in chapter 15.

GETTING STARTED

After a period of optimism and relative progress in the 1920s, the international outlook became steadily more threatening in the course of the 1930s.

MEG	NEAB	NICCEA	SEG	LONDON	WJEC	TOPIC	STUDY	REVISION 1	REVISION 2
✓	✓		✓			**The decline of the League of Nations**			
✓	✓		✓			The impact of the Great Depression			
✓	✓		✓			The Manchurian crisis, 1931			
✓	✓		✓			The Abyssinian crisis, 1935			
✓	✓		✓			**German expansion under Hitler**			
✓	✓		✓			Hitler's violations of the Treaty of Versailles			
✓	✓		✓			The policy of appeasement			
✓	✓		✓			Assessment of the policies of the 1930s			

WHAT YOU NEED TO KNOW

The decline of the League of Nations

▷ **The impact of the Great Depression**

The late 1920s saw the sudden decline of leading world economies, beginning with the American, and the collapse of trade, as well as the collapse of financial and commercial confidence, as illustrated by the Wall Street Crash of October 1929.

Economic consequences

The US depression spread to the rest of the capitalist world, bringing with it:

(a) sharp reductions in industrial and agricultural output, with massive shrinkage of investment and commercial enterprise – shares were at a very low ebb;

(b) collapse of international trade – import/export firms did little business, debts were recalled and shipping and transport suffered;

(c) collapse of prices, and caution due to deflation in the markets;

(d) reduction of industrial production – there were no profits and little new investment; short-time working and unemployment soared;

(e) poverty and idleness for the unemployed and their families – those on social welfare benefits could not even afford to buy at lower prices.

Political consequences

There were serious results for governments. Democracies, shaken by accusations of neglect, experienced grave crises; some newer democracies collapsed altogether and gave way to authoritarian regimes. All, except the Soviet Union, with its insulation from external markets and its command economy, experienced similar problems:

(a) shrinkage of their tax base – those governments which wanted to maintain welfare services crippled themselves by having to tax more highly;

(b) escalation of the cost of social benefits in support of the unemployed and the poverty-stricken, which landed governments with ever bigger welfare payments;

(c) cutting of interest levels, which penalized investors and those on fixed incomes, while the bleak outlook discouraged enterprises from borrowing new money;

(d) demand for protective practices such as the enactment of higher tariffs and commercial embargoes. This brought more bureaucratic interference in business and encouraged the nationalization or other control of vital or failing industries.

Interference with trade and industry led to diminished contacts between nations and mutual suspicions, and led to dangerous side effects:

(a) It was to the disdavantage of debtor countries, many of which could no longer raise money in the USA. Some, e.g. Chile, defaulted on their debts; others were squeezed into supplying raw materials at rock-bottom prices, or were drained of their gold, which was syphoned off to the USA.

(b) It eroded foreign investment and stimulated financial nationalism.

(c) It led to doctrines of national self-sufficiency, and the desire to achieve independence from outside supplies, e.g. Nazi idea of autarky.

(d) It tempted governments into the development of military capacity, expansion of their forces and rearmament, so as to assert their will and remedy unemployment.

(e) It produced imperialistic ideas in pursuit of raw materials or lands under neighbours' control, e.g. the Nazi idea of *Lebensraum*.

(f) It encouraged the growth of nationalism on the part of colonial and client countries in South America and the Far East, and even of Japan.

▷ The Manchurian crisis, 1931

Japan's attitudes and ambitions

Japan had imposed the *Twenty-One Points* on China at the time of the First World War, and at the peace conference demanded the right to acquire former German colonies in the Far East. Britain and France supported these claims.

Japan was a founder-member of the League of Nations, but never felt quite welcome there. The Japanese tended to think of the League as a white colonialists' club, and did not participate whole-heartedly in its work.

Meanwhile, Japan continued to entertain its ambitions in Manchuria. The territory of Kwantung, around Port Arthur, had first been leased to Japan in 1905, and the Japanese had made large investments in the area, building the South Manchurian Railway (SMR) and developing the country's enormous resources.

Japan was ruled by a weak parliamentary democracy, but the traditional military elements never fully accepted it, pressing for increases in the military budget and for greater freedom of action for the officers of the Kwantung army in Manchuria.

In September 1931 they took the bold step of acting on their own initiative to take over control of Manchuria.

Japan seizes control

A bomb outrage on the SMR provided the Japanese with the excuse to act, and they swiftly occupied Mukden and then the entire province. China appealed to the League, but there was some reluctance by member states to become involved so far away, and decisive action was not forthcoming.

A commission of inquiry, the *Lytton Commission*, was dispatched by sea to the Far East. Its report did not appear for over a year. When it did, it recognized Japan's interests in the area, but nevertheless acknowledged China's sovereignty there, demanding that the Kwantung army be withdrawn.

The Japanese refused to withdraw, but withdrew from the League instead, and proclaimed the former Manchu ruler, Pu Yi, as Emperor of their puppet state of Manchukuo. The League took no action. The whole episode marked a stage in the League's decline, and showed how it would allow determined aggression to succeed. The example was not lost on Mussolini or Hitler.

▷ **The Abyssinian**
crisis, 1935

Italian ambitions in Abyssinia

Mussolini saw Italy as a major power with naval ambitions in the Mediterranean area, and the ambition to build a colonial empire in Africa like Britain or France. Geological surveys in eastern Africa had shown the presence of oil; Abyssinia was weak, lying between the small Italian colonies of Eritrea and Somaliland.

A dispute over the exact location of the frontier in the Ogaden region followed a dispute at the tiny oasis of Wal Wal. Following a skirmish, Mussolini claimed the territory and compensation for the lives of Italians killed there.

Emperor Haile Selassie refused to give way, and referred to the League.

The League and Abyssinia

Haile Selassie appealed to the League on three occasions in 1935, on the final occasion successfully, but by then the war had already begun.

The League condemned Mussolini's actions, but was reluctant to apply sanctions because Britain and France wanted to retain his friendship. At Stresa in April 1935, Italy, Britain and France announced 'close and cordial collaboration' to ensure compliance with the peace treaties, and went on to condemn German rearmament.

When Mussolini invaded Abyssinia in October, there was a good deal of dithering before sanctions were finally agreed; but Germany would have nothing to do with them, and in any case they did not extend to coal, oil or steel, commodities which Mussolini needed most. Nor did Britain close the Suez Canal to the passage of Italian troops – on the grounds that such a closure would be illegal under the original agreement under which the canal had been built.

Furthermore, in December 1935, Britain and France concluded a 'compromise' with Mussolini (the Hoare–Laval Pact) under which most of Abyssinia was awarded to Italy in return for a narrow corridor of land connecting Abyssinia to the sea. This pact forced the resignation of its British originator, Sir Samuel Hoare, and was universally condemned; Mussolini decided that the Stresa Front was not worth the paper it was written on, and abandoned it, while Hitler noted that the League powers lacked determination and could be defied with impunity.

Mussolini completed his conquest by May 1936 and proclaimed Victor Emmanuel III the new Emperor, driving Haile Selassie into exile in Britain.

German expansion under Hitler

▷ **Hitler's**
violations of
the Treaty of
Versailles

Initially, Hitler's protests against the Treaty of Versailles aroused little hostility; it was regarded as natural, and even as right, that he should wish to escape from the limitations it imposed upon him. Only when his aggressive intentions became obvious did Europe become alarmed.

The early steps

When, in January 1935, Hitler arranged a plebiscite in the Saar, there were few who were surprised or disappointed with the result. The Saar was clearly part of Germany, and many regarded its reunion with the Reich as natural and justified. In any case, it had not been forbidden by the treaty.

In March 1935, Hitler revoked the disarmament clauses of the treaty and began building up a large army. There were many who defended this on the grounds that the restrictions on him had been unreasonably tough; others were inclined to blame France for its harsh insistence on the letter of the law, which had driven Hitler from the Geneva Disarmament Conference the previous year.

In June 1935, Britain actually signed a naval rearmament treaty with Hitler, allowing him to rebuild a German fleet up to 35 per cent of the British navy. At the time, Britain was keen that Hitler should not become the ally of Mussolini; Baldwin also naively believed that Hitler would keep within the agreed limitations.

The remilitarization of the Rhineland

In March 1936, Hitler broke both the Versailles Treaty and the Locarno Agreement and began to remilitarize the Rhineland. Neither Britain nor France liked this development, but neither thought it was sufficient justification for war, and though for a time the air was thick with paper protest, they allowed the incident to pass without retaliation. Little attempt was made to refer the matter to the League; in any case, even if Britain and France had, the burden of enforcement would have been entirely up to them, and they were unwilling to shoulder it.

The Spanish Civil War, 1936–39

After he had supported a right-wing military dictatorship on the part of Primo de Rivera after 1923, King Alfonso XIII abdicated in 1931, and a republic was set up.

There were many quarrels between the conservatives and the progressives:

(a) The republicans and their socialist allies sought to reduce the influence of the army and the church, and help to create a more equal society with better chances for the peasantry; but the upper classes resisted this bitterly.
(b) Left-wing parties favoured anti-clerical policies and nationalization – state control of industry, banks, etc. The upper classes favoured the church and private enterprise.
(c) Left-wing parties supporting the republic included different socialist groups and a sizeable Communist Party that wished to cultivate close relations with the USSR; the right-wing parties preferred fascist support from Italy and Germany.
(d) Republicans encouraged demands for home rule by provinces such as Catalonia, which right-wing parties thought would lead to the disintegration of Spain; they favoured policies to strengthen and centralize the government.

In 1936, liberals and socialists formed a *Popular Front*, winning power to form a government of the left, with a majority of seats, though not of votes cast. Right-wing groups, angry because they feared a domination of the government by the communists, plotted against the republic. Extremists on both sides resorted to violence, perpetrating atrocities against their opponents.

The disorder provided an opportunity for military revolt by disaffected soldiers, and there were risings in five garrison towns.

General Franco seized the opportunity to bring in rebel troops from northern Africa, and later took control at the head of the nationalists. He expected a quick and easy victory, but was forced to engage in a long, bitter struggle against the republic, which was still supported by the vast majority of the people.

From the start, Mussolini and Hitler supported the nationalists. Mussolini hoped to counter British power in the Mediterranean, and to assert his power around what he called 'Mare Nostrum'. Hitler also sent munitions, planes and troops and even a battleship to intercept republican shipping. At one point the Luftwaffe practised its skills in the blitz of the Basque town of Guernica.

Stalin, on the other hand, supported the republic, but not very vigorously since he had denounced Trotsky for 'world revolution' and did not wish to encourage it. He therefore sent very limited help and insisted on being paid for it. The republic shipped its entire gold reserve to the Soviet Union, but when it got to Odessa it was stolen.

Western opinion was deeply divided: half felt threatened by the spread of communism to Spain; the other half were more afraid of the growth of fascism.

The governments of France and Britain, not knowing on which side they should intervene, were anxious to preserve their neutrality. Volunteeers from the democracies, and even from the USA, joined in on the republican side, forming the *International Brigades* to fight against the nationalists. However, they were not numerous, had limited support and made little difference to the outcome of the war.

The matter was referred to the League of Nations, but no action was decided upon. This was allegedly because the war was a civil war rather than an international crisis, and so the League was supposed to have no right to intervene.

The League powers established a *Non-Intervention Committee* to denounce intervention, but no one took it seriously, least of all Germany and Italy.

Measures were agreed at the *Nyon Conference* (1937) to check interference with shipping (what was called 'piracy'). Attacks by 'unknown' submarines in the Mediterranean were somewhat lessened, but this was really only because Mussolini was afraid of being caught.

The war ended in 1939 only with the complete victory of the nationalists.

The policy of appeasement

Collective security – the belief that if enough powerful states banded together to preserve peace, would-be aggressors would be deterred from their ambitions – came to an end with the collapse of the Stresa Front after 1936. Hitler was now more difficult to restrain.

Origins of appeasement

By 1937, Britain and France had both begun to rearm while assuring their peoples that they were doing no such thing. In Britain, a new Prime Minister, Neville Chamberlain, was prepared to do everything possible to preserve peace against a background that was becoming ever more menacing. Chamberlain, whose knowledge of taxation details and municipal drainpipes was perhaps greater than his experience of international diplomacy, developed three approaches to dealing with the questions of the 1930s: first, reliance on the League of Nations as an agency for resolving problems; when that failed, second, direct settlement with Hitler by negotiation, to satisfy his demands; and, third, if all else failed, rearmament so that Britain could fight to defend its interests.

By 1937, he had little hope that the League of Nations would be able to accomplish anything. So he attempted a negotiated agreement with Hitler, hoping to be able to meet his demands. This policy was known as one of *pacification*, or, as it became known, 'appeasement', after the French expression *appaisement*.

The Anschluss with Austria

The union of Austria with Germany, rather illogically, was forbidden in the Treaty of Versailles. France had taken steps in 1931 to counter even a customs union between the two, and in doing so had helped to precipitate the financial crisis in that year.

Hitler had failed to achieve a Nazi takeover in 1934, but his failure still rankled and he returned to the idea in 1938. He bullied the Austrians into submission, and secured the promotion of sympathetic Nazis to key positions in the Austrian government. Then he encouraged Austrian Nazis to stage disturbances, and, on the pretext of restoring order, marched in German troops. The whole plan was carried out quite bloodlessly, and then Hitler staged a plebiscite to show the world how popular he was.

The western powers were quite alarmed. Nevertheless, they thought of Austria as Hitler's 'backyard', believing the Austrian people to be German by speech and culture; so there was nothing very wrong in uniting them under the same government. They also had the evidence of the recent plebiscite – though some among them were quite aware that its results were likely to be suspect. They were undecided what to do; they certainly had no intention of involving the Soviet Union. In the end, all they did was to strike Austria's name from the membership list of the League of Nations.

The Sudetenland crisis and the annexation of Czechoslovakia

It was against Czechoslovakia later in 1938 that Hitler made his next move. He seized on the opportunity of taking up Sudetenland complaints that German-speaking citizens were being badly treated by the Czech government, and demanded that the remedying of these grievances be given top priority. Like Austria, Czechoslovakia had never been part of Germany before, but this did not prevent Hitler from threatening to intervene there unless his complaints were given an immediate hearing.

Chamberlain, trying to resolve the crisis peacefully, sent the *Runciman Mission* to the country in August to investigate their grievances. Runciman reported that the German areas might be given home rule within the Czechoslovak state, but the Czechs were reluctant to act, and the crisis rumbled on. Hitler began to make dire threats that the problem had to be resolved before the end of September. Thoroughly alarmed, Chamberlain flew to Germany three times in order to reach a solution.

He flew on 15 September to *Berchtesgaden*, where Hitler demanded the immediate cession of the Sudetenland to Germany. Chamberlain consulted the French government, and offered ,to cede to Germany all areas of Czechoslovakia where the German population exceeded 50 per cent. The areas were to be determined by plebiscite. The Czechs were forced to agree to this, even though they had not been consulted.

Chamberlain flew to *Godesberg* in the Rhineland on 22 September, only to find to his dismay that Hitler now demanded that German troops occupy the whole of the Sudetenland by 1 October, thus pre-empting any plebiscite results. Chamberlain was very angry that Hitler had quite brazenly moved the goalposts. He could hardly have been surprised when the Czechs rejected this new demand. France was bound to honour its treaty obligations to help Czechoslovakia; the USSR, too, was bound to act, but only if France moved first. In Britain, schoolchildren were set to filling sandbags and trying on gas masks.

On 29 September, Chamberlain again flew to Germany, this time to *Munich* for a conference with the representatives of Britain, Germany, France and Italy. Neither Czechoslovakia nor the USSR was invited. Agreement was reached in the early hours of 30 September. The Godesberg memorandum was accepted in its entirety: German troops were to march into the Sudetenland, with Hitler making the 'concession' that the occupation be completed by 15 October instead of 1 October. Parts of Czechoslovakia were to be ceded to Poland and Hungary, and final boundaries other than for the Sudetenland (which was to go entirely to Germany) were to be decided later by plebiscite. Hitler also signed an agreement, the famous 'piece of paper' in which Britain and Germany pledged their joint commitment to peace.

It was this paper which Chamberlain waved triumphantly on his return to Heston Airport the following day. 'I believe it is peace in our time', he told the cheering crowds in Downing Street later that evening.

Perhaps it would have been if Hitler had been the reasonable man Chamberlain thought him to be. If so, the price might have been worth paying. But Munich did not teach Hitler to be reasonable; it taught him that ruthlessness pays.

Germany was much strengthened; Britain and France had shown that they were unreliable friends and allies, and that they would give in to threats of force. Some critics, like Churchill, believed Munich was a humiliation, and that it was time to call Hitler's bluff. To the critics, it seemed unlikely that Hitler would have dared attack a mobilized and powerful Czechoslovakia, especially if it had the backing of Britain, France and the USSR. As it was, Munich marked the high water mark of appeasement; peace had been bought, but at too high a price.

Hitler was now convinced that he could do as he liked. In March 1939, disorders in Czechoslovakia gave him the excuse he needed; he marched into Prague and occupied the whole country, dividing it into two halves, making the western half a protectorate of the Reich, and responding to the demands of the Slovaks for home rule by granting independence to Slovakia in the east.

If Chamberlain wondered if Czechoslovakia was the last of Hitler's territorial demands in Europe or the first of his steps towards world domination, he did not have to wait long to find out.

The end of appeasement

Only a week after the fall of Prague, Ribbentrop's intimidation of the Lithuanian Foreign Minister was followed by the seizure of Memel and its surrounding territory and its annexation by East Prussia.

Any hope that Mussolini might offer a voice of restraint was dashed when Mussolini used the Easter holiday to launch a surprise attack on Albania, an invasion so ham-fisted in its execution that, as was said at the time, it could have been repulsed by any reasonably well-trained fire brigade. After conquering this tiny kingdom, Mussolini went on in 1940 to invade Greece, which took even longer.

In the interval, Britain had offered guarantees to Poland (which was actually much more difficult to defend than Czechoslovakia), and then to Greece, Romania and Turkey. This was far from the earlier policy of appeasement, and was said to represent exactly the opposite: 'A guarantee a day keeps the dictator away'. Hitler's response was to sign the *Pact of Steel* with Mussolini, and to denounce the Anglo-German naval treaty of 1935.

In May, Britain stepped up rearmament, and introduced military conscription.

The Polish crisis, 1939

Also in March 1939, Hitler made common cause with Albert Forster, the Nazi Gauleiter of Danzig, to secure improved conditions for German-speaking citizens in the city. Hitler demanded the union of Danzig with the Reich, and, at the same time, permission to open a strategic road and rail link across the Polish Corridor to join Germany proper with Danzig and with East Prussia.

In spite of the ideological uncertainty which he felt, Chamberlain tried to make good his pledges of support for Poland by securing a promise of Soviet help. A British delegation of junior officials, headed by a Foreign Office mandarin, was sent to Moscow; the Soviet Union countered by suggesting a triple alliance of the USSR, Britain and France, together with a military convention and a guarantee to border states in eastern Europe. Eastern European states were unwilling, since they feared Soviet protection as much as they feared Soviet hostility. In particular, Poland was unwilling to allow Soviet troops on its soil, even to defend it, and Chamberlain, doubting the efficiency of the Soviet army after the purges, was disinclined to put pressure on Poland to override its objections. Military discussions were equally fruitless, and the British negotiators were finally left empty-handed.

In the meantime, however, the Germans and the Soviets had agreed the Molotov–Ribbentrop Pact – a non-aggression pact that was to run for ten years, with a secret protocol under which the Soviet Union was to secure dominance over the Baltic states and a demarcation of areas of influence in Poland, for when the country should be partitioned between the two. Stalin, conscious of his weakness, preferred peace as the ally of the Germans rather than war as the ally of the British and French.

The war began on 1 September, when German troops invaded Poland.

▷ **Assessment of the policies of the 1930s**

Two attitudes only seemed possible towards Hitler in the 1930s – appeasement or defiance. The western powers tried the first, but when it failed to deliver the required results, swung towards the other.

The attitudes of the Axis powers

Germany

There were forces at work in Germany, mainly in the army, which would have been willing, as late as 1938, to overthrow Hitler and to replace him with someone more moderate and reasonable in his views, but such forces were inclined to blame the weakness of the democracies rather than their own hesitation for their inaction.

Hitler had considerable appeal to the German people: he had restored their self-respect, undone the hated treaty, created work and prosperity, and built up Germany's armed forces again. In diplomacy, he had run rings round the professionals and held people like Chamberlain in furious contempt: 'I have only one worry, namely that Chamberlain, or some other such pig, will come forward at the very last moment with some proposal or with some treachery. He will go flying down the stairs, and I'll jump on his belly personally in front of all the photographers!'

Though *Mein Kampf* was ridiculed at the time, it became ever clearer as time went on that Hitler meant much of what he had written there quite literally, and the book revealed his vulgar, unstable and paranoid character. The Anti-Comintern Pact showed his profound antipathy towards communism, while the Axis Pact and the Pact of Steel with Mussolini showed his militaristic leanings. All the same, until the Allied declarations of war, Hitler thought that his mixture of lies and bluff might succeed in winning successes and avoiding open conflict.

His only regret came to be that his diplomatic allies and his party supporters within Germany lacked his drive and his grim conviction, and finally were too weak to bear the burden he laid on them.

Italy

Mussolini, originally Hitler's model, lacked both the megalomaniac vision of his ally and the material means of accomplishing his country's ambitions. He was reluctant to be engaged in such an enormous struggle, believing he was subordinating his interests to those of his Nazi ally; he preferred his own more local concerns. Thus he was only a half-hearted ally when it came to destroying the Jewish nation, or fighting in a world struggle against the Soviet Union.

By 1943, his support was a liability to Hitler rather than an asset.

The western democracies

Britain

There were many domestic problems confronting Baldwin's and Chamberlain's governments in the 1930s, and memories of the First World War were so raw and hideous that they preferred to deal with domestic matters rather than squander their resources on re-armament and war. In any case, there was considerable sympathy in Britain for Hitler's objectives and methods, and the British leaders hoped to the last that they could negotiate solutions that would satisfy his demands.

The upper classes feared communism more than fascism, and did not seriously want an agreement with the Soviets even when they could have got one. They did not trust their French allies either: not only did they have left-wing governments, but they were militarily weak and quite prepared to betray their allies.

France

The French were very conscious of their own weakness, and ever since Versailles had been playing a role which their resources were not able to sustain. The governments of the Third Republic were weak and short-lived, their army behind the times and no match for the German army, and their mechanized forces very much under strength, as de Gaulle pointed out in 1936.

They had alliances with a number of European states such as Czechoslovakia, but thought they had to have Britain behind them before they could fulfil their treaty obligations. They suspected that Britain was pushing them into a war, and at the last minute would abandon them and leave them to face the music alone. This can clearly be seen in September 1939, when France took care not to declare war first.

The Soviet Union

Self-preservation was uppermost in Stalin's mind in 1939, taking precedence over his carefully rehearsed communist ideology. He was aware of the effects which his army purges had produced in the strength and discipline of his fighting forces, and he was as anxious as Lenin had once been for a 'breathing space'.

The western democracies were offering him war, and a war in which he would bear the main burden; Hitler was offering peace and security, and, for good measure, a slice of Poland to gratify his patriotism. The Non-Aggression Pact, of course, was a million miles from the sentiments of *Mein Kampf*, but Stalin hoped that Hitler would not carry out the threats which that book contained.

 GLOSSARY

Anti-clericalism Opposition to the power and influence of the church. In Roman Catholic countries like France and Spain, it meant opposition to the important part played by the church in politics and education, and led to the growth of left-wing political parties committed to the reduction and elimination of church influence. They wanted the complete separation of church and state, and they were prominent in the Popular Front governments of France and Spain during the mid-1930s. In Spain, where anti-clericalism led to attacks on churches and violence against nuns, it alarmed many into supporting Franco and the Falangists during the 1930s civil war.

International Brigades These were civilian volunteers, organized into military units, who fought on the republican side in the Spanish Civil War. They were left-wing sympathizers, mainly from Europe and the USA, most of whom believed that in fighting against Franco they were advancing the cause of international socialism. They showed much bravery and idealistic commitment, but in the end they were no match for the professional soldiers of Franco, and his German and Italian allies. The total numerical strength of the brigades never exceeded 20,000, but included many well-known intellectuals such as George Orwell and W.H. Auden.

Non-Intervention Committee Fear that the Spanish Civil War might bring about the involvement of other European powers led almost 30 European governments to agree not to assist either side in the war. This non-intervention agreement of 1936 had originally been proposed by Britain and France, and the Non-Intervention Committee held its meetings in London. Almost from the outset, Germany and Italy broke the agreement and their example was soon followed by Soviet Russia. Other states proclaimed their intention to stand by the agreement, but many secretly traded with one side or the other and often with both. The committee continued to meet with increasingly little effect until it became certain that Franco would win; by then the meetings of the committee had become pointless.

Pact of Steel An agreement signed in May 1939 by which the loose alliance between Germany and Italy was strengthened. It signalled Italian approval of the German takeover of Czechoslovakia, and German approval of the Italian conquest of Albania. It was not a precise and formal alliance, but Hitler and Mussolini agreed to act together to safeguard European civilization in this 'the seventeenth year of the Fascist Era'. It was thus an agreement of the two fascist powers to act together internationally in the fascist interest. The Axis Pact of the following year turned it into a formal alliance.

EXAMINATION QUESTIONS

 Question 1   (a)   Why did Chamberlain follow a policy of appeasement?   (15 marks)

(b)   In what circumstances and for what reasons did Britain abandon appeasement?   (15 marks)

 Question 2   (a)   'The Munich Agreement was a great success for Britain and France.' Do you agree or disagree with this statement? Explain your answer.   (15 marks)

(b)   Hitler had always declared his hatred of Russian communism. Yet in August 1939 the Soviet Union signed an agreement with Germany. Why did the Soviet Union do so?   (10 marks)

EXAMINATION ANSWERS

Question 1   *Outline answer*

(a)   A lot of marks are involved here, so this will require a detailed discussion with several reasons developed. Chamberlain's overwhelming desire for peace and his horror of war were widely shared; memories of the First World War were still vivid, and there was the widespread belief that the Second World War would be even more destructive. Guernica reinforced that belief. Chamberlain had the notion that in dealing with Hitler he was dealing with a reasonable man with justifiable grievances. The grievances, over the Saar, the Rhineland, Austria, the Sudetenland (not a Versailles grievance!), Memel and the Polish Corridor need to be looked at in the argument (but not presented in narrative form). The paradox that Chamberlain wanted peace and believed the British people wanted peace, and yet that he needed time for Britain to rearm, needs to be looked at. Some assessment would reinforce an award of the top Level: for example, was Chamberlain taken in by Hitler? Did he really believe that a signature on a piece of paper would be a reliable guarantee of peace? Was Chamberlain just playing for time?

(b)   Here both circumstances and reasons are required. Crucial in causing Chamberlain to abandon appeasement was Hitler's seizure of Prague and the break-up of Czechoslovakia in March 1939. The seizure of Memel and the Italian attack on Albania confirmed that appeasement had failed. Chamberlain was now convinced that the dictators could no longer be trusted. Chamberlain's response was to offer treaty guarantees to Germany's smaller neighbours including Poland, to accelerate rearmament and to introduce conscription, and to attempt to negotiate an alliance with the Soviet Union. It is important that all this is discussed before tackling the Polish crisis in detail. The Nazi–Soviet Pact made war virtually inevitable, but it is worth pointing out that, even up to the very last minute, Chamberlain had not completely abandoned appeasement and was prepared to buy peace at a price, even though the price was not high enough for Hitler.

▷ Question 2(a)   *Tutor answer*

From Munich Chamberlain brought back a piece of paper – his agreement with Hitler which seemed to promise 'peace in our time'; peace lasted less than one year. Munich was not even a diplomatic triumph. Chamberlain's three trips to see Hitler began with a plan to cede those parts of the Sudetenland with 50 per cent Germans to Germany, continued with a demand by Hitler for the whole of the Sudetenland by 1 October, and ended with Hitler 'giving way' and agreeing not to take the whole of the Sudetenland until 15 October. Hitler, in fact, had conceded nothing and gained all. It has been strongly argued by those with hindsight that the Czechs, with their 35 divisions and their virtually impregnable frontier defences, would have given a much better account of themselves than the Poles did in the following year. And the Soviet Union would have been on the side of the Czechs instead of regarding the western allies with suspicion and eventually entering into negotiations with Germany. The Munich settlement undermined what international confidence remained in the League of Nations, and in the two leading members of it, Britain and France. The settlement gave Hitler the impression that nothing would be denied to him, and that Britain and France were weak-willed and could be safely ignored. Thus Hitler now believed that Britain and France would seek to avoid war at any cost, and this gave him the self-confidence to proceed to even more outrageous demands. If Britain and France had any justification, it was that by postponing war at Munich they gained time to rearm. Perhaps in 1938 this belief was not unreasonable, but in fact it gave Hitler time too, and many experts say that Munich gave Hitler time to pull even further ahead in armaments and trained men. So it is difficult to see how Britain and France could regard Munich as a success except in the short-term postponement of war. In the long term, France had gained time, but not enough to avoid the disaster of 1940, and Britain had gained time, but not enough to avoid the darkest days of 1940 and 1941.

Note: This is strongly argued one way. Those who claim Munich as a success and substantiate their argument can also reach top Level, as can those who attempt a closely argued balancing act.

▷ Question 2(b)   *Student answer with examiner's comments*

'Not what is required. These are Hitler's reasons, not Stalin's.'

'Nor in Asia either.'

Hitler had seen with some alarm the negotiations between Soviet Russia and the western powers in the summer of 1939. They raised the spectacle of Germany having to fight a war on two fronts. Hitler had no intention of abandoning the aims stated in Mein Kampf, *but by coming to an agreement with Stalin he could postpone the inevitable war with Russia until a time of his own choosing. He knew that Stalin was annoyed about Munich and that Russia felt isolated.*

From Stalin's point of view he seemed to have no option but to negotiate with Germany. The Anti-Comintern Pact threatened Russia with attack both in Europe and in Asia, and Russia had no allies in Europe. Czechoslovakia had been sacrificed at Munich and Stalin had not been invited to the discussions. He doubted the sincerity of Britain's and France's new hostility to Hitler in the spring of 1939, and their unwillingness to put pressure on Poland convinced him that Britain and France were not seriously seeking a Russian alliance. He had no alternative but to buy time by coming to an agreement with Germany. He did not doubt that Hitler would eventually turn against him, but thought that for the moment Hitler would be preoccupied in the West. The recent purges in the Russian army meant that time was needed for consolidation and reorganization. And there were immediate advantages to be gained. A new partition of Poland would move Russia's frontier 200 miles further west, giving greater strategic security, and the free hand Hitler offered in Estonia and Latvia could be extended unilaterally to Lithuania and Finland. Moreover Hitler offered to buy Russian grain and oil in return for capital goods. Stalin probably reflected that he had got the better bargain.

Examiner's decision on the student answer
The second paragraph contains an excellent answer. The digression in the first paragraph will not deprive it of top Level, but might lead to a mark of 9/10 rather than 10/10.

SUMMARY

In this chapter you have learned more about the developments of the 1930s, especially relating to:

▷ the economic and political consequences of the Great Depression;

▷ the decline of the League of Nations in the 1930s, with regard to:

▷ Japanese expansion into Manchuria and China,

▷ the Italian conquest of Abyssinia,

▷ its later inability to check the advances of Hitler;

▷ the outbreak of the Spanish Civil War and its political consequences;

▷ the policy of appeasement, and the reasons for its failure.

The chapter concludes with an assessment of the international policies of the 1930s.
   The history of the Second World War follows in chapter 12.

Chapter 12

The Second World War, 1939–45

GETTING STARTED

When Britain and France decided to make a stand in support of Poland, the policy Hitler had pursued in the 1930s eventually produced a war. This war was the most important conflict that the twentieth century had witnessed.

MEG	NEAB	NICCEA	SEG	LONDON	WJEC	TOPIC	STUDY	REVISION 1	REVISION 2
	✓		✓*	✓		**Germany on the attack**			
	✓		✓*	✓		The Nazis conquer Europe			
	✓		✓*	✓		**Japan on the attack**			
	✓		✓*	✓		The beginning of the Pacific war			
	✓		✓*	✓		**The Home Front**			
	✓		✓*	✓		British society during the war			
	✓		✓*	✓		The impact of the war			
	✓		✓*	✓		**Germany and Japan on the defensive**			
	✓		✓*	✓		Hitler's empire crumbles			
	✓		✓*	✓		The defeat of Japan			

* Coursework only

WHAT YOU NEED TO KNOW

Germany on the attack

▷ **The Nazis conquer Europe**

In 1939, Britain and France can be blamed for their unpreparedness, the USA for its isolationism and the Soviet Union for the shortsightedness of its Non-Aggression Pact with the Nazis. But weakness and shortsightedness are excusable. It is impossible to defend or excuse Hitler's policy of expansion and aggression, and Germany's leaders must bear the major responsibility for the war.

German successes in Poland and western Europe, 1939–40

Poland

When German troops crossed the frontier on 1 September 1939, Britain and France honoured their obligations by going to war with Germany, but they could not do much to help Poland. Tactics soon to be repeated in the west rapidly crushed Poland; against Germany's armour the Polish cavalry fought gallantly, but in vain.

The German attack was swiftly supported by a Soviet invasion from the east on 19 September, with the forces of the Red Army moving forward to recover those areas lost as a result of the Russo-Polish War of 1920–21. The Poles found themselves caught between the upper and the lower grindstones, and by early October virtually all organized resistance was at an end.

When Finland refused the Soviet demand for bases in November, a 'Winter War' began, the tiny Finnish army fighting against the immensely superior numbers of the Soviets. The defensive successes of the Finns excited western admiration, and plans were even discussed to send them help through Norway and Sweden, a scheme blocked by the determination of the Swedes to maintain their neutrality. Norway's neutrality, however, was compromised by Allied mine laying in Norwegian waters.

Western Europe

Meanwhile the British and the French in the Maginot Line and the Germans in the Siegfried Line faced each other along the Franco-German border. The worst things that happened were air sorties to drop thousand of pamphlets over enemy cities. Both sides seemed confident that their lines were impregnable; both sides expected to overwhelm the other with a tremendous offensive, and so avoid the trench stalemate of the First World War. Along the Belgian part of the border, however, French defences were primitive and incomplete.

This did not prevent a mood of overoptimism among the British people, encouraged by a number of incidents in the war at sea, such as the defeat and scuttling of the German pocket battleship *Graf Spee* in the River Plate in South America. This feeling of complacency was reinforced at Christmas 1939, when Gracie Field's broadcast home from 'somewhere in France' included the popular song:

> We're going to hang out the washing on the Siegfried Line
> If the Siegfried Line's still there.

By the spring of 1940 this inactivity had been given the name of 'phoney war' by an American observer.

In the spring of 1940, however, the stalemate was abruptly broken. The Allies were taken by surprise when, on 9 April, Germany attacked Denmark and Norway. Denmark was easily overrun, but the Norwegians were a tougher nut to crack. British attempts to establish a foothold in central and northern Norway were not successful, and were weakened by a lack of air support – though severe damage was inflicted on the German fleet. Before the last resistance in Norway had ended in early June, the Germans had invaded the Low Countries on 10 May. On that day British misfortunes in Norway helped to cause the replacement of Chamberlain's government by a coalition government headed by Winston Churchill.

The nature of blitzkrieg warfare

At the outset of the war, the German army was able to demonstrate in reality the tactics it had been preparing in training during the 1930s. Later, these tactics were also employed by the Japanese in the Far East. This method of fighting was called the *blitzkrieg* because of the weight of the attack, and the lightning speed with which it was put into effect.

Its four stages followed swiftly one after the other:

(a) dive-bomber attacks on critical communication points – roads, bridges, railway installations and airfields;
(b) paratroop drops to take possession of key strategic points;
(c) columns of tanks moving into enemy territory – light tanks in front, covering heavier tanks behind to knock out military installations;
(d) forward infantry in armoured cars or on motorbikes, followed by the main body of infantry transported quickly by lorry or railway train.

This technique superseded at a stroke traditional defensive tactics, dispensing with conventional lines of communications and making useless static lines of defence such as the Maginot Line, which prided itself on its impregnability. Battles in future were much more fluid, and covered vast areas of territory, e.g. the tank battle for Kursk in central Russia in 1943 involved thousands of tanks of various sizes on both sides, and covered an area nearly as big as England.

The fall of France and the Battle of Britain, 1940–41

The *blitzkrieg* previously seen in Poland was now repeated in the west. Much of Rotterdam was obliterated by German air attack. The Dutch had no answer to the Luftwaffe and the Panzer divisions, and Holland was overrun in five days. The Belgians surrendered in little more than a fortnight, just as British and French troops sent to help were being cut off by a German drive to the Channel ports to the south of them. The

British air force gave the troops some cover, while the British navy during six days organized the evacuation of nearly 340,000 British and French soldiers from Dunkirk. Whether Hitler's interference had slowed down the German advance or not, the 'miracle' of Dunkirk was at the same time a disaster which brought the loss of the British Expeditionary Force's guns and transport, and inflicted on British Fighter Command heavy losses of aircraft. Desperate French pleas for Spitfires were turned down by the British, and with France on the brink of collapse, Britain prepared to defend itself against attack.

Despite Churchill's offer of a political union with France to bolster flagging French resistance, France signed an armistice with Germany on 22 June 1940 in the same railway carriage in Compiègne as the Germans themselves had been forced to accept an armistice in 1918. By this, the Germans came into possession of all France's Channel and Atlantic coasts, and France, with Paris under enemy occupation, moved its capital to the small spa town of Vichy.

Churchill inspired the British people with speeches, but the British army lacked numbers and equipment, and the navy could not defend Britain without air cover. Only the British air force could save the country from the fate of France – mercifully, unknown to the Germans, it had recently been equipped with radar, a newly invented radio tracking device which enormously helped in the effective deployment of its strength. Hitler, who until as late as July had continued to hope that Britain would make peace, found that Britain was prepared to continue alone with the struggle, and had no alternative but to attempt an invasion of Britain for which he was totally unprepared. His plan depended on the Luftwaffe being able to establish a superiority in the air sufficient to counterbalance the weakness of the German surface navy in comparison with the British. Goering, the commander of the Luftwaffe, thought this was possible, and Churchill was under no illusion as to the importance of the struggle to come: 'The Battle of France is over. I expect that the Battle of Britain is about to begin.'

When the battle began in mid-July, the Luftwaffe had the advantage in overall numbers, but not in terms of fighters alone. But since German bombers had to have a fighter cover, the Germans were only able to deploy about half their bomber strength for the operation. Moreover, the German Messerschmitt 109 had an operational radius which barely allowed it to reach London, while the RAF, operating over its own bases, could stay in action longer. The fine summer made it a grandstand spectacle for those living in the south-eastern counties: for six weeks children in some areas slept in air raid shelters rather than in their own beds. On one day alone, the RAF claimed to have shot down over 180 German aircraft.

There may have been some exaggeration here, but none the less it is certainly true that the Germans suffered losses about twice as heavy as those of the RAF. Furthermore, British aircraft production was beginning to outpace its German rivals. By early September, when the Germans attempted to secure victory by switching the attack to London – thus relieving the enormous pressure on the exhausted pilots of Fighter Command – the Luftwaffe found it had met its match. In October, the invasion plans were indefinitely shelved. Churchill commented soberly: 'Never in the field of human conflict was so much owed by so many to so few.'

That was not the end of the story. German night 'blitzes' began before the end of the year, and continued until well into 1942. Though they had little strategic significance, they caused considerable damage and loss of civilian life. They also gave the civilian population the feeling that they were 'in the front line' with the troops, with their own vital job to do.

The Mediterranean war

Italy's entry into the war in June 1940 at first seemed almost an irrelevance; but soon the threat to Britain's lifeline in the Mediterranean became evident. Much shipping used the Suez Canal route, and Britain's oil supplies arrived from the Middle East via the Mediterranean. When Italy came in on the German side, these communications were threatened. The British garrison and dockyard in Malta were very close to Sicily, and the Italian troops who had invaded Egypt were dangerously close to the Suez Canal. The Italian attack on Egypt from Libya might have achieved more, but for Mussolini's embarrassingly unsuccessful invasion of Greece, begun in October. By December the British were able to counterattack, clearing the Italians out of Egypt and overrunning eastern Libya.

The Italian navy suffered such losses at the battle of Matapan that it was forced thereafter to stay in harbour. Mussolini's humiliation was further emphasized by the defeat of his armies in Abyssinia in April 1941, and the restoration of Emperor Haile Selassie.

Italy's weakness was a source of irritation to Hitler, and its defeats made it a liability. In the autumn of 1940 Romania and Hungary felt themselves obliged to sign what amounted to treaties of alliance with Germany; Bulgaria followed in March 1941. Once the adhesion of Yugoslavia had been secured, the Balkans would effectively be in Germany's pocket, and Mussolini could be rescued from the Greeks. Hitler was in a hurry as he was already planning Operation Barbarossa – his invasion of Russia. But he was forced to delay it for six weeks: Yugoslavia decided to resist. It took two weeks for Yugoslavia to be crushed, and another month for Greece to be overrun. The British thinned their troops in north Africa to send aid to Greece, and they went on to give the German parachutists some bad moments in Crete in May 1941; but by the end of that month the Germans and Italians controlled nearly all of south-eastern Europe, and the Italians, with German help, had recaptured Libya and once again invaded Egypt. Only Tobruk (as in the first Italian offensive in 1940) held out behind their lines, until it was eventually forced to capitulate in June 1942.

The invasion of the USSR, 1941, and the 'Great Patriotic War'

The Soviet alliance with Nazi Germany in August 1939 had been an odd marriage of convenience. The Nazi leader, whose followers had fought a running battle in the streets with their communist opponents, and whose hatred of communism fills the pages of *Mein Kampf*, had merely postponed his quarrel with the Soviet Union in order to avoid a war on two fronts by dealing first with Britain and France. Stalin succeeded in buying a little time. Such was his suspicious nature that he ignored western warnings that a German attack was imminent, believing them solely to be designed to drag the Soviet Union into the war. His own intelligence services seem to have underestimated the German preparations, for the German attack of 22 June 1941 took the Soviets completely by surprise. Soviet middle-ranking officers were so intimidated by memories of the recent army purges that they dared take no initiative in the field without first clearing it with their superiors. One Red Army unit radioed: 'We are being fired on. What shall we do?' The answer came back from Headquarters: 'You must be mad. And why is your signal not in code?' It is hardly surprising then that in the confusion bridges were captured intact, hundreds of Soviet planes were destroyed on the ground and no concerted defence was attempted.

Lack of preparedness, the political timidity of Red Army officers and the impact and precision of the German attack cost the Soviets heavily in the first few weeks. The fluidity and unfamiliar speed of the German *blitzkrieg* trapped whole Soviet armies behind the German lines: 650,000 prisoners were taken by October, and about 700,000 more found themselves encircled at Kiev. While Hitler and his generals haggled about their objectives – to seize the coal and the industry of the Don Basin and move on to capture the oilfields of the Caucasus, or to make an all-out effort to seize the political initiative by marching into Moscow – the German juggernaut smashed its way forward, reaching the outskirts of the Soviet capital, and 450 miles to the north-west beginning a siege of Leningrad that was to last nearly three years.

The onset of winter gave the Soviets their first real respite. In many areas, the very success of their offensive had caused the Germans to overreach themselves: they lacked suitable airfields and had to fight without air cover, or they had left their supplies of petrol and ammunition far behind them. Moreover, the expected anti-Bolshevik uprising never came: Soviet citizens, communist and non-communist alike, forgot their differences, accepted Stalin's leadership and turned the German invasion into the Great Patriotic War. Transferring more of their factories further east beyond the Urals, the Soviets began to build up their strength for eventual victory.

But with the spring came the renewal of the German advance. German forces pushed towards the Volga River and the Caucasus, and in August 1942 came up against Stalingrad, a city the Soviets decided to turn into a fortress to check the German advance. As the Germans seemed poised for victory, the Soviets counterattacked, fighting street by street, and building by building in the most savage hand-to-hand combat of the war. In mid-November, Marshal Zhukov was ready to intervene, with no fewer than twelve armies. Pouring troops into the city, he also sent Generals Rokossovsky and Yeremenko in a wide sweep north and south of the city, in a pincer movement to cut off the entire German force, thus besieging the besiegers. A vast German fighting machine was soon entirely cut off and encircled.

A break-out and a withdrawal from Stalingrad would probably have saved the bulk of the German Sixth Army at an early stage, but Hitler would not hear of it. The forces on their flanks – mainly Italian and Romanian – were crumbing rapidly, and disaster seemed inevitable. In January the Soviets advanced on Rostov, threatening to cut off Kleist's Army Group 'A' in the Caucasus. Thanks partly to the Germans still fighting in Stalingrad, they narrowly escaped, but nothing could be done to save the Sixth Army itself. Throughout the intensifying winter cold, the surrounded Germans fought on hopelessly. On 3 February 1943, frozen and starving, the German army, originally numbering well over 300,000 men, surrendered, their commander, von Paulus, earning the dubious distinction of becoming the first German Field-Marshal ever to be captured in battle. After Stalingrad, Hitler's leadership lost its magic: the Soviet Union was now on the attack and the effect on German morale was immense.

Japan on the attack

▷ **The beginning of the Pacific war**

It has been suggested that the Second World War began not in the west in 1939, but in the Far East in China in 1937. Japan had a controlling grip on nearly all China's coastal provinces by 1939. In 1940, Japan took advantage of the fall of France and Holland to help itself to the lands of French Indochina and the Dutch East Indies.

The Japanese made no secret of their belief that it was their destiny to dominate eastern Asia and the Pacific. They were short of raw materials and wary of the Soviet Union, against which Japan had fought a short and unsuccessful war in 1939. But in April 1941, Japan escaped the possibility of a Soviet attack when the two countries met and signed a neutrality pact. The Japanese were now relieved of any threat of a 'stab in the back' and left free to pursue their own designs.

Pearl Harbor and its results

The Japanese plans to bring the whole of south-east Asia under their economic and military control met one chief obstacle – the USA. The Americans countered recent Japanese expansion by demanding immediate withdrawal, and placing an embargo on the supply of oil and other vital materials to Japan. Britain fell into line by reopening the Burma Road, which had been closed by the British in response to pressure from Japan in 1940. This action renewed the supplies of arms and raw materials to nationalist China in 1941. The Japanese had no intention of giving way, but allowed negotiations with the United States to continue in the hope of reaching a settlement.

The Japanese Prime Minister, General Tojo, however, believed that Japanese plans were certain to lead to war against the USA and Britain, and decided to strike a crippling blow first. Despite heavy commitments elsewhere, Japan could call on eleven divisions, over a thousand aircraft, a powerful modern fleet and bases adequate to the task. Furthermore, the Japanese hoped to secure at least the tacit support of native populations by declaring their aim to be the establishment of a *Greater East Asia Co-prosperity Sphere*, which would put a stop to European colonial exploitation in the interests of the whole area.

The basic Japanese strategy was to seize the richly productive areas of south-east Asia in a lightning attack, thus making themselves self-sufficient in oil and vital raw materials, and able to protect their gains by building an impregnable defensive perimeter around the whole area to deter the Allies from trying to dislodge them later. Accordingly, before any declaration of war, on 7 December 1941, Japanese aircraft operating from nearby aircraft carriers attacked the US Pacific fleet at Pearl Harbor in the Hawaiian islands. The results were spectacular. It was early Sunday morning, and the base was taken completely by surprise. There were thousands of casualties, five battleships were sunk and over 200 aircraft destroyed on the ground. At the same time, the US air base at Midway was blitzed and heavily damaged.

It was odd that the simultaneous departure of most Japanese merchant vessels for their home ports, and the sudden radio silence they imposed, passed apparently unnoticed. US naval intelligence, however, was not asleep, and the Japanese code had already been broken. Important naval vessels had been withdrawn from the base before the attack took place, and the conclusion is inescapable that it did not take the Americans quite so much by surprise as their government pretended. It seems that Washington needed this outrage to take place in order to justify the declaration of war on Japan that speedily followed. Hitler and Mussolini shortly afterwards fulfilled their obligations under the Axis Pact by declaring war on the USA.

The war on the mainland

Japan now embarked on a two-pronged attack with its greatest strength on the right. Six divisions would move against the British in Malaya and southern Burma; one division would seize Hong Kong, and two would be sent against the Americans in the Philippines. Finally, two more would converge on the weaker Dutch East Indies.

Hong Kong held out for seventeen days with little artillery and no air support, until the Japanese captured the water supplies and further resistance became impossible.

The danger of a Japanese attack against Singapore had been clear since July, but because of Britain's overriding interest in the desert campaign, nothing had been done to prepare for it. Instead of the great fleet necessary, the naval base held only the warships *Prince of Wales* and *Repulse*, together with a handful of cruisers and destroyers. Aircraft available were few in number and old. The British army commander, Lt.-Gen. Percival, had nearly 90,000 men, and was opposed by smaller numbers of Japanese; but they had 200 tanks, whereas he had none, and they also had the support of over 500 aircraft.

The attack began on 8 December, from the Malayan side. Two days later the Japanese sank both the *Prince of Wales* and the *Repulse*, thereby securing complete control of the sea. At the same time, the superiority of their Zero fighters assured them of control of the air. The defending troops were continually out-thought and out-manoeuvred, and were finally bottled up in Singapore itself. The landward side of the base was almost defenceless, the bulk of its heavy artillery being useless, since it was sunk in concrete emplacements facing outwards to the sea. Reinforcements arrived just in time to surrender on 15 February 1942.

Britain was staggered by the blow. Singapore had been thought one of the great fortresses of the empire, yet it had fallen, and fallen almost without a fight. The 80,000 British prisoners outnumbered the Japanese who had defeated them, and now were imprisoned by them in conditions of barbaric severity.

Later during 1942, the Americans lost the Philippines; Japanese troops overran Burma and threatened India, and the Japanese invasion of New Guinea seemed on the verge of success, and was a direct threat to the security of Australia. For a time, everything went in accordance with the enemy's plans.

The Home Front

▷ **British society during the war**

It is sometimes said that war is the catalyst of social change; certainly the years between 1939 and 1945 saw big changes in British society.

British society at the beginning of the war

The interwar years had brought great improvements in education, living standards and diet, housing conditions and social welfare; in spite of the slump there were generally better wages and smaller families than before.

Even so, social standards left much to be desired. There were vast inequalities of income between the poorer working classes and the better-off; career opportunities for many people were still cripplingly limited; and the government still did relatively little to assist the handicapped and the unfortunate.

The social consequences of the war

The war did much to remove the remaining inequalities in British society:

(a) Wages and social conditions for the majority of people rapidly improved, and as the privileges of the upper classes were whittled away, the numbers engaged in domestic service almost entirely disappeared.

(b) The war produced a greater sense of equality and cameraderie between the classes than previously, especially under the stress of enemy attack.

(c) The government took a livelier interest in welfare than before; Churchill said, 'There is no better investment for the future than putting milk into babies.' This was reflected in measures such as:

  (i) the *Beveridge Report* (1942), promising a comprehensive social insurance system which would protect people 'from the cradle to the grave';

  (ii) the *Butler Education Act* (1944), which abolished school fees in many schools, and created more equal opportunities in the 'tripartite system' of grammar/technical/secondary modern schools.

▷ The impact of the war

The Second World War had a more direct effect on the civilian population than the war of 1914–18. This can be seen in a variety of ways.

The Blitz

Blitzkrieg attacks in 1940–42 devastated cities and caused considerable damage and heavy civilian casualties. These air raids made necessary the creation of elaborate communications systems, effective fire-fighting organizations and first-aid and hospital facilities for the injured. Air-raid wardens patrolled the streets, and every large public building, school and factory had its own team of fire-watchers. Other jobs included rescue workers, volunteer firemen, ambulance drivers, rest-centre helpers, and behind these the forces of the Home Guard and the Special Constables.

London suffered most heavily from these attacks, which occurred almost every night during the autumn of 1940 and during 1941 and 1942, and in which the areas around London's docklands were systematically devastated. Major provincial cities, such as Sheffield, Liverpool, Manchester, Southampton and Plymouth also suffered. In Coventry, for example, over 550 civilians died in a raid on 14 November 1940 which destroyed not so much the engineering works as the city centre and the cathedral; other cities similarly attacked thereafter were said to have been 'coventrated'.

After the Blitz, 1944 witnessed attacks by German pilotless aircraft, the V1s, also known on account of their noisy little engines as 'buzz-bombs' or even 'doodlebugs'. These engines cut out when the V1 was above its target, and the sudden silence was a warning to those below to take cover as the flying bomb fell to earth. Later came the V2s, supersonic missiles launched from the continent and against which there was no defence. These might have been a serious threat to morale had their launching sites not been captured soon after the Allied invasion of Europe.

Altogether over 50,000 British civilians died from enemy air attack during the war, but this was less than the number killed in German raids on Polish cities in 1939, on Dutch cities in 1940 or on Soviet cities in 1941 and 1942. It was also ten times less than Germany's own air-raid casualties in the later stages of the war.

The evacuation

An attempt was made in Britain in 1939 to avoid unnecessary bombing casualties by evacuating children from high-risk areas to safer areas in the countryside. These town children, clutching their gas masks, were taken by train to foster homes in rural England. One of the things which struck people in the reception areas was the poor physical condition of these children. Numbers of them were infested with vermin, chiefly head-lice: flat, greyish-white parasites which crawled over the scalp, and there laid their eggs, called 'nits', which they cemented to the roots of the hair. Some of these children had never seen a cow, and thought that milk came from bottles.

Many evacuees returned to the cities during the 'phoney war', only to be involved in new evacuation schemes organized when German air raids began in earnest in the autumn of 1940. The 'black-out', i.e. the rigorous banning of all artificial lighting in the open – vehicles moved at night with headlights covered except for little slits – made night travel hazardous in all countries which were at war, and was even enforced after December 1941 in vulnerable east-coast states of the USA.

Fig. 12.1 Schoolchildren are evacuated from London, 1 September 1939

Women at war

Women volunteers were encouraged to serve in their own branches of the services, in the army, navy and air force, though not on active service; later in the war, young single women were even conscripted for military service. Women also served in uniform in the nursing services and in the Women's Land Army, where they did necessary agricultural work. In the services, too, women were often chauffeurs and clerks, or served in domestic capacities.

In 'civvy street', women did even more man's work than they had been permitted to do in 1914–18. They worked in munitions factories, and in factories producing clothing, boots, medicaments and other vital war supplies. They did not go down the mines, but they worked in surface jobs. They delivered letters, worked on the railways, drove lorries, trams and buses, and worked as conductresses ('clippies'). Oddly enough, even at the time of Germany's greatest need in 1944–45, fewer women were in war work there than in Britain. It must, however, be remembered that Germany used thousands of foreigners under conditions of extreme duress as 'forced labour'.

Food supplies

It was highly important to maintain food supplies, although the supply of most other consumer goods quickly dried up. In Britain, an effective system of food rationing was introduced in January 1940, as U-boat attacks on British shipping lanes began to strangle imported supplies. Customers had to register with their normal shopkeeper, and in order to obtain their supplies of tea, sugar, butter, margarine, cooking fats, meat, bacon, eggs, etc., had to surrender coupons taken from their ration books. Later in the war, a more flexible 'points' system was devised for tinned goods of all kinds, where purchases were deducted from a points 'score' allowed to each consumer. Later still, clothes and even furniture were also rationed. Rationing grew more severe as greater shortages threatened. In 1946 even bread was rationed, though (unlike the First World War) potatoes never were. Curiously, rationing was never as severe as it was under the Attlee government when the war was over.

Fresh vegetables and fruit – provided it was native fruit (things like bananas disappeared entirely, and children at the end of the war had never seen them) – were fairly readily available. Spare plots of land, even parks, were dug up and planted; it was considered rather unpatriotic to have flowers in your garden when you could be growing carrots and onions. 'Dig for Victory' was the slogan persistently presented to the public throughout the war.

Although there were anxious moments for Britain's food supplies during 1941, the British people were quite adequately fed during the war, and the physical fitness of the civilian population, especially children, showed a marked improvement over that in the 1930s. This was not the case in Europe, drained of its food supplies to feed Germany. Rationing there was severe, and malnutrition was common – especially in major cities where people were denied access to the resources of the countryside. Military operations interrupted food distribution in areas of hostility such as western Russia; anyway, priority was given to the troops. Thousands died of starvation. In contrast, the German people, cushioned by food imports from other areas of Europe, were adequately fed until the closing stages of the war. Allied soldiers crossing from Holland into Germany were struck by the contrast between the gaunt, half-starved Dutch civilians and the well-fed Germans.

The Home Guard

In Britain the invasion danger of 1940 led to the revival of the Local Defence Volunteers (the LDV, derisively nicknamed 'Look, Duck and Vanish'). This was soon to be transformed into the Home Guard. All able-bodied male civilians, except children and pensioners, had to serve in it, unless they were engaged in other war work, in order to assist in the defence of the country against invasion.

Subsequent generations may have laughed at their fictionalized exploits in *Dad's Army*, but at the time they were taken very seriously, though with their broomsticks and their ancient weapons they would have had little chance against invading Panzer divisions, no matter how great their fighting spirit.

Censorship and propaganda

All countries at war censored the news and selected the information which the public should be given. Much of the censorship was necessary for obvious security reasons, and much was justified in the name of public morale. In Britain posters constantly reminded the population that 'Careless Talk Costs Lives'.

Even so, propaganda news broadcasts from Germany could be listened to without penalty; indeed, 'Lord Haw-Haw' (so called because of his drawling accent) gained a large following in Britain without any significant impact on British morale. Those who listened to him did so for his entertainment value, not because they believed what he said. His technique of using accurate information gleaned from prewar guidebooks ('Trinity church clock is two minutes slow') gave a touch of authenticity to his much more fanciful comments on the course of the war.

In Europe, however, listening to Allied broadcasts was an offence which in occupied territories was usually punishable by death. Nevertheless, broadcasts from London, prefaced by a morse-code 'V' (for 'Victory') signal beaten out on a drum, and on Sunday evenings heralded by a full performance of the national anthems of all the occupied countries, were listened to by many, and uplifted even British audiences. They gave comfort to those suffering occupation, and encouragement to the resistance movements (to whom they often sent coded messages) which increasingly plagued the Germans in many countries from 1942 onwards.

Both sides, of course, used propaganda, hammering home their messages by constant repetition in the flimsy newspapers, on the radio and on a wide variety of wall-posters. Unwelcome news was concealed until it could be hidden no longer, and even minor victories were inflated into triumphs. Enemy leaders were ceaselessly reviled for their shape, appearance or sexual prowess (or usually lack of it), as much as for their actions and policies. The Germans, with commendable honesty, called the department under Josef Goebbels by the name of the *Ministry of Propaganda*, while in mealy-mouthed Britain the parallel department was called the *Ministry of Information*.

Travel restrictions

Restrictions on news were accompanied by restrictions on travel. Railways and roads were needed for troop movements, and civilian travel was discouraged. Petrol was strictly rationed for private cars, and then only to be used for important business purposes. Buses and trains were few, uncomfortable and invariably late and overcrowded. 'Don't you know there's a war on?' became the universal excuse for even the grossest inconveniences.

The arrival of American forces in increasing numbers made security of vital importance. From late 1943, preparatory activity was unmistakable: roads were marked into yellow parking lots for tanks and armoured vehicles. Civilians living within 10 miles (16 kilometres) of the coast in the south-east were not allowed to cross county boundaries except on urgent business; everybody else was urged to stay away from the seaside and have 'holidays at home'. But nothing could prevent the locals seeing the huge concentration of weapons and equipment building up on the roads in May and early June 1944, and the sight of gliders moving across the coast at dusk merely confirmed what everyone had suspected for some time – the invasion of Europe was imminent.

Civilian hardship

In Britain this hardship was bearable, as it was in Germany until the final days of chaos in 1945. The Japanese expansion in south-east Asia often brought death, destruction and atrocities in China, and Europeans falling into Japanese hands suffered terrible privations in notorious prisoner-of-war camps. Other nationalities avoided undue hardship only if they collaborated with the Japanese, and they speedily learned to hate their new taskmasters as much as they had European colonialists.

In occupied Europe it was a different story. Everybody shared in the privation, and, as resistance movements grew, German retaliation against civilian populations reached heights of barbarity such as the obliteration of the Czech village of Lidice and the French village of Oradour-sur-Glane. It was not uncommon to execute ten innocent and randomly chosen civilians for every one German assassinated.

The Germans reserved their most unspeakable inhumanity for the Jewish population of Europe, of whom about 600,000, or about a tenth, came from Germany itself. Anti-Jewish measures had become a feature of increasing frequency in Germany since the middle of the 1930s, and these culminated in 1941 with what came to be called the 'final solution', worked out in detail in a highly secret conference at Wansee in early 1942, a solution from which Hitler took pains to distance himself. Jews were rounded up, taken to special concentration camps in isolated localities often in Poland, there robbed and stripped, deprived even of the gold in their teeth-fillings, and, other prisoners having been first forced to dig their grave-pits, finally and without warning exterminated by the thousand in gas chambers.

The horrors of these happenings, scrupulously recorded on film after the liberation of the camps, and still fully documented, were so hideous that even respectable historians have thought them exaggerated – even totally fabricated – and have tried to play them down; but there is absolutely no doubt that they occurred, and that the majority of Germans are heartily ashamed of them. There were acts of heroism and sacrifice by those of many nationalities (including German) who intervened to save Jewish lives at grave risk to themselves. Nevertheless, in this appalling *Holocaust*, 6 million Jews died, probably accounting for about half of all the civilian deaths of the Second World War.

Germany and Japan on the defensive

▷ **Hitler's empire crumbles**

By 1943, Germany's war effort had peaked. All the ranting or persuasion of which Hitler was capable could not squeeze any more energy from his exhausted people. The final catastrophe, to which he had for so long closed his eyes, loomed ever closer.

The Soviet 'steamroller'

After Stalingrad the Germans were never again able to mount a major offensive on the Eastern Front. For the first two summers, 1941 and 1942, the Soviet Union had been on the defensive, turning to the offensive only in winter. But in the summer of 1943 it hit back. After destroying the massed German tanks at the battle of Kursk, the Red Army went on to recapture large areas of the Ukraine and White Russia, and overran the Crimea. The British and the Americans sent limited but useful supplies of materials down the long and hazardous sea-lanes to Murmansk; but in the main it is true to say that the Soviets won the 'Great Patriotic War' by their own efforts.

Stalin, and the communists in the west, demanded the opening of a *second front*, conveniently discounting the efforts his allies were making in north Africa and Italy; but Soviet casualties were extremely heavy, and Stalin might well be forgiven for thinking that their allies were willing to fight the Germans to the very last Russian. To him, any respite would ease the terrible strain.

In January 1944 Soviet forces entered Poland, but in the early part of the year they concentrated on liberating Romania, Bulgaria and Hungary from the German occupation. Although the Soviets were close to Warsaw in the summer of 1944, an anti-German rising of Polish patriots proved to be premature. In crushing it, the Germans did the Soviets an unexpected service in destroying much of the anti-communist leadership in the city.

After a brief pause, the Soviet forces moved on again in January 1945, occupying East Prussia and reaching the River Oder. They fought their way against stiff German resistance to the outskirts of Berlin, while to the south they liberated Austria and Czechoslovakia. Within a few days, Hitler had committed suicide, the Nazi regime had collapsed and Germany had surrendered.

The Italian campaign

The Germans had taken over control of the campaign in north Africa in 1942, and in September, at the first battle of El Alamein, General Rommel, their commander, tried but failed to break through towards the Nile Delta. In October the British Eighth Army led by General Montgomery attacked the Germans – again at El Alamein – with overwhelming superiority both on the ground and in the air, and the Germans were forced into retreat. Montgomery maintained the forward momentum of his advance, and Tobruk, Benghazi and finally Tripoli fell to the advancing troops.

Surprise American landings in Morocco and Algeria threatened Rommel's rear and communications; he abandoned Libya in order to concentrate on the defence of Tunisia and on his lines of communication with Italy. German reinforcements delayed the inevitable, but finally succeeded only in swelling to 160,000 the German army that surrendered there in May 1943. Within two months the first invasion of Europe followed: the Allies landed in Sicily, swiftly overran it and crossed to the mainland of Italy. Although Mussolini's government handed over to Marshal Badoglio, who soon surrendered, the Allies in the confusion that followed missed the opportunity to seize Rome.

The Germans took control of most of the country, briefly re-establishing Mussolini as the puppet ruler of the short-lived Salo Republic in northern Italy, and setting up the powerful defensive Gustav Line in the south. Heavy fighting followed, particularly around the monastery of Monte Cassino, but not until June 1944 did the Allies enter Rome. Half the Italian peninsula still remained to be conquered piece by piece.

D-Day and the invasion of Europe

When Churchill and Roosevelt met at Casablanca in January 1943, they had agreed on the timing of an invasion of France, and further details were discussed when they met Stalin at Tehran in November. Supreme command was entrusted to US General Eisenhower.

The actual invasion took place, after a brief postponement caused by the weather, on D-Day, 6 June 1944. The Germans had been led to expect the attack nearer Calais, with the advantage of a shorter sea crossing, and so the attack on the Normandy coast took them somewhat by surprise. Speed and secrecy, superiority in the air and the use of parachute troops – all essential to earlier German success – guaranteed success to the Allies now. An oil pipeline, PLUTO, kept their vehicles refuelled with less need for cross-Channel tankers which would be exposed to U-boat attack. Within a month German resistance crumbled. Once Normandy was cleared of German forces, the Allied advance was rapid.

Paris was recaptured on 25 August, and the Rhine in Holland was reached in September. A German counterattack in the Ardennes was defeated in December. Once the Allies crossed the Rhine in March 1945, resistance in the west virtually ended.

▷ **The defeat of Japan**

The Japanese fell short of their objectives in 1942: China remained undefeated; India was still in British hands, and Australia still lay unconquered to the south. More important, the US Pacific fleet was damaged but not put out of action.

'Island hopping' against Japan

Japan's resources were inadequate to hold the vast empire it had just acquired. The Japanese loss of four aircraft carriers at the battle of Midway in June 1942 was a serious blow, and a token of the fate in store, for the Pacific war was to become largely a battle for air supremacy based on such carriers.

The Americans, led by General MacArthur, turned to the offensive and captured the island of Guadalcanal, after a bitter six-month battle, in February 1943. The Americans now developed the tactics of *island hopping*, by which they captured one island and by-passed the next, so keeping their enemies permanently at a disadvantage, since they were unaware where the next blow would fall.

In this struggle, the Americans developed a whole new military strategy:

(a) US forces, spearheaded by highly mobile, yet strongly armoured Marines, concentrated superior forces on a narrow front in striking at the island aimed at; isolated Japanese garrisons, on the other hand, frequently threw their lives away rather than surrender, which they considered dishonourable.

(b) The Americans ensured command of the sea and the air, cutting off the defenders from the hope of assistance. This enabled them to dictate the pattern of the struggle and to maintain the advantage of surprise, since the Japanese forces were kept in the dark about American intentions.

(c) US forces always had great technical superiority. Though the Japanese showed great courage and fortitude in defence, they were always finally overwhelmed.

(d) The element of surprise enabled the Americans to hop over Japanese strongpoints without endangering their own communications, so that substantial enemy garrisons were cut off and mopped up later.

Between November 1943 and February 1944, the Americans reduced Japanese outposts, gaining valuable experience in amphibious operations along the way.

Fig. 12.2 The Pacific theatre of war, 1942–45

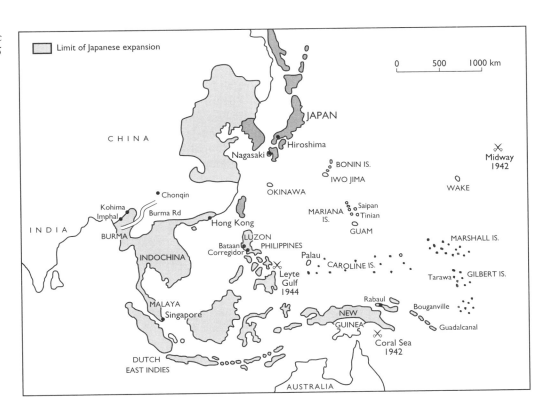

At the same time, the Australians advanced along the coast of New Guinea, while the Americans took Bougainville, cutting off the important air base at Rabaul in New Britain, with its garrison of over 100,000 men. The Gilbert and Marshall Islands fell to superior US forces, and the Japanese naval base at Truk in the Caroline Islands was heavily damaged by attack from carrier aircraft.

In the light of these reverses, the Japanese fell back on their second line of defence in the Palau, Mariana and Bonin Islands. Thus, when three divisions of US Marines landed on Saipan in the Marianas in June 1944, the result was the naval battle by which the Japanese tried to restore their defensive position – the battle of the Philippine Sea. The Japanese had a formidable fleet at their disposal, including five battleships and nine carriers. The Americans were numerically superior, but the Japanese thought they could rely on land-based planes from Guam to restore the balance. However, US fighters shot down two-thirds of the opposing aircraft, while US bombers destroyed the bases at Guam on which the Japanese placed such reliance. US submarines sank two Japanese carriers, and, as the enemy started to retreat, aircraft sank another and damaged four of those remaining. The toll of Japanese planes was catastrophic: they lost so many that US pilots called their encounter 'the great Marianas turkey shoot'. The US forces were now free to continue their advance, and went on to seize the heavily defended islands of Saipan, Tinian and Guam.

Japan's defences crumble

At the same time, British forces began a counterattack in Burma. Brigadier Wingate and his Chindits, who had already been infiltrating the jungle, were able to launch an offensive across the River Irrawaddy preparatory to the reconquest of Burma.

These reverses brought the fall of General Tojo's cabinet in Tokyo and a change in the Japanese government. The new government, however, did not believe that the war was already lost. Ten new divisions of troops were raised, and efforts were made to strengthen the defence of the Philippines against MacArthur's impending attack. But by now Japan's forces were outnumbered by more than four to one and their chances of victory were receding rapidly.

The prelude to the invasion of the Philippines came with the battle of Leyte Gulf in October 1944. MacArthur's fleet, expecting reinforcements from Admiral Halsey's powerful Third Fleet, was faced by everything the Japanese could muster, reinforced by seven Japanese battleships from Singapore. Halsey was decoyed away in pursuit of four Japanese carriers. None the less, both US fleets were overwhelmingly successful in the engagements that followed, most of the opposing capital ships and carriers being sent to the bottom, and over half of their aircraft being shot down. The Japanese Navy Minister commented: 'Our defeat at Leyte was tantamount to the loss of the Philippines. And when the Americans took the Philippines, that was the end of our resources.'

Leyte and Mindoro fell before the end of 1944. In January 1945, US troops embarked on the reconquest of Luzon; Bataan and Corregidor were also recaptured. In March US troops seized control of Iwo Jima, and went on in April to assault Okinawa, both islands within 800 kilometres of the Japanese mainland, and veritable rabbit-warrens of underground defences. Japan fought tenaciously to hold the islands; the Americans suffered 4,000 casualties at Iwo Jima and 12,000 at Okinawa. Air attacks by *kamikaze* suicide pilots on US ships and bases made these casualties even heavier.

Meantime Mandalay and Rangoon had fallen to British troops, and Burma was rapidly being cleared of Japanese forces. Nevertheless, powerful armies remained undefeated, and the Japanese were not prepared to humiliate the Emperor or themselves by accepting the Allied demand for unconditional surrender.

The atomic age begins

In these months, the Americans came to the conclusion that the Japanese would defend every inch of their territory to the last, and that there would be casualties of astronomical dimensions when an invasion of the Japanese mainland was attempted. So it was decided to drop the most deadly of modern weapons, the atomic bomb, on Japan.

The first was dropped on the city of Hiroshima on 6 August 1945, killing about 80,000 of its population and wounding a further 100,000. Three days later, while Japan was still reeling under the shock, a second was dropped on Nagasaki. Because of the geographical configuration of the area, this caused rather fewer casualties, but even so, there were about 75,000 killed and wounded. No one as yet, in either town or elsewhere, had any inkling of the much more insidious danger that would be caused through radiation, or of its long-term consequences.

The USSR, previously kept in the dark about atomic developments, seized the opportunity of the confusion to earn itself a seat at the peace conference by declaring war on Japan, invading Manchuria, and landing troops on the Japanese island of Sakhalin. Shortly afterwards the Emperor brought pressure to bear on his government to agree to capitulate, and the Japanese surrendered unconditionally to General MacArthur on the deck of the US battleship *Missouri*, anchored in Tokyo Bay. The war in the Pacific came to an end.

Causes of the Japanese defeat

The main cause of Japan's overwhelming defeat was the mismatch between the country's ambitions and its capabilities. The *military clique* ruling the country, trading on the obedience and the submissiveness of the whole nation, and its long tradition of respect for its rulers and the Emperor, met little opposition. Its thinking combined military fanaticism with messianic fervour for the future. They were able to sell their wildly unrealistic plans as well within the bounds of possibility, and, in a country where there was little independent thought, let alone critical public opinion, there was little to prevent them putting their plans into effect.

The *resources* of the country were one of its main limitations. Its population, though increased in recent years by almost 25 per cent, was still only about 60 million, with many of them at the peasant level, and little of the intended emigration to territories recently acquired had occurred. Some of the urban centres, like Tokyo with its population of well over 3 million, were densely packed and highly developed, but much of the country was still very rural and backward. Japan's own resources had been rapidly developed, and the country was strong in manufacturing, but it was lacking in many necessary materials like timber and oil, and it had only limited supplies of coal. Manchuria was as yet only partially developed, though it was rich in many industrial materials, and the search further afield for the commodities needed was only just beginning.

This was the reasoning lying behind the Greater East Asian Co-Prosperity Sphere, the main force driving Japan's foreign policy throughout this period. But it was not easy to control the enormous *colonial areas* that came into Japan's control. This was partly due to geographical factors: they covered much of the Pacific hemisphere; they were separated by hundreds of kilometres of sea; communications between them were poor; and their riches were not easily accessible. Furthermore, the native peoples, promised their freedom and independence by the imperial government, found themselves mere serfs, and chafed under the often brutal Japanese regime. National resistance movements sprang up, refusing cooperation and sabotaging essential installations.

Most of Japan's energies had been expended on the *war with China*. The country occupied a vast area and stretched over most of the continent of east Asia, containing millions of inhabitants and dwarfing the armies sent to conquer it. Even if conquered (which it never was) it was going to take far more in the way of resources to hold it in submission than the country was ever likely to yield. China alone was likely to provide an insuperable barrier to Japanese imperialism.

Japan, however, had taken on not only the Chinese, but Britain and the Commonwealth, and the USA at the same time, and, late in the war, the Soviet Union for good measure. The *combined might* of Japan's foes, their population, resources and industrial capacity were such that no one in his right mind would ever have contemplated taking on such a formidable combination. The overwhelming superiority of the Allies in the air, at sea and eventually on land, as well as the ingenuity of their strategists, became clearer as time went by, until by 1945 they were all but irresistible. The advanced character of their scientific research and their nuclear potential was not revealed until the last moment, but clearly this was something in which the Japanese could not begin to compete.

Perhaps the most fundamental error of the Japanese leadership was their *reliance on force*. Japan was the prisoner of traditional concepts of power politics. Its leaders failed to realize that peaceful penetration of the Pacific would have served the country's purposes better than did aggression, and would have saved the enormous expenditure that war involved. The success of Japan's postwar 'economic miracle' and the commercial supremacy that went with it provides a much better indicator of the country's real potential.

GLOSSARY

Battle of the Atlantic   This was the battle to keep open the Atlantic shipping lanes. These carried supplies from the USA, both as a friendly neutral from 1939 to 1941 and as a powerful ally of Britain from December 1941 onwards. The German U-boats inflicted much damage, and in 1942 they were sinking more shipping than could be replaced in the shipyards. But by 1943 the Allies had gained the upper hand: aircraft could patrol most of the Atlantic from land bases; and especially equipped destroyers, radar and convoys all contributed to the defeat of the U-boats, which in 1944 suffered such heavy losses that the German navy temporarily suspended U-boat activity, and could only make a token resumption in the final stages of the war.

Blitz   This German word for lightning has come to mean concentrated and repeated bombing from the air; it was first used in connection with the air attacks on British cities from late 1940 to early 1942.

Chindits   The word 'Chindit' is a corruption of the Burmese word *chinthey*, which means 'brave lion'. It was a reference to the dedicated soldiers who fought in difficult jungle conditions under Wingate's command. They were sometimes called 'Wingate's circus'.

Co-prosperity Sphere   This is the Japanese equivalent of the German *Lebensraum*. Japan's aim was to bring south-east Asia under economic (and political) domination, and this was temporarily achieved at the height of its military power in 1942.

Holocaust   Anti-Semitism had been a major theme in Hitler's *Mein Kampf*, and violence against German Jews intensified after the Nazis achieved power. But the decision to exterminate the Jewish race did not become official policy until 1941, by which time the Germans had overrun countries such as Poland with large Jewish populations. Himmler was personally responsible for the extermination policy, but other Nazi leaders were well aware of what was going on, and approved of it. Concentration camps, such as Auschwitz, became centres for the killing of Jews; here cyanide gas was used. In the Soviet Union, *Einsatzgruppen*, execution squads, machine-gunned their victims into large death-pits. Most of the Jewish populations in European territories under German control were wiped out. It is estimated that at least 6 million Jews lost their lives. Such a deliberate policy of genocide, and on such a huge scale, is unprecedented in modern times.

Phoney war   This name is popularly given to the war on the Western Front from 3 September 1939 to 10 May 1940, during which time the opposing armies sat tight in the Maginot and Siegfried Lines, and the only skirmishes were those between reconnaissance patrols. Of course, it was not a phoney war in Poland, or at sea.

 EXAMINATION QUESTIONS

▷ **Question 1**   Describe two of the following battles or campaigns of the Second World War, and in each case show how it contributed to the eventual defeat of Germany:

(a)   the Battle of Britain;
(b)   the Battle of the Atlantic;
(c)   the Battle of Stalingrad;
(d)   the Normandy landings.

(30 marks)

▷ **Question 2**   (a)   Why were the Japanese so successful in the early stages of the war in the Pacific?

(10 marks)

(b)   Why were the Japanese increasingly unsuccessful in the later stages of the war in the Pacific?

(10 marks)

(c)   Was it necessary to use the atomic bombs to force the Japanese to surrender?

(10 marks)

▷ **Question 3**   'Hitler's greatest mistake was the invasion of the Soviet Union in 1941.'

(a)   Why did Hitler invade the Soviet Union?   (8 marks)

(b)   For what reasons did the invasion turn out to be a disaster for Hitler and Germany?

(10 marks)

(c)   Did Hitler make any other mistakes in the Second World War?   (12 marks)

EXAMINATION ANSWERS

 Question 1 *Outline answer*

At the highest Level, Level 4 in this instance, an answer sharply focusing on how the chosen battle or campaign contributed to Germany's defeat is required; good description will not get you beyond Level 2. Thus it will not be enough simply to say that the Battle of Britain thwarted German invasion plans or that the Battle of Stalingrad prevented the Germans from capturing the Caucasus oil. It will be expected not only that the consequences of the battle or campaign are clearly brought out, but that each is shown in the overall context of the war and of the effectiveness of its contribution to Germany's ultimate defeat. So the Battle of Britain meant the survival of Britain, and without Britain's survival there would have been no European base for the USA and no second front, and the USSR would have had to fight single-handed or give up the struggle. The Battle of the Atlantic saved Britain from starvation both of food and war materials. It made the seas virtually safe for the Allies and dangerous for the Axis powers. It made possible the enormous build-up of men and materials that led to the invasion of France, and ultimately to the successful invasion of Germany from the West. The Battle of Stalingrad saw the collapse of the last major German summer offensive in the Soviet Union. Stalingrad destroyed the myth of German invincibility, forced the Germans on to the defensive and ended their dreams of conquest. It was the first major step towards their ultimate defeat. The final step was the invasion of Normandy. This led to the liberation of France and the Low Countries. It was the second front which relieved the pressure on the Soviets and helped them to accelerate their overrunning of eastern Europe. It brought the land war to Germany's own soil, forced the Germans to face impossible odds on two fronts, and made Germany's defeat inevitable.

 Question 2 *Tutor answer*

(a) From the outset the Japanese had the advantage of surprise: the attack on Pearl Harbor was swift and sudden, and the Americans suffered heavy naval losses which were to handicap them in the early stages of the war, until they could be replaced. While the Americans were not geared up to full-scale war, the British were so closely engaged in north Africa and in protecting Britain that they had few resources to spare for the defence of their bases in the Far East. Hong Kong was virtually surrounded by Japanese-occupied China, and could not realistically expect to hold out for long, and Singapore's defences relied on gun emplacements facing out to sea – a landward attack was neither anticipated nor catered for. This was in part because the British believed Malaya's jungle too impenetrable to be campaign territory. But the Japanese had trained to become skilled jungle fighters, moving swiftly and silently, and using aircraft from carrier bases in support. The British could send only two battleships without air cover to the area, and they were speedily sunk. The Japanese were despised by both British and Americans as 'little yellow men', and thus their superb fighting skills were grossly underestimated by their enemies. The Japanese took pains to conceal their aim to dominate south-east Asia economically and politically, and posed, at first, as liberators coming to drive out the colonial powers, so the native populations tended to be friendly. Within six months of the attack on Pearl Harbor, the Japanese had carved out for themselves a huge empire and began to conceive of themselves as invincible.

(b) Japan's early successes led to the overstretching of its limited resources. Japan had not only acquired Siam, Burma, Malaya, the Philippines and most of the Dutch East Indies, but had to man a 2,400 kilometre front in China. Japan did not have the men to deliver a knock-out blow to China, to conquer India, or to mount an invasion of Australia; and yet, in the summer of 1942, all three were being attempted. But by now the USA had recovered from Pearl Harbor and was building new ships, especially aircraft carriers, faster than Japan. The Americans could anticipate every Japanese move, since the Japanese secret codes had been broken even before the war started, but now the Allies had the resources to make use of this information. Bitter experience had taught the Allies the importance of air cover at sea and the vital significance of aircraft carriers. It had taught them, too, to develop effective jungle fighting techniques, and these led the British to turn the tables on the Japanese in Burma in

1944. The American strategy of island hopping left Japanese garrisons isolated and without supplies, and brought the Japanese mainland within target range of American bombers. The Japanese, so dependent on overseas supplies for their war effort, were gravely handicapped by the loss of sea and air control, and the overseas sources were now threatened as the Japanese came increasingly to be regarded as conquerors rather than as liberators. Japan needed a quick war for certain success; in a war of attrition it was increasingly likely that it would end up on the losing side.

(c)   By the end of 1944 it was clear that Germany was heading for defeat, and that the full might of the Allies would soon be turned against Japan. The man responsible for leading Japan to disaster, Prime Minister Tojo, had already been forced to resign. Even so, heavy American casualties were expected when Japan was finally invaded: probably a million if the Japanese defence of Okinawa was anything to judge by. The Japanese were already using *kamikaze* suicide pilots in attacks on American ships, and the Allies expected that Japan would defend itself to the last man. By the summer of 1945 it had been decided to force an end to the war by dropping atomic bombs on Japan; this might save millions of lives, both military and civilian. The necessity of this has been questioned. Japan's cities were being destroyed by Allied air raids, and Japan's war production was badly hit both by the air raids and by the cutting off of overseas supplies. Japan could not prolong the war indefinitely and might have to come to terms even before a mainland invasion. If the Allies had been prepared to modify their unconditional surrender proposals before the atomic bombings, the 'doves' in the Japanese cabinet might have gained the upper hand over the 'hawks'. Certainly the Japanese had put out feelers for peace weeks before Hiroshima and Nagasaki. And the threat of Soviet intervention made peace even more urgent from Japan's point of view; the Japanese did not want Manchuria over-run, and the islands of northern Japan exposed to Soviet attack. After the atomic bombings, the Allies did modify unconditional surrender with their promise to respect the position (but not the political power) of the Emperor. Had this been agreed in July 1945, the bombs might not have been necessary, but the point has been much argued by historians, without any agreement.

▷ Question 3   *Student answer with examiner's comments*

'This is about Soviet weakness – what about other reasons for Hitler's attack: ideological, strategic, supplies and oil, "Lebensraum"?'

'Some exaggeration here: "most" would apply only to the most senior officers.'

'This is very disjointed: it needs a well-knit and coherent argument; some points, e.g. Stalin's leadership, need to be developed.'

'Useful on the Battle of Britain, but the second mistake is vague (it might have been better to avoid the USSR) and the references need to be explained.'

(a)   *Hitler believed that the Russians would be easy to beat. He had lulled them into a sense of false security by the Molotov–Ribbentrop Pact and he knew that Stalin regarded British warnings of a German attack on Russia as a ploy to get Russia into the war. Hitler knew the Russian army was in chaos; Stalin had shot most of his officers, and the Russian army had disgraced itself in the war against Finland.*

(b)   *The weather was colder than expected and the diesel oil froze, immobilising Hitler's tanks. The Germans had not been equipped for winter campaigning and the Russians were – the Cossack horses could deal with the cold better than the German mechanised transport. Stalin was a great leader. The British and Americans gave the Russians very little help, but the Japanese did not help the Germans either. Russia is a very big country. There was much partisan resistance to the German invaders.*

(c)   *His other mistakes were switching tactics during the Battle of Britain, and refusing to allow his generals to retreat. In the first Hitler ordered his airforce to switch their attacks from British airfields to British cities as a reprisal for a British air-raid on Berlin. This enabled the RAF to recover, to repair their damaged communication centres and airfields, and to secure eventual victory. This made a German invasion of Britain impossible as the Germans had not won control of the air. The other mistake occurred at Stalingrad, in North Africa and at other places in Russia in 1943–44. Hitler had become power-crazy and had lost the war single-handed.*

Examiner's decision on the student answer
Overall the answers avoid narrative and try to present reasons and explanation, but the arguments require greater precision, and clearer and more logical presentation. The answers are all rather brief, and not strong enough for the highest mark Level (Level 4). These will be at the lower end of Level 3, scoring about 6 marks each out of 10.

SUMMARY

In this chapter you have studied an outline of the Second World War, including the following topics:

▷ the war against Germany:

   ▷ German successes in Poland and western Europe,

   ▷ the nature of *blitzkrieg* warfare,

   ▷ the German invasion of the Soviet Union, its early successes and later failure,

   ▷ the major engagements of the war with Germany,

   ▷ causes of the defeat of Nazi Germany;

▷ the war against Japan:

   ▷ Japanese expansion in the Pacific area,

   ▷ the major engagements in the war with Japan,

   ▷ the start of the atomic age, with the attacks on Hiroshima and Nagasaki,

   ▷ causes of the defeat of Japan;

▷ the Home Front in Britain:

   ▷ attitudes of the British people towards the war,

   ▷ censorship and propaganda,

   ▷ the evacuation, food supplies and rationing,

   ▷ the effects of the war on Britain, the Blitz and the Home Guard,

   ▷ the impact of the war on the British economy and society.

The USA, 1919–41

 GETTING STARTED

During the nineteenth century, the United States had been a political and economic backwater, cut off from the rest of the world and exercising little influence there. In the twentieth century, however, it acquired a position of world importance.

MEG	NEAB	NICCEA	SEG	LONDON	WJEC	TOPIC	STUDY	REVISION 1	REVISION 2
✓	✓	✓	✓*	✓	✓	**US society in the 1920s**			
✓	✓	✓	✓*	✓	✓	The US economic boom in the 1920s			
✓	✓	✓	✓*	✓	✓	Politics in the USA			
✓	✓	✓	✓*		✓	Social developments			
✓	✓	✓	✓*	✓	✓	**US external relations: the rise and fall of isolationism**			
✓	✓	✓	✓*		✓	Origins of isolationism			
✓	✓	✓	✓*		✓	The growth of isolationism			
✓	✓	✓	✓*	✓	✓	**The New Deal**			
✓	✓	✓	✓*	✓	✓	The Wall Street Crash and the beginning of the Depression			
✓	✓	✓	✓*	✓	✓	The New Deal takes effect			
✓	✓	✓	✓*	✓	✓	Assessment of the New Deal			

* Coursework only

 WHAT YOU NEED TO KNOW

US society in the 1920s

▷ **The US economic boom in the 1920s**

In 1919 the USA seemed the strongest country in the world. In Europe, both the winners and the losers of the First World War had been exhausted by their efforts and sacrifices. The USA had suffered, too, but relatively lightly in comparison. US goods were available to markets starved of consumer products during the war years, while European countries were struggling to switch from wartime to peacetime production. This gave the Americans the upper hand in economic dealings.

The development of US industries

Manufacturing industry, especially in some concerns, such as automobiles, developed rapidly to satisfy apparently inexhaustible demand. By the mid-1920s, cars were being made at the rate of over 3 million a year; the typical four-cylinder car, which in 1913 cost $1,500, could be bought for $600 in 1927. Henry Ford, who wanted all his employees to have a car of their own, and said they could choose any colour they liked so long as it was black, produced sturdy low-maintenance cars that came to be known as 'tin lizzies' and were ideal for the rough dirt roads of rural America. They were mass produced on production lines capable of producing one every few seconds. Heavy industry, too, was busy extending the railway network and producing locomotives, or building scores of new ships to make good wartime losses.

But it was perhaps the consumer durables industry that made the biggest strides, for the USA was rapidly becoming in the 1920s the land of domestic gadgetry. Electric household appliances such as cookers, heaters, washing machines and fridges were produced in vast numbers; sales rocketed, many purchasers influenced by the new advertising industry and taking advantage of the hire-purchase revolution that was developing at this time to pay for their goods by instalments.

At the same time, the industrial financial structure became more far-reaching and more complex. Elaborate manufacturing and commercial monopolies appeared, even in spite of the existing trust laws, and massive business empires were set up in the form of cartels, holding companies and the like; large-scale integration of allied businesses also took place. At the same time, the number of banks grew, and other financial concerns such as insurance and credit corporations. Those successful in such businesses were able to earn enormous salaries.

Inequality in the USA

This economic prosperity, however, was spread very unevenly among the population. There were older industries, such as textiles, where improvements were limited, and where the labour force, many of them immigrants lacking the protection of effective trade unions, worked long hours for miserable wages, and often lived in squalor. A commentator wrote of their lot in the 1920s: 'Poverty becomes more painful in the shadow of great wealth; idleness more demoralizing beside the feverish activity of competition. America can show greater contrasts in such matters than any other country I know.' In particular, US agriculture suffered a recession after the First World War. US farmers, many of whom were now able, using the new agricultural machinery, to bring larger areas under the plough, had overextended themselves and had borrowed heavily from the rural banks in order to increase the size of their farms; but the more they extended their production, the further farm prices fell and the more their troubles increased. Worse still, the thin soil of the prairie states, loosened by clearing and by the plough, was easily exhausted, producing what became known as the 'dust bowl' effect as the light sandy soil turned to dust and simply blew away. The same dismal picture was true of the struggling farmers of Tennessee, and those of the tobacco states and the cotton states of the Deep South: misery and poverty were the main feature of their lives.

Commercial policies

America inherited protectionism from the days of its economic weakness, when traders and manufacturers needed tariffs to shelter their struggling businesses. They were now strong, but could not be weaned away from tariff protection, which they continued to demand from their governments.

(a) *1922, Fordney–McCumber tariff* forced tariffs higher than ever before. It set up a Tariff Commission empowered to vary tariff levels on different articles of trade. In the 1920s, there were 37 such variations; all but five of them were increases, and those five were of only trifling importance. The revenue from these tariffs was used to help another favourite business interest – the cutting of taxes.

(b) *1930, Hawley–Smoot tariff* was an emergency measure enacted at the time of the slump. Since the USA enacted tariffs on foreign imports, these countries retaliated by erecting tariff barriers against American goods; this produced retaliation against retaliation, and the USA raised its tariffs even higher. The effect of tariff legislation was to impede further an already flagging commerce.

These tariffs were evidence of US distaste for contacts with the outside world, and a desire to limit such links, as was US immigration policy – though in fact many US manufacturers would have benefited from a free inflow of cheap immigrant labour which had not yet organized itself into trade unions.

▷ Politics in the USA

US political parties

There were two main parties; each formed an amalgam of different interests.

Republicans

Traditionally, the Republicans were the party of the north of the United States. The party's symbol was the elephant. It generally had conservative leanings: it wished to keep expenses and taxes low; it regarded government regulation as evil; it held to the idea of free enterprise; and it upheld the rights of the separate states. Republicanism stood for 'America First' and tended towards isolationism. It was sometimes seen as operating in the interests of big business.

Democrats

Traditionally, the Democrats were the party of the southern states. Their symbol was the donkey. The party often operated in the interests of the downtrodden and of minorities, and wished to help them financially and socially through a policy of reform. The Democrats were not so hostile to state action and wanted a strong central government. They saw the USA as having an important world role, and were less inclined to isolationism. The Democrats were sometimes suspected of having socialist leanings.

Republican rule in the 1920s

President Woodrow Wilson, who had been Democrat President since 1912, became increasingly unpopular towards the end of his term, not least because of his marked obsession with the First World War, and America's role in European and world affairs. Traditionally, Americans rejected the tiresome and expensive entanglements in which this involved them, and looked upon the 'New World' as the 'Land of the Free', a place where they would be able to turn their backs on imperialism and power politics. America's determination to revert to isolationism and to expand business opportunities unfettered by external commitments led to a Republican victory in the presidential election of November 1920.

Warren G. Harding, 1921–23

Warren G. Harding was the new President. He was a rather lack-lustre character who surrounded himself with political cronies from his home state of Ohio. Harding achieved little, and his friends, who soon became known as the 'Ohio gang', seemed chiefly concerned to feather their own nests, indulging in corrupt and even criminal activities under the President's unwitting protection. The worst of these abuses was the *Teapot Dome scandal*, in which large areas of oil-rich lands were sold off to speculators in squalid backroom deals. Harding's realization of what was going on hastened his death in 1923, when he was succeeded by his Vice-President, Coolidge.

Calvin Coolidge, 1923–29

Calvin Coolidge gained a reputation for honesty by his successful handling of Harding's poker-playing friends, some of whom he sent to gaol. Known as 'Silent Cal' for never using two words when one would do, he was generally just as disinclined to act as he was to speak, and hence did nothing at all. This did not mean that he was stupid. On the contrary, he was a shrewd politician, and he demolished his opponents in the presidential campaign of 1924. Coolidge believed that America would prosper if the government left things alone: 'The business of America is business', he said. And, as America prospered, the Republicans took the credit for their inaction.

Herbert Hoover, 1929–33

Herbert Hoover replaced Coolidge in 1928. Coolidge's terse remark that 'he did not choose to run' did not stop the Republicans striding to victory again. Hoover was considered by many to be the strong man behind the scenes in Coolidge's administration, and he was well known abroad for his postwar work in Belgium. As Secretary of Commerce he warned against excessive tariffs, the financial weakness of American banks and the dangers of share dealings on borrowed money. But by the time he had become President it was almost too late to avert financial disaster.

 **Social developments**

There was a streak of stand-offishness and intolerance in US attitudes after the First World War, parallel with its tariff policies in commercial matters.

Immigration policies

The USA was a melting-pot of many different nationalities, all of whom were originally immigrants to the American continent. Many of them wished to turn their backs on the poverty and humiliation of their origins and to enjoy a new and freer life in America.

The new nation had shown little conscience in its dealings with the aboriginal population of what they called 'Red Indians', most of whom had been wiped out in a succession of wars in the nineteenth century. By 1900, the Americans had enacted immigration laws restricting the inflow of Chinese and Japanese, and against Mexican immigrants ('wet-backs'). There were restrictions, too, which excluded the sick, the diseased, paupers, prostitutes, anarchists and alcoholics.

(a) *1917, Immigration Act* introduced literacy tests for new immigrants, partly at the request of labour, which saw the chance to limit immigrant numbers, and partly because of reformist groups, who for racist reasons did not wish to see American 'stock' coarsened by intermixture with 'inferior' breeds. There was a 'Barred Zone', including India, Indochina, Siam and other parts of Asia, from which immigration was absolutely forbidden. Wilson resisted the proposal, but the law was passed over his presidential veto.

(b) *1921, Immigration Act* introduced the 'quota' system, by which the number of new immigrants from any nation was to be limited annually to a quota of 3 per cent of the total number of persons of that nationality already resident in the USA, the total number being limited to 350,000 per annum. This law markedly favoured the English, Irish, Germans and Scandinavians.

(c) *1929, National Origins Act* reduced the annual total to 150,000 and barred the immigration of those who might become chargeable in future to the state. These regulations seemed strangely at variance with the inscription at the foot of the Statue of Liberty which still stood guard over New York harbour:

> Give me your tired, your poor,
> Your huddled masses yearning to breathe free,
> The wretched refuse of your teeming shore,
> Send these, the homeless, tempest-tost to me:
> I lift my lamp beside the golden door.

Prohibition

Reformers had long recognized that drunkenness and poverty went hand in hand. A strong Temperance movement in the 1850s had dwindled during the Civil War, but in 1873 the Women's Christian Temperance Movement was formed in Ohio and spread rapidly, aided by churches of all denominations. That women were prominent in the movement is not surprising in view of the deprivation and violence, and the broken homes, caused by drunkenness. Churches were also concerned with the sinfulness of drinking, and some employers were worried about the effect drink had on worker efficiency. Carrie Nation, a lady from Kansas, gained renown for demolishing drinking saloons with a hatchet, and her example helped to lead to the Anti-Saloon League of 1893. Before the First World War, reformers had prevailed upon the government to ban the immigration of alcoholics, and several states and a large number of districts had gone 'dry', i.e. had enacted laws banning alcohol altogether.

The war gave the movement further impetus. It was considered unpatriotic to devote scarce grain to making alcohol instead of using it for food; furthermore, drunkenness would impede the war effort. At the same time, the economic and political importance of women was enhanced by the war. In 1919, the Eighteenth Amendment to the US Constitution prohibited the importation, transportation, manufacture and sale – though not the consumption – of alcoholic liquors throughout the United States. Despite the veto of President Wilson, it became law as the Volstead Act later that year.

At first only 2,000 enforcement officers were appointed to cover 32,000 kilometres of frontier and coast, apart from seeking out illegal stills within the vast interior of the USA. Pent-up demand for alcohol soon produced the criminal fraternity willing to satisfy it, and while the gangs prospered both by smuggling the drink (boot-legging) and running the establishments in which it could be consumed (speak-easies), the general public showed its contempt for a law which was mistakenly attempting to enforce the state's view of public morality. Gangsters and crime flourished. Alphonse ('Al') Capone controlled a thousand armed gunmen in Chicago alone. Rival gangs of crooks, engaged in the drink trade, or organized gambling, or in protection rackets, fought over their 'territories'. Bloodshed was frequent, though not always as spectacular as the St Valentine's Day massacre of 1929, when the whole of Bugsy Moran's rival gang was ruthlessly mown down by machine-gun fire. The sums of money involved were huge: Capone's mob took $60 million a year, of which a third went into Capone's personal account, to be spent on flashy diamonds or armour-plated motorcars. Some argued that the boom of the 1920s was in part the beneficial result of Prohibition, but by the end of the decade most Americans felt that Prohibition was a disastrous failure. Roosevelt was soon to show that he agreed.

The 'Red Scare'

Though many Americans were of Russian origin, the country was highly alarmed at the revolutions of 1917 and the seizure of power by the Bolsheviks. They agreed with the forcible ending of Tsarist tyranny, but looked with dread on a system of government that confiscated private fortunes, nationalized industry and instituted the methods of the police state. The end of the First World War brought to America sudden unemployment and a number of violent strikes, in the course of which there were several bomb outrages. As a result the legal authorities arrested about 6,000 suspects, many of them immigrants, and deported about a thousand more. There is no doubt that this reaction smacked of overkill, but it certainly stirred up in the USA a hatred of anarchists and 'Red' agitators.

Nicola Sacco and Bartolomeo Vanzetti were two self-confessed anarchists, arrested in 1920 for robbery and murder. Some of the evidence against them was faked and their trial was certainly a shot-gun affair, with even the judge in their case referring to them as 'those anarchist bastards'. They were swiftly convicted, and, in spite of several appeals to higher courts, were executed in 1927.

Vanzetti put his finger on the truth when he said in the course of an appeal: 'I am suffering because I am a radical, and indeed I am a radical; I have suffered because I was an Italian, and indeed I am an Italian.' He was certainly right that it was difficult to be a radical or an immigrant in the United States at this time.

Fundamentalism and science

Americans in the 1920s accepted the advances of science and technology and benefited from their results. Pleasing though this progress was, it worried a lot of people who felt that it was the work of the Devil that things should come to them so easily. They felt that the scriptures, prayer and moral improvement were all being sacrificed on the altar of materialist advance.

In 1919, a large Bible conference launched a campaign to prevent the teaching in US schools of Darwin's theory that man and apes are descended from a common ancestor. In a changing society they hoped to find certainty by affirming their belief in the literal truth of the Bible. As a result, a number of states in the 'Bible belt', including Tennessee, banned the teaching of Darwinian theories, since they seemed to contradict the biblical version of Divine creation.

In 1925, revealed religion and scientific theory clashed in the courtroom in Dayton, Tennessee, in the Scopes Trial, or 'Monkey Trial', as it soon became known. John Scopes, a high-school teacher, had purposely chosen to teach evolutionary theory to his biology class so as to provide a test case for the state's anti-evolutionary law. The case excited intense interest. In the end, the jury brought in a guilty verdict, later upheld in the Tennessee Supreme Court, though they reduced the penalty imposed to a nominal $100 fine.

The victory of fundamentalism swiftly led to its defeat. Its teachings were exposed to ridicule, the blinkered prejudice of its supporters laughed at throughout America. Though evolution could not legally be taught for many years, the attempt to ban it only gave the theory wider publicity.

Forms of southern extremism and populism

The *Ku Klux Klan* formed another outlet for narrow-minded conservatism in the south. This organization, a not very secret society of hooded figures performing apparently harmless rituals, promoted all kinds of hatred, expanding the numbers of its membership to around 5 million in 1924. For some years the Klan was a political force that could not be challenged. Anyone who did might attend the next torch-light lynching or branding not so much as a bystander as a victim. Its members tended to be white, Anglo-Saxon by descent and Protestant in religion – hence the nickname WASPS. One of their pamphlets revealed how numerous were their enemies: 'Every criminal, every gambler, every thug, every girl-ruiner, every home-wrecker, every wife-beater, every dope-peddler, every moonshiner, every crooked politician, every Papist priest, every shyster lawyer, every black spider . . .' Although they specially condemned foreigners, Jews and Roman Catholics in their propaganda, they chiefly singled out the 'inferior negroes' as the major threat to society, and it was against them that they mainly directed their violence. While criminal gangsters dominated the cities of the north, the rural south saw a spate of lynchings and occasional burnings of any black who was judged by the Klan to have stepped out of line.

Other brutal forms of *populist* tyranny were to be found in the south at this time. One such populist figure was Huey 'Kingfish' Long, effective dictator of Louisiana before his assassination in 1935. He was an excellent example of the US political 'boss'. He gained complete control of his state by bullying and coarse abuse, winning ignorant whites by his common touch and corrupting his fellow politicians. He silenced the hostile press, kidnapped his opponents and surrounded himself with an armed bodyguard worthy of the gangsters of the north. He was not without national ambitions, and served for a time in the US Senate in the early 1930s. He was the perfect example of the glib and dangerous populism that from time to time threatened the country.

It is not surprising that phenomena such as these gave the USA the reputation of being a land of growing lawlessness in spite of its increasing prosperity.

US external relations: the rise and fall of isolationism

▷ **Origins of isolationism**

A number of factors combined to generate a powerful feeling in favour of keeping America free from external complications.

Historic and political

Many of the first- and second-generation immigrants came from Europe in distressing circumstances: they were poor, persecuted for their religious and political beliefs, refugees from alien governments, etc. They turned away from their unhappy pasts.

They rejected the ideas of the 'Old World' – power politics, aggression, imperialism, even conventional diplomacy – and looked for something better.

They came from a variety of different national backgrounds, but did not wish to continue the quarrels that had poisoned their lives in the past; they wanted a new life in which they would live together in peace and freedom.

Geographic and economic

They prided themselves on their self-sufficiency, and did not wish to be dependent on foreigners for imports; they wished to set up their own independent economy.

They were separated from the Old World by nearly 5,000 kilometres of sea, in a continent they had made their own. They had no wish to interfere in European affairs, and wanted Europe to avoid meddling in American affairs (the *Monroe Doctrine*).

They wanted to keep their taxes low, and to avoid the expensive entanglement of an elaborate foreign policy; in particular, they did not want to be obliged every few years to sort out at their own expense the problems of Europe.

The Republicans, who won power in the 1920s, made a point of advocating America for the Americans, and non-participation in outside problems.

▷ **The growth of isolationism**

President Wilson had generated a good deal of interest in European affairs, and played a big part in the later stages of the war; he dominated the peace conference and wanted a key role for America in the League of Nations. But Republican sympathizers were anxious to revert to 'normalcy', i.e. to isolationism.

Postwar external policies

Mistrust of the outside world could be seen under Harding, Coolidge and Hoover in laws restricting *immigration* and severe *tariff laws* in 1921, 1922 and 1930.

The Republicans also contracted out of the peace process: the US Senate refused to accept the Treaty of Versailles, or US participation in the League.

In 1921, there was a *Joint Declaration of Congress* which simply announced a separate peace with Germany, leaving out any reference to either the League of Nations or war guilt. The only aspect of the new peace which merited the attention of the Republicans was *war debts*, which they insisted should be paid in full. (In fact, only Finland repaid the whole of its debts.)

But the USA was never totally isolated. It played a part in the following:

(a) *1922, Washington Naval Disarmament Conference*, in which the powers fixed the relative naval strengths of the five great naval powers (USA, Britain, Japan, France and Italy) in a proportion of 5:5:3:2:2.

(b) *1924, Dawes Plan*, aiming to reduce the burden on Germany after its rapid inflation by rescheduling the payment of postwar reparations.

(c) 1926, USA accepted the *Court of International Justice*, but refused to take part in any cases which involved the USA.

(d) *1928, Kellogg–Briand Pact (Pact of Paris)*, renouncing war as an instrument of policy. The USA became one of its 65 signatories.

(e) *1929, Young Plan*, reducing German reparations by more than half, so as to create the conditions for the repayment to the USA of debts during the Depression.

(f) *1930, London Naval Disarmament Conference*, resisting pressure for more naval building (especially from Japan), and restricting new building of battleships and submarines.

(g) *1931, Hoover Moratorium*, delaying the repayment of European debts to the USA.

(h) *1934*, though continuing to reject membership of the League, the USA joined the *International Labour Organization*, taking part in its discussions and abiding by its rulings.

Isolationism in the 1930s

President Roosevelt, leader of the Democrats, was less enthusiastic than the Republicans about isolationism, but circumstances at first led him to continue with it:

(a) *1934, Johnson Act* forbade all loans or other financial assistance to countries which had not repaid their war debts – this meant most of them.

(b) *1935, (First) Neutrality Act* prohibited loans or trading credits to belligerent countries, placed an embargo on direct and indirect shipments of arms or munitions, and barred Americans from travelling on the ships of belligerent nations. This expressed disapproval of rearmament programmes in Europe.

(c) *1937, (Second) Neutrality Act* banned Americans from volunteering for foreign wars, or taking part in them. This was a reaction to the Spanish Civil War (1936–39).

Cultural contacts with the world

The USA was a very open society, and its activities were hard to muzzle. In the 1920s and 1930s, the country had great influence on the rest of the world, especially in publishing, music and films; these contacts continued unabated even in the years of isolation.

Publishing
There was a good deal of important critical writing against the cult of mediocrity and of materialism by writers such as Walter Lippmann, Joseph Wood Krutch and Henry L. Mencken, exposing bourgeois complacency and vulgarity in a variety of newspapers and periodicals.

At the same time, great imaginative writing was produced by Sinclair Lewis, Scott Fitzgerald, James Farrell, John Dos Passos, Thornton Wilder and John Steinbeck, and important works of theatre by such people as Eugene O'Neill. Much of their work still gives penetrating insights into the life of the period.

Music

The rise of radio broadcasting spread the fame of popular and jazz music fast throughout the nation, and yielded an audience beyond the American continent. By the end of the 1930s, there were over 15 million radio sets and 900 broadcasting stations in America. The growth of small-town America produced juke boxes and crowds of young people sipping cokes and discussing the merits of Guy Lombardo and Duke Ellington.

Syncopation and jazz go back to before the First World War with figures such as Scott Joplin and 'ragtime' bands like that of Jack 'Papa' Lane in New Orleans. Between the wars there was a great era of composition and technique, and famous performers such as Fats Waller (piano), Louis Armstrong (trumpet), Benny Goodman (clarinet), Charlie Parker (alto sax) and Dizzy Gillespie (trumpet). The exuberance of their improvised playing produced many different jazz styles, running parallel with more conventional popular music in the orchestral style, culminating by the time of the Second World War in 'big-band' leaders such as Glenn Miller.

This new era of US music dominated the whole cultural scene by the 1930s.

Film

The motion picture made little impact until David Griffith's *Birth of a Nation* in 1915, but afterwards there was a great creative upsurge of film making, coupled with the development of Hollywood and the 'star system'. A few figures dominated the whole movie scene: Mary Pickford, 'America's sweetheart'; Douglas Fairbanks, handsome and athletic; Charlie Chaplin, comedian extraordinary; Pearl White, whose escapades left the audience breathless each week; and so on.

The advent of sound in 1927 with *The Jazz Singer* revolutionized film. It led to a host of new stars such as Clark Gable, Irene Dunn, Charles Boyer, Hedy Lamarr, Rudolph Valentino, Myrna Loy, Errol Flynn, Jean Harlow, Bette Davis and Olivia de Havilland. The 1930s also saw the lavish productions of the big film studios like Metro-Goldwyn-Mayer (MGM) and Twentieth-Century Fox.

For people faced by the grim reality of depression and unemployment, the cinema provided an opportunity for escape into a world of make-believe and wealth. It spread American values and attitudes all over the world, wherever there was a white screen and a projector.

The 'Good Neighbor' policy

At the same time as the USA professed isolationism, a movement gained momentum to promote friendship between the various republics of the American continents. As early as 1889, regular 'pan-American' conferences were being held to resolve problems and promote political unity; in 1923, a conference at Santiago set up the first pan-American arbitration machinery.

Under Roosevelt, the USA played a more prominent role in the movement, and took part in a number of conferences:

(a) *1933, Congress of Montevideo* agreed that no American republic should interfere in the affairs of another, even to collect debts. However, the USA did not always respect this, as seen in the cases of Haiti and Cuba until 1934.
(b) *1936, Congress of Buenos Aires* remodelled relations between them, and laid down principles of what came to be called 'hemispheric defense'.
(c) *1938, Congress of Lima* declared in favour of international law, equal sovereignty and individual liberty.
(d) *1939, Congress of Panama* forbade acts of war in America's 'neutral zone'.

Roosevelt's policies were not universally popular:

(a) In the USA, he was accused by his critics of hobnobbing with Latin American dictators such as President Vargas of Brazil.
(b) Foreign countries were suspicious of his motives: foreign governments sometimes thought that 'Good Neighbor' policies were no more than a cloak for *dollar imperialism*. Indeed, by 1939, the United States had invested over $3bn in Latin America and $4bn in Canada.

The end of isolationism

The increasing aggressiveness of the European dictators in the later 1930s revealed to Roosevelt that the USA could not continue indefinitely to isolate itself from Europe, though it took some time for public opinion to come round to his opinion.

(a) 1939, Congress accepted that the countries now at war in Europe were allowed to buy arms and supplies, but strictly on a 'cash-and-carry' basis, i.e. they had to pay for them when they bought them, and transport them themselves. On the face of it, this was even-handed; in reality it favoured the Allies, who controlled the sea.

(b) June 1940, US declaration of help and support for the Western Allies.

(c) July 1940, pan-American countries at Havana promised to protect European colonies (chiefly British in the West Indies) in the New World.

(d) September 1940, peacetime Conscription Act; this was followed by a 'destroyers-for-bases' agreement giving Britain 50 old ships in return for the right to build bases in British-controlled territory stretching from British Guiana to Newfoundland.

(e) January 1941, in Britain's 'darkest hour', Roosevelt made his *Four Freedoms Speech* in Congress:

> In future days, which we seek to make secure, we look forward to a world founded upon four essential freedoms.
> The first is freedom of speech and expression, everywhere in the world.
> The second is freedom of every person to worship God in his own way.
> The third is freedom from want – which means economic understandings which will secure to every nation a healthy peacetime life for its inhabitants.
> The fourth is freedom from fear – which means a worldwide reduction of armaments to such a point that . . . no nation will be in a position to commit an act of physical aggression against any foreign neighbor.
> This is no vision of a distant millennium. It is a definite basis for a kind of world attainable in our own time and generation.

(f) March 1941, 'Lend-Lease' provided help more liberally for Britain.

(g) August 1941, Roosevelt and Churchill, meeting on a battleship off Newfoundland, issued the *Atlantic Charter*, in which they outlined their plans for a more peaceful future to be achieved by Allied cooperation.

US policy in the Far East

Japan's relations with the USA worsened as the 1930s continued:

(a) 1938, Prime Minister Konoye announced Japan's *New Order* in Asia. America reacted angrily, imposing trade restrictions on Japan, though after a time these were relaxed.

(b) 1939, continuing Japanese refusal to compromise led to tightening of restrictions, especially on commodities such as oil, scrap metal and rubber.

(c) 1940, after the fall of France, Japan began the construction of bases in Indochina.

(d) September 1940, Japan signed the *Tripartite Axis Pact* with Germany and Italy.

(e) April 1941, Japan concluded a *Non-Aggression Pact* with the USSR.

(f) May–July 1941, Japan began moving troops into Indochina; the USA retaliated by freezing Japanese assets, and strengthening the defences of Hawaii and the Philippines.

(g) 7 December 1941, Japanese carrier-based bombers carried out dawn raids on Pearl Harbor (Hawaii), Midway, Wake and Guam.

The United States declared war on Japan on 8 December; Japan's allies, Germany and Italy, declared war on the USA on 11 December.

The New Deal

Three Republican Presidents shared the optimism and progress of the 'Roaring Twenties', and could see no end to the tide of rising prosperity. But they were soon to be undeceived.

▷ The Wall Street Crash and the beginning of the Depression

There had already been signs of economic stress before 1929; a feature of it was the speculative craze in the late 1920s. The prospect of inexhaustible markets inflated the value of companies, and speculation inflated the value of shares. Speculators even borrowed to buy shares, hoping to be able to repay the loans out of the profit they made when the shares were sold. (This was called 'buying on the margin'.) Such a style of business could not long continue.

The collapse of the stock market

Problems soon turned into a crisis:

(a) Food prices were rapidly collapsing. Some farmers borrowed and remortgaged in order to survive; others abandoned the struggle against low prices and soil erosion, and moved into the towns to seek work.

(b) In industry, goods in search of a market were stockpiling; rising tariffs kept foreign goods out of the USA, but at the same time prevented foreigners acquiring dollar credits with which to buy US exports.

These signs of weakness were ignored by a soaring stock market, but later in 1929 wary and experienced dealers began to sell, and confidence was gradually undermined until, in October 1929, the *Wall Street Crash* produced such a catastrophic fall in share values that panic replaced the former optimism, and a flood of frantic selling occurred.

Those who had 'bought on the margin' could not repay their debts. This had a knock-on effect: creditors of those who could not pay, could not themselves pay their debts. Banks, too, had 'played the market' and were caught in the same trap: many of their assets were irrecoverable loans, and though they foreclosed on farmers who could not pay their mortgages, they could not sell the farms so repossessed. Hundreds of small rural banks in the Midwest closed their doors and went into liquidation, taking with them the current accounts of businessmen and the entire savings of the mass of their customers.

President Hoover finds no remedy

President Hoover tried to stem the crisis with words of reassurance, but his confidence was regarded with suspicion, and the feeling grew that the Republicans were simply hanging on and hoping for the best. ('In Hoover we trusted, and now we are busted!') He did, however, make some real efforts: he reduced taxes to increase people's ability to buy goods, and he put through Congress an *Emergency Relief and Reconstruction Act* in 1932 which provided employment on federal public works projects, and gave loans to states with public works programmes of their own.

These were valuable measures, many of them foreshadowing with uncanny accuracy the later reform measures of the New Deal, but they were not popular among Republicans, since they smacked of state initiative and went against the grain of free-enterprise economics.

By 1933 there were nearly 13 million unemployed – there had been only 1 million in 1929 – and the whole banking system was on the verge of collapse. Hoover's candour and his honesty were forgotten; his critics seemed to be winning all the arguments as the situation deteriorated. The shanty towns of unemployed, nicknamed 'Hoovervilles', gave him and his government a more permanent and less welcome niche in history.

The presidential election of 1932

Rightly or wrongly, the American electorate blamed the economic disaster on the Republicans in general and on Hoover in particular. There seemed little prospect of another Republican victory in the coming presidential election in November 1932, so the future seemed to depend on the Democrats and their choice of candidate.

Franklin D. Roosevelt had good political experience: he had served in the Wilson administration, and had been the vice-presidential candidate in 1920. He had become Governor of New York State in 1928, a tough post which was often a valuable stepping-stone for politicians with presidential ambitions. The fact that his legs were paralysed as a result of polio in 1921 was no liability – on the contrary, it showed that Roosevelt was a fighter in his personal as well as his public life, and that he was ready to tackle any handicap. Yet although he spent most of his time criticizing Hoover for his errors, Roosevelt had no clear-cut programme of his own for getting the USA out of depression.

He promised a 'New Deal' for the American people, telling them that they had 'nothing to fear but fear itself'. The best he could do was to promise a period of 'experimentation', saying that it was his intention to tackle the problem vigorously.

But Roosevelt was no economist, and the American people had to take him on trust. The presidential election in November gave him a large electoral majority, but he had four months of waiting, while the economic situation worsened, before the constitution allowed him to take over from Hoover.

▷ The New Deal takes effect

The strategy of the New Deal

Roosevelt employed a much more 'hands-on' style of leadership than his predecessors, and surprised them by his speed of action. His philosophy aimed at:

(a) *relief* – many Americans needed help desperately if they were not to starve;
(b) *recovery* – he felt the government had to lead America out of the Depression;
(c) *reform* – efforts had to be made to remedy the evils present in society.

His methods at the time were thought of as extremely radical:

(a) He used federal powers to the limit; opponents thought he went beyond his powers and accused him of behaving unconstitutionally.
(b) He surrounded himself with a talented cabinet, men like Harry Hopkins (in charge of Federal Relief) and Frances Perkins (Secretary of Labour and the first woman member of the cabinet).
(c) He employed the services of a 'Brains Trust' of professionals – experts in finance, economics, etc., and other academics.
(d) He took pains to keep in touch with the people, using his fireside chats over the radio, and holding press conferences twice a week at the White House to ensure proper coverage of his work.

The 'Hundred Days'

During the first hundred days of his presidency it was necessary for Roosevelt to deal with the immediate crisis so as to restore the nation's confidence. His work produced an immediate flood of legislation:

(a) He ordered the temporary closure of insolvent banks while their books were audited and balanced; he also banned the export of gold and silver bullion. Later he devalued the dollar by almost half.
(b) *Emergency Banking Act* gave federal guarantees to deposits in sound banks only, thus forcing the weaker banks out of business, but restoring confidence in the sound banks and in the currency. Later, the *Glass–Steagal Banking Act* separated commercial and investment banking, and restricted the use of banking credit for speculative purposes.
(c) *Securities Act* reduced speculation and fraud by requiring full public information on the details of new securities. This was followed by a *Stock Exchange Act* which restricted marginal and speculative dealings; it also led to the setting up of the *Securities and Exchange Commission*. Later a *Federal Deposit Insurance Corporation* was set up guaranteeing bank deposits under the Glass–Steagal Act.
(d) *Economy Act* reduced government spending by 15 per cent, in particular reducing public-sector salaries. These emergency cuts were later restored.
(e) *Agricultural Adjustment Act* destroyed crop surpluses, reduced cultivated acreage, and tried to sustain farm prices and encourage cooperative practices. Later a *Federal Farm Loan Act* set up a Federal Farm Credit Administration to support farm mortgages and create new ones.
(f) *Home Owners Loan Corporation* (HOLC) was given wide powers of borrowing in order to finance home owners in trouble with their mortgages.
(g) *Federal Relief Act* widened federal aid in the form of relief, and was the origin of a number of agencies which were later of great importance (see below).

Finally, Prohibition, with its organized crime and uncontrollable corruption, was swept away: 'I think now would be a good time for beer', the President said.

The New Deal in the remainder of Roosevelt's first administration

Measures for the longer term had been initiated during the Hundred Days, and the cost of them steadily mounted into billions of dollars. These agencies were known by their initials and were popularly referred to as 'alphabet agencies'. They included:

(a) *Civilian Conservation Corps*, to provide temporary work in conservation projects which enabled young men to get back to work at a modest salary. They were engaged in reafforestation, flood control and soil conservation, and built dams and laid roads and telephone lines. By 1940, the CCC had employed $2^1/_2$ million such young men at a salary of about $30 a month, some of which they sent home to their families.

(b) *Federal Emergency Relief Administration* was set up to provide relief in the form of work for adult unemployed; it spent over $3bn in aid to those in need of it, and 4 million benefited from this by 1940. There was a *Public Works* and a *Civil Works Administration*, and they undertook the construction of roads, houses, libraries, hospitals, swimming pools and many other public buildings. In 1935, they were replaced by the *Works Progress Administration*, which continued with public works such as the Hoover Dam on the Colorado River, and also provided employment for musicians, writers and artists.

(c) *Tennessee Valley Authority* was created to coordinate flood control in an area of severe agricultural depression, to turn thousands of square kilometres into fertile land, to provide much needed hydroelectric power through a series of dams, to improve navigation, to protect the environment and to supply cheap electricity. Needless to say, the scheme provided much employment. It turned out to be a vast undertaking, spreading across seven separate states.

(d) *National Recovery Administration* tried also to help industry: until 1935 it introduced joint committees of workers and employers to control conditions, and opened the way for more democratic management. Trade unions were for the first time actively encouraged. The *Wagner Act* (1935) extended their powers, creating a *National Labour Relations Board* to guarantee workers' rights. Many firms adopted a minimum wage. Child labour was forbidden. Firms which cooperated with the NRA were awarded a blue eagle badge, and advertising was used to persuade the public to show preference for products bearing the blue eagle.

(e) *National Resources Board* was set up in 1934 as the first gesture towards the safeguarding of the environment. It started work on a survey of the natural wealth of the USA in timber, minerals and land, for the benefit of future planners.

(f) It continued its monitoring of agriculture:
  (i) *Grazing Act* forbade further sales of federally owned land.
  (ii) *Farm Security Administration* helped evicted smallholders and sharecroppers to find new homes, and it provided loans to restart businesses.
  (iii) *Farm Resettlement Administration* removed poor land from cultivation, extended loans to resettled farmers and improved rural facilities.

(g) *Social Security Act* (1935) began provision for old age pensions and unemployment insurance, though no attempt was made to extend the cover to health.

All this activity told the Americans that *laissez-faire* had been abandoned and that their government was actually attempting to do something about economic and social problems. As unemployment figures began to fall and the country slowly began to claw its way out of the Depression, the New Deal often got the credit for the improvement. It was not surprising that, in the 1936 presidential election, Roosevelt won the majority vote in all but two of the states.

Opposition to the New Deal

The New Deal had many critics and opponents. Roosevelt had made the Depression his personal responsibility, but not everyone was happy with his methods.

(a) The destruction of crops and livestock seemed scandalous when so many were poor and hungry.

(b) Businessmen feared the power of the trade unions, previously restricted by law and now unmuzzled. Moreover, they thought the heavy clamp-down on monopolies and monopolistic practices an infringement of economic freedom; after all, promoting monopolistic practices was a sure-fire way of restoring the health of an industry, and they expected the President to look more kindly on it.

(c) Although Roosevelt had been careful not to 'demoralize' the unemployed with the US equivalent of the 'dole', his public works schemes were often attacked for providing too much relief and too little actual work. Many of his critics regarded him as a socialist.

(d) Above all, the politicians felt that parts of his legislation were unconstitutional, in that they undermined the powers of the individual states and were part of an insidious process of creating a single vast unitary state.

(e) The US Supreme Court, the watchdog of the American constitution, declared eight major Acts of the New Deal legislation unconstitutional, including the Agricultural Adjustment Act. Even the Tennessee Valley Authority seemed to threaten the powers of the various states over whose territory it spread. In the Supreme Court, Justice Roberts said:

> The expressions of the framers of the Constitution, the decisions of this Court interpreting it, and the writings of the commentators will be searched in vain for any suggestion that there exists . . . in the Constitution the authority whereby every provision from that instrument may be subverted, the independence of individual states obliterated, and the United States converted into a central government exercising uncontrolled police powers in every state of the union.

When Roosevelt's position was confirmed by the election of 1936, he tackled the problem. There were still judges in office who had been appointed by Republican Presidents, and they were now rather elderly. Roosevelt suggested that judges should retire when they reached 70; if they refused, he proposed to appoint additional judges, raising the maximum number from nine to fifteen.

His opponents took the hint and were less obstructive from then on. Shortly afterwards he was able to appoint five new judges after recent deaths or retirements. The Court's younger members were more sympathetic to the New Deal, and its attitude was softened. Even so, a good deal of time was spent during his second administration on reviving or amending legislation rejected by the Supreme Court during the first.

The New Deal in Roosevelt's second administration

There was not so crowded a legislative programme as in his first, and there was more emphasis on social rather than economic problems.

(a) *1937, Agricultural Adjustment Act* attempted to remedy the damage done to Roosevelt's agricultural policy by the Supreme Court. Farming was boosted and at the same time federal action against monopolies in industry was intensified.

(b) *1937, Federal Housing Act* set up a *Housing Authority* to undertake slum clearance and build low-cost housing for the workers. A *Federal Housing Administration* was also set up to assist the HOLC to refinance and insure existing small mortgages; by 1940 it had supplied $4bn in aid.

(c) *1938, National Electricity Authority* was set up, leading to the building of 8,000 kilometres of transmission lines, and the widespread provision of cheap power.

(d) *1938, Fair Labor Standards Act* specified minimum wages and maximum hours, and increased the control over the use of child and sweatshop labour. This led in its turn to the *Fair Employment Practices Committee* (1941), which had the main effect of extending labour protection to negroes.

The upturn in the economy in the mid-1930s was jolted by a 4 million increase in unemployment in 1938. Roosevelt attacked economic selfishness, claiming that 'while private enterprise nodded, one-third of the population remained ill-fed, ill-clothed and ill-housed'.

The setback was temporary, and caused in part by a government fear of inflation which had caused federal aid to be restricted. The renewed recovery in 1939 and 1940 was probably as much the result of increasing rearmament as of government policy.

Roosevelt had a surprisingly tough fight against the Republican candidate Wendell Willkie in the 1940 presidential election. It might have been even tougher but for the European war, which persuaded Americans not to risk a change of government at that time.

▷ **Assessment of the New Deal**

Roosevelt's New Deal has been said to follow the policy and advice of one of his advisers, the British economist J.M. Keynes. Keynes wanted governments to spend their way out of the recession by initiating necessary public works, thus creating employment and with it spending power to stimulate the demand for goods. He dismissed the need for balanced budgets and wanted spending to be financed by borrowing rather than by heavier taxation. Such a policy he believed to be justified for as long as there were labour resources standing idle which could be productive.

Roosevelt's grasp of economics fell short of this. He was prepared to borrow in the short term, but was instructed by the pundits at the Treasury to look for balanced budgets in the long term. He feared that 'priming the pump' (i.e. putting more money into circulation by government works programmes) might increase spending power to the point of inflation. Thus Roosevelt's critics thought he was doing too much, but Keynes's disciples thought he was too cautious and was doing too little.

Hopes of a major boost to the construction industry from the Works Progress Administration were disappointing. The National Recovery Administration was already experiencing internal difficulties when it was declared unconstitutional in 1935. The Agricultural Adjustment Act had been a boon to farmers, but it too was declared unconstitutional in 1936.

Production and trade improved in the late 1930s, but not to the levels of the 1920s until the USA joined the Second World War in 1941. Unemployment remained stubbornly high: 7,700,000 in 1937 was the lowest rate since 1930, but unemployment was to return to over 10 million in 1938 and was still over 8 million in 1940.

There were other limits to the success of the New Deal. Social security was far from being the comprehensive welfare service which its advocates had in mind: indeed, it failed to give any protection at all to the most vulnerable sections of American society. Domestic servants, migrant workers and farm labourers were not covered by it, and hence did not qualify for wage protection or for limitation of hours of work. Because of professional opposition and widespread political prejudice, the Social Security Act did not offer any health insurance scheme, with the result that many sick people could not afford medical care. Likewise most black people, especially in the south, enjoyed few of the benefits either of welfare services or of industrial protection, and thousands lived in conditions scarcely better than when they had been slaves. One of them, employed as a laundry worker in the north in Brooklyn in 1939, recalled the conditions under which she had worked in 1937:

> Conditions in the laundry where I worked are a hundred times better than they were two years ago, but they are still far from ideal.
>
> I worked as a press operator before we were unionized. 'Slavery' is the only word that would describe the conditions under which we worked. At least 55 hours a week. It was speed up, speed up, eating lunch on the go, perspiration dripping from every pore, for at least ten hours a day. When I reached home sometimes I was too tired to prepare supper. I would flop across the bed and go to sleep . . .
>
> The toilet at our place wasn't fit for animals, and there was only one for men and women. When I complained, the boss said: 'There ain't many places paying ten dollars a week now, Evie.' That ended my protests, because I didn't want to get fired.

It is therefore easy to exaggerate the achievements of the New Deal by representing it as the coming of a new era. But Roosevelt was the first US President to take upon himself the nation's struggle, and to fight it in the full glare of publicity from press and radio. To the Americans, the Depression was a terrifying and appalling experience. If Roosevelt could not completely defeat it, at least he could inspire his people to make a fight of it.

GLOSSARY

Anarchist A person who believes in the abolition of government and man-made laws. Anarchism was an important movement in late Tsarist Russia, where its outrages included the assassination of a Tsar. To the mass American public in the early 1920s, an anarchist was a figure in a dark cloak, speaking with a heavy eastern European accent, and carrying a large smoking bomb. Anarchist activities in the USA inflamed popular prejudices and made it impossible for Sacco and Vanzetti to be given a fair trial.

Balanced budget The aim of orthodox government finance. It was generally believed that it was necessary for governments to strive for a balanced budget, i.e. that government expenditure should be covered by government revenue (income from taxes), and that if a government spent more than its income (i.e. had an unbalanced budget) then dire economic consequences such as inflation would occur. This orthodoxy was criticized in the 1920s and 1930s by the economist J.M. Keynes, who suggested that economies in depression could be kick-started into life by increased government expenditure financed through borrowing.

Cartels Organizations in which a number of businesses within an industry join together for the purpose of maintaining prices, controlling wages and limiting competition. Cartels are usually very large – they need to be if they are to be effective – but they are usually loosely knit and tend to fall apart after a time. An alternative method of extending control within an industry is when a company buys such a large quantity of another company's shares that it in effect owns the company it has bought into. In such a case the buying company is known as the *holding company*. Sometimes the holding company is not engaged in business at all, but simply exists to own other companies.

Dollar imperialism The spread of American influence by economic means. The USA had been strongly critical of political empires like those of Britain and France, and took every opportunity to deny that it was an imperialist power (i.e. engaged in the expansion of empire). But the USA had strong economic interests in Central and South America, and it preserved these interests in two ways: by heavy overseas investment where the USA had trading interests; and by using the strength and international position of the dollar to control the currency and much of the trade of its neighbours. The *Organization of American States* was founded in 1890 by the USA for commercial purposes, and through it, at least until after the Second World War, the USA was able to dominate its members both economically and, to a large extent, politically.

Laissez-faire A government policy of leaving things alone, especially in industry and agriculture. Thus governments should intervene as little as possible in the lives and activities of their citizens.

Protection A policy of encouraging the development and prosperity of domestic industries by using heavy tariffs to keep out imports. This policy seemed to work during the 'boom' years of the 1920s, but it had the effect of depriving foreign countries of dollar earnings with which to buy American goods. Thus it was a major contributor to the Depression.

Tariff A tax levied on foreign imports, usually at the port of entry. Alternatively known as a *customs duty*, its collection is the responsibility of customs officers. Tariffs have often been used by governments as effective weapons in the battle for world trade, but they invite retaliation and are usually counterproductive in the long term. Many tariffs are protective in purpose, i.e. intended to protect home industries, but some are levied purely to raise revenue.

US political system The United States is a *federation* of 50 states, most of them on the North American mainland. There were originally thirteen British colonies, which united after the American War of Independence. Each state has its own capital (e.g. Richmond, Virginia) and its own political system; but there is a federal government in Washington, DC, with powers superior to those of the states.

The *constitution* is the instrument under which the USA is governed. It is a written document which may be amended with the consent of the states. The 22 amendments are listed at the end of the document. The interpretation of the meaning of the constitution is in the hands of the Supreme Court.

Presidents are elected for a fixed term of four years every leap year; if they die or are incapacitated, they are succeeded for the rest of their elected term by their Vice-President. They are elected indirectly, i.e. by the votes of an electoral college in which each state has as many electors as it has members of Congress. These are chosen in each state by the ordinary voters, but since they are all pledged to vote for a particular presidential candidate, the electoral college results are known within hours of voting, and long before the electoral college meets.

Congress is made up of two Houses: the House of Representatives and the Senate. Each state has two Senators, irrespective of its size, but the size of the body of Congressmen going to the House of Representatives varies proportionately according to the size of the state's population. The House of Representatives is elected every two years, the elections in the intervening years between presidential elections being known as *mid-term elections*. The Senate is partially renewed in thirds every two years, so that it is entirely renewed every six years.

The *Supreme Court* has judges who are nominated by the President in office when a vacancy occurs. It is the most important court in the land, taking precedence over all other courts, and it has the special duty of interpreting the constitution.

Each state has its own state militia, just as it has its own police force. In cases where the state militia is inadequate, federal troops may be used for the preservation of law and order.

▷ EXAMINATION QUESTIONS

 Question 1   (a)   Why did the wealth of the USA grow so rapidly throughout most of the 1920s?

(10 marks)

(b)   Did all Americans share in this growing wealth in the 1920s? Explain your answer.

(10 marks)

(c)   Why were so many Americans so much poorer in the 1930s?   (10 marks)

▷ **Question 2**   (a)   The Wall Street Crash. The policies of President Hoover. Roosevelt's promise of a New Deal.

Which of these was the most important reason for the election of Roosevelt as President in 1932? Refer to all three of the above in your answer.   (10 marks)

(b)   In 1932 there were almost 13 million unemployed in the USA, and there were still over 8 million in 1940. Does this mean that the 'New Deal' was a failure? Explain your answer.

(10 marks)

(c)   Why was there opposition to the 'New Deal'?   (10 marks)

▷ EXAMINATION ANSWERS

 Question 1   *Outline answer*

(a)   Here you will need to refer to the vastness of the USA with its various natural resources. The fact that the USA emerged from the war virtually unscathed and did not need to rebuild damaged or out-of-date industries gave the USA a head start in postwar trading conditions. The US policy of maintaining high tariffs meant that US industries faced only minimal competition from abroad, even when mainly European competitors had recovered from the war. The exploitation of America's vast natural resources was in its early, most productive stages, with the most up-to-date technology to assist production. The new consumer industries – earlier in the USA than elsewhere – accounted for much of the growth: motorcars, domestic electrical goods, new synthetic fibres (e.g. rayon). Above all, the prevailing climate of enterprise, and *laissez-faire* policies on the part of successive Republican administrations, encouraged unfettered economic activity, and it has even been suggested that Prohibition made its contribution through the vast 'black economy' it created.

(b)   Those who benefited from the booming economy were mainly white, middle-class town dwellers. You will need to explain how and why, with falling agricultural prices and the spreading 'dust bowl', agriculture did not share in the boom. Foreclosed mortgages brought homelessness and unemployment to the American countryside. Those who suffered most were the American blacks of the south, who were usually the first to become unemployed in the countryside. In the towns, the blacks were usually employed in the most menial and poorly paid jobs, and did not share in the growing affluence. And, of course, there was always a hard core of unemployed, both black and white. Relief for the poor varied from area to area and state to state, but at best it was inadequate, at worst virtually non-existent.

(c)   Descriptions of the Wall Street Crash will not provide a direct answer to this question. In so far as the Crash led to individual bankruptcies, put banks out of business when they could not recover their loans, and put workers out of jobs when firms collapsed, it will be relevant. The worsening agricultural situation (with several dry summers) accelerated agricultural unemployment, and the shortage of cash led to a fall in consumer demand and further commercial bankruptcies. Poverty, which in the 1920s had been largely confined to agricultural workers and black industrial workers, now spread right across the white community, and hit the middle and upper classes as well as the workers. Massive unemployment needs attention, but do not give Hoovervilles more than a reference – a description of them is unnecessary in this context. Even those in work suffered wage cuts or cuts in working hours, and it was only a very small minority who continued to prosper during the worst years of the Depression. In reality, America still had the same potential as before, but its industrial capacity and its human resources were standing idle, and were only gradually reactivated.

▷ Question 2(a)   *Tutor answer*

Without the Wall Street Crash, Hoover's Republican policies, which seemed to have served the USA so well in the 1920s, could well have continued. If the Wall Street Crash had not occurred and America had continued to prosper, the American electorate might have seen no reason to abandon Hoover, and there would have been little call for a New Deal policy from a Democratic President. It is just possible that the electors might have thought it time for a change; but a landslide victory, such as actually occurred in 1932, would have been extremely unlikely. It was the Wall Street Crash which highlighted the unwillingness of Hoover to adapt his policies to changing needs, even though he did belatedly attempt to legislate to check the financial panic, tackle mortgages and encourage public works. By 1932 the nature of the catastrophe brought on by the Wall Street Crash was too calamitous to be dealt with by gentle legislative tinkering: banks were failing, unemployment was accelerating and business confidence was evaporating. Amid the ruins of the American economy, voters were ready to listen to any voice, even the Democratic Roosevelt's, which promised a break with the past and hope for the future. It was the effects of the Crash which made them listen to Roosevelt. His New Deal promises lacked substance, but offered hope. Without the Crash his vague promises would not have been necessary and would certainly not have been so convincing.

▷ Question 2(b)   *Student answer with examiner's comments*

'Spelling.'

'The HOLC was not able to protect all mortgage holders in difficulties.'

'The alphabet agencies need to be focused on their effectiveness in dealing with unemployment.'

'Only here is there any attempt at detail.'

(b)   The New Deal was not a failure. Banking was dealt with by closing down incompetant banks and giving the others goverment backing. Farmers were encouraged by the AAA to destroy crops and carry out improvements. The goverment stopped people losing their homes through being unable to meet morgage repayments. Unemployment was dealt with by the WPA, the CCC and the TVA. The NRA encouraged high standards in the production of goods. Trade unions were given more power. Old-age pensions and unemployment insurance were provided. The salaries of public servants were cut to save money. Roosevelt gave 'fireside chats' over the radio to gain public support, and he made everyone happy by getting rid of Prohibition, with its speakeasies, bootlegging and organised crime, so that everyone could now enjoy beer, whiskey and wine again. So with all this it is obvious that the New Deal was not a failure.

Examiner's decision on the student answer

Overall this is not answering the question. It is a brief New Deal narrative, with no attempt to assess how the unemployment figures are related to success/failure.

▷ **Question 2(c)**   *Student answer with examiner's comments*

> *(c)   In order to push the New Deal Roosevelt had to propose laws to Congress rather than Congress proposing laws to him. This seemed to make the President very powerful, and many people thought that the President had gained too much power into his own hands. Among these were the Supreme Court who felt that the President was using Federal power to reduce that of individual states. That is why they declared so much of his New Deal legislation unconstitutional. Others, especially business men, thought that the new laws placed too many restrictions on business, and that the President had become a socialist. His attempts to help the aged and the poor led to accusations of creating a 'nanny' state, in which people became dependant on the state and stopped trying to help themselves. This criticism was even made of some of the Alphabet Agencies intended to put people to work; men were being paid salaries when there was no work for them to do. Even the hungry poor and the unemployed were alarmed at agricultural policies which aimed at the destruction of surplus food and the raising of food prices. Of course the Republicans, as Roosevelt's opponents, criticised the New Deal anyway, as was only to be expected from a political opposition.*

Examiner's decision on the student answer

This is doing what is asked. It has good coverage and depth, and would reach top Level. The spelling, although not perfect, would not affect the mark.

SUMMARY

This chapter has dealt with the main points in the history of the USA in the years between the wars. In your revision you should focus on:

▷ the growth of the industry and commerce of the United States;
▷ social divisions in the United States;
▷ political parties and policies in the United States;
▷ immigration and race relations;
▷ Prohibition and gangsterism;
▷ the fundamentalist controversy;
▷ extremism and populism in the United States;
▷ the growth and decline of isolationism in US external policies;
▷ the Wall Street Crash and the Depression;
▷ the Hundred Days and the New Deal;
▷ opposition to the New Deal and assessment of its importance.

Further material is to be found:

▷ on the part played by the USA in the Second World War, in chapter 12;
▷ on the later development of US history, in chapter 14;
▷ on the US role in postwar affairs, in chapters 15 and 18.

Chapter

14

The USA, 1941–80

GETTING STARTED

After 1945, the United States became one of the world's superpowers, and achieved a unique importance both in its home policies and in world affairs.

MEG	NEAB	NICCEA	SEG	LONDON	WJEC	TOPIC	STUDY	REVISION 1	REVISION 2
			✓*	✓	✓	**The impact of the Second World War on the USA**			
			✓*	✓	✓	The changing world position of the USA			
			✓*	✓	✓	McCarthy and McCarthyism			
			✓*	✓	✓	Industrial progress			
			✓*	✓	✓	**Social change**			
			✓*	✓	✓	Social trends after the war			
			✓*	✓	✓	**Political changes in the postwar USA**			
			✓*	✓	✓	Presidential changes after 1945			
			✓*	✓	✓	The affair in Dallas			
			✓*	✓	✓	Later Presidents			
			✓*	✓	✓	**Civil rights in the USA**			
			✓*	✓	✓	The struggle for black emancipation			
			✓*	✓	✓	The 'New Frontier' and the 'Great Society'			
			✓*	✓	✓	Social problems under Nixon			
			✓*	✓	✓	The feminist movement			

* Coursework only

WHAT YOU NEED TO KNOW

The impact of the Second World War on the USA

▷ **The changing world position of the USA**

After it finally abandoned isolationism in 1941, the United States played a major part in the Second World War, and continued this role thereafter.

The United States and the Second World War

In the Pacific
Pitched headlong into the struggle when Japan attacked Pearl Harbor, the United States was strong enough by 1943 to start a counteroffensive, and by 1945 it had reoccupied

186

the Philippines, captured Okinawa and Iwo Jima and was poised for an invasion of Japan itself. In August of that year, the war came to an end quite suddenly with the dropping of atomic bombs on the Japanese cities of Hiroshima and Nagasaki. After this, the entire Pacific area became a US sphere of influence.

In the western hemisphere

Here US forces also played a leading part. An Anglo-American landing in north Africa ('Operation Torch') under General Eisenhower in 1942 linked up with Montgomery's Eighth Army advancing westwards from Egypt; together, they drove the Axis armies into Tunisia, forcing them to surrender there in 1943. Allied troops conquered Sicily, and then fought their way northwards up the length of the Italian peninsula. In 1944, US troops invaded southern France, occupied the whole area of Vichy France and poured through the Belfort Gap into upper Alsace, where they contributed to the Allied invasion of Germany across the Rhine in 1945. Meanwhile, other US forces had crossed to the Normandy beaches on D-Day and played their part in the liberation of northern France. Recapturing Paris, they pressed through the Ardennes against the last desperate resistance of the German army and accomplished their advance towards the Rhineland in the concluding weeks of the war.

At sea and in the air

US efforts both at sea and in the air contributed magnificently to the final victory. Apart from its role in the Pacific, the US navy shared the burden of policing the Atlantic, while the US air force took a leading part in the bombing of Germany with massive daytime strikes to complement RAF bombing raids by night. By the end of the war, Britain had become a vast aircraft carrier moored off the coast of Europe, groaning under the tonnage of war material that the Americans had stockpiled there.

The United States at the end of the war

Throughout the war, the United States formed the 'arsenal of democracy', sending a ceaseless stream of weapons, supplies and equipment into Europe from the New World. By the time the war ended, the Americans had built about 12,000 ships, 100,000 tanks and nearly 300,000 aircraft, many of them flown to Europe by young pilots who had just completed their training in Canada or the United States. The United States lost about half a million servicemen in the war, and its financial spending topped $400bn, a sum greater than that spent by the rest of the Allies put together.

Though President Roosevelt died shortly before the end of the war, there seemed little danger that the United States would once more return to isolation. The USA was now, with the USSR, one of the world's two superpowers: it was one of the main founder-members of the United Nations Organization, set up at the San Francisco Conference in July 1945, and it footed the bill for its headquarters to be set up shortly afterwards in New York.

The USA took part in the partitioning of Germany in 1945, and afterwards garrisoned its Zone there, as well as contributing towards the joint garrisoning of Berlin. The USA lent a supporting hand to the tottering economies of western Europe with the *Marshall Plan* in 1947, and was the mainstay of the North Atlantic Treaty, establishing NATO, in 1949. By 1950, the European powers had come to take the presence of the Americans in Europe almost for granted.

President H.S. Truman, 1944–52

Harry Truman, who had been Roosevelt's Vice-President and who had succeeded to the White House when his predecessor died, was scarcely known in Europe while Roosevelt was alive. Nevertheless he served almost two full terms and achieved considerable success. Truman's main concern, like Roosevelt before him, was with social policy, in a country which, though rich, had great areas of submerged poverty, especially in rural areas and in poor non-white city precincts. Truman at first modestly confined himself to putting the finishing touches to Roosevelt's New Deal.

In September 1945 he set out his programme of *Twenty-One Points*, aiming to build more working-class housing and to extend social security benefits. In 1946 he secured the passing through Congress of an *Employment Act*. However, economic controls, planning and interference with free enterprise stuck in American gullets, and he was steadily compelled to abandon any semblance of state direction. The Republicans gained control of Congress in the mid-term elections of 1946 and proceeded to put through the *Taft–Hartley Act* in 1947: US employers were freed by it from some irksome restrictions, but others equally damaging were imposed on the trade unions. Republicans also made clear that they preferred tax cuts instead of the extension of social services.

Somewhat unexpectedly, Truman was returned for a second term in 1948 and continued with his social policies, but he never enjoyed the support of a sympathetic Congress, and pushed through his reforms in the teeth of their opposition. In 1949 he brought in his *Fair Deal*, modelled on the New Deal of 20 years before. Social security measures were extended, working conditions and hours were further regulated, minimum wage levels were introduced alongside subsidies and other support for poorer rural areas, and a new Housing Act extended the provision of low-cost homes for those on lower incomes. Truman had ambitious plans for more public works schemes, but some of his proposals earned congressional disapproval and had to be abandoned.

▷ McCarthy and McCarthyism

The rise of the communist threat in Europe after the end of the war alarmed and disturbed Americans, who came to suspect that there existed a conspiracy aiming to overthrow democratic methods of government. As after 1919, the Americans experienced a 'Red scare' from 1949 to about 1954.

The domestic impact of the 'Cold War'

By 1948, the Soviets had taken over in eastern Europe and had tried to oust the western powers from Berlin at the time of the blockade; and in 1949 they exploded their first atomic bomb.

In China, the nationalists, America's wartime allies, were overthrown by Mao Zedong in 1949. Americans found the 'loss' of China difficult to accept, and suspected that it heralded an alliance between the Soviet and the Chinese communists.

Such developments were only to be explained by treachery and conspiracy, a hunch strengthened by recent developments. In 1949 *Alger Hiss*, who had had a distinguished career during the war, had been one of Roosevelt's advisers at Yalta and had chaired the founding sessions of the United Nations at San Francisco, was accused of being a communist agent, and was convicted by a federal court on a charge of perjury. There followed the confession of *Klaus Fuchs*, accused of selling atomic secrets to the USSR in 1950. His accomplices, *Ethel and Julius Rosenberg*, were also arrested, and were convicted and executed as traitors in 1953.

This provided an opportunity for the scare-mongers to suggest a widespread communist conspiracy in the USA, with 'Reds under the bed'.

Joseph McCarthy and the 'UnAmerican Activities Committee'

This committee, originally founded before the war, came to be used in 1945–46 to root out communists from government service. It was used in 1947 to inquire into whether the US film industry had been subverted by 'celluloid communists'.

In this nervous atmosphere, Joseph McCarthy, a right-wing Republican and junior Senator for Wisconsin, seized his chance to launch a crusade against the communists. In February 1950 he accused the State Department of 'harbouring known communists', and claimed to have a list of the names of 205 of them. His rather amateur campaign against Dean Acheson failed, his charges dismissed as 'a fraud and a hoax'; shortly afterwards his denunciation of Owen Lattimore, expert in Far Eastern affairs in the State Department, also collapsed.

But otherwise, McCarthy had it all his own way, his cause further supported by the outbreak of the Korean War in June 1950. Truman declined to extend this war to China, but could not prevent the enactment of the *McCarran Internal Security Act* (September 1950) which required every 'communist front' organization in the USA to register, and banned 'subversives' from entering the United States.

The end of McCarthyism

Many Americans were disturbed by McCarthy's campaign, but dared not denounce him for fear of incurring his hostility; for a time 'guilt by association' meant that anyone might be accused of disloyalty if an acquaintance was a suspect.

Republicans in particular were not averse to referring to the Democrats' 'twenty years of treason', and stressing the respectability of their own political creed.

McCarthy continued his 'Red hunting' even after Eisenhower became President in 1952, but in 1954 he unwisely attacked the US army. The committee hearings were televised, and Americans were able to see McCarthy's bullying tactics for themselves. Public opinion swung about, and his reputation abruptly collapsed.

The Senate passed a vote of censure on him, and his career was finished; his death in 1957 went almost unnoticed by many who had feared him shortly before.

▷ Industrial progress

In the fifteen years after the war, the United States was already well on the way to being an economic superpower as well as a military one.

The development of US industry

Between 1945 and 1970 the economy grew at the astonishing rate of 3.5 per cent per annum. Between 1945 and 1960 the workforce grew from 54 million to 68 million job-holders, and this generated an abundance that was the envy of the world. With the post-war 'baby-boom' and the sharp decline of the death rate through the development of new 'wonder drugs' such as penicillin and cortisone, the population increased from 150 million in 1950 to 181 million in 1960: postwar Americans were the richest and the healthiest people in the world.

Automobiles remained the most important factor in this bonanza. Car and truck sales averaged 7 million per annum in the 1950s, and with them there was a similar expansion in service stations, garages, motels and highway construction, and an enormous boost to the oil industry. Americans by now had become not only the richest, but the most mobile nation in the world, millions of them moving to the 'sunshine belt' between California and Florida in search of better jobs and greater opportunities. Real estate, low taxes and a large infusion of military spending all helped in the boom.

Big business grew bigger in the postwar era. Not only did mergers bring together many firms in the same economic sectors, but they also led to vast conglomerates in unrelated fields – for example, International Telephone and Telegraph (ITT) brought into common ownership not only communications, but house construction, retail food outlets, an hotel chain and insurance as well.

This went hand-in-hand with the enormous development of credit institutions, not only for the hire-purchase of new cars, but for the enormous development of domestic technology, much of it electric, e.g. air conditioners, refrigeration equipment, automatic clothes washers and driers, and, of course, television. The new spending patterns got under way in 1950 when the Diners' Club introduced the *credit card*, soon to be followed by American Express and a host of others.

New industries also mushroomed into growth. The *chemical industry*, led by du Pont, turned out a never-ending flow of products, many of them in the consumer field, such as aerosols, dacron and new plastics such as vinyl. *Electricity and electronics* also developed very rapidly. As well as producing over 6 million television sets every year, other devices, such as electric blankets, hair dryers and so on, multiplied, spurred on by efficient Japanese competition. Around 1960, the computer revolution began, heralding the post-industrial revolution. Perhaps the most rapid growth was to be seen in the *aerospace industry*, growing very rapidly in the civil sphere, but also stimulated by multi-billion contracts from the Pentagon to supply sophisticated military hardware.

Industrial decline

At the same time, many traditional industries declined. Railroads were increasingly over-taken by road freight, coal mining declined as the competition from alternative fuels grew, and textiles also decayed, the traditional materials wool and cotton being steadily replaced by nylon, orlon and polyester.

Agriculture also changed drastically. Modern methods produced more than the consumer could buy; food prices dropped. The only way that farmers could keep in business was by reducing unit costs through economies of scale and the use of fertilizers, pesticides and the latest in elaborate farm machinery. Small farmers got squeezed out, to be replaced by 'agribusiness' enterprises; the number of farmers fell from 25 million to 14 million in the years 1945 to 1960, and welfare dependency in rural areas increased.

Social change

This was the period of what the US economist J.K. Galbraith called 'the Age of Affluence', with an enormous increase in what might be called 'middle-class' families and a sharp drop between 1945 and 1960 in 'poor' families, from about 40 per cent to less than 25 per cent. The change could also be seen in other ways.

▷ **Social trends after the war**

The 'teenage' era

The most obvious feature of the new America was the rapid spread of college education, with about 4 million students being enrolled annually in upwards of 2,000 colleges and universities in the United States. Until the end of the 1960s, these college campuses were quiet, orderly places where students pursued their courses and avoided politics or radicalism of any kind.

Teenage culture also flourished. Youngsters had money to spend and set the tone in popular taste, with their discos, clubs and generous spending on clothes and personal luxuries. It was the era of popular television, with Lucille Ball in *I Love Lucy* and Phil Silvers in *Sergeant Bilko*. This was also the era of Elvis Presley, the first rock'n'roll super-star. Though he was a showman of traditional stamp, Presley was the herald of a new era of sexual permissiveness, later to be graphically depicted in the movie *Grease*.

American women and family life

The war had disrupted traditional social patterns when millions of women had entered the labour force. After the war, they were confronted with a dilemma: whether to continue with their outside work, which many of them wished, or to stay at home, as many men wanted them to do.

The United States became more child orientated after the war. Working women earned the criticism that they were unfeminine, and many of them tried to provide in the home for their husbands and their families the sort of ideal environment that illustrated magazines led them to expect. Many were torn between the two ideals portrayed in the cinema by the wholesome image of Doris Day and the outrageous sex symbol of Marilyn Monroe.

The 'togetherness' ideal of the 1950s and 1960s, characterized by picnics, outings to parks and beaches, backyard barbeques, television watching and holiday excursions, could not gainsay the fact, however, that the working woman was emerging in the American culture. The female workforce expanded from 17 million in 1945 to over 25 million by 1960. The 'career woman', too, later depicted in films such as *Working Girl*, tended to glamourize the lifestyle of professional females, especially in city life.

In the 1960s, however, women adopted more positive attitudes, resenting the traditional domination of men. Feminists began to demand equal rights for women, better education, more career possibilities, greater control over their own bodies. They particularly resented Stokely Carmichael's wisecrack that 'In our movement the position of women is horizontal.' In the 1960s, many of them were working in jobs traditionally closed to them. By this time, nearly half the workforce was female.

The culture of 'conformity'

Suburban society and a mass culture generated a new type of American character – one that avoided individualism and aimed at conformity with others. This was curiously at variance with America's business ethic, but was perhaps regarded as 'safer' by the dominant commercial classes.

In business, an 'organizational ethic' was stressed, with employers encouraging their workers to dress, look and act alike. When appointments to senior positions were being made, great importance was laid on how the interviewees' wives dressed and behaved. Great stress was laid on the importance of being a good 'team player'; anything that smacked of individualism was frowned on.

In ordinary life, many lost the firm moral framework that their parents had once had: they were cast adrift morally, and searched for approval in their peer groups; many turned to the very uncertain tutor of television for guidance. Young people consumed their social values as they did their breakfast cereals. By the end of the 1970s, people were aghast at any expression of individuality, regarded as eccentricity, and cultivated a colourless acceptance of the dominant thinking of the period. PC values ('political correctness') began to dictate not only social behaviour, but social values and even what was regarded as acceptable vocabulary. Words like 'short', 'fat', 'black' and 'crippled' were severely discouraged. The results were sometimes as unintentionally comic as they were fashionably inescapable.

Political changes in the postwar USA

▷ **Presidential changes after 1945**

With the United States as one of the great world superpowers, the belief grew up that the question of political leadership was perhaps more important than ever before. For a democracy to be successful, the choice of the leader was a vital one.

The alternation of the Democrats and the Republicans

Harry S. Truman, 1945–52

Truman held office for most of the 1940s, after four terms to which Roosevelt was elected. By 1950 there was a feeling that perhaps it was not a good idea that the Democratic Party should hold power for so long.

In 1951 the *Twenty-Second Amendment* to the US constitution was passed, limiting future Presidents to two terms of office, and preventing any leader from doing what Roosevelt had done in 1932, 1936, 1940 and 1944. Supposedly a token of respect for George Washington, who had had the good sense to withdraw from politics after eight years in the late eighteenth century, the measures actually concealed a deep-seated American fear of presidential dictatorship – a danger which became all too apparent in the days of Richard Nixon.

The later years of the Truman presidency became empty and rather sterile because of the resistance of a hostile Congress to his wishes, and no one was very surprised when the Republicans came back to power with President Eisenhower in 1952.

Dwight D. Eisenhower, 1953–61

Eisenhower, one of the heroes of the Second World War, was a soldier rather than a politician. He had only a limited interest in the machinations of politics, and never thought like a whole-hearted party man. As a result he was never entirely accepted by the grandees of the Republican Party.

His main interest was in overseas policy and in military affairs, in which he had spent so much of his professional career. In domestic matters, Eisenhower was a conservative. He had no wish to reverse the policies of the New Deal or the Fair Deal, but he tried to avoid too much spending, and generally supported the interests of the prosperous middle class on whom he relied for support. After 1956, when the Democrats recovered control of Congress, he vetoed several attempts by reformers to push through expensive housing and welfare schemes. In economic matters, too, he showed the same caution.

Though there were recessions in 1953 and 1957, and a steel strike in 1959 which involved him in conflict with the trade unions, Eisenhower was President at a time when the economy of the country was generally flourishing.

His skills were those of a business manager; he liked to appoint the best men to the jobs, and then leave them to get on with them. He liked to be on the golflinks every afternoon. But for much of the time he was not in the best of health. He suffered a moderately severe stroke in 1957, and much of his work fell on his ambitious Vice-President, Richard Nixon. On the other hand, his supporters always said that Eisenhower worked very hard, but that he liked to cultivate an impression of indolence to put his critics off their guard; certainly his mastery of language can be seen from the skilful and detailed changes he made to the drafts prepared by his advisers for his speeches – something that always impressed Winston Churchill.

John F. Kennedy, 1961–63

Kennedy, the rising Democratic star, became President in 1961. His opponent for the presidency was Richard Nixon, who felt that his long years of apprenticeship under Eisenhower virtually entitled him to the office. He was, however, narrowly defeated. Their TV confrontation showed Nixon in a poor light: with his five o'clock shadow and sweating under the studio lights, he was soon earned the ironic gibe: 'Would you buy a second-hand car from this man?' Kennedy was a much more attractive figure: self-possessed, a New Englander, a Roman Catholic, and, at the age of 43, the youngest candidate ever to become President. Youth and energy were the keynotes of his presidency, soon to be translated into legend under the name of 'Camelot'.

In social policy he shared the ideals of most Democrats, and carried on the work where Truman left off. The same spirit of liberalism showed itself abroad in the form of the *Peace Corps*, founded in 1961 to allow skilled helpers to provide help for undeveloped nations. He also put forward his *Alliance for Progress* with Latin America, to increase cooperation with the countries in the western hemisphere and to help to raise their often desperately low standards. In Europe, too, he suggested sweeping tariff cuts in the so-called *Kennedy Round* of tariff negotiations, so as to encourage the growth of American trade with Europe.

His actual achievements, however, fell far short of his expectations. In 1963, he was still in the planning stage for further sweeping changes in policy.

▷ **The affair in Dallas**

Kennedy travelled to Texas in November 1963 with his Vice-President Lyndon B. Johnson, in the hope of reunifying southern Democrats who had recently split into liberal and conservative factions. Texas was a large state with an important bloc of electoral votes which Kennedy had won only narrowly in 1960 and now hoped to win again.

The murder of the President

Kennedy arrived at Dallas airport in Texas on the morning of 22 November, from where his motorcade proceeded to downtown Dallas shortly after noon. The motorcade turned into Elm Street and drove past the Texas Book Depository Building, from which three shots rang out, fatally wounding the President in the head and neck. He was rushed to Parkland Hospital nearby, where shortly afterwards he was pronounced dead.

Within hours, the police arrested Lee Harvey Oswald, a loner with a rather chequered background. On his way to court two days later, Oswald was confronted by Jack Ruby, a Dallas nightclub owner, who shot Oswald at pointblank range and killed him.

Meanwhile, aboard the presidential plane only a few minutes after the assassination, Johnson was sworn in as President of the United States.

Repercussions of the assassination

The murder of the President was greeted with dismay not only in America, where people wept openly in the streets, but also in foreign countries, and even in countries of the Soviet bloc. A number of curious circumstances surrounding the event, however, prompted speculation about it which has continued until the present time.

President Johnson appointed a Special Commission, headed by Chief Justice Earl Warren, to re-examine all the evidence, and ten months later the commission reported that there was no evidence that anyone assisted Oswald in the assassination.

No evidence has ever been found to refute their conclusion, although numerous efforts have been made to put the murder down to some kind of conspiracy, and over a thousand books have been written to challenge the Warren Commission findings.

For many, the passing of J.F. Kennedy marked the end of an era of youth and optimism, when apparently all things were possible, and the beginning of a long tunnel of despair in the shadow of the Vietnam crisis.

▷ Later Presidents

Though Kennedy was followed by a number of important Presidents, none of them quite enjoyed his personal prestige or authority, and the consensus which he seemed to foreshadow in support of domestic reform rapidly fragmented.

The presidency in the 1960s and 1970s

Lyndon B. Johnson, 1963–69

Johnson had the difficult task of effecting an orderly transition of power that ensured stability and continuity of US government. This he accomplished with remarkable success. Hard-bitten and cynical, and with an intimate knowledge of the more sordid and less idealistic side of politics, Johnson provided a complete contrast with his predecessor; none the less he managed to complete in about five years most of the tasks which his predecessor had set himself.

He pushed through Kennedy's programme and tightened the discipline of the Democratic Party, an accomplishment which may well have been beyond Kennedy. But increasingly the USA became obsessed with the entanglement in the fruitless struggle in Vietnam. Though Johnson was returned to power successfully in 1964, by the time of the presidential election in 1968, American opinion was so nervy and domestic criticism so violent that Johnson refused to run for re-election.

Richard Nixon, 1969–74

Nixon brought the Republicans back to power in 1968. In his campaign he played up the domestic problems of the government in the 'long, hot summer' of 1968, but made particular capital out of Johnson's inability to solve the Vietnam problem. Nixon gave the promise that, if he were returned, he would finish off the war. Nevertheless he won by only a fairly slender margin of electoral votes.

Though his external policies were unquestionably successful, Nixon soon earned himself the reputation of being a rather self-centred and shifty character with no vision for solving domestic problems. He showed little enthusiasm for reform, and though he did not attempt to undo any of the reforms already made, he showed no desire to go any further. Indeed, he showed some resentment towards critics, radicals and students, all of whom he lumped together under the name of 'pinkos'. The troubles on the university campuses and in the cities dwindled during his term of office, but this was less because he had found a way of solving them than because of the harshness with which he clamped down on them.

He made a number of positive moves in social policy, such as the appointment of a *Council for Urban Affairs*, but it was generally the US economy that occupied the centre of his attention. The massive amount of overseas spending, not least on the defence of other nations, brought a big outflow of currency and weakened the dollar. The result was that the 1970s saw a curious new phenomenon, 'stagflation', in which economic recession and high unemployment (about 4 million in the early 1970s) combined with a steadily rising level of wages and prices. Nixon made strenuous efforts to restore the Republicans' reputation as the 'businessmen's party', and to bring expenditure under control. He tried to freeze wages and prices; he introduced a surcharge of 10 per cent on imports to redress the adverse balance of payments; he cut back on government spending and thus on borrowing, so as to reduce interest rates; and finally he devalued the dollar. This provided a temporary respite, but later in the 1970s trouble with the economy started again. What America needed, he felt, was a steady spell of sound Republican administration to put the country back on track.

The Watergate affair, 1972

Nixon was convinced that only the Republicans could save America, especially with himself in charge, so he embarked on a process at the end of which he hoped to be able to repeal the Twenty-Second Amendment, so as to permit himself a third, and perhaps further terms as President. This immediately aroused the latent fears on the part of all liberals of presidential dictatorship.

But it was the *Watergate Scandal* that put an abrupt and shameful end to his political career. A newspaper campaign, building on small and unsubstantiated rumours that Nixon had been engaged at the time of the 1972 presidential election in burglary (at the Watergate Hotel, which gave its name to the affair and which was the Democrat Party HQ at the time of the election campaign), theft and misrepresentation, eventually ruined him when the truth about Nixon's 'plumbers' (i.e. his agents and 'fixers', acting on his instructions) came to light. It became known that in the course of pursuing his re-election – his Campaign for the Re-Election of the President was perhaps appropriately known as CREEP – Nixon had not always stayed on the right side of the law.

The knowledge that the President of the United States should have so little regard for obedience to the law came as a terrible shock to most Americans. He did his best to excuse himself by inventing a new constitutional doctrine known as the *presidential prerogative*, which more or less meant that the President could do as he liked – a doctrine that not even George III had thought of.

The real quality of Nixon's presidency was revealed when, after much wriggling, he agreed to produce certain clandestine tapes which showed how far he trusted his intimate advisers, having recorded every word they uttered in the Oval Office. When played, these tapes contained a considerable number of mysterious blanks where the words used had been deleted, but they also showed to the American people that their President was foul-mouthed, mean-minded and petty, and not above breaking the law when it suited him. Congress reacted by threatening to impeach him for his misdeeds. Rather than face disgrace, he resigned office in August 1974, handing over to his Vice-President Gerald Ford, who promptly pardoned him for whatever he had done, so closing the book on one of the most unsavoury episodes in American history.

The end of the 1970s

The presidential election of 1976, marking the two hundredth anniversary of the US Declaration of Independence, saw the end of the brief spell of office of Gerald Ford, whose performance most people agreed was exceptionally mediocre, and the return of a Democrat rather than a Republican to the White House.

Jimmy Carter, 1977–81

Carter had a rather bucolic background – he was a peanut farmer from Georgia in the Deep South – and presented an image quite different from the somewhat sleazy impression being projected at the time by smart Washington society. His modest, sincere manner came like a breath of fresh air to a jaded and dispirited capital.

But though he promised well, he achieved relatively little. At home he grappled without much success with the problems of the weakening dollar, an adverse balance of payments, high rates of interest and of domestic unemployment, and steadily advancing inflation.

Perhaps his most serious problem was the energy crisis. The unpopularity of the USA in many parts of the Middle East generated retaliatory measures by the *Organization of Petroleum Exporting Countries* (OPEC) to raise the price of oil, of which the Americans, in spite of their own massive resources, were major importers. The resultant crisis gave President Carter a lot to occupy him. The United States decided that it ought to make better use of its own natural oil and gas supplies: it made efforts to extract oil from coal and shale; it undertook engineering research to produce more efficient car engines; it imposed maximum speed limits; and there was even talk of rationing for a time. But many of the sensible remedies put forward by Carter were not popular with Congress, and in the end little came of them.

One of Carter's main concerns was with *human rights*, which he assiduously pursued in his domestic policies. Abroad, too, he adopted a rather righteous stance. After the overthrow of the Shah of Iran, one of his leading allies in the Middle East, he protested against the brutalities of the regime of the Ayatollah Khomeini, who replaced him. Relations with Iran were so bad that in 1979 Iranian students seized a large number of US hostages and held them for over a year. The Carter administration, in spite of its great world strength, seemed powerless to do anything about it. An attempt at a rescue by a 'hit squad' of US helicopters was a disastrous failure. It was only at the end of the Carter presidency that the problem was solved.

Though Carter had done something to restore American self-respect after Nixon, the hostage affair too was a humiliation, and few people were really sorry when he was replaced at the 1980 presidential election by the Republican Ronald Reagan.

Civil rights in the USA

In 1945, Americans aimed to recapture the prosperity of the Roaring Twenties, and soon came to enjoy the benefits of the greatest industrial power ever. At the same time, a variety of disadvantaged groups embarked upon their long slow struggle to achieve their fair share of the American dream.

▷ **The struggle for black emancipation**

After the war, in which black Americans had played a substantial part, the struggle against discrimination continued. The *National Association for the Advancement of Coloured People* (NAACP), originally founded in 1909, but with a membership in 1945 of well over a quarter of a million, continued to chip away at the judicial foundations of segregation, and was soon encouraged by the success of a number of distinguished black athletes, like Jackie Robinson, who was allowed to take part in major ball games.

Early successes

Truman was the first President to promote civil rights causes. He was well aware of the importance of the black vote in northern states, and in 1946 he set up a Committee on Civil Rights to draft a programme in favour of greater equality. He tried to ban lynching, to abolish discrimination in interstate commerce and to enforce the decisions of the *Fair Employment Practices Committee*, in which he had taken an interest since its foundation in 1941; unfortunately the Republicans were strongly against his proposals, and southern Democrats generally ignored them.

He had some success in barring discrimination in government offices, and in the armed forces, where his executive order could not be challenged. But by 1952 it was obvious that reform still had a long way to go.

Eisenhower took this process further. As a leader of the Republicans, Eisenhower had more clout in Congress than Truman had ever had. Soon after his inauguration, he appointed Earl Warren, Chief Justice of California, to be Chief Justice of the Supreme Court, where he ruled in *Brown* v. *Topeka Board of Education* that separate schools for negro children were unconstitutional, saying that though theoretically they were 'equal' with white schools, in practice they were much inferior. The southern states tried to ignore the ruling, but Eisenhower insisted, and when the state militia refused to enforce it he ordered federal troops in Little Rock, Arkansas, to escort black students into school and protect them against the prejudices of white southerners.

This was immensely encouraging to black people. In 1955, in Montgomery, Alabama, Rosa Parks initiated the modern civil rights movement by refusing to give up her seat at the front of a bus to a white man who demanded it. Under the leadership of Dr Martin Luther King, Jr, the black civil rights leader, this developed into a full-scale boycott of the city's buses. King declared: 'Integration is the great issue of our age, of our nation and of our community. We are in the midst of a great struggle, the consequences of which will be world-shaking.' Helped by a Supreme Court ruling that bus segregation was unconstitutional, the protesters eventually forced the city bus company to abandon the practice, and also to begin to employ black drivers and black mechanics. Soon protests spread to other blacks who objected to whites-only cafés, hotels, libraries and drug stores, or who objected to being barred from public parks and other places of public resort. By 1960, a fully fledged civil rights movement had come into being.

It had its first success in 1957 when Eisenhower passed a *Civil Rights Act*, attempting to prevent negro voters from being deprived of their votes.

Civil rights under Kennedy and Johnson

Kennedy declared himself in favour of civil rights from the start of his campaign, and won the approval of large numbers of black people by securing the release of Dr King from gaol in Birmingham, Alabama, where he had been imprisoned for his part in the recent campaign.

When he became President, he appointed a number of negroes to important federal offices, e.g. Robert Weaver, who became Head of Housing. He also appointed negroes to judicial offices, but he counterbalanced this by choosing a number of segregationalist judges for the southern courts. The President's actions were strongly supported by his brother, Robert Kennedy, who became Attorney-General; but critics, including King himself, accused him of 'tokenism' in his actions (i.e. doing something once in order to create an impression of doing it regularly).

Kennedy again used federal troops to enforce desegregation in 1962, when they gave protection to black students entering the universities of Mississippi and Alabama. He came out strongly against discrimination when he said in 1963:

> We preach freedom around the world, and we mean it. And we cherish our freedom here at home. But are we to say to the world – and much more importantly to each other – that this is the land of the free, except for Negroes; that we have no second-class citizens, except Negroes; that we have no class or caste system, no ghettoes, no master race, except with regard to Negroes? Now the time has come for this nation to fulfil its promises.

To show support for the legislation Kennedy was putting forward, civil rights leaders organized a march on Washington. Addressing a meeting of over 200,000 supporters in front of the Washington Memorial, Martin Luther King passionately affirmed his belief in the rightness and the inevitability of his cause:

> I have a dream that one day this nation will rise up and live out the true meaning of its creed: We hold these truths to be self-evident, that all men are created equal. I have a dream that one day on the red hills of Georgia, the sons of former slaves and the sons of former slave-owners will be able to sit together at the table of brotherhood.

After the rally, Dr King met with President Kennedy to discuss the issues raised; unfortunately Congress still continued to stall and little practical was done.

Johnson, for all that he came from the American south, was able to deliver far more than Kennedy had. With his familiarity with the levers of political power, he managed to force through Congress far more of Kennedy's programme than many thought possible or likely. He managed to get Kennedy's *Civil Rights Act* through Congress in 1964, outlawing discrimination in housing, jobs and education. A *Public Voting Act* in 1965 resulted in an increase in the number of registered black voters in the southern states, and led to a higher proportion of them actually using their votes. Another *Civil Rights Act* followed in 1968, attempting to end discrimination in the sale and leasing of domestic accommodation. In other areas, too, he was active. In 1965 he increased job opportunities for underprivileged young blacks through his *Equal Opportunities Act*. However, though the situation was much improved, the same hostile attitudes lingered on in many walks of American life, especially in the south.

▷ **The 'New Frontier' and the 'Great Society'**

The Democrat leaders Kennedy and Johnson were not only involved during their presidencies in reforms relating to conditions for the black citizens of the United States, but concerned themselves too with remedying the problems of other sectors of society in relation to living and working conditions.

Kennedy's 'New Frontier'

Kennedy invoked the spirit of the old pioneer in his appeal for what he called a 'New Frontier' policy, directed not against the untamed wilderness of the western lands, but against the twentieth-century evils of poverty, inequality and deprivation. He set as his goals a fairer, freer and more equal society, where the spirit of adventure should be restrained within a civilized framework.

He aimed at comprehensive reform: medical care for the elderly, federal aid for education, housing reform, and reform of immigration and of working conditions. Many of his ideas, however, remained in the blueprint stage, partly because of a hostile Congress and partly because of the expense that would be involved. For example, his $2½bn federal aid proposal for schools was rejected, even though Kennedy took great care not to make it appear that he favoured Catholic schools.

But he had a number of smaller successes:

(a) *1961, Area Redevelopment Act* provided limited funds for economically depressed areas.
(b) *1962, Manpower Retraining Act* provided nearly $500 million to retrain unemployed workers in new skills.
(c) *1962, Minimum Wages Act* increased the federal minimum wage and extended it to cover nearly 4 million more workers.

In the economic sphere, Kennedy was accused of being a reckless spender, and he tried to reassure his critics by keeping a close watch on federal spending.

When the steel industry hiked the price of steel by $6 a ton in 1962, he restrained them, but his own ideas of 'deficit financing' on the Roosevelt model caused more disquiet and seemed to threaten inflation.

The recovery that occurred in 1963, however, was due less to his ideas than to big increases (of about $50bn) in defence expenditure because of the Cold War and in order to facilitate the moon shot. As Kennedy said: 'No single space project in this perod will be more impressive to mankind nor more important for the long-range exploration of space . . . than putting a man on the moon.'

At the same time, his critics argued that it was Kennedy's extravagant programmes that initiated the dangerous upward spiral of state spending that was to create the serious budgetary difficulties of the 1970s and 1980s.

Johnson's 'Great Society'

A man of humble origins, Johnson believed that state action could be a real way of improving the lot of the disadvantaged; in this sense he was much more the inheritor of the New Deal commitment than was his more highly esteemed predecessor. He invoked memories of the dead President to prise reforms out of Congress, at the same time promising to keep a check of federal spending. He was thus able to put far more on the statute book than Kennedy ever had.

(a) *1964, Economic Opportunity Act* authorized the spending of over $1bn to further his anti-poverty programme.
(b) *1964, Office of Economic Opportunity* (OEO) was created to administer the programme – especially involving the poor themselves in devising such programmes.
(c) *1964, Jobs Corps* was set up to help the poor find work.
(d) *1965, Housing and Urban Development Act* provided funding for creating up to 250,000 units of low-cost housing, and $3bn more for 'urban renewal'. To help with this, he created a *Department of Housing and Urban Development*.
(e) *1965,* the provisions of *Medicare* for the elderly and *Medicaid* for the poor were extended in spite of bitter opposition from organized physicians.
(f) *1965, Education Act* at last began to supply federal funds to support elementary and secondary schools which were willing to enrol low-income students.
(g) *1964, Immigration Act* was the first comprehensive overhaul of immigration policy for nearly 40 years, and scrapped the 'quota' system, introducing a new non-racist system based on skills and education.

(h) 1965–66, a large number of smaller measures went into law, requiring, for instance, the accurate labelling of products of household use, the provision of true information on rates of interest charged on loans and credit purchases, and new measures for conservation, wildlife preservation and highway safety.

The pace of reform slowed to a trickle after 1966 with the build-up of disaffection in the rundown suburbs of older cities, and with the mounting expenditure on the Vietnam War. These were among the problems inherited by Nixon in 1968.

Fig. 14.1 'The Train Robbery'. *Punch cartoon*, January 1967

Social problems under Nixon

In the presidency of Nixon, four social issues overlapped, highlighted by a series of 'long hot summers' during the late 1960s.

Civil rights

The moderate successes of Martin Luther King, until his assassination by a white extremist in 1968, led to more radical expressions of black aspirations in the *Black Power* movement, and to the growth of 'black consciousness'. Radicals such as Stokely Carmichael and James Meredith advocated more direct methods, and radical groups like the *Black Muslims* (Elijah Poole and Malcolm X) and *Black Panthers* believed in violent methods against white opponents.

This example was followed by other minorities:

(a) Puerto Rican students in New York demanded greater respect and the right to pursue their own studies in high-school and college curricula.
(b) Aboriginal Americans demanded 'Red' power, and particularly repayment for their ancestral lands confiscated during the 'Indian Wars'.
(c) Mexican-American ('Brown Power') militants waged a campaign for greater rights for poor farm workers ('Chicanos'), particularly among grape-pickers in California's San Joaquin Valley.

Urban decay

In the poorer, more crowded quarters of great cities, black protest linked naturally with urban poverty and unemployment, and there were serious outbreaks of violence in areas which should have benefited from Johnson's urban renewal plans.

In the *Watts* suburb of Los Angeles, there was a week of burning and looting in 1965, injuring 1,100 persons and destroying $40 million worth of property. This dismayed the authorities, since conditions in Watts were better than in many other areas.

In *Newark* (New Jersey) and *Chicago* (Illinois), similar riots followed in 1967. In the former, 26 people were killed in rioting, and in the latter 43. Order was restored only with patrolling tanks and soldiers carrying machine guns.

In *Washington*, serious riots occurred in 1968, when buildings were burned within a few blocks of the White House, and soldiers mounted machine guns on the Capitol steps. In all these riots, over 80 per cent of the fatalities were black rioters.

Student protest

Students – dubbed 'draft-dodgers' by an ungrateful Nixon – also figured prominently in the protest movement. The Vietnam issue was one issue at stake; there was also inequality, unemployment and the cynical materialism of the administration.

The movement spread by 1969 to other countries, most notably Japan and France, where student disaffection was a main cause of the downfall of President de Gaulle.

The revolt was accompanied by an 'alternative lifestyle' that older Americans rejected contemptuously. Skirts were voluminously long or microscopically short; rings were worn in places where they had never been seen before; hair was worn long and free by men as well as women; 'flower-power' ruled. Many strummed soulful guitars, and sang the lyrics of Bob Dylan. Serious issues mingled with pot smoking and bra burning in various music festivals and rallies.

A number of university campuses were affected by demonstrations and 'sit-ins', perhaps the most famous being at Berkeley, California.

▷ The feminist movement

Betty Friedan, in *The Feminine Mystique* (1963), led the modern women's liberation movement, rebelling against what she called the 'split-level home' and calling it a 'comfortable concentration camp'.

'Consciousness-raising' women's groups sprang into being all across America, demanding equal pay for equal work, equal access to the professions, equal treatment before the law, and an end to the overt or unwitting 'sexism' of their menfolk.

Johnson was aware of the sentiment and tried to remedy it in his *Civil Rights Act* of 1964, but this did little for women's grievances.

In 1966 they founded the *National Organization for Women* (NOW), for fairer treatment for women, but their more radical wing expressed hostility to men. They had some successes:

(a) *Equal Rights Amendment* was revived in Congress in 1970 after being buried in apathy for about half a century; it only narrowly missed ratification.
(b) Better *job opportunities* for women in jobs hitherto closed to women, e.g. fire-fighters, police, auto mechanics and even building workers.
(c) In the Supreme Court, in *Roe* v. *Wade* in 1973, the right of women to have abortions on demand was upheld.

Another expression of the same spirit was seen in the open avowal of homosexuality by former 'closet queens' and of female lesbians, with parades chanting 'Say it loud, gay is proud!' It was not long before cases were being brought against the service authorities by 'gays' who wanted their rights acknowledged.

Pressures subsided in Carter's presidency, after he caused something of a scandal by appointing the black and rather outspoken Andrew Young as US Ambassador to the UN. He dropped him in 1979, losing much of the black vote at the 1980 election, even though he appointed another black ambassador.

▶ **GLOSSARY**

Agribusiness   Large-scale farming. Farms were bought up and amalgamated by big business interests with available capital, and thus the means to invest in the latest heavy machinery. Economies of scale meant that such farms survived the Depression, while small farms went to the wall.

CREEP   The Campaign to Re-elect the President. An aptly named organization of Nixon's close aides who were working to secure his re-election to the presidency. It was this shadowy organization, formed in 1972, which was responsible for the break-in at the Democratic headquarters in the Watergate Hotel, Washington, which led to the Watergate affair and Nixon's eventual resignation in 1974.

Electronics   The branch of physics and engineering which led initially to radio and television, and eventually to the replacement of radio valves by transistors. The widespread development of electronic techniques led to a virtual revolution in the communications industry in the 1970s and 1980s, and this revolution is still continuing.

Fair Deal   The domestic programme of President Truman, intended to continue the work of Roosevelt's New Deal. Its main concerns were to deal with poverty and old age, to assist farmers, and to promote civil rights. Much of the programme was obstructed by a hostile Congress from 1946, so the achievements of the Fair Deal were disappointingly limited.

Kennedy Round   President Kennedy's attempt to foster international trade by tariff cuts, first through Congress, and then at the diplomatic level through the General Agreement on Tariffs and Trade (GATT), which negotiated tariff reductions for participating countries.

NAACP   The National Association for the Advancement of Colored People. This was formed in the USA in 1909, but it was not until the 1950s and 1960s that it became a powerful black movement, especially so under the control of Martin Luther King. Its aim was to enlighten both blacks and whites on the evils of racism, and it played an effective role in the movement for civil rights, fighting civil court cases and organizing non-violent demonstrations and protests.

Political correctness (PC)   Part of a code of social behaviour whose aim is to avoid giving offence to minority groups and interests. It developed in American universities in the 1960s, and it has spread throughout the western world. Offensive expressions referring, for example, to blacks and homosexuals are banned, and the 'rules' of PC have tended to become more extensive and more rigid. Offenders against PC can often lose out on promotion or even lose their jobs, so that an incautious word or an unintentional remark can be costly.

The rigidity of PC has also, in many instances, made it ludicrous: that Maths books cannot have questions on men filling a trench, but must have it filled by 'persons' for fear of upsetting feminists, is counterproductive, and tends to hold up to ridicule both PC and the feminists. As a consequence there are signs that in the late 1990s PC has lost some of its momentum, but in the late 1970s and the 1980s it was a powerful influence, especially in the USA, where it made some positive contribution to more liberal attitudes, especially concerning race, feminism and homosexuality.

▶ **EXAMINATION QUESTIONS**

▷ **Question 1**   (a)   In what ways were blacks discriminated against in the United States in the years immediately following the Second World War?   (10 marks)

(b)   How far had there been an improvement in the condition of the blacks by the end of the 1960s?   (10 marks)

(c)   Feminists in the 1960s claimed that women were as much discriminated against as the blacks had been in the 1940s and 1950s. Do you agree? Explain your answer.   (10 marks)

▷ **Question 2**

Fig. 14.2 An American anti-communist cartoon of the late 1940s

YEAH — SO HELP ME GOD !

LOYALTY OATH

(a)   How valuable is the cartoon in helping historians to understand American attitudes towards communism in the late 1940s and early 1950s?   (5 marks)

(b)   Why was McCarthyism so strong in the USA of the early 1950s?   (8 marks)

(c)   Why did McCarthyism fail to survive the mid-1950s?   (10 marks)

(d)   Was anti-communism still strong in the USA during the 1960s and 1970s? Explain your answer.   (7 marks)

 EXAMINATION ANSWERS

▷ **Question I**   *Outline answer*

(a)   Here you will need to pinpoint a variety of ways in which the blacks were treated as second-class citizens. Some distinction between the northern and southern parts of the USA would be useful. Thus while it was possible for some blacks to exercise voting rights in some of the northern states, this was virtually impossible throughout the south. Segregation, too, was almost universal in the south, e.g. on buses, in hotels, in schools and in public sports and entertainment; while in the north such segregation often occurred, it was not, as in the south, backed up by state law and state enforcement. In jobs, blacks were at the bottom of the economic heap in both north and south; thus it followed that poor housing for blacks was inevitable. Black success in the professions was rare enough to attract media notice: there were very few black officers in the US armed forces in the Second World War, and the first black actress to win an Oscar won it in 1940 for playing a domestic servant in *Gone with the Wind*.

(b)   The improvements were political and social. You need to discuss the early support for racial integration by such unlikely persons as the Republican President

Eisenhower, and you will need to consider the aims and methods of the civil rights movement and in particular the work of Martin Luther King. Thus civil protest, white sympathy and federal intervention led to desegregation on buses and in public places, and to moves to end segregated schooling (e.g. Little Rock, Arkansas). Efforts to give blacks a political voice were ineffective in the south in the 1950s, but began to have an effect after the Johnson legislation of the 1960s. However, the economic condition of the blacks was difficult to tackle. More entered public life and more prospered in the professions, but the vast majority of blacks were still the worst housed and the lowest paid, the most unskilled, and the first to lose their jobs in times of rising unemployment.

(c) This is, of course, an exaggeration. There was no specific discrimination against women, except on certain golf courses and in men's clubs. But women were expected to be homemakers and housewives, and those who pursued careers, especially if they had young children, were often frowned upon and even ostracized. Abortion was not a choice available to most women. The professions were difficult to enter, and promotion was difficult to achieve, especially if a woman's career was interrupted by child bearing. A woman could vote, but entering politics was entering a man's world. Economically, however, except for the poorly paid single woman (equal pay was beginning to make its appearance in the professions, but not in the business world), women shared the economic status of their husband or families, and were not necessarily living in poverty or squalid housing as the blacks were.

▷ Question 2(a)   *Tutor answer*

The cartoonist is here trying to depict the communist in the worst possible light. He is made to look evil, and he is shown taking the oath of loyalty to the USA, while wearing the communist insignia on his back. The cartoonist obviously assumes that communism and loyalty to the USA are incompatible. The fact that this is a published cartoon demonstrates that the cartoonist expected to strike a sympathetic chord with at least some of the American public, but it is not clear whether the cartoon represents the opinion of a minority or the majority. To the historian the cartoon would be valuable both in the attitude it depicts and in the implicit assumptions that it makes. It certainly seems to illustrate from the McCarthy era a viewpoint which we know from other sources to have been fairly typical of the period.

▷ Question 2(b)   *Tutor answer*

The American fear of communism was not entirely removed by the fact that the Soviet Union was the USA's ally in the Second World War. After the war, mutual suspicion between the USSR and its western allies developed almost as soon as hostilities ended. Americans were concerned at the Soviet domination of eastern Europe, their intransigence over Berlin, and their refusal to accept or to allow others in their political sphere to accept Marshall Aid. The rapid collapse of nationalist China convinced many Americans, not of Chiang Kai-shek's incompetence, but of his betrayal by traitors from within his own ranks and by the US State Department. When the Soviet Union exploded its first atomic bomb in 1949, and it became clear that atomic secrets had been betrayed to the Soviets by agents working in the USA, the Americans developed something like paranoia about the traitor within. They saw their security, their prosperity and their way of life threatened by an international communist conspiracy bent on world domination. The outbreak of the Korean War in 1950 confirmed their suspicions. McCarthy played effectively on these fears, and became the mouthpiece of those who saw every liberal as a subversive communist, and all who did not share their opinions as suspect.

▷ **Question 2(c)** *Student answer with examiner's comments*

'So, how did this help to end McCarthyism?'

'So, was it a mistake to attack public figures, and did his committee's appearance on TV enhance or damage his reputation?'

> *In 1953 the Korean War came to an end. McCarthy attacked important public figures and his committee was shown in action on TV. He decided to accuse a general of communism. Eisenhower, although of the same political party, did not like McCarthy. Many people in the USA were rather ashamed of the way in which they had supported the communist 'witch-hunt'.*

'Was this a mistake?'

'These points require explanation and development.'

Examiner's decision on the student answer
A brief answer, in which no reasons appear at the beginning, but reasons are hinted at towards the end. The student knows something, but fails to make use of the knowledge. This would be only Level 2 at about 4/10.

▷ **Question 2(d)** *Student answer with examiner's comments*

> *Communism was still feared by most Americans in the 1960s and 1970s. The Cold War was still at its height, the Russians had the hydrogen bomb, and many believed that the Vietnam War was an attempt by the communists to take over the whole of South-East Asia. Spy-planes, soon to be replaced by spy-satellites, heightened the tension, but World War Three did not seem as close as it had during the Korean War. The humiliation of withdrawal from Vietnam in the early 1970s made the Americans even more rather than less determined to face up to the challenge of communism and to prevent its expansion both internationally and at home.*

Examiner's decision on the student answer
This is still rather brief, but is more sharply focused than (c). It needs more development, and would not achieve the highest Level. It would probably be Level 3, scoring about 7/10.

SUMMARY

In this chapter you have studied the history of the USA in the later part of the twentieth century, and have dealt with the following topics:

▷ the effects of the Second World War on the United States;
▷ Truman and the 'Fair Deal';
▷ the rise and fall of Senator McCarthy; 'McCarthyism';
▷ modern industrial and social change in the USA;
▷ the development of American feminism;
▷ later Presidents: Kennedy, Johnson, Nixon;
▷ civil rights and social problems in the USA.

Further information on the role of the United States in international affairs in the later twentieth century will be found in chapters 15 and 18.

The development of the Cold War, 1945–63

 GETTING STARTED

There developed over the next half-century a bitter struggle between East and West – the American- and the Soviet-dominated blocs of powers – which came to be known as the *Cold War*, because it was fought not with conventional weapons, but with the more insidious weapons of propaganda. It ended only with the collapse of the Soviet bloc at the end of the 1980s. It is to the history of this Cold War that we now turn.

MEG	NEAB	NICCEA	SEG	LONDON	WJEC	TOPIC	STUDY	REVISION 1	REVISION 2
✓	✓	✓	✓	✓	✓	**The beginning of the Cold War**			
✓	✓	✓	✓	✓	✓	The emergence of rivalry between the superpowers			
✓	✓	✓	✓	✓	✓	The situation in postwar Europe			
✓	✓	✓	✓	✓	✓	**The Cold War in the Far East**			
✓	✓	✓	✓	✓	✓	The origins of the Cold War in the East			
✓	✓	✓	✓	✓	✓	The Cold War in Korea			
✓	✓	✓	✓	✓	✓	**The Cold War after the death of Stalin**			
✓	✓	✓	✓	✓	✓	An era of 'summits'			
✓	✓	✓	✓	✓	✓	The Cuban missile crisis, 1962			

 WHAT YOU NEED TO KNOW

The beginning of the Cold War

▷ **The emergence of rivalry between the superpowers**

Even at the time when they were allies against Nazi Germany, the communist leadership of the Soviet Union and the leaders of the western powers never fully trusted each other: relations were formal rather than cordial. Though they shared common aims, they did little to share their strategies and were generally unhelpful to each other. Western planes, for example, were denied the use of Soviet landing grounds in the later stages of the war, even though this would have been very convenient to them.

The breakdown of the wartime alliance

After the war each side distrusted the intentions of the other. US leaders like Roosevelt and Truman gave generous names to their objectives, talking of peace, freedom and security; but the Soviets saw American aims as being imperialism and world economic domination. The USSR, on the other hand, claimed to be fighting for communism and for world revolution; but the western powers suspected that this ideological camouflage disguised its underlying aim of territorial expansion.

By May 1945 the Red Army had poured into central and eastern Europe, and was now anxious to consolidate its gains, deliberately building barriers of secrecy and incomprehension in order to prevent relations of familiarity or friendliness with the West. This was the origin of what later became known as the *Iron Curtain*.

The United Nations, set up at the San Francisco Conference in April, to the Soviets seemed already to be an American-dominated body which could not be expected to offer genuine mediation in the event of a struggle between East and West.

Beliefs and attitudes of the wartime leaders

Stalin thought that the only thing to do was to secure firm control of his bargaining counters in Europe if he was going to have something to negotiate with in trying to prevent a western takeover. His former allies saw this as Soviet ruthlessness and aggression, but Stalin knew that the struggle with Nazi Germany had seriously sapped his strength, and now he tried to prevent the West from finding out how desperately his resources were overstretched.

Truman, at the same time, was more intransigent than Roosevelt had been. The dropping of atomic bombs on Japan in early August strengthened his resolution. At their meeting in Potsdam only a week or two before, Truman had deliberately concealed the bomb's existence from Stalin; now his Secretary of State, James Byrnes, felt able to suggest: 'The bomb might well put us in a position to dictate our own terms.' Truman's own feelings fell little short of elation: 'If the bomb explodes – and I think it will – I'll have a hammer on those boys!' (the Soviets).

The exact opposite was the case. Soviet leaders regarded the American action as evidence of bad faith, and this reinforced their opinion that Truman was hatching some evil plot against the Soviet Union. Had they been aware of it, they would have found unwelcome confirmation of their view in the order issued to Montgomery in the closing stages of the war by *Churchill*, to keep the German armies intact 'in case they had to be used against the Russians'.

The crisis in Iran

Not only were relations bad in Europe, but soon the Soviets found themselves eased out of Iran by the western allies. Soviet influence there was replaced by the USA, as was said later, 'not with troops and revolution, but silently with dollars in support of the status quo'.

The oil concessions promised to the USSR failed to materialize, and before long Iran became an American satellite. The Soviet Union became all the more determined to resist further encroachments on its sphere of influence, its leaders referring in Moscow to the American strategy as 'the Iranian method'.

▷ The situation in postwar Europe

By May 1945 much of eastern Europe had been 'liberated' by the advancing Soviet troops and was now occupied by the Red Army. Before the mistrust already described grew up between the former allies, it is unlikely that Stalin had any intention of retaining these conquests permanently; but as suspicion deepened, he concluded that the only way to be safe was to establish Soviet control of these territories through the establishment there of governments submissive to Soviet wishes.

Eastern Europe

This control was not difficult to bring about. The prewar dictatorships had maintained themselves in power chiefly through ruthless police forces and a corrupt bureaucracy, which the democratic movements of the time were too weak to challenge. All that had to be done was to graft on to the existing system the objectives of the 'revolution', supposedly on behalf of the people. The Soviet leadership had an excuse for this in that during the war the former right-wing leaders had sided with the Nazis and now seemed ripe for destruction. Really, the only thing that was different was that in 1945 the western powers suddenly discovered an interest in the fate of these peoples, while in the interwar years they had simply disregarded them.

In *Poland*, efforts were made in 1945 to merge the wartime government in exile under Stanislaw Mikolajczyk and the newly formed Committee of National Liberation, operating under Soviet sponsorship from Lublin; but this broke down and the communists took control, forcing Mikolajczyk to flee to safety in London.

Much the same thing happened in *Hungary*, where the Prime Minister phoned in his resignation while on holiday in Switzerland, when the communists ousted their colleagues in a government coup.

In *Bulgaria*, on the other hand, Nikola Petkov, leader of the Agrarian Party, was arrested by the communists and actually hanged, and a 'people's democracy' was established there at the end of 1947.

There was a similar coup in *Czechoslovakia* early in 1948: non-communists were not allowed to stand in the elections; Jan Masaryk, the son of one of the founding fathers of the country, was found dead below an open window in mysterious circumstances; and President Benes despairingly resigned.

The opposite was happening in Turkey and Greece. In *Turkey*, the government was unpopular; the army was weak and in need of re-equipment; in addition it was under some pressure from the USSR to open the Straits to Soviet warships. At the same time in *Greece*, British forces were struggling to bring the country under British control. British-backed Prime Minister Tsaldaris silenced the communist opposition and engineered an election victory under British supervision which made possible the return of the discredited monarchy. The result was a civil war in which the British lent every assistance to the right-wing government to crush the communist insurgents. Stalin looked on, but, anxious to have a free hand himself in the countries his troops had occupied, decided not to intervene.

The Truman Doctrine

Britain, whose resources had been exhausted by the Second World War, declared that it could no longer afford the heavy expenses of its campaign in Greece, and the government gave notice of its intention to pull out in 1947. The Americans then decided to act, the Secretary of State Dean Acheson saying: 'If the British are getting out of Greece and Turkey, and if we don't go in, the Russians will.'

The result was the *Truman Doctrine* in March 1947, whereby the President promised to support 'free peoples' against 'attempted subjugation by armed minorities or by outside pressures'. He did not name communism as the enemy, but no one had any doubt about what he meant.

In the course of the next few years, he provided over $400 million in aid with a view to strengthening the governments of Greece and Turkey against internal enemies.

Western Europe

In 1945, the Allies had poured into Germany and occupied it. They agreed that Germany should be demilitarized, denazified and democratized. For a time they wanted to deindustrialize it, too, until it became obvious that such a policy was not very practical. They worked out a formula for reparations to be paid to the victors, and they set up a central Control Council to decide matters affecting Germany as a whole.

Such agreements could not long mask the fundamental lack of trust between the powers. The idea of treating Germany as a whole, so that an agreed peace settlement would follow and the occupying forces then withdraw from the country and leave it to itself, became steadily more improbable; instead, East and West used Germany to promote their own separate visions of the future.

The appalling physical destruction of German agriculture and industry, leading to the threat of mass starvation, together with the breakdown of civil and military discipline, forced the Allies to take complete control of Germany. Even after a partial recovery, none of the occupation zones was very viable, and the Allies had to go on importing large quantities of foodstuffs and other materials.

At the same time, the USA rebuffed Soviet requests for assistance. In 1945, the Soviet government asked for a $1bn loan, partly to meet occupation costs. Unfortunately, the US government 'lost' the request. When the Americans got round to it months afterwards, Truman promised to 'discuss' the loan, but attached such conditions to it that the Soviets came to the conclusion that they would be better off without it. The decision to cancel the wartime lend-lease agreements was looked on by the USSR as further unfair pressure, and an act which entitled the Soviets to disregard their promise to their allies not to exceed certain agreed limits in their reparations demands.

The Marshall Plan

Events then moved swiftly. At the end of 1946, the British and the Americans merged their zones into a single economic unit known as *Bizonia*. In June 1947 there followed the *Marshall Plan*, an ambitious programme of financial aid for Europe. Over the next few years, about $15bn were to be made available for postwar reconstruction. It was the work of the US Secretary of State George Marshall, and formed the western counterpart to the Truman Doctrine.

Theoretically, the plan was open to all states: 'Our policy is directed not against any country or doctrine, but against hunger, poverty, desperation and chaos; its purpose should be the revival of a working economy in the world.' Unfortunately, the Soviet Union claimed to discern behind the apparent generosity of the plan the sinister hand of economic imperialism, and turned it down.

Nevertheless in February 1948 the *European Recovery Programme* to dispense Marshall Aid was established, followed in March by a defence pact setting up the *Brussels Treaty Organization*.

The Berlin blockade

In March 1948, the USSR withdrew from the Central Control Council at work in Germany. In June, the western powers introduced a new German currency intended for use in all the zones, but the Soviets rejected the proposal when the US authorities refused them the right to print it as required.

The Soviet authorities had already been harassing western communications with their zones in the city. Officials inspected western trains crossing Soviet-controlled areas en route for Berlin; barges on the canals were stopped and minutely examined; queues of lorries at autobahn checkpoints lengthened as the Soviets kept road traffic waiting. MIG fighters 'buzzed' western aircraft in the air corridors leading to Berlin, and at least one was forced down and its crew killed.

Finally, in June 1948, the USSR stopped all east–west traffic and a blockade of the city began. The Soviets turned off the gas and the electricity, bringing cold and discomfort to Berliners (mercifully, the water supplies were mainly situated in the allied zone of Berlin). Stalin hoped that the Allies would give in and evacuate the city; he never imagined they would attempt to succour the garrison and the city's 2 million inhabitants by air.

General Lucius Clay, US Commander in Europe adopted a stubborn stance: 'When Berlin falls, West Germany will be next; if we mean to hold Germany against communism, we must not budge.' East and West stood suddenly on the brink of war.

The Berlin airlift

For eleven months, an enormous fleet of aircraft kept open the lines of communication between the West and the beleaguered Berliners. Dakotas, Skymasters and even the huge Globemasters, each of which could carry over 20 tons of cargo, began a massive airlift of supplies into the city's airports.

Clay thought at first that the Allies could fly in only 600 tons of freight a day, but as timing improved, the figure rose to 8,000 tons, with planes landing at the city's two (later three) airports every 90 seconds. Altogether over 2 million tons of supplies were flown in, including foodstuffs, petrol (in square drums) and even coal, for fuelling the city's bakeries – it was more economical of space to fly in the flour and the coal than to fly in bread already baked.

Eventually Stalin tired of his 'brinkmanship' and gave up the struggle, raising the blockade in May 1949 even more abruptly than he had imposed it.

Results of the Berlin crisis

The Berlin crisis produced a hardening of the hostility between East and West, fixing the outline of the Cold War in Europe for the next 40 years:

(a) Two German states came into being, each sponsored by its occupying power:
   (i) in the west, there was the *Federal Republic of Germany*;

(ii) in the east, there was the *Democratic Republic of Germany*.

Since the Germans were not yet fully trusted, neither republic was fully independent at first, but by 1955 they had become sovereign states.

(b) Meantime, as the result of a joint Anglo-American initiative, the Brussels Pact was enlarged in April 1949 to form the *North Atlantic Treaty Organization*, to which Canada, Iceland, Norway, Denmark, the Benelux countries, France, Portugal and Italy adhered, later to be joined by Greece, Turkey and West Germany. For some years, Spain was not allowed to join because of its fascist government.

The Soviet response was to:

(a) develop the *Cominform*, already refounded in 1947, as a vehicle for communist planning and propaganda;
(b) launch in 1955 the *Warsaw Pact*, comprising the Soviet Union and its smaller eastern European allies;
(c) develop its own atomic bomb. In September 1949 the Russians exploded their first bomb, from which developed a long-lived nuclear stand-off.

The two alliances confronted each other across the Iron Curtain until 1990, when the forces of world communism suddenly disintegrated with the initiation of reforms in the Soviet Union and the dissolution of the Warsaw Pact in 1991.

The Cold War in the Far East

▷ **The origins of the Cold War in the East**

The communist threat also made itself felt in China, where Chinese communist forces seized power in 1949. In the United States, President Truman found himself under pressure from McCarthy and his supporters (see also chapter 14) to clamp down on what was said to be a Red conspiracy in the USA involving traitors, spies and even senior members of the State Department; they were suspected of sharing with an odd mixture of academics, movie actors and homosexuals the wish to overthrow freedom and democracy in favour of a Stalinist dictatorship.

The Chinese Revolution, 1949

Riddled with corruption and inefficiency, the Chinese Nationalist Party (the Guomindang) had been crumbling since 1946. All the efforts of General Stilwell, the US liaison officer with the nationalists, to use American money and resources to prop up the Chinese nationalist regime failed.

In 1949, Jiang Jie Shi, the nationalist leader, was finally defeated and forced to flee to Taiwan, where he set up a right-wing dictatorship. In Beijing, the leader of the Chinese Communist Party, Mao Zedong, established the People's Republic of China in the autumn of 1949.

Before long, Mao introduced sweeping changes in Chinese politics and society, and launched vigorous external policies to reclaim his country's historic boundaries, after many years of betrayal by the 'unfair' treaties.

The American reaction

In the USA, the McCarthyites contrived to suggest that the success of the communists in the Chinese Revolution was all America's fault, and that a little more diligence on the part of the United States could have stopped it from happening.

In April 1950 an American defence committee produced a document known as NSC 68 (National Security Committee paper no. 68) advancing the view that the communists' victory in China and the Soviet atom-bomb tests were both part of the same pattern – the rising tide of world communism. The committee recommended that the USA should: 'strike out on a bold and massive program of rebuilding the West's defensive potential to surpass that of the Soviet world, and of meeting each fresh challenge promptly and unequivocally . . . This new concept of the security needs of the nation calls for an annual appropriation of the order of 50 million dollars, or not much below the former wartime levels.'

Thus a note of toughness crept into US dealings with both the Soviet Union and China.

The Cold War in Korea

The peninsula of Korea had been since 1910 a dependency of Japan. The wartime Allies had agreed that in future it was to be 'free and independent', and at Potsdam in 1945 it was agreed that the parallel of 38°N should be the demarcation line between the Soviet occupation forces in the north and the Americans in the south. During 1947 the UN tried to hold elections for the Korean people to choose their own government, but the Soviets refused to admit UN observers to their zone, and no elections took place. In the south, however, it was a different story.

The division of Korea

Elections in the south led to the formation there of the Republic of Korea in 1948, under Syngman Rhee; at the same time, the USSR set up the People's Democratic Republic of Korea in the north, under Kim Il Sung. In 1948–49, Korea was evacuated by the occupying powers, though the separate political regimes they had established were both left in existence.

Each republic claimed authority over the whole country and refused to admit the existence of the other. In practice, neither regime had much to recommend it. In the north, Kim Il Sung embarked on policies every bit as authoritarian as those of Stalin himself, while Syngman Rhee's corrupt police state in the south brutalized and terrorized its opponents to such an extent that western news correspondents were forbidden to report it.

The only thing that the two leaders agreed on was that they could no longer accept a divided nation, though they did not begin to agree on the form that the eventual reunion should take.

The outbreak of the Korean War

In June 1950, powerful North Korean forces crossed the 38th parallel into the south, setting in train a civil war which lasted rather more than three years.

Which side caused the war is difficult to decide with any certainty. The favourite western version of events was that, acting on orders directly from Stalin, Kim produced an unprovoked and quite unexpected attack on the south. Stalin is supposed to have launched the attack in a bid to show that it was he, not Mao Zedong, who was the master of the communist world, his intention being to supplant the United States in the Far East, and to threaten Japan, his former enemy, and now the main base of US forces in the Pacific area.

In fact it is unlikely that Stalin would have been keen on such an adventure. His forces were still feeling the effects of the Second World War, and in any case were far too heavily committed in Europe to be easily redeployed in the Far East. At the same time, his atomic weaponry was totally inadequate for an international confrontation. Furthermore, he had little faith in the long continuance of Syngman Rhee's government in the south, where he had fared badly in elections only about a month before the invasion. Indeed, Stalin seems to have accepted Kim's assurance that the war would be only a little local one, and would be swiftly decided without anyone having the chance to intervene.

Above all, Soviet representatives had recently walked out of the Security Council as a protest against China's exclusion from membership of UNO by the USA. If the Soviet leader knew that a war was about to be launched, it seems unlikely that he would have deliberately absented himself from the only body which could have effectively vetoed international intervention in the conflict, thus leaving the field clear for his opponents. Nevertheless this was the explanation of the affair which the western powers chose to accept.

UN intervention in the Korean War

The USA, acting with exemplary swiftness, brought an emergency motion before the Security Council recommending action, and this was carried.

The Soviet view was that the illegal exclusion of Mao's delegation from the Security Council, as a result of US pressure, rendered all the other activities of the Council illegal, so that there was no need to veto them; indeed, had there been a need, there was no reason why the Soviet delegation should not have returned to the table.

The United States, on the other hand, backed by an alliance of western powers created almost overnight, took the view that the absence of the USSR from the discussions of the Security Council was a different thing from a veto and so did not invalidate UN proposals.

What had been in its early stages a civil war soon became international. The USA prevailed on the Security Council to appoint General MacArthur as Supreme UN Commander, and created a sixteen-nation Joint Expeditionary Force – most of whom were Americans – to assist the South Korean government. At the same time, the North Korean government signed pacts of financial and military support with the USSR and the Chinese communist government.

The war in Korea

The war was a long-drawn-out affair, with fighting from one end of the country to the other:

(a) In their initial attack, the North Koreans seized the South Korean capital, Seoul, and penetrated deep into the country, pinning back the South Korean and UN forces into the Pusan pocket.

(b) Then the war swung the other way: with the assistance of a seaborne landing behind the North Korean lines at Inchon, Seoul was retaken; the communists were defeated and steadily driven back to the Yalu River in the far north of the country.

(c) Chinese intervention followed, with the 4th and the 5th Red Armies coming to the support of the North Koreans; UN and South Korean forces were driven back, and the campaign ended in an armistice in 1953 close to the 38th parallel – the point at which it had first begun.

Fig. 15.1 The war in Korea, 1950–53

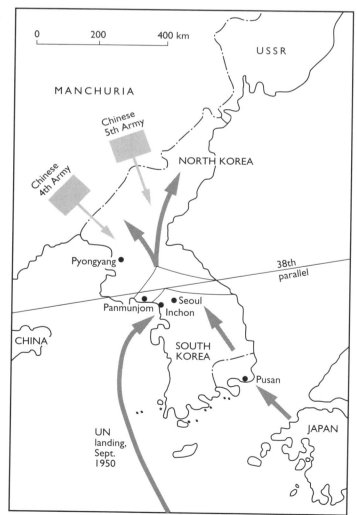

The armistice was the outcome of tedious and protracted negotiations at Panmunjom, where there were endless disputes even about the shape of the negotiating table. In the end almost nothing was decided, and the peace was little more than an interruption of the hostilities, with no agreement about the future of the two Koreas.

The results of the Korean War

The war produced an unsatisfactory stalemate, protracting the division of the country until the present time – a worse solution perhaps than if the powers had left the civil war to settle itself. But the cost was large:

(a) The South Koreans and UN forces lost nearly 70,000 dead, 85,000 captured and over 200,000 wounded; the North Koreans even more. Nearly half a million civilians were killed and over 4 million wounded or made homeless.

(b) Economic progress was set back for a generation: most of the country's economic resources – coal, iron, electricity and other resources – remained under the control of North Korea and were relatively slow to develop.

(c) Politically, North Korea was under the iron fist of Kim Il Sung until the 1990s, when he was succeeded by his equally unpleasant son; South Korea was governed by the tyrannical and unrepresentative regime of Syngman Rhee until 1960, when he was deposed by Park Chung Hee, who was assasinated in 1979.

There were also important international consequences of the war:

(a) The most lasting result for the UN came as a result of the dispute in the Security Council over the crisis. This was the decision of the General Assembly in the *Uniting for Peace Resolution* (November 1950) that if the Security Council was deadlocked, the General Assembly could, by a two-thirds majority, take action in its stead. To the present, however, it is doubtful whether the resolution would be effective, i.e. whether a two-thirds majority in the General Assembly would really be capable of overriding a Security Council deadlock.

(b) Diplomatically, there followed a number of regional pacts:
(i) the *ANZUS Pact*, a defence agreement between the USA and Australia and New Zealand;
(ii) a defence agreement between the USA and Japan;
(iii) various smaller agreements were unified in 1954 in the form of the *South-East Asia Treaty Organization* (SEATO), incorporating Australia, New Zealand, Thailand, Pakistan, France, Britain, the Philippines and the United States. Alongside this there was the *Central Treaty Organization* (CENTO), formerly known as the Baghdad Pact until the defection of Iraq in 1959, and incorporating also Turkey, Pakistan, Britain and Iran, with the USA as an associated power. Both these organizations lasted until well into the 1970s, and were looked upon as important bulwarks against the spread of communism.

The Cold War after the death of Stalin

The death of Stalin in March 1953 was in some ways a turning-point in the Cold War. The new leaders of the Soviet Union were willing to travel abroad to talk with their opposite numbers in the West. Khrushchev and Bulganin were fêted in western capitals, while astute politicians such as Richard Nixon (Vice-President of the USA, 1953–61) and Harold Macmillan (British Prime Minister, 1957–63) saw the chance to make some political mileage out of visits to the USSR.

▷ **An era of 'summits'**   For a time, tensions remained high between East and West; later the two sides seemed more willing to meet each other to negotiate about their differences.

Continuing tensions between East and West

From 1953, the Soviets seemed willing to negotiate. Shortly afterwards:

(a) Soviet troops were withdrawn from Finland and from Austria, and the USSR signed a treaty accepting the independence of Austria and its future neutrality.
(b) Khrushchev visited Belgrade and took a much more flexible line than Stalin, telling Marshal Tito there was 'more than one road to socialism'.
(c) In July, there was an armistice in Korea after months of wrangling.

The USA, however, did not seem impressed. Eisenhower's Secretary of State, John Foster Dulles, remained unrelentingly anti-Soviet. In his very first speech, he declared: 'To all those suffering under Communist slavery, let us say: "You can count on us!"'

East Germany

His assurances, however, did little for the workers who rebelled in June 1953; their government used tanks to crush the revolt, and Khrushchev's policy turned out to be every bit as harsh as Stalin's before him.

Dulles began a build-up of nuclear weapons, including the new and more powerful H-bomb, in an effort to 'place more reliance on deterrent power'; but in August the Soviets themselves tested an H-bomb, and the Americans lost their short-lived advantage over their rivals.

Taiwan

Tension between the Chinese communists on the mainland and the exiled nationalists on Taiwan had steadily been increasing, and Dulles, firmly convinced that Mao was little more than a Soviet puppet, rallied to the support of Jiang Jie Shi. Early in 1955, the communists began shelling the nationalist-held off-shore islands of Quemoy and Matsu. The USA called in its Pacific fleet, and even threatened the use of nuclear weapons against the mainland.

Indochina

Here there was a war between the French, seeking to re-establish their rule after the war, and a nationalist guerrilla force led by Ho Chi Minh, which was anxious to get rid of the colonialists. At first, the Americans had no wish to be seen propping up a decadent colonial regime, but the French were clever enough to play on McCarthyite fears of creeping communism, and eventually secured their help.

In April 1954 Eisenhower began to worry about the future of south-east Asia, and came to agree that a communist victory in one country might send them all tumbling like a row of dominoes into enemy hands.

His *domino theory* seemed all the more plausible when the French were finally overthrown at Dien Bien Phu in May 1954 and began withdrawing from the country, leaving it in the hands of Ho, who seemed to prefer communist policies.

In July, the *Geneva Conference*, under the joint chairmanship of Britain and the Soviet Union, agreed to neutralize Laos and Cambodia, and to divide Vietnam in two along the 17th parallel, leaving the north in the hands of the communists, and the south in the hands of Bao Dai, the French puppet emperor. The plan was for the two halves shortly to hold elections for the reunification of north and south under a common government.

Unfortunately, by the time the elections were due in 1955, Bao Dai had been deposed in the south and a republic set up under Ngo Dinh Diem; he refused to take part in the elections and set about increasing the armed forces in order to prolong his control of the country.

At the same time, the prospects for international harmony seemed to brighten. The Soviets adopted a less strident tone, and in Moscow *Izvestia* produced the headline: 'A New Era in International Relations Has Begun', while in the USA even Secretary of State Dulles seemed less hawkish.

The Soviet twentieth party congress and its results

In February 1956 Khrushchev used the occasion of the twentieth party congress of the Soviet Communist Party to announce basic changes in Soviet thinking:

(a) He made a dramatic and unexpected attack on Stalin, accusing him of tyranny and self-glorification. He rejected the *cult of the personality* and said: 'It is foreign to the spirit of Marxist-Leninism to elevate one person, and to transform him into a superman having supernatural powers akin to those of a god. Such a man supposedly knows everything, sees everything, thinks for everyone, can do anything . . .'

(b) To the eastern European countries he offered greater tolerance by his emphasis on 'different roads to socialism'.

(c) To developing countries he promised financial support for peaceful socialist development instead of inevitable revolution.

(d) To the West he offered an olive branch by announcing his idea of *peaceful co-existence* instead of deepening conflict.

Khrushchev's 'debunking' of Stalin, whose whole reputation had rested on his supposed infallibility, naturally undermined the respect in which his eastern European puppets were held, whose authoritarian behaviour was closely modelled on Stalin's own:

(a) In *East Berlin*, industrial workers called a general strike which the government had to crush by bringing in tanks; the party leader, Walter Ulbricht, got a nasty shock before he re-established his authority.

(b) In *Poland*, political and economic grievances led to revolt; the popular communist leader, Wladislaw Gomulka, previously deposed by Stalin on a charge of 'Titoism' – the unforgivable sin of thinking for himself – had to be reinstated.

(c) In *Hungary* in 1956, Ernö Gerö, first Secretary of the Communist Party after Matyas Rakosi, was forced by popular pressure to restore Imre Nagy as Prime Minister. Nagy introduced liberalizing measures, freed the media from state control, did away with the one-party system and called fresh elections. Worse still, he proposed to leave the Warsaw Pact. To staunch communists his political reforms were bad enough, but his intention to break ranks with his allies seemed to threaten the whole cohesion of eastern Europe and in particular the security of the USSR.

The West welcomed these developments exultantly; the Soviets even had the idea that the Americans were giving the Hungarian dissidents secret financial backing. But while the world's attention was diverted by the Suez crisis, the Soviets moved in tanks and troops and brutally restored order, carrying off Nagy and unceremoniously executing him in favour of a 'safer' leader in the person of Janos Kadar.

The Suez crisis, 1956

This crisis caused tension of a different sort. Here the USA caused grave offence in Britain by refusing to give its backing to the Anglo-French invasion of Egypt, designed to overthrow the Egyptian leader, Colonel Nasser, and stem the rising tide of Arab nationalism. In the UN Security Council, the world witnessed the unusual sight of the USA and the USSR voting together against Anglo-French imperialism. The two countries had to withdraw their troops, while President Nasser's reputation soared high in the Arab world. Both Britain and France lost face, and it was a long time before their leaders forgave either the United States or the United Nations.

1958, however, saw the restoration of the usual alignment of the powers. In this year, Britain intervened in Jordan to support its right-wing, English-educated King, Hussein, this time with American approval. Simultaneously, Britain landed its own troops in the Lebanon in response to a left-wing coup in Iraq, which it imagined threatened to turn the Middle East into a Soviet sphere of influence.

International summit meetings, 1955–61

Geneva, November 1955

President Eisenhower and Eden and Faure, the Prime Ministers of Britain and France, met the Soviet leaders, Khrushchev and Malenkov, in Switzerland to try to reduce international tensions. Nothing much came of it: no progress was made on any of the three main problems discussed – disarmament, the reunification of Germany, or the promotion of more friendly relations between the communist and the non-communist worlds.

The only success of the summit was that it helped to establish the genial personality of Eisenhower with the other leaders, and to arouse hopes, especially among the Soviets, that in future some progress might be possible.

In fact, Khrushchev took part in 1959 in two meetings of foreign ministers first suggested by the British Prime Minister, Harold Macmillan, and went on to meet Eisenhower in the President's Maryland retreat of Camp David, where the two men agreed to attempt another summit meeting in Paris the following year.

Paris, May 1960

About a fortnight before the summit was due to take place, an American U-2 plane, a high-level reconnaissance aircraft on a secret camera mission, was forced down 2,000 kilometres inside the Soviet Union on a flight from Peshawar. The Soviets later produced its pilot, Gary Powers, an agent of the Central Intelligence Agency, whom they were holding prisoner.

Khrushchev was furious and rounded on Eisenhower, accusing him of deceit. The President denied the accusations. Khrushchev found it hard to decide whether Eisenhower was so incompetent that he did not know what was happening behind his back, or whether he was so dishonest that he intended to brazen it out even when he was caught in the act. Shortly afterwards, Eisenhower admitted responsibility for the act, but went on to say that it was America's right if necessary to spy on the Soviet Union.

That pleased Khrushchev scarcely better. He abandoned all efforts at better relations and roundly denounced the Americans, threatening them: 'On the ruins of destroyed imperialism the victorious peoples will create with tremendous speed a civilization a thousand times higher than the capitalist system, and will rebuild their bright future.' He demanded that flights be stopped forthwith and, before Eisenhower had time to make any promises, went on to demand a formal apology, an act of submission that the USA angrily refused to make. The summit broke up amid mutual recrimination.

Vienna, June 1961

Ill-feeling still persisted at this meeting, at which Khrushchev agreed to meet with the youthful President Kennedy, recently elected in the United States. Little was achieved, however, because of the revival of the Berlin problem.

The Berlin crisis, 1961

This had recurred even before the Paris summit. In 1958 the Soviets had stated their intention of withdrawing their troops, so as to declare the whole of Berlin a 'demilitarized free city' and bring pressure on the western powers also to withdraw. They were unwilling to do this, and in any case had not yet even given diplomatic recognition to the Democratic Republic of East Germany. Khrushchev clearly hoped to force the West to do one thing or the other.

The problem was made worse by a steady flow of political refugees from East Berlin to the West, a flow which, after the Paris summit, reached 2,000 a day and threatened to become a flood. By the time of the Vienna summit, the question could no longer be ignored.

At Vienna, Khrushchev decided to separate the question of the refugees from that of the western recognition of East Germany, and tried to resolve the refugee question alone. On 12–13 August, on Khrushchev's orders, a wall was built dividing East from West Berlin. It was built practically overnight out of rough concrete blocks and was patrolled by uniformed East German guards armed with machine guns. This provided the West with a cheap propaganda victory – East Berlin was the socialist paradise where you had to build a wall to stop the grateful workers from getting out!

Later that autumn the East German government, still seeking recognition, began creating difficulties at crossing points in the city, threatening a new blockade. For a time American and Soviet tanks faced each other at Checkpoint Charlie on the Friedrichstrasse, muzzle to muzzle, 50 metres apart. President Kennedy visited the city and drew great cheers from the crowds when he declared 'Today in the world of freedom the proudest boast is *Ich bin ein Berliner!*'

The early 1960s therefore saw the question of East–West relations as far from a solution as it had ever been.

▷ **The Cuban missile crisis, 1962**

Throughout the postwar period, the USA seemed reluctant to allow the United Nations any scope for operating in the western hemisphere, preferring that problems there should be settled by the *Organization of American States*, in which the United States was the main member – an eagle among a flock of sparrows. It was in this hemisphere that the next crisis broke.

The coming of the crisis in Cuba

Since it became independent in the Spanish–American war of 1898, the island had been dominated by the USA. Sugar was its main export, and the USA its main market. Cuba's capital development, including its railways, electricity and telephone services, was in the hands of American companies; US Marines were permanently stationed in the south-east of the island in the base at Guantanamo.

The USA supported the dictatorship of a former army sergeant, self-promoted to general, Fulgencio Batista, who ruled Cuba wisely 1933–44, but in his second period of rule after 1952 increasingly became intolerant and tyrannical. He dealt severely with his opponents, used US dollars in lavish bribes for his supporters, and turned a deaf ear to all demands for reform.

It was against his rule that Fidel Castro, a young law student, rebelled. His first attempt was unsuccessful and he was gaoled, but in 1956 he tried again, starting a guerrilla war in the mountains of eastern Cuba to rid the country of Batista. At first he was a democrat and a nationalist who wanted to end US domination, but his weakness forced him to cultivate communist support.

Public opinion gradually hardened against Batista. At the end of 1958 he was forced to flee to Dominica, and Castro, aged 32, became ruler of Cuba. His communist leanings soon became evident: land was seized and redistributed to the poor peasantry; large measures of state control were enacted; American enterprises found themselves 'nationalized', and an entente with the USSR was engineered.

The 'Bay of Pigs' affair, 1961

When Kennedy became President, he inherited a rather half-baked CIA plot to send in a band of volunteers trained in Florida and backed by American hardware to overthrow Castro's government. Kennedy decided to let the coup proceed, but he was mistaken in placing such reliance on the CIA, whose calculations were disastrously inept.

Their 'scenario' of an island yearning for deliverance from the rigours of communism was very wide of the mark: in fact American intervention produced world indignation and a storm of nationalist protest from all ranks of Cuban society.

The 1,500-strong band of assorted invaders was mopped up within a few days, Castro's jets shooting down their flimsy air cover. The whole 'Bay of Pigs' affair was embarrassing for the USA: Kennedy's government lost face on account of its support of 'banditry', and Castro was driven further into the arms of the Soviet Union.

The Cuban missile crisis, October 1962

Worse was to follow. During 1962, encouraged by the Soviet Union, Castro began to install intermediate-range ballistic missiles (IRBMs) at launch sites scattered throughout Cuba. Supplied by the Soviets, these could be fitted with nuclear warheads. They were capable of destroying every American city within a radius of 4,000 kilometres, including New York and Washington. Only Seattle would escape.

Kennedy reacted vigorously, and on 22 October proclaimed a blockade of Cuba by the US navy to prevent further missiles being put ashore, and threatened unlimited nuclear retaliation not only against Cuba, but also against the Soviet Union by inter-continental ballistic missiles (ICBMs) if any US city were attacked. For a few anxious days Washington was on red alert, and the President and his advisers did not go to bed. Then the Soviets mercifully backed down – as one American official said: 'We were eyeball to eyeball; but I think the other fellow just blinked.'

Khrushchev offered to remove his rockets from Cuba if the Americans would remove theirs from Turkey, where there were NATO bases. He declared: 'Your rockets are in Turkey. You are worried by Cuba. You say it worries you because Cuba is 144 kilometres from the American coast. But Turkey is right next to us!'

Kennedy would not budge an inch – publicly, that is – for fear of upsetting the Turks, his NATO allies. Privately, however, he had already decided to withdraw his rockets from Turkey, so that this was not much of a concession; and the withdrawal took place quietly shortly afterwards. In anticipation of this, Khrushchev announced agreement on 27 October; shortly afterwards the missile sites were dismantled and the rockets recrated and returned to the Soviet Union.

UN Secretary-General U Thant attempted to intervene, but his efforts were largely irrelevant and were ignored by both sides. The settlement, which showed more flexibility on the part of the USSR than it did on the part of the USA, was arrived at bilaterally and reflected no credit on the United Nations.

Importance of the Cuban missile crisis

The missile crisis, when for a few days the world stood on the brink of nuclear destruction, produced significant results:

(a) A 'hot-line' telephone and telex link was set up between Washington and Moscow to prevent a future crisis and to avoid the frightening possibility that nuclear war might break out by accident.
(b) Khrushchev, condemned by Soviet hard-liners for his so-called 'adventurism' in diplomacy, was overthrown in a Kremlin coup and was succeeded by the ageing Brezhnev, who followed a much more cautious path.
(c) Most important, the weaknesses of the two sides in the Cold War had been revealed to their leaders. The USSR was beginning to find itself grossly overburdened by escalating arms expenditure, and was anxious to reduce its commitments. The USA, whose vulnerability to rocket attacks had been thrown into sharp focus by the crisis, was also quite anxious to negotiate. The result was the *Nuclear Test Ban Treaty* in 1963, ending all forms of testing except those carried out underground, where there was less risk of damaging 'fallout' from the explosions.

This treaty was the first stage of a process which steadily gained in momentum after the Khrushchev–Kennedy era towards a reduction in the dangers of the arms race, by way of increasingly ambitious treaties restricting the spread of nuclear armaments.

It is from 1963 that we can begin to trace the development over the next 30 years of reduced tension between the major powers. This process of arriving at a better understanding was referred to as *détente*.

The process also involved the beginnings, and the growth, of the *Sino-Soviet split*, a quarrel between the USSR and China over matters of communist principle as well as over details of policy tactics, which had been simmering under the surface for some time. It now broke out into a public dispute.

GLOSSARY

Brinkmanship   The art of going as close to war as a leader dares without actually starting it. Thus a national leader may take his demands to the brink of conflict but then withdraw, or compel his opponent to withdraw. It is a game of 'diplomatic chicken' in which the defeated party suffers considerable humiliation.

Cold War   A conflict stopping short of military action, but being conducted by both sides with economic and propaganda weapons, and often making frequent use of the media. Thus the struggle between the USA and the USSR after 1945 was of long duration, but never reached the point of open military conflict except very occasionally and by accident.

Confrontation   The situation of being face to face with an enemy and on the brink of conflict. The situation may be resolved by open war, as in the case of the war in Korea, or else by negotiation, as in the case of the Iran crisis of 1946, or by the withdrawal of one of the parties, as in the case of Stalin over the Berlin crisis of 1948–49.

Containment   The act of enclosing or limiting the development of some opposing force, often by pacts or alliances. Thus the US government tried to confine communism to the areas in Europe where communism was already in control, and to resist its extension to other areas of Europe, seeking to achieve this through Marshall Aid, the Truman Doctrine and NATO.

Coup From the French *coup d'état*: a sudden and illegal change of government; a forcible seizure of power. Thus the communists attempted a coup in Greece in 1946, and successfully brought one about in Czechoslovakia in 1948.

Iron Curtain A frontier or boundary rigidly dividing one ideology from another, characterized by the lack of free movement of people and ideas between them. Thus the frontier in Europe dividing the pro-Soviet communist states of eastern Europe from the non-communist states of western Europe was called the 'Iron Curtain'. In the case of China, a similar barrier was sometimes known as the 'Bamboo Curtain'.

Satellite A smaller state under the influence of a larger neighbour, like a planet in orbit round the sun. Until the late 1980s and early 1990s, most states of eastern Europe were satellites of the Soviet Union. Some central American states have sometimes been called satellites of the USA.

Stand-off A situation of deadlock or stalemate where two powers stand apart from each other in mutual suspicion, and where their economic and military capacities are about equal. Thus a stand-off in the form of mutual nuclear deterrence was achieved by the 1960s with the concept of what became known as Mutual Assured Destruction (or MAD): neither the USA nor the USSR could start a nuclear war because they knew that such a war would destroy them both.

Status quo From the Latin *status quo ante*: the situation as it was before. A power which is likely to lose by an alteration of the existing state of things will on this account object to changes in the status quo.

EXAMINATION QUESTIONS

 Question 1 (a) 'Khrushchev was less committed to the Cold War than Stalin.' Do you agree? Explain your answer. (10 marks)

(b) Why was the United Nations unable to reduce Cold War tensions during its first 20 years? (10 marks)

▷ **Question 2** Study Sources A and B and then answer *all* the questions that follow.

Source A

We have decided, in response to urgent representations from our comrades in South Korea, to liberate South Korea from the tyranny of Syngman Rhee. Our troops have met little resistance and are everywhere being welcomed as liberators.

(North Korean communiqué, June 1950)

Source B

Urged on by the USSR and China, the forces of North Korea have invaded South Korea in defiance of the Potsdam agreement. The communists of the North obviously intend to take over the South and destroy its democratic freedoms. South Korean troops are offering strong resistance. (American press report, June 1950)

(a) Sources A and B are both about the start of the Korean War. How do the sources differ in the accounts they give? (7 marks)

(b) Explain why Sources A and B differ in what they say. (8 marks)

(c) 'The Korean War was an unnecessary waste of men and resources.' Do you agree? Explain your answer. (10 marks)

EXAMINATION ANSWERS

 Question 1 *Outline answer*

(a) Don't be in too great a hurry to agree with this statement. It is true that Stalin's suspicion of the West, and his determination to make the USSR's western frontiers secure, helped to bring about the Cold War. The ideological differences and the Soviet race to produce atomic weapons intensified it. But Stalin had limited objectives. He came to an agreement over Iran in 1946, although he later believed that

American influence in Iran was not part of the agreement. He did not interfere to help the communists in Greece, and he did eventually back down over the Berlin blockade. His assistance to the communists in China was lukewarm at most, and despite contemporary American allegations to the contrary, he had no hand in the Korean War. Khrushchev's protestations of a thaw in the Cold War were belied by some of his actions. Perhaps he was only collectively responsible for the suppression of the East German and Polish revolts of 1953, but he was personally responsible for the suppression of Hungary in 1956. His warmer relations with Eisenhower were soured by the U-2 incident, and the Cuban missile crisis came closer to turning the Cold War into a hot war than anything in Stalin's time. Neither Stalin nor Khrushchev wanted war: Stalin because he wanted time for the USSR to recover from the war and to catch up with the USA in nuclear capability, and Khrushchev because he knew that neither side would emerge as a winner in a nuclear war. Khrushchev rather than Stalin took the world to the brink of war; the experience made him one of the early architects of *détente*.

(b) The United Nations was not set up or designed to end the Cold War. The period 1945–65 was one in which the United Nations tackled trouble spots in various parts of the world with varying success, e.g. Palestine, Congo. But it was the age of the superpowers. If the USA or the USSR was directly involved, any action by the United Nations required their approval or was subject to their veto in the Security Council. The UN had no powers to bring the superpowers to heel. So the UN could only protest feebly at the Soviet invasion of Hungary in 1956, but with the support of both superpowers it could act more vigorously against Britain and France in Egypt in 1956. The basic ideological and strategic reasons for the Cold War were not likely to be influenced by any resolution of the UN, and the UN itself was ideologically divided and capable only on rare occasions of acting in concert. The UN attempted to mediate over the Cuban missile crisis in 1962, but the outcome was determined not by the UN, but by the brinkmanship contest between the two superpowers. The UN was relegated to the role of giving its approval to decisions over which it had no direct influence; it welcomed the first Test-Ban Treaty and recommended it to all its members, but it neither initiated nor drafted it. The superpowers paid lip-service to the UN and made use of it; the USA benefited from the UN's headquarters being in New York, and made use of its majority support in the UN to turn the American defence of South Korea into a United Nations' war; Khrushchev used the UN as a stage for his shoe-thumping and histrionics. The UN during these years achieved success in many fields, but ending the Cold War was way beyond its reach.

▷ Question 2(a)   *Tutor answer*

The only thing that the two sources agree upon is that North Korean troops have moved into South Korea. According to Source A, the purpose is to liberate South Korea; according to Source B, the purpose is to destroy South Korean democracy. Source A implies that the troops are responding to demand from the south, while Source B suggests that they are responding to urging from China and the Soviet Union. Source A does not mention China and the Soviet Union, and Source B makes no mention of 'urgent representations' from the south. Source A's reference to the tyranny of Syngman Rhee contrasts with Source B's reference to the 'democratic freedoms' of the south. The breach of the Potsdam agreement referred to in Source B has no echo in Source A. The sources disagree on the South Korean response to the invasion: Source A claims that there is little resistance and that North Korean troops are everywhere welcomed 'as liberators', while Source B talks of 'strong resistance' to the invaders.

▷ Question 2(b)   *Tutor answer*

The differences can be explained by the origins and purpose of the sources. Source A is an official communiqué issued by the North Koreans to justify their invasion. It is likely that this is mainly intended for consumption in North Korea, where news was strictly censored, rather than as an international justification, but it could serve as a propagandist declaration of defiance against the rest of the world. The propagandist element is clear in the specific reference to Syngman Rhee, hardly the champion of the 'democratic freedoms' Source B talks about. Although Source B is not an official report, it is from an American newspaper. In the state of the Cold War at the time, this is likely to reflect the American hostility to communism and fear of its spread; an American newspaper, if it is to remain in business, must reflect, to some extent at least, the opinions of its readership. In referring to the 'unprovoked attack', the 'defiance of the Potsdam agreement' and the 'democratic freedoms' of South Korea, the newspaper could well be preparing public opinion in America for the American intervention which was to follow. The two sources are on opposite sides in the Cold War, and this is reflected in their respective content.

▷ Question 2(c)   *Student answer with examiner's comments*

'A narrative approach.'

'Something of an argument here.'

> *The North Koreans invaded the South on June 25, 1950. Their troops soon occupied Seoul, the Southern capital, and within three months had taken all of South Korea except the Pusan pocket. By then the Americans, in the name of the United Nations, had intervened, and following a US marine landing at Inchon, liberated the whole of South Korea and invaded the North. When the American and UN forces had almost reached the Yalu river the Chinese joined the war, and the American and UN forces were driven right back into South Korea, losing Seoul again. Slowly the UN forces recovered, reoccupied Seoul, and after much negotiation an armistice was signed in 1953 which restored the boundary between North and South much as it was before the war started. So it had all been a waste of time, and in order to achieve nothing nearly three million people had been killed and many more wounded. So I agree with the statement.*

Examiner's decision on the student answer
The narrative approach leads to only one point of argument. The answer is confined to the events of the war, and does not take into account the wider implications: the permanent division of Korea, the reluctance of the UN to become so actively involved in later conflicts, US attempts to prevent the spread of communism in south-east Asia by using economic aid (the Colombo Plan). Some argument does emerge from this answer at the end, but the narrowness of the approach and the narrative treatment will restrict it to around half marks.

SUMMARY

In this chapter you have dealt with the Cold War up to the Cuban missile crisis of 1963. You have covered:

▷ the breakdown of the wartime alliance;

▷ Soviet expansion in Europe and the Iron Curtain;

▷ the Berlin crisis of 1948–49;

▷ the Cold War in the Far East and the Korean War, 1950–53;

▷ changes in eastern Europe on the death of Stalin;

▷ the U-2 incident and the building of the Berlin Wall;

▷ the Cuban missile crisis.

You will find further material relevant to the Cold War in:

▷ chapter 17, on the history of modern China;

▷ chapter 18, on the later history of the Cold War.

Chapter

16 China to 1949

GETTING STARTED

China is one of the world powers of the twentieth century, but was slow to come to prominence. It started to emerge between the wars, but it was only in 1949 that the world began to take notice. It is to China that we now turn.

MEG	NEAB	NICCEA	SEG	LONDON	WJEC	TOPIC	STUDY	REVISION 1	REVISION 2
				✓	✓	**China under the nationalists**			
				✓	✓	China in 1911			
				✓	✓	China under the Guomindang (Kuomintang)			
				✓	✓	**China under Jiang Jie Shi**			
				✓	✓	The growing clash with the communists			
				✓	✓	The conflict with the Japanese			
✓				✓	✓	**The Chinese Civil War**			
✓				✓	✓	The prelude to the civil war			
✓				✓	✓	The civil war			

WHAT YOU NEED TO KNOW

China under the nationalists

▷ **China in 1911** China had long been isolated from the rest of the world, regarded by many as a distant exotic place about which little was known. At the start of the twentieth century, it was weak and disorganized, a target for the greed and cunning of the imperialists. Reformers made attempts to bring it up to date, but these efforts foundered on the conservatism of the ruling dynasty.

Foreign influences in China

Under the Manchu dynasty, the country had long been the victim of powerful and ambitious foreign states.

(a) *Russia*, the largest of these, had nibbled at China's borders from the west and had succeeded in extending Russian influence in border regions such as Mongolia and Manchuria. Before 1914 the Russians had occupied Port Arthur on the Yellow Sea.

(b) *The western powers*, such as Britain, France and Germany, had infiltrated the country at points along the eastern seaboard. They had secured *treaty ports* such as Kaiochao, where they exercised extraterritorial rights and could act independently of the Chinese authorities, draining off the country's trade to their own profit.

(c) *Japan*, China's Far Eastern neighbour, was able to prove its strength by winning a war against China in 1895 and imposing its will on its much larger neighbour.

The Chinese, who in any case felt an extreme distrust of outside influences, seemed powerless to prevent the country's exploitation by such groups of marauding foreigners. One after the other, they came to impose on the country what patriotic Chinese regarded as *unfair treaties*.

The condition of China in 1911

Meanwhile, the mass of the Chinese peasantry lived under the heel of autocratic land-lords in conditions of grinding poverty, scratching a bare living from the soil with their primitive tools, and always at the mercy of famine and flood.

Heavily taxed, ignorant, oppressed, their womenfolk scarcely more highly valued than the cattle in the fields, the Chinese peasantry were the prey of the local gentry and of imperial officials who were scarcely less corrupt and selfish. In the distant areas of this vast country, the tyranny and greed of both these groups went unchecked and even un-noticed by the central government.

In the towns, foreign big business was another source of exploitation, this time by industrialists and traders who were interested only in making as much profit out of their Chinese workforce as they could.

A minority of middle-class Chinese, many educated overseas, were deeply ashamed of the depths to which their once-great country had sunk, and seized the chance of the death of the old Empress Ci Xi (T'zu hsi) in 1908 to press for reform for the people. Many were attracted to the western ideas of *self-determination* and *democracy*. Some even claimed to be socialists. But their chances of success were slight, for the bulk of govern-ment officials were unwilling to share power with anyone, and were doing too nicely out of the existing system to want to change it.

Their resistance to change brought the final overthrow of the dynasty in 1911, when a number of revolutions in the main Chinese cities such as Gwangzhou (Canton) sent the new boy-emperor, Pu Yi, and his court scurrying into exile, their luggage loaded with the country's treasures. Overnight the whole rotten pyramid of Manchu rule collapsed. The new leader was Sun Zhongshan (Sun Yat-sen), one of the bright hopes of the budding republican movement. He returned from the USA, where he had been on a lecture tour, to become the first President of the Provisional Chinese Government in Nanjing (Nanking).

Sun Zhongshan was rightly respected as an intellectual, a statesman and a revolu-tionary. He aimed, with the support of the masses, to purify and modernize the govern-ment and the country. His dream was to realize a new way of life for China based on his *three principles* of democracy, nationalism and the people's welfare.

▷ China under the Guomindang (Kuomintang)

Unfortunately, the new republic faced an uncertain future. Apart from a dedicated few, the Guomindang (the National People's Party) was weighted down by opportunists who were neither able nor willing to fight for the democratic future they claimed to believe in. For more than 20 years, China faced threats to its stability and progress from a vari-ety of sources.

China and the monarchists

For some years, Dr Sun was overshadowed by the former Manchu general Yuan Shikai (Yuan Shih-kai), the strong man of the old regime with no love of republican principles. He seized power in northern China and was the first of the *warlords*. By a series of manoeuvres, Yuan made himself President, moved the government back to Beijing (Peking) and set about the task of strangling the infant republic. By 1914 he had altered the con-stitution to give himself wider powers, aiming to exclude Dr Sun from power. Sun was a politician rather than a soldier, and Yuan by his ruthlessness and by his powerful allies did not find it too hard to get his own way.

Yuan refused to be constitutional head of state, banned the Guomindang, and dis-solved the Chinese parliament. During the First World War, Japan as one of the Allies attacked the German-occupied parts of Shandong (Shantung) Province, and presented the notorious *Twenty-One Demands* to Yuan in January 1915, forcing him to agree. These set up Japanese control of Shandong, increased Japanese influence in Manchuria, and gave military and economic privileges to Japan that made China into a mere protectorate. So bitterly did the Chinese resent these concessions that the day on which Yuan signed them became known as 'National Humiliation Day'.

These events effectively prevented Yuan from pursuing further his idea of restoring the empire with himself as Emperor. Faced with widespread revolts in the south-west provinces, and with public opinion in the north almost equally hostile, his life came to an abrupt and unexpected end in 1916 when he died, as was said at the time, 'from a fit of pure displeasure'.

The Guomindang, meanwhile, had established itself in the southern city of Gwangzhou, and a split between north and south threatened. The former Premier in the north, Duan Qirui (Tuan Ch'i-jui) seemed bent on setting up a military dictatorship, and declared war on Germany in 1917, signing away Chinese rights in Shandong in secret agreements with Japan. The end of the war brought humiliation to China at the Versailles Conference, when the Japanese and their allies confirmed all the exactions they had demanded of Duan. All this added strength to the *May 4th Movement*, protesting at the shabby way the country had been treated, and demanding social and political reforms. This brought Duan's government to an ignominious end.

China and the warlords

For a decade from 1918 to 1928, China was plagued by civil war, and central control over the country was shattered. The western areas like Mongolia and Tibet declared their independence, while the remainder of the country was ruled by a small number of powerful warlords, and a greater number of small warlords, together with a very large number of roving bands of robbers loosely bound together by their lust for plunder. One such warlord is said to have been a Christian, and is supposed to have baptized the soldiers of his army with a hosepipe.

These private armies numbered altogether about 2 million men. They financed themselves by brutal extortion, causing chaos and suffering over wide areas of the countryside. The lot of the Chinese peasant had never been a very happy one, and this predicament made it even worse.

None of the promised reforms ever materialized, however badly they were needed, and the social and economic condition of the countryside remained at a low level. What was wanted was a government with the determination and the strength to permit the peasant to own his own land and work for his own and his family's salvation, but no government was bold enough to do this. It is scarcely surprising that the peasantry wished above all for the creation of a strong, stable and reformist government: this no doubt explains the fact that so many of them eventually placed their hopes in the Chinese Communist Party and in Mao Zedong (Mao Tse-tung).

During this period of anarchy in China, Sun Zhongshan strove to safeguard the Guomindang, though its authority was restricted to a narrow strip of the coastal plain between Shanghai and Gwangzhou. More than once he was forced to flee to Japan for safety, but still he persevered. In 1925 he died of cancer, amid scenes of nationwide mourning. His rather uninspiring features appeared on postage stamps, and a huge memorial was built to him in Nanjing.

Origins of the Chinese Communist Party

As long as he lived, Dr Sun never managed to get very far in his plans for China. He never fully controlled the army, and he lacked most of the tools for a successful social revolution. He appealed hopefully to the western democracies for their support, but got very little practical response. In its disillusionment, the Guomindang turned to the Soviet Union for help.

In 1918 a *Society for the Study of Marxism* was formed at Beijing university, and three years later, at a girls' school in Shanghai, the Chinese Communist Party was founded, originally called the Gong Chan Dang (Kung ch'an dang), or 'Share Production Society'. Mao Zedong was one of the official delegates at the first meeting of the party in 1921.

Mao was born in 1893 in Hunan in southern China, his father a well-to-do peasant who was a supporter of the Manchu, and who constantly quarrelled over politics with his son. Mao was a studious boy and in 1911 joined the Junior College in Changsha. When, a few months later, the revolution began, he left and joined the revolutionary army. A year later he left the army and joined the Teacher Training College in Changsha, eventually taking a humble job as assistant librarian in the university of Beijing. By this time he was a convinced radical, and he went on to work as a trade union organizer at about the time that the Communist Party was launched. Another early member of the party was Zhou Enlai (Chou En-lai).

Sun Zhongshan, though himself a moderate parliamentary socialist distrustful of Bolshevism, eventually agreed to accept Soviet help. He sent the young soldier Jiang Jie

Shi (Chiang Kai-shek) to train in the USSR to become head of a new Military Academy near Gwangzhou, and agreed that the Guomindang itself should be organized along Bolshevik lines by a communist agent, Michael Borodin, who was sent from the USSR for the purpose.

In 1926 Jiang, whose suspicions of the communists were never very far below the surface, succeeded Sun to the Chinese leadership and formed a 'United Front' between the right- and left-wing groups in the Guomindang. This uneasy alliance succeeded in crushing the warlords in the Northern Campaign in 1928–29, and giving the communists their first real taste of authority in China.

China under Jiang Jie Shi

Jiang ruled China for rather more than 20 years, yet like Sun Zhongshan never fully succeeded in imprinting his authority on the country or on his own followers. His mistrust of his communist rivals was always for him a more urgent priority than providing his country with an honest reforming government.

▷ **The growing clash with the communists**

One of the reasons why Jiang had been so successful in his campaigns was that his allies, the communists, won the support of the peasantry by offering them radical land reform. Behind his advancing armies, communist-inspired *Peasant Associations* had been set up. These were a threat to the right-wing leaders of the Guomindang.

The Shanghai massacres, 1927

As early as April 1927, Jiang had come to the conclusion that his communist allies were more dangerous than his enemies. While he was engaged in the siege of Shanghai, he was approached by representatives of the business and banking groups there, who offered him their help if he crushed the communists. Jiang recognized that their financial backing was important, and chose to throw in his lot with them.

His troops rounded up known communists and trade unionists and imprisoned them, rooting out all the evidence they could find on their activities. Quite suddenly, the communists in the Guomindang found themselves arrested. In a bloody purge, about 5,000 of them were shot in batches, and those who escaped death were cowed into silence. One who escaped was Zhou Enlai, who happened to be an old colleague of the soldier detailed to shoot him, and who prevailed upon him to let him go free.

Soon afterwards Jiang allied himself even more closely with the propertied and banking classes by marrying the sister-in-law of Sun Zhongshan and sister of the Chinese minister of finance, in a Christian ceremony. Relations with the Soviet Union were now broken off, and Borodin was sent packing back to Moscow. To Jiang it seemed more sensible to ally himself with the leaders of the million or so rich and influential city families, right-wing though they were, than to the hundred million peasant families in the countryside, as the communists wished to do.

The Northern Campaign, 1928

It was not until 1928 that Jiang's *Northern Campaign* restored the authority of the central government to China. By a variety of methods – force, threats, diplomacy, intrigue, trickery and even poison – the warlords were subdued and Beijing was occupied by the nationalists. Once again China had a strong central government.

His communist rivals were driven into the west and south, chiefly in Jiangxi (Kiangsi) and Hunan; but though they built up quite a following among the peasants, their position was far from strong. The peasants had little money to give them, they had few weapons, and there was little shelter or protection in the inhospitable regions in which they lived. All the same, they had the talents of a capable soldier in Zhu De (Chu Teh), who built up the Jianxi Red Army in preparation for the coming struggle. It was at this time that Mao developed the principles of guerrilla conflict, so that his men could win the war when it came.

The Long March, 1934–35

In the period 1930–34, the Guomindang launched no fewer than five 'extermination campaigns' against the communists in Jiangxi. There was so little hope of Mao's survival that a Moscow newspaper actually published his obituary in 1930. But the communists were not ready to give up the ghost. They fought well, showed themselves more mobile and daring, and were helped by the fact that communist propaganda was well received at a time when the landlords were pushing up the peasants' rents.

All the same, the superior resources of the Guomindang in the end began to tell, and Mao decided in October 1934 to break out of Jiang's encircling ring of fortifications and to move into safer territories.

The original aim of the Long March, which began with 100,000 supporters and finished with little more than a fifth of that number, was to move Mao's headquarters about 160 kilometres to the west, where the danger from the nationalists would be less. But so intense were the attacks upon them that the marchers were forced to continue westwards almost to the borders of Tibet, and then were driven northwards towards Yan'an (Yenan) in Shanxi (Shensi). The Chinese expert, Edgar Snow, tells us that the marchers passed over eighteen mountain ranges, five of which were snow-capped, through eleven different provinces of about 200 million people, occupied 62 cities and towns, and engaged the armies of ten different warlords, besides evading or defeating the nationalists sent against them. They penetrated areas which no Chinese army had entered for nearly a hundred years. The march was destined to become part of Chinese political mythology, its episodes lovingly retold for the young, its glories always freshly burnished.

The marchers were not only continuously harrassed by hostile forces; they were confronted by swamps, steep ravines, scorching deserts and blinding snow. They crossed the Yangtse Kiang (Yangzi Jiang) and forced their way in the teeth of hostile machine-gun fire across a wooden bridge over the River Tatu, from which most of the planks had been removed, leaving the soldiers only the supporting chains to balance on. Mao's own wife perished on the march. The journey was over 3,000 kilometres, and took a year and a half to complete. As the marchers proceeded, they gathered new recruits and set up local soviets. Nevertheless, when they reached their destination in the mountainous and inaccessible province of Yan'an, they were in a broken and battered condition as well as sadly depleted in numbers. But the foundations of future communist power in China had been well and truly laid.

▷ **The conflict with the Japanese**

In these years the Chinese were faced not only with political division at home, but with the threat of Japanese invasion as well.

The Manchurian affair, 1931

The Japanese had secured many advantages in China under the Versailles Treaty, confirming their control of many of the areas where the Germans had earlier established themselves. They secured Kiaochow and much of the valuable silk-producing province of Shandong. They also extended their rights in northern China, gradually gaining control over Manchuria. The USSR regarded Manchuria as being within its own sphere of influence, but the Japanese rejected Soviet claims, and gradually brought the province under the control of what they called the Kwantung Army, the Japanese garrison in the area. When the local warlord tried to counter the growth of Japanese influence, he was murdered in 1928. His son made efforts to recover the position, but these only increased Japanese determination to annex the province.

In September 1931 the Kwantung Army, smarting under a recent decision in Tokyo to cut their pay and privileges, staged an incident on the South Manchurian Railway near the capital, Mukden, and within a short time took over control of the city and the whole province, in defiance of the wishes of the civilian Japanese government. Jiang Jie Shi offered very little resistance, not least because he preferred a Japanese to a Soviet occupation of Manchuria.

At first, the Tokyo government accepted a ruling from the League of Nations that it had to give up the province, but the persistence of the Kwantung Army in its original intentions only strengthened suspicions of Japanese duplicity. Shortly afterwards there was a change of government in Japan. The new Prime Minister, Inukai Tsuyoshi, was much more right wing than his predecessor, and gave his backing to the military dissidents in Manchuria.

There was sporadic fighting during 1932, but otherwise Japan was hardly opposed. The League of Nations responded to Japan's refusal to comply with its wishes by sending a special commission under Lord Lytton to Manchuria, but its recommendations were ignored, and Japan, which had long harboured the suspicion that the League was no more than a white men's club, resigned its membership. Manchuria was renamed Manchukuo, and Pu Yi, the boy emperor deposed in 1911, was made the puppet emperor there. In the meantime, Japan landed a force in Shanghai, fought against the nationalist 19th Army, and backed up its aggression with a bombing blitz on the city – the first to reveal the terror that could be produced in a densely populated urban area by concentrated air bombardment. Though it was victorious, Japan was condemned by the League; and in this instance, the League's pressure was successful in bringing about a Japanese withdrawal from Shanghai.

Early in 1933 the Japanese continued their expansion southwards from Manchuria. In May of that year there was a brief truce, but the Japanese paid little attention to it, and went on fortifying Manchuria as their main base and maintaining their penetration of China.

In 1933, they took the north-east province of Rehe (Jehol) and its main city Chengdeshi (Chengtehshih); this was added on to Manchukuo and brought their frontier to within 150 kilometres of Beijing. They went on in 1935–36 to occupy much of the province of Hebei (Hopei), in which Beijing itself was situated. During the whole of this time Jiang's attitude was one of appeasement: he firmly believed that it was only after crushing the communists that he could expect to win the national struggle with the Japanese. He therefore concentrated his efforts against Mao, ignoring the communists' call for a patriotic war.

The Xian (Sian) incident, 1936

At the end of 1936 Jiang went to Xian in southern Shanxi (Shensi) to organize a massive attack against his enemies there, but his army, consisting largely of men from the area bordering on Manchuria and much influenced by communist propaganda, refused to fight. Jiang was kidnapped by his own troops and forced to agree to a new 'United Front' with the communists. At first he refused, but Mao sent Zhou Enlai, now one of his foreign affairs advisers, to negotiate with him, and Jiang at last agreed.

Mao saw a double advantage in this: he secured himself in future against nationalist attacks, and he now also had the support of the nationalists in furthering the patriotic war against Japan, in the course of which he hoped to be able to show to the peasantry who their real friends were.

It is difficult to see what Jiang got out of it. For him, loyalty to the pact would have meant a change of political objectives and priorities, and would have gone against the grain of all his thinking. Indeed, Jiang deounced the pact as soon as he got back to Chonqin (Chungking), and continued in his old style of plotting against his communist allies. Only the western press took the pact seriously.

The war with Japan

Full-scale war between China and Japan began in 1937 with the so-called China 'incident' – the very name betrayed Japan's desire to play the whole episode down. The 'incident' was brought about when the Japanese claimed that their troops had been fired on during a night patrol. This was the excuse they needed to strike back with all the troops they could muster in a war which was to last until 1945.

Within a month, the Japanese had seized Beijing and Tianjin (Tientsin). Soon the whole of north-eastern China was in their hands as far as Nanjing. Nationalist forces were easily defeated, and Jiang had to move his capital to the mountain stronghold of Chonqin. Here he was prepared to sit out the war with Japan, leaving the fighting to the more patriotic communists, who used their limited resources to their best effect, so as to hinder the Japanese advance. He seems to have hoped that the two sides would wear themselves out, leaving him free to pick up the pieces.

Europe was very much absorbed by its own problems in the 1930s, and only the Soviet Union seems to have wished to play any part in the Sino-Japanese struggle. The USSR, however, helped the nationalists rather than the communists; Stalin seems to have thought that the Guomindang was his only possible ally against the Japanese threat, and this was in line with his use of popular national movements as a weapon against the imperialist powers. Especially after the Xian Pact, which apparently allied the communist and the nationalist sides together, Stalin began to supply the Guomindang with a meagre trickle of arms and supplies.

With the attack on Pearl Harbor in 1941, the Sino-Japanese War merged into the Second World War, and soon the other western powers also began to send supplies to the nationalists. The Japanese air force cut the Burma Road which connected Chonqing with the outside world, but the United States began instead to fly in masses of supplies and armaments by heavy transport aircraft across the Himalayas. Little positive resulted from it. This was partly because Jiang's supporters were getting ever more greedy and ruthless, his whole government sinking steadily deeper into lethargy and corruption; and partly because his main idea seemed to be to stockpile whatever resources he could get his hands on, so that he could renew his attack on the communists when the war was over. Jiang claimed that he was 'trading space for time', but the US General Joseph Stilwell said that this was 'just a catchy way of saying he would never attack'.

The US government in particular became increasingly irritated, and at one point actually contemplated switching its aid to the communists instead. Then the USA's natural caution came to mind, and the Chonqin regime continued to be the main beneficiary. At least the United States could claim that in supplying Jiang with aid it was tying down a large number of Japanese troops who otherwise would be fighting against the Americans in the Pacific theatre of the war.

In contrast, Mao's troops were much more active and successful in their struggles. They employed their guerrilla tactics to good effect, and soon had the Japanese forces virtually prisoners in the towns they had captured. They built up their hold most successfully in the rural areas, and soon came to control wide areas of the north, where something like a hundred million people lived. This gave spectacular confirmation for Mao's view that 'the towns are the fish that swim in the sea of the Chinese peasantry'.

The communist armies rarely risked open conflict, but their steady persistence continuously frayed the nerves of the scattered Japanese garrisons, and they soon had the feeling that they were winning. Towards the end of the war, quarrels broke out between Jiang and his American advisers. Roosevelt revised his high opinion of the nationalist leader, and his request for a big increase in the flow of supplies was sharply turned down.

The end of the war

In August 1945 two atomic bombs were dropped on Japanese cities, and within a few days the Japanese surrendered. The struggle now began in earnest for the future control of China.

By this time the nationalist regime had lost whatever support it originally possessed among the peasant masses, and though it still continued to have the backing of the USA and the USSR, its future looked less than encouraging. It now relied almost exclusively on the propertied classes, such as the landlords and the financiers, and had abandoned its democratic aspirations in favour of simple oppression. Jiang used his secret police to terrorize and imprison his opponents, spending his accumulated finance and resources to make friends and influence people.

All the same, there were few who would not have predicted victory for the nationalists in the forthcoming struggle.

Achievements of the Guomindang

Jiang succeeded in making constructive changes in the Chinese political system:

(a) He embarked after the anarchy of the warlords on a policy of strengthening the central government by bringing provincial rulers under central control.
(b) He improved communications, building 5,000 kilometres of new railways and about 160,000 kilometres of new roads, together with better postal and telegraph services.

(c) He reformed education, increasing the number of secondary schools fivefold, and creating new universities. Technical instruction was improved.

(d) He reformed the currency and reorganized the banking system.

(e) He introduced social reforms in dress, housing and diet, and improved the lot of women in Chinese society, e.g. abolishing foot binding for girls.

(f) He increased the industrialization of China and imported heavy machinery, persuading many foreign powers to limit their extraterritorial concessions and winning control over the country's tariff system.

(g) In foreign affairs he helped to restore the country's self-esteem, ending many of the 'unfair treaties' with the imperialist nations.

At the same time, critics maintained that the Guomindang should have done more:

(a) Nationalist control was strongest on the eastern seaboard; the western provinces such as Tibet became independent, and Mongolia was virtually taken over by the USSR.

(b) Even on the east coast there were a number of provincial governors who, though they nominally supported the Guomindang, followed policies of their own, often more left wing than the official policy.

(c) In the countryside, power was vested in the *pao chia* system, each *pao* consisting of a hundred families and each *chia* of ten families; in effect power passed into the hands of influential families, many of them landlords, who operated the system for their own benefit. As a result, taxes and rent for the poorer peasants remained very high, and they could not get justice in court.

(d) Social reform, such as the *New Life* movement (1934) soon degenerated into trivialities, laying stress on dress, good manners and consideration for others. In practice, westernization mirrored the least attractive features of modern life – fast cars, European clothes, multiple stores, smoking in public, etc.

(e) Party members came to rely on their perks and privileges, and the wealthier came to dominate the awarding of government contracts. By 1939, for example, the whole of Chinese banking had passed under the control of the Four Big Families, who made millions out of financial manipulation.

(f) After the war, inflation raged unchecked, and embezzlement and corruption among even the rank and file of the party became commonplace.

(g) The military training of its soldiery was hasty and slipshod, and many of its troops were of doubtful loyalty; their officers took their responsibilities lightly, and supplemented their income by selling off their equipment.

The Chinese Civil War

The end of the Second World War led directly to the outbreak of a civil war in China, when at last the nationalists and the communists embarked on their struggle for supremacy. It is to this war that we now turn.

▷ **The prelude to the civil war**

Few people outside China understood the hollowness of Jiang's position, and most people, especially those in the West, continued to look forward to the day when Jiang would begin to reform and modernize China. The fact that this was not going to happen took a long time to sink in.

Attitudes of the Chinese

Jiang had little to show for all the support he had received during the war. His preparations for resuming the reins of power were sketchy, and the Americans were not alone in comparing the high living, corruption and profiteering in Chonqin with the dedication and sense of purpose in the communist-controlled areas.

Mao had worked very hard to disrupt Japanese communications, and had established large pockets of territory under Chinese communist control; indeed, at one point during the war his forces had been attacked by the nationalists – the result, said Jiang, of a misunderstanding. He also produced a book in 1940 called *New Democracy*, in which he showed how China could move on naturally from Sun's 'democratic' revolution to a more advanced 'socialist' revolution under communist leadership.

Attitudes of China's neighbours

The USSR
The Soviet Union declared war suddenly on Japan in 1945, and invaded Manchuria, seizing towns and cities, but giving very little aid to Mao's forces. Instead the Soviets signed a pact with the nationalists in which Stalin promised to support Jiang, and undertook not to interfere in Chinese domestic affairs.

The USA
The Americans continued their long-standing commitment to the nationalists; they had a deep fear of any action which might result in the strengthening of communism in the Far East. Hence they airlifted Jiang's troops to whatever areas the Soviets had liberated, so as to forestall the communists there. Soon, too, US troops were landed in Beijing, Nanjing and Shanghai, and with the tacit approval of the Soviets set about silencing the communists.

Meanwhile, the Americans tried to prevent civil war by bringing the two sides together and persuading them to negotiate a settlement. In September 1945 they arranged a meeting between Jiang and Mao in Chonqin, but were depressed by the inflexible attitudes shown by both parties during a month of negotiations, which eventually came to nothing.

President Truman sent General Marshall to China to bang a few heads together, but with little result. He managed to arrange two ceasefires, but both were short-lived. Marshall disliked Jiang even more than Mao, and actively encouraged a third political group, the *Democratic League*, which had some middle-class backing and which was campaigning for a democratically elected parliament and a style of government modelled on the West.

Unfortunately, Jiang, as soon as he got to know there was another contender in the field, moved against the Democratic League, using his secret police to wipe it out by assassinating its leaders and rounding up its supporters. By 1947 it was clear that a coalition government was out of the question. A decision had to be reached by force.

▷ **The civil war**   General Marshall's efforts were shattered in 1946, when open fighting broke out between the two sides and the missions of US advisers were withdrawn.

The position of the nationalists
Jiang's prospects at first looked good. He had considerable financial resources and enjoyed international backing. His armies were well rested and well supplied, and outnumbered the communists by about four to one. He had stockpiled vast quantities of material and armaments. He had a modern air force; the communists could not muster a single plane. He felt confident that he could sustain two simultaneous campaigns: one in Manchuria to prevent it falling into Mao's hands, the other in the broad river valleys which lay between his main strongholds of Nanjing and Beijing.

But this picture of strength was misleading. Many of his soldiers were half-trained and ignorant, with very little idea what they were fighting for. Jiang himself made gross strategic blunders. The whole regime was shot through with corruption and incompetence, and inflation was rife. The only way of getting anything done seemed to be to have a bottomless purse and to be willing to grease palms all round. This was a solution which provoked the derision of the communists and the blind fury of the peasants.

In 1947 the nationalists' position steadily deteriorated. After bitter fighting, Jiang's armies in Manchuria were reduced to immobility in the cities they captured, their communications severed by communist guerrillas controlling the countryside. The only way to sustain the garrisons was by air. At the same time, the efforts he made to break northwards towards Beijing were frustrated by other communist bands in the broad plains between.

The communists take the offensive
In 1948 the communists went on the offensive, abandoning the use of guerrilla tactics and going over to large-scale and sustained military movements. They were heartened by the lack of resolve of their opponents, and strengthened by the large quantities of

military equipment that began to fall into their hands. Desertions, sometimes of whole regiments with their weapons, swelled communist ranks until it was they who enjoyed the numerical advantage over their enemies.

One by one, the great Chinese cities began to fall to them. In November 1948 Mukden fell to Mao, and the whole province of Manchuria passed into communist control. At the end of the year, Jiang finally lost his battle to control the river plains, losing control of the Yangzi Jiang (Yangtse Kiang) on which Nanjing stood.

In January 1949 he also came off the worst in the battle of the Huai (Hwai) Valley, losing about 200,000 dead and about 300,000 prisoners. There was now nothing to stop the communists in their advance northwards.

In the same month, the National Liberation (Communist) Army entered Beijing in a carnival mood, leaving Jiang with only the tattered remnants of his forces. In desperation he called a national assembly, but this met just in time to receive his final resignation as leader, after which he and the last loyal nationalist elements fled to the offshore island of Taiwan (Formosa), where they established a government-in-exile which lasted until after his death in 1975.

In October 1949, Mao, in a drab cloth cap and worn clothes, was greeted thunderously by an immense crowd in Beijing, and installed as the leader of the new People's Republic of China.

Importance of the Chinese Communist Revolution of 1949

Population increase and western imperialism had by 1910 undermined traditional Chinese society. After the collapse of the Manchu dynasty, the Guomindang had tried to reunify the nation, but it lacked the wisdom and the selflessness to achieve it, and relied too exclusively on the old weapons of hierarchy and obedience. It made honest attempts at reform, but the effects of these were limited and the old ruling classes remained in power. As time went by, the Guomindang attempted less and less; in the end it simply exploited the country it meant to reform.

The revolution brought great changes in the nature of Chinese society:

(a) It marked the end of 30 years of government by the Guomindang, and the failure of that regime to reform and modernize China. During this time the people were exposed to the arbitrary tyranny of the warlords, and to high taxation and bad government by their own nationalist leaders.

(b) It brought a revolution in land ownership: the land was taken from the landlord class, and redistributed among the peasantry.

(c) It led to the reform and modernization of Chinese government and in particular to its effective centralization under a single control, and to the further industrialization of the country.

(d) It produced big social changes for Chinese citizens, especially women and children, though there turned out to be little recognition of civil rights.

(e) The deaths of the first generation of revolutionary leaders in the 1970s and 1980s brought about the promise of greater liberalization under younger leadership.

It brought great changes in China's world position:

(a) A Sino-Soviet Friendship Pact was signed in February 1950 between Stalin and Mao, and by 1952 the USSR had surrendered all its privileges in Manchuria. For some years, Mao followed a policy of what he called 'leaning to one side', i.e. the communist side.

(b) Other foreign authorities and influences were excluded from China, apart from a few coastal presences such as Britain in Hong Kong (until 1997) and the Portuguese in Macao nearby. For some years, Chinese attitudes were markedly hostile to foreigners; liberalization did not come until after the death of Mao.

(c) It led to a series of border disputes between China and neighbouring states for the recovery of lands lost under the 'unfair treaties'.

(d) It eventually produced a realignment of world power; instead of a dual confrontation of the USA and the USSR, there was a triple confrontation between the United States, the Soviet Union and communist China.

GLOSSARY

Anarchy This is a state of chaos resulting from a lack of government or a struggle between rival would-be governments. It implies that a country is ungoverned, and sometimes that it is ungovernable.

Extraterritorial rights These are rights granted by the government of a country to the nationals of another country, usually within a restricted area. Here they are governed in accordance with the laws of their home country instead of those of the country where they are living. This concession, together with other privileges, is often used as an inducement to foreign nationals to establish residence there: for example, in the international area of Shanghai. But such privileges often encouraged xenophobia among the native Chinese.

Guerrilla tactics These are the methods employed by those fighting an informal war. Such people do not usually wear uniforms and their actions are not regulated by an accepted code of military behaviour; they are loosely organized and may even manufacture their own weapons. It was at this time of guerrilla war in China that Mao developed his famous four principles of guerrilla warfare:

> When the enemy advances, we retreat.
> When the enemy halts and encamps, we harass them.
> When the enemy seeks to avoid battle, we attack.
> When the enemy retreats, we pursue.

In Spanish *guerra* means 'war', and *guerrilla* means 'little war'.

Imperialist Someone who supports or works for the expansion of empire. European and Japanese imperialists in the nineteenth and early twentieth centuries regarded China as easy prey for their imperialist ambitions, and hoped to extend their territories, or at least their influence, at China's expense.

Unfair treaties These were so regarded by the Chinese because they had been forced upon China by more powerful states such as Russia, Britain and France. Britain, for example, had secured Hong Kong as early as 1842, and had gone on to take more treaty ports and to force the Chinese to accept the commercial policy of 'the open door' (in effect, free trade). The Chinese often felt that the foreigners had made use of the country's political weakness to force humiliating terms on them, and to deprive them of territories that were rightfully theirs. Not until the Chinese had a powerful government were they in a position, in the second half of the twentieth century, to secure the reversal of most of these treaties.

Warlords When China lapsed into anarchy soon after the fall of the Manchu dynasty, political power devolved into the hands of the governors of the provinces. The more ambitious of these became virtually independent, collecting taxes that should have gone to the government, raising armies and warring with their neighbours. Thus they were known as warlords. They kept China in chaos until they were suppressed in the 1920s by the Guomindang.

Xenophobia Hatred of foreigners. Chinese feared both commercial exploitation and the loss of political independence at the hands of privileged foreigners. Thus the end to exploitation and 'China for the Chinese' were political aims common to all major Chinese political parties from the 'Boxers' onwards.

EXAMINATION QUESTIONS

▷ **Question 1** Study the sources below, and then, using the sources and your own knowledge, answer the questions which follow.

Source A

We swept across a distance of more than 6,500 miles on our own two feet, across 11 provinces . . . The Long March is a manifesto. It declares to the world that the Red Army is an army of heroes and that Jiang Jie Shi and the like are as nothing. It shows Jiang's complete failure. The Long March also tells the 200 million people in 11 provinces that only the road of the Red Army leads to their liberation. It has sown many seed in 11 provinces, which will bear fruit and yield a crop in the future. To sum up, the Long March has ended in our victory and in the enemy's defeat. (Mao Zedong)

Source B

In fact the Long March was a great retreat. Only about one-tenth of those who started out survived it. And after it the communists were still on the point of being completely destroyed. (James Pinckney Harrison, historian)

Source C

Heavy fog was all around us. There was a high wind and it began to rain. As we climbed higher there was a terrible hail storm. The air became so thin we could hardly breathe. It was impossible to speak. The cold was so dreadful that our breath froze and our hands and lips turned blue. Men and animals staggered and fell into chasms, disappearing for ever. Those who sat down to rest or go to the toilet froze to death on the spot. (A Red Army soldier)

(a) Source B differs from Source A. Does that mean that Source A is unreliable? Explain your answer. (8 marks)
(b) Does Source C support Mao's or Pinckney's view of the Long March? (7 marks)
(c) Which of these sources is the most valuable to historians? Explain your answer. (10 marks)

▷ **Question 2** (a) What was the importance of the Long March for the Chinese Communist Party? (10 marks)

(b) How was China affected by the war with Japan (1937–45)? (10 marks)
(c) Why were the communists able to defeat the Guomindang in the civil war? (10 marks)

 EXAMINATION ANSWERS

▷ **Question 1** *Outline answer*

(a) Not necessarily. Mao in Source A is concentrating on the positive achievements of the march: the survival of the Red Army from Jiang's 'extermination campaigns', and the indoctrination of the peasants in the lands through which the Long March took place. Pinckney correctly labels the Long March as a great retreat, pointing out the appalling wastage rate and the continued danger from the Guomindang. Mao does not deny this, but sees the Long March as a symbolic victory, while Pinckney sees it in practical terms as a near disaster.

(b) Again, in a practical sense, the Red Army soldier supports Pinckney. The huge loss of life which Pinckney pinpoints is not surprising in the light of the suffering that the Red soldier relates. But in showing the appalling suffering, which Mao and others survived during the march, the soldier is perpetuating Mao's legend of a triumph over hardship, even though he does not go so far as Mao does in claiming victory out of defeat. Even so, the soldier's picture of intense suffering is the stuff heroes are made of, so there is greater affinity between Sources A and C than the source content alone might indicate.

(c) It really depends what the historian is looking for. If the historian wants to understand the importance of the Long March for the subsequent history of China, then Mao's words are ideal. If the historian wants a bald comment on the immediate, rather than the long-term consequences of the march, then Pinckney is useful. But if the historian wants an eyewitness account of the actual suffering on the march, then the Red Army soldier's experiences are valuable and typical. But it is probable that an historian will be more concerned with the long-term importance of the march – as a heroic feat, as an inspiration and as a legend – and Mao's words in Source A show that legend in the making.

▷ **Question 2(a)** *Tutor answer*

In the short term, the Long March allowed the Chinese communists to survive. The 'extermination campaigns' of the Guomindang had made the Red Army's position in Kiangsi virtually untenable, and the 20,000 who reached Yenan were the hard-bitten survivors who would live to fight another day. The march gave the Red Army new leaders. After the disasters of the early months, Mao Zedong's influence grew and so did that of his immediate associates. By the time the march ended, Mao was its undisputed leader, and the leaders of the Long March were to dominate the Chinese Communist Party for at least another generation. Mao was quick to establish the march as a communist legend. The suffering became a kind of purification, and those who had been on the march became heroes whose exploits were to be admired and imitated. In a more practical sense, the behaviour of the marchers had won over the peasantry in many of the provinces through which they passed, not least because they treated the peasantry with respect, while the Guomindang robbed and pillaged at will. And the march took on a patriotic note which perhaps it hardly deserved. Mao was able to suggest that the march had been deliberately aimed to reach north China so that the Red Army would be in a better strategic position to challenge the Japanese invaders who had already overrun Manchuria, and were doubtless intending an attack into northern China as their next move. The very survival of the March demonstrated the incompetence of the nationalists and the skill and determination of the communists. Overall the Long March came to symbolize the heroism, the patriotism and the socialism of the Chinese communists, and the party was able to get mileage out of its memory for many years to come.

▷ **Question 2(b)** *Tutor answer*

The war brought great suffering to the people of China. The Japanese air force had unchallenged control of the skies, and Chinese cities were often mercilessly bombed, with heavy civilian casualties, before being occupied by ground forces. Suffering did not end there. Massacres of civilians occurred throughout Japanese-occupied China, and since Japan was not a party to the Geneva Convention, the Japanese took few prisoners, and many of the Chinese troops captured were slaughtered. The loss of much of its eastern seaboard deprived China of its ports and business centres, so external trade fell off alarmingly, and widespread shortages occurred. The Japanese invasion showed Jiang and the nationalists in a bad light. Jiang preferred to defeat the communists before tackling the Japanese; the communists preferred to fight the Japanese, and got most of the credit for the Xian agreement by which communists and nationalists agreed to suspend their civil war in order to fight the common enemy. When the war merged into the Second World War, the nationalists gained increased American aid, and the communists were virtually given the cold shoulder by Stalin. But Jiang's close links with the USA and Britain laid him open to Mao's charge of associating with 'imperialists', and consolidated Mao's grip on the peasantry. In the later stages of the war, Jiang was busy preparing for the civil war to come, so that Mao got the credit for his determined guerrilla war against the Japanese, while Jiang got the blame for the wartime inflation and his failure to get to grips with the invaders. Although the war ended with Jiang in an apparently very strong position, his nationalists had very little following in the Chinese countryside, and the advantages of his American connection were soon dissipated. Mao had used the Japanese war to advance the communist reputation for Chinese patriotism, and Jiang's days were numbered.

▷ **Question 2(c)**   *Student answer with examiner's comments*

'An exaggeration.'

'A word that indicates that the answer is loosely strung together instead of being woven into an effective argument.'

'Not quite, but they despaired of him.'

First The Guomindang was unpopular. Their troops were undisciplined: they treated the peasants badly, they did not always obey orders, and some deserted to the communists. Also Jiang was corrupt: he and his officers kept all the American aid to build fortunes for themselves. Also Jiang was blamed for the rapid inflation which destroyed the spending power of the Chinese money. Large amounts of Japanese war-time equipment fell into communist hands in North China. The communists were popular because they treated the peasants well, and had fought relentlessly against the Japanese. The Red Army was well led, and well disciplined. Also it had control of the countryside, while the Guomindang held the cities only. The fact that the Guomindang had American help made them overconfident, and even the Americans abandoned Jiang in the end.

Examiner's decision on the student answer
This contains all the information which could be built into a good answer; it needs more development in places – it looks almost in note-form – and the various points need more effective linking together. It would probably score 7/10.

SUMMARY

In this chapter you have learned about the following:

▷   China in the early twentieth century, and the fall of the Manchu Empire in 1911;

▷   Sun Zhongshan and the formation of the Guomindang;

▷   China under the warlords: origins of the Chinese Communist Party;

▷   changing relations between the Guomindang and the Communist Party;

▷   the struggle with Japan, and the Sino-Japanese War, 1937–45;

▷   the Chinese Civil War, 1946–49, and the communist victory;

▷   achievements of the Guomindang, and the importance of the 1949 revolution.

Further information on China is to be found in:

▷   chapter 17, on communist China after 1949;

▷   chapter 18, on the importance of China in world affairs after 1949.

China after 1949

▷ **GETTING STARTED**

The year 1949 marked the establishment of communist rule in China after almost 25 years of conflict between the nationalists and the supporters of Mao Zedong.

Mao's view of communism was different from that of his allies in the Soviet Union. But he was not dissimilar from them in his patriotism. He continued the long tradition of resistance to the 'foreign devils', seeking to rid the country of selfish and intrusive interests and trying to recover the lands that had been lost under the 'unfair treaties'. Nor were his fundamental aims very different from the Soviet equivalent. He wanted to build a classless society, no longer dominated by the profit motive, and one in which the individual could find fulfilment.

MEG	NEAB	NICCEA	SEG	LONDON	WJEC	TOPIC	STUDY	REVISION 1	REVISION 2
✓	✓*			✓	✓	**China under Mao Zedong**			
✓	✓*			✓	✓	Mao's policies in China after 1949			
✓	✓*			✓	✓	Later policies of Mao			
✓	✓*			✓	✓	Social policies of Mao Zedong			
✓	✓*			✓	✓	Chinese foreign policy after 1949			
✓	✓*				✓	**China after Mao Zedong**			
✓	✓*				✓	Repercussions of Mao's death			
✓	✓*				✓	The end of the 1980s			

* Coursework only

 WHAT YOU NEED TO KNOW

China under Mao Zedong

Mao governed China until his death in 1975, and in that time revolutionized the whole nation.

▷ **Mao's policies in China after 1949**

The three strands of his policy – political, economic and social – were closely woven together to form the pattern of the new society for which he aimed. In their way, these strands were similar to Dr Sun's original three principles. However, partly because Mao had more widespread backing than the early reformers, and partly because he did not hesitate to crush resistance when it showed itself, Mao Zedong had far more success than his predecessors.

Political developments

Before the final fall of the Guomindang, a conference of about 650 communist delegates from all over China met in Beijing to discuss the future form that the People's Republic should take. They, and other left-wing bodies, chose a central government council under Mao as chairman, and this body ruled China for the next five years. In the interval they arranged for national and local elections of communist representatives to form the *National People's Congress*.

In September 1954 this body finally came into being. Thereafter the communist deputies met regularly, and it became the supreme governing body of the country.

Deputies elect the Chairman of the Republic and the members of the State Council, which is the equivalent of the cabinet and is presided over by the Prime Minister. The first President was Mao Zedong, and the first Prime Minister Zhou Enlai.

The constitution contained a statement of civil rights, including equality for women and the universal right of voting. The main difference between this system and the western democratic system is that in China, as in the Soviet Union, political power is in the hands of the all-powerful Communist Party, which controls the elections, supplies all the candidates for election, and monopolizes the membership of the various governing bodies. The party itself is organized on lines very similar to the state, with periodic congresses and a ruling Politburo most of whose personnel are the same people as those who occupy senior positions in the government.

Opposition therefore finds it hard to express itself legally. The party, on the other hand, reaches right down to the roots of Chinese society. With over 20 million members, it forms a well-organized network of influence to control events and to carry out what it sees as its necessary work of education and propaganda among the people.

Few Guomindang supporters of Jiang accompanied him to Taiwan; most stayed in China in a mood of 'wait and see'. Some even returned from abroad in the same spirit; at last there seemed to be a chance that they could devote their talents to the service of their country. These people were the *bourgeoisie*, and therefore in theory were enemies of the working-class revolution. But Mao knew that their skills and experience were necessary to rebuild China; so he encouraged them to stay, hoping to re-educate them to accept socialism as the goal for which they were working.

Economic policy: agriculture

Farming was the foundation of the Chinese economic system, and this had been ravaged by decades of civil war, the disruption and neglect of the Japanese occupation, and the customary series of natural disasters such as periodic flooding.

The first task facing the new government in 1949 was that of changing small privately owned farms into large communally owned farms:

(a) First, the landlords' land was taken over and redistributed among the peasants, so that each of them owned his own holding. This first stage was achieved by the *Land Reform Law* (1950), so fulfilling what had originally been one of Sun Zhongshan's objectives – 'the land to the tiller'. But though this ended the ancient abuse of landlordism, it did not in itself bring about agricultural efficiency. Had things been left like this, there would have emerged a new class of conservative land-owning peasants hostile to the continuance of the revolution. Besides, with holdings of so small a size – the average was less than 1 acre – mechanization and new farming methods would never have developed, and the whole country would have remained poor and backward.

(b) The needs of the peasants for such things as seed and markets made it possible to go on to the next stage and start to organize cooperatives. By the *Land Reform Law* (1952), the *collective* principle was introduced: the land still remained in the peasants' ownership, but now about a hundred families were working together and sharing out their produce. By 1954, it is calculated that almost 200 million people were members of such collectives. *Mutual aid teams* were built up, together with cadres of selected communist leaders, giving guidance to the farmers and actually working alongside them in the fields. These *lower-stage cooperatives* had a good deal of independence, sharing the land they worked on, and dividing up the produce between them by agreement.

Economic policy: industry

China in 1949 was even more backward industrially than Russia had been in 1917. There was some light industry, mostly foreign-owned before the revolution, and the Japanese had set up some heavy industry – mining, smelting and engineering – in Manchuria during their occupation of the province. China's own industry was chiefly made up of small handicraft workshops.

Early steps did little more than restrain inflation and cut back on the massive unemployment left by the disruption of the war. Foreign firms and those owned by supporters of the former Guomindang were confiscated, but small Chinese-owned businesses continued in private hands. Indeed, until the decade 1956–66, small capitalists were allowed 5 per cent interest on their investment – another example of the communist leadership treading softly at first for fear of creating enemies.

Much more remained to be done, but for two or three years, while China was engaged in the Korean War, 40 per cent of China's budget went on national defence spending.

In 1951 the *State Planning Commission* took over about 80 per cent of heavy industry and about half of light industry. It also turned its attention to the further industrialization of the country, and drew up its first *Five-Year Plan*, which came into operation in 1953.

Planning was centrally organized and tightly controlled, concentrating chiefly on the development of the heavy industries. To this extent it was modelled on the Soviet pattern. Indeed, under the 1950 Sino-Soviet Treaty of Friendship, the USSR gave extensive economic aid and guidance, and provided, over fifteen years, in excess of 300 modern industrial plants, with training for the Chinese who operated them, at a cost of over $3,000 million in loans.

By 1956, however, Mao was coming to the conclusion that Soviet-style planning was not well suited to China's needs. His relations with the USSR in any case were beginning to deteriorate, and Soviet aid was ended in 1960.

But in the interval, coal, iron and steel, chemicals and machine tools were among the main beneficiaries, and alongside these was the production of electricity for domestic and industrial purposes. Steel output alone rose from about 150,000 tons per year to about 5½ million in 1957, and overall there was a national growth rate of about 12 per cent per annum. Heavy industry benefited the most, but there was also a considerable growth in consumer manufacture.

Social reform

This was perhaps the area where the greatest effort was needed to lift the people out of the primitive conditions in which they had for so many centuries been obliged to live. Work began in 1949 to overhaul social life in the same radical fashion, in living conditions, housing and education, but it was not for many years that the situation genuinely improved.

▷ **Later policies of Mao**

'Thought reform', 1950–57

There was at the start little resistance to the rule of the new communist regime. Here at last was a government which got things done, even if its actions were not popular with everybody. Few opponents were spared. People's courts imposed summary justice in which nationalists and landlords were persecuted, and about 2 million perished. Surviving opponents changed their views; doubters learned to keep their mouths shut.

The party cadres played a vital part in organizing the overhaul of Chinese thinking; theirs was the main responsibility for political education. In the early years there were three major campaigns:

(a) 'thought reform' among the intellectuals in 1950;
(b) the Three-Anti Campaign against corruption, waste and bureaucracy in 1951;
(c) the Five-Anti Campaign against bribery, tax evasion, fraud, theft of government property and theft of state economic secrets, also in 1951.

Thought reform aroused horrified reactions in the West, where it was regarded as 'brainwashing' through the subtlest of psychological tortures; on the positive side, it helped to reconcile the individual with social attitudes through a process of self-criticism and confession. It was nevertheless deeply dreaded by opponents of the regime.

The 'Campaign of the Hundred Flowers', 1957

By 1957, however, it was possible to lighten social pressures. Mao took the view that the only way to achieve permanent socialism was to convince the people of its rightness; repression could not be substituted for persuasion for ever. Hence for a time restrictions were lifted in what became known as the *Campaign of the Hundred Flowers*: 'Let a hundred flowers bloom and a hundred schools of thought contend.' Ordinary people, together with bourgeois and intellectuals, were encouraged to find fault with the communist system. The leadership allowed this to happen freely for a time, and then clamped down. Those who had spoken their minds were now silenced, and sometimes were forced to publish humiliating retractions, headed by words such as 'I confess my guilt to the people.'

Mao, having persuaded his critics to reveal themselves, was now able to silence them. The basic socialist framework of the new China was not to be questioned – that was no less than counterrevolution!

Agricultural reform after 1955

Second-stage collectives, called *communes*, began to appear in 1954 as the next step in the collectivization of farming. Here it was not unusual for 300 or 400 families to work in teams on the land, their back-up services now being much more extensive.

By 1956 the drive to form these larger collectives was intensified. Individual peasants were still entitled to own a small portion of land as their own, but 95 per cent of the land was now merged into the communes, which bought the tools, the cattle and the buildings from individual families.

By 1958 there were about 28,000 communes throughout China, each one having 40,000 to 50,000 workers in it. Collectivization had thus been achieved in Mao's own way, not through force and cruelty, but steadily, firmly and through conviction. The lessons of Stalin's method seemed to have been learnt: the occasional natural disasters brought famine and even deaths, but there was no attempt to wipe out an entire class of citizens as there had been in Soviet punishment camps.

As well as agriculture, these large new units also undertook industrial developments, embarking on ambitious drainage, irrigation and even hydroelectric schemes. Furthermore each one ran its own schools, clinics, libraries, theatres and shops, all of them collectively owned and operated. The aim of the large self-sufficient community seemed to have been realized. All the same, these things were often on so large a scale that life became regimented and impersonal. Nor were they always efficiently managed. For these reasons in recent years the size of the commune has been reduced to something like 25,000 people.

The 'Great Leap Forward', 1958

In the early 1950s, the Chinese leadership hesitated to antagonize the population by too rapid a takeover of industry and by too much compulsion. About half of the smaller businesses remained in private hands.

But in 1958 there came the *Great Leap Forward*, an attempt to step up both agriculture and industry, and to achieve 'the work of 20 years in a single day'.

By the end of the First Five-Year Plan (1953–57), Mao was becoming increasingly concerned that China's economy was seriously unbalanced. This was for a number of reasons:

(a) Over 70 per cent of new investment had so far gone on heavy industry; only about 7 per cent was devoted to agriculture. Steel production was a fine thing, but if it could not be turned into tractors, tools and machinery, it was of little help to the collective farms.

(b) Industrial growth was heavily concentrated on the eastern coastal strip, partly because this was the most accessible place for the foreign firms that had first developed there. There was a disturbing drift of population to the eastern cities; these had grown in about ten years from 60 million to about 90 million people.

(c) Agriculture was beginning to lag behind industry, but as in Stalin's USSR there was a need for agricultural surpluses for export and to feed the growing cities. Unless the balance was redressed, the old enemy, famine, might strike.

(d) Mao had for some time been losing faith in the usefulness of centralized planning on the Soviet model. He feared it might produce a generation of technocrats who might be tempted to use the revolution for their own purposes. Furthermore, central control was not likely to succeed in a country so large and often with such primitive land communications.

The government therefore encouraged the same local self-sufficiency in industry as existed in the communes. The leadership assisted the growth of small-scale industry throughout the countryside, beginning with 600,000 'backyard furnaces' to boost iron and steel output. They were manned by the peasants in the communes, aided by men from the local cadres with the necessary specialist skills. They made not only metals, but farm tools, machinery, spare parts and other things in day-to-day demand. The workers in their dungarees – 'blue ants' as they were called, after their unceasing efforts – constructed dams, reservoirs, irrigation channels, flood control systems and other massive earthworks, often working only with the most primitive of hand tools.

In terms of economic success, however, the Great Leap Forward was more of a stumble. The new furnaces produced steel of a very poor quality, and their other products were sadly inadequate. Some of their earthwork schemes were grandiose and were left half-finished. Worse still, they led to a neglect of agriculture, whose encouragement was one of their main aims. Hard times followed: food rationing had to be reintroduced in 1959, lasting until 1961. Many peasants were starving and the death rate went up from malnutrition and its consequences. Some modern estimates suggest that about 20 million people died – a figure not far short of Stalin's tally of casualties in the USSR in the 1930s. China's industry recovered in the 1960s, but the effects of these overambitious schemes lasted for many more years.

The Cultural Revolution, 1966

Mao's suspicions of the technocrats lingered on after the Great Leap Forward, and surfaced again in 1966. Part of his trouble was that he felt that the Soviet method of modernization was too bureaucratic and institutional, and sacrificed everything to industrial productivity, whereas he had the idea of shaping socialist man from his soul outwards. He, like the early Lenin, harboured deep misgivings about expertise: he thought that experts were more likely to set about buttressing their class privileges than to further the people's revolution.

He therefore aimed to keep the revolution moving rather than to encourage the emergence of a new administrative élite. His *Red Guard*, mostly impressionable schoolboys, whose energies could be easily unleashed against what Mao called the 'capitalist roaders', were to be kept busy reading his 'little red book' (*The Thoughts of Chairman Mao*) and then agitating in public to smash up the four 'olds', defined as 'old ideas, old culture, old customs and old habits'. Temple decorations, sculpture and college and university libraries were vandalized; scientists and teachers were 'denounced' as counterrevolutionary and made to scrub out the latrines instead of continuing with their professional activities.

The Red Guard was so busy stressing the importance of keeping the revolution moving that no one had time to put in a full day's work. Planning and output went by the board, and numerous dislocations in every sector of Chinese society led to breakdowns and shortages once again.

The Chinese found that, far from accelerating their progress, ideology turned out to be a barrier to development. It was only after the fury had died down that education and productivity recovered once again.

Though China exploded its first atomic device at Lop Nor in 1964, the overall level of Chinese technology lagged far behind the West. This was partly due to the persistence of small industrial workshops, which the Chinese seemed to prefer to large enterprises, and partly also to the belief in Maoist China that 'socialism is a way of life rather than a way of industrial growth'. For masses of Chinese, poverty and backwardness continued to be the main feature of their lives.

▷ **Social policies of Mao Zedong**

Since the revolution of 1949, there is no doubt that social conditions in China have vastly improved. Modern buildings have been put up, the people are better housed and better fed, there are fewer beggars on the street, and the whole atmosphere of the country has become more enlightened and progressive. This improvement can be summarized under a number of headings.

The position of women

In feudal China, women were often regarded as the mere possessions of men. They were subject to barbaric practices such as the binding of the feet of baby girls; they were married off in childhood and were actually sold in hard times by their husbands and fathers. In 1931 the Guomindang had passed a law for the betterment of the lot of women, but for the majority of them, who lived in regions distant from the eastern coastal strip of the country, the law had little effect. Women had to wait until 1949 for any real improvement.

In 1950 the *Marriage Law* grappled with this problem: it abolished child marriage, banned infanticide, i.e. the custom of murdering unwanted girl babies, and imposed heavy penalites for bigamy. In recent years, women have been treated with more consideration. With the introduction of public nurseries, laundries and restaurants, and in particular with strict limitations on the size of families, women have been freed from the more toilsome aspects of domestic work, while at the same time finding new opportunities for education and employment in society.

Public health

At the time of the revolution, life expectancy in China was low and a large number of children died during infancy. Ordinary infectious diseases such as measles and influenza caused a high mortality, and deficiency diseases such as rickets were common. The extension of medical services and the provision of hospitals and qualified doctors have therefore been a high priority in social policy.

The result over half a century has been the creation of a hygiene-conscious people, with greatly improved conditions of health and cleanliness. New medical and surgical techniques have been pioneered. The ancient art of acupuncture has been extended and brought up to date. There have even been campaigns to stamp out the common house fly.

Population

This is perhaps the most serious problem confronting the Chinese people in the twentieth century. The reduction of infant mortality together with the conquest of disease has meant that an already large population has exploded massively in size, shooting up from about 450 million in 1950 to 1,000 million towards the end of the century. In the 1960s it was already increasing at a rate of 50,000 every day.

The government therefore publicized the need for effective measures of birth control. But quite suddenly the whole campaign was halted on the grounds that the problem was not as serious as had been supposed. Perhaps Mao was responding to political pressures so as to ensure that China would be in a proper state of military preparedness. Mao took the view that the overall density of the population was low; that the cultivated area could easily be increased to feel all the new mouths; and, more importantly, that the country's population growth was below the level needed to sustain the drive towards modernization.

All the same, wiser counsels prevailed. The 1970s saw a return to population control. Recent years have seen an enormous increase in the single-child family, a development which not only makes possible greater child care, but ensures that the overall increase in population is kept well in hand. Control involves restraints which would be unacceptable to the West: there is an official minimum marriage age of 25 for women and 27 for men; a 5 per cent pay rise is given for the first-born, together with various child benefits such as health care and education – but further benefits are withheld if there is a second child, and a third brings pay cuts of 5 per cent and the withdrawal of earlier benefits. There is also severe social disapproval for couples with large families.

Education

In 1949 the main emphasis in Chinese schools was on simple literacy, since the majority of the population at that time could not read or write. The government, too, tried to bring more children into schooling: in the period 1949–59, numbers in schools went up from about 25 million to nearly 100 million. The existing patchwork of Chinese schools – private, state and mission schools – was also merged into a truly national system.

There was also a heavy emphasis on politics: primary school children, for example, were taught arithmetic by getting them to calculate the number of American casualties in Vietnam.

One problem was the enormous number of characters in the written language. Efforts were made to simplify them and to reduce them in number, or even to substitute a 26-letter alphabet on the model of the Roman one. But the task proved to be long and unpopular, and the traditional Chinese script persists to the present day.

With the Cultural Revolution in 1966, furthermore, education came to a halt from the village schools at the bottom to the universities at the top. For nearly two years the system was disrupted: there were no classes, no examinations were set, and two years of school-leavers entered the labour market without qualifications. When schools were reopened, there was a new emphasis on combining theory with practice. The skills approach as well as the more traditional academic approach was welcome. Practical subjects appeared on the curriculum; open-book examinations became more common, and stress was laid on skills as well as on academic achievement.

In the 1970s there was a campaign against Confucianism, the philosophy most associated in the Chinese mind with ancient authority and scholarship. At the time of Mao's death, education was still a battleground between left and right; but the emphasis on scientific and practical subjects still survived, and schools eventually tired of 'struggling and criticizing', as they had in the Cultural Revolution, and got back to the business of teaching.

Welfare and working conditions

Hard work and poverty were the inheritance of most Chinese in 1949. With the introduction of trade unions at the time of the revolution, and the creation of a trade union federation in 1950 (though controlled by the state), conditions steadily improved.

Conditions of work were reformed; leisure and holiday facilities were introduced. Retirement was fixed in accordance with the type of occupation at 45–55 for women and 55–65 for men. Smaller families have meant that more money is left for leisure pursuits, and though these do not compare with the range available in the West, the Chinese are now provided for better than ever before.

National minorities

Almost one-sixth of the population are not in fact Chinese. There are Mongolians, Tatars, Tibetans and many others, nearly all of whom have their own languages, customs and religions. Until the Chinese constitution of 1954, the attitude of the Chinese leadership towards these peoples seemed to be a tolerant one, and the constitution itself referred to them as 'national autonomous areas', going on to say that they formed 'inalienable parts of the People's Republic of China'. Mao, however, laid more stress on the phrase 'inalienable parts' than on 'national autonomous areas'.

In the 1950s, for example, Tibet, reoccupied as an ancient historic province of China, was shown less and less respect for its different ways until its people were driven into rebellion in 1959. Then violent military action was taken against this distant country, its monasteries were closed and its religion was extinguished. Eventually its ruler, the Dalai Lama, was driven to take refuge in India and was briefly replaced by a pro-Chinese puppet, the Panchen Lama.

After 1960, however, the conduct of the Chinese towards their subject peoples mellowed somewhat. Efforts were made to preserve their own languages and cultures, and they were linked up to the Chinese economic system instead of being subordinated to it. By 1980 the Chinese seemed to be more sensitive than before to the charge that they were in the habit of riding rough-shod over their neighbours.

▷ Chinese foreign policy after 1949

Ignorance about communist China in the early days led to fear of Chinese intentions in their external relations, causing the Americans, for example, to refer to China as 'this new Frankenstein'. The world might have been forgiven for thinking that China was bent on a policy of reckless expansion.

The 'unequal treaties'

The attitude of the communists towards foreign settlements in China was one of baleful hostility. As far as they were concerned, foreigners had no right to be in China and were to be persuaded to leave, or squeezed out by force if they refused.

When, for instance, the British gunboat *Amethyst* sailed up the Yangzi in 1949 with supplies for the British community in Nanjing, it was trapped in the river by shore-based artillery for three months before escaping under cover of night and being chased by hostile batteries 200 kilometres down-river. Other foreign stations in China were treated equally brusquely by the Red Army.

The communists regarded the concessions to these foreigners, under the 'unfair treaties' of the nineteenth century, a gross affront to their national dignity, and systematically reabsorbed the areas granted to them. The last of them to go was the tiny colony of Macao, close to Hong Kong, which was to be restored to China in 1999, after nearly 450 years of Portuguese control.

Fig. 17.1 China and Asia, 1949–70

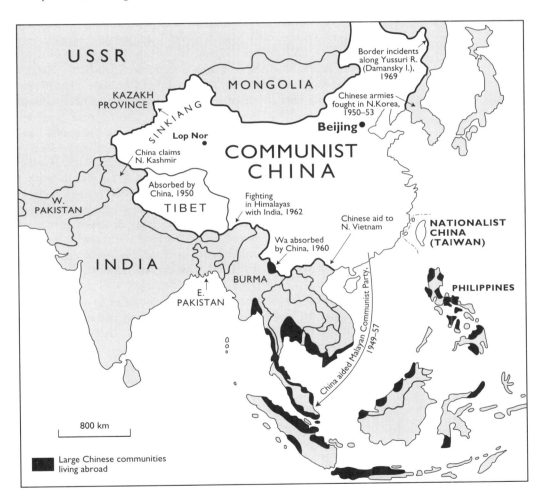

Border wars

China found itself involved in wars along its frontier on several occasions after 1949, often with the purpose of recovering lands lost earlier which the Chinese regarded as being their own:

(a) In 1951, Mao found himself involved in a costly war against the United Nations and the USA when he supported the neighbouring North Korean regime, which was both politically and racially akin to communist China. As a result North Korea was re-established.

(b) In 1950, Mao reabsorbed Tibet, where the situation degenerated into persecution and violence in 1959. Control was finally established.

(c) In 1960, Mao nibbled at the frontier of Nepal, and went on, after sporadic fighting, to take control of Wa, a mountainous region on the border with Burma.

(d) In 1962, there was sporadic fighting in the mountains above Assam. The Chinese also laid claim to Ladakh, a part of northern Kashmir, and there was quite serious fighting with Indian troops 'on the roof of the world'. China eventually secured control of desolate areas which it claimed were rightfully Chinese.

(e) In the 1960s, China at first supported Ho Chi Minh in North Vietnam, though it later drew back rather than be involved in the Vietnam War with the USA.

(f) Large Chinese communities lived abroad in Singapore, Malaysia, Indonesia and elsewhere, often in sufficient numbers to appear to be a threat to these countries. But in fact China showed little interest in them, and never claimed sovereignty.

The Sino-Soviet split, 1960–70

Perhaps the most serious of these conflicts was that with the Soviet Union. After his 30-year *Treaty of Friendship and Alliance* with Mao, Stalin was one of his staunchest supporters, lending him considerable military and technical support in the task of building up Red China. But communist China was much less docile than the Soviet satellites in eastern Europe, and Mao was far from being a puppet. Often it was Stalin who had to fall in with Chinese wishes, as when he agreed to withdraw from Port Arthur in Manchuria. Ironically, it was only after Khrushchev debunked his predecessor in 1956 that Mao came into the open as one of Stalin's champions.

On the surface there was little disagreement, but behind the scenes Mao's irritation with Khrushchev mounted. The problem came to a head at a conference in Bucharest in 1960, when Khrushchev laid great stress on changing East–West problems and openly advocated an understanding with the capitalist West. As a result, Mao welcomed the fall of Khrushchev in 1964, but this did not change things much.

Under Brezhnev the USSR moved closer to *détente* with the West, and Chinese anger with the USSR increased. This showed itself in central Asia.

In the 1960s, they began to fortify their remote north-western frontier with the Soviet province of Kazakhstan, and were later involved in actual fighting with Soviet forces along the Yussuri River, which formed the frontier between Manchuria and the USSR, particularly over certain islets in it whose ownership had never been formally included in any agreement. By 1970, Sino-Soviet relations had deteriorated to the point of open conflict.

In 1980 communist China condemned the Soviet occupation of Afghanistan, denouncing it as an 'imperialist adventure', and for a time Sino-Soviet relations cooled even further. As the 1980s wore on, the Chinese regarded the Soviet Union with ever greater estrangement.

The conflict with Vietnam, 1960–80

The Vietnam War revealed much the same sort of picture. Here, South Vietnam received support from Kennedy and then from Johnson in its struggle with Ho Chi Minh, who headed an army from the north in his fight to free the country from foreign control and set up his own communist regime there.

The death of Ho Chi Minh in 1970 did not make the North Vietnamese any more inclined towards peace, and President Nixon renewed the American offensive, launching massive air strikes in the north and even in Cambodia, where there was a good deal of support for the nationalist cause. The offensive failed, however, and it was only after it had been abandoned that a ceasefire agreement was signed in 1973, under which US troops were to be withdrawn.

Throughout this time, North Vietnamese communists sought the support of China and the USSR. The Soviets responded, contributing a supply of armaments, tanks, trucks and aircraft parts. China was less enthusiastic. It had to overcome a long history of suspicion between China and Vietnam, and it was less than pleased with the promptness of the Soviet response – China even denied the Soviets the use of Chinese air-strips while they were flying in supplies.

When the war was over, Vietnam continued to be the object of Chinese suspicions. Vietnamese troops, having reunified the country, spilled over into neutral Laos and Cambodia (Kampuchea), and China was so upset that there was a short frontier war between China and Vietnam, from which it was the Chinese who had to retire first.

Worse still, in 1978 Vietnam signed a treaty of friendship with the Soviet Union, and thus became a 'Soviet pawn' in south-east Asia, as irritating to the Chinese as the Soviet 'pawn' in Cuba had been to the Americans.

China after Mao Zedong

In January 1976, Zhou Enlai died and was replaced as Premier by the almost unknown Hua Kuofeng. This was intended by Mao as a concession to strident voices on the 'left', who pressed for more radical and sweeping changes in line with their communist ideology, and who had recently brought about the fall of the much more populist Deng Xiaoping. Then, in September 1976, Mao himself died.

▷ **Repercussions of Mao's death**

Leadership changes

The 'right', or moderates, now felt themselves strong enough to order the arrest of prominent 'leftists', such as the *Gang of Four*, including Mao's wife, Jiang Qing (Chang Ching), herself. Hua Kuofeng slipped into Mao's job as Chairman, and brought back Deng Xaioping as Premier. Later he and his colleagues were replaced by other rightists, such as Li Xiannian, Zhao Ziyang and Hu Yaobang.

The political position became confused, especially since all these different groups called themselves the rightful heirs of Mao. One Chinese commentator at the time observed that 'when the snow thaws, the road becomes very muddy'.

Changes in external affairs

After the death of Mao, there was also significant change in China's relations with the outside world:

(a) China patched up its relations with the USA after 1971, and in that year was finally admitted to the United Nations, with a permanent seat on the Security Council in place of Taiwan (Nationalist China had still retained this from 1945).

(b) In 1987 China concluded the agreement to allow Hong Kong to rejoin China in 1997. As a result, China reached agreement with Britain and the USA for further financial and technical help.

(c) In 1985 China patched up its quarrels with Japan after 40 years without an official end to the war, when it agreed to employ the latest in Japanese techology, especially in the newer industries.

Domestic changes

After Mao's death, those who had been silenced by the Cultural Revolution had their revenge. The 'Gang of Four' was brought to trial by the 'rightists' for a long catalogue of crimes, including the charges they had themselves brought against their opponents in the 1960s. After a protracted trial a number were executed, though Jiang Qing's life was spared, presumably in anticipation of a recantation.

However, Deng himself was much less influenced by political theory than Mao had been – indeed, he was so little attached to political labels that he asked, 'What does it matter whether a cat is black or white so long as it catches mice?'

Hence there was some relaxation in China after Mao's death. For a while, more criticism of communist policies was permitted. In front of 'Democracy Wall' in Beijing – a stretch of wall set aside for political posters (or *dazibao*) – there was a sort of 'Speaker's Corner', where greater freedom showed itself in the open-air debates that took place.

Fig. 17.2 Democracy
Wall, Beijing

Industrially, vast new plants were being set up, like the Baoshan steel plant near Shanghai, and Deng was trying once again to attract foreign investment by offering special conditions to investors such as low rents and taxes, and in particular cheap labour with which to produce goods. Some people found such concessions distasteful, and reminiscent of earlier foreign privileges, but the Chinese leaders swallowed their pride in the interests of modernization.

Deng also allowed workers to return to the cities of the eastern seaboard, and a small measure of private enterprise began to reappear. Cash incentives also returned to economic life. State concerns became more market conscious and turned out fewer goods of shoddy quality. In the market place, a wider range of goods became available, and television sets and household appliances found their way into thousands of Chinese homes. By the 1980s, the government was even learning to look on tourists not as 'foreign devils', but as valuable sources of foreign currency.

▷ **The end of
the 1980s**

But perhaps liberalization went too fast for the older members of the Politburo. Freedom of speech, however reassuring to foreign observers, seemed threatening to many members of the Chinese leadership.

Domestic repression

The end of the 1980s produced student demonstrations which, far from urging on their leaders as they had during the Cultural Revolution, now seemed to threaten the whole basis of communist authority. These demonstrations turned to riots in which radical youngsters challenged the rule of the stumbling gerontocracy (the word is derived from the Greek for 'old man', and is an unkind way of referring to a government in the hands of doddering oldies).

This led to a sharp clampdown in Beijing, where tanks appeared on Tiananmen Square in the city in a confrontation with thousands of unarmed opponents. For a time the protesters had things their own way, and government forces seemed nonplussed by their reckless bravery.

But brute force eventually prevailed. Hundreds of rioters were killed and the rest dispersed as the rising was savagely put down. Thousands of arrests followed as the government tried to stamp out the embers of the revolt. The Chinese leaders, moved as much by panic as by harshness in their actions, created world hostility by their severity, not least on the part of China's future nationals in Hong Kong.

Foreign changes

The catastrophic collapse of Soviet communism in 1991 left the Chinese Politburo very much isolated as the sole remaining major communist power in the world. It might well have reacted by saying 'I told you so' to the Soviet leadership, having warned them for so long about the dangers of playing with capitalist fire; but by now Boris Yeltsin, in deep trouble on his own account, was impervious to their protests.

With the ideological foundations of communism irretrievably weakened, China faced a vexing dilemma: whether to persevere with the authoritarian course it had chosen for itself after Tiananmen Square, and so continue to face the world in isolation; or whether to risk further liberalization, and possibly bring down on its own head the fate that awaited the Soviet Union. In the mid-1990s, with Deng retired from public life, the Chinese Politburo had not yet had the courage to make up its mind.

 GLOSSARY

Autonomous Autonomous means self-governing, from the Greek word for self-rule. It usually applies to an area which is part of a larger state or union, but yet is virtually independent. Thus Tibetan opposition to communist China before 1959 usually claimed autonomy within China rather than complete independence.

Cadre This is a nucleus of regular soldiers in a regiment who are the best trained, and therefore the most reliable. By extension, communists apply the word to the hard core of party supporters who can be trusted to educate and lead other members or persuade waverers to join.

Confucius A Chinese thinker who lived from about 551 to 479 BC. He became Minister of Justice in Shandong Province, but his schemes for improving the lives of citizens were ignored by local rulers, and he wandered around China in search of a wise ruler who would put his ideas into practice. When he returned home, he set up a school in which his ideas were taught. His main concerns were love and respect for one's fellow-men, and the need for forgiveness and repentance. He was widely respected as the founding father of Chinese scholarship.

Maoism and Stalinism They are similar in that they both seek to apply in practice the ideas set out by Karl Marx. But they have significant differences; not simply differences that are based on national variations, but more fundamental ones:

(a) Stalinism was based on the urban proletariat – the railway workers, the factory workers and the town dwellers. Maoism is peasant based and is a rural communist movement originally independent of the towns. Mao believed that the cities were no more than 'the fish which swam in the sea of the peasantry'.

(b) Stalinism was inherited from Lenin's small body of dedicated communist leaders who organized a *coup d'état* in the cities and largely ignored rural opinion; Maoism was a spontaneous peasant rising, fighting a war of liberation under his leadership. This war was a guerrilla war. Mao observed that 'political power grows out of the barrel of a gun'.

(c) Stalinism was class based and was perhaps closer to Marxist theory than Maoism. Mao hesitated to make enemies of the Chinese bourgeoisie (middle class); he saw that they had their own parts to play in modernizing and strengthening the country. It was only if they acted disloyally to the revolution that he treated them as class enemies.

(d) Stalinism made extensive use of coercion and terror, e.g. with the show trials of the purges; Mao preferred to educate and persuade rather than to terrorize. Hence the great emphasis under Mao on thought reform, mutual criticism sessions, and analysis and discussion among comrades seeking the truth. Even opponents were sometimes persuaded of the error of their ways – it was the Chinese who first perfected the technique of what later became known as 'brainwashing'. Even so, former landlords and political dissidents suffered especially at the time of the Korean War. But Mao never approached Stalin's record in the ferocity of his terror.

(e) Stalin set perhaps too much store by the achievement of a high level of industrial output; Mao believed that 'economism' was the wrong road to follow. Maoism preferred to create 'new socialist man', a man who had the right attitude and beliefs; industrial production could come later, if it was really needed. To Mao, keeping up with the capitalist Joneses and competing for the consumer market – as Mao believed Khrushchev was doing after Stalin – seemed almost to be treachery to the true socialist ideal.

(f) Stalin tolerated, even encouraged, a high level of party bureaucracy, setting up a ruling clique which lost touch with its revolutionary roots. Mao saw this as ending in the same kind of tyranny as had existed under colonialism or landlordism – the rule of an unfeeling minority chiefly anxious to preserve its own privileges, powers and status. It was in order to prevent this from happening in China that Mao devised the Cultural Revolution.

Politburo   The ruling political committee of the Communist Party. The word is an abbreviation of the phrase 'political bureau'.

 ## EXAMINATION QUESTIONS

▷ **Question 1**

Source A

Fig. 17.3   Poster showing Chinese villagers engaged on a flood prevention scheme at the time of the Great Leap Forward

Study Source A and then answer the questions which follow.

(a) What can you learn from this source about the Great Leap Forward? (7 marks)

(b) Was the Great Leap Forward an 'utter and complete failure'? Explain your answer.
(13 marks)

▷ **Question 2** Study Sources A and B below, and then answer the questions which follow.

Source A

Those in command of the Red Guards, according to material posted around the city, are now trying to restrain their 'extreme' actions which have aroused discontent among the people and created an 'unfavourable international impression'. The beatings and killings of workers, party cadres, and the attacks on foreigners are now said to have been the result of 'provocations by bad people', although the press has repeatedly called the activity of the Red Guards 'completely legal' and 'revolutionary'. (*Pravda*, Moscow, 23 September 1966)

Source B

I was once called to attend a 'denunciation meeting'. Horror made me feel very chilly in the hot summer afternoon when I saw a dozen or so teachers standing on the platform on the sports ground, with their heads bent and their arms twisted into the 'jet plane' position. Then, some were kicked on the back of their knees and forced to kneel, while others, including my English-language teacher, an elderly man with the fine manners of a gentleman, were forced to stand on long, narrow benches. He found it hard to keep his balance, and swayed and fell, cutting his forehead. A Red Guard, with fists clenched, yelled 'Get back on to the bench!' He did not want to be seen as soft on a 'class enemy'. Blood trickled down the teacher's forehead. (Jung Chang, *Wild Swans: Three Daughters of China*, 1993)

(a) Which would you regard as the more reliable evidence, Source A or Source B? Give reasons for your answer. (10 marks)

(b) To what extent is Source A supported by Source B? (8 marks)

(c) Was the Cultural Revolution merely an attempt by Mao to make his position stronger? Explain your answer. (12 marks)

(d) Why did the Cultural Revolution come to an end? (10 marks)

 EXAMINATION ANSWERS

▷ **Question 1** *Outline answer*

(a) The poster gives an impression of strength: of the muscular giant in the foreground, and the feverish activity going on in the background. The smile indicates a degree of self-satisfaction, from which it can be assumed that the other workers shown were in happy spirits also. But note that the flood control depends absolutely on labour. There is no heavy machinery to be seen in this poster. You might also query whether, since it seemed necessary to the authorities to issue this poster, it portrays things as they really were. If nothing else, it could have been intended as a morale booster.

(b) The Great Leap Forward is best remembered for the poor-quality steel of its back-yard furnaces, and for communes so stretched and diversified that they could not provide the labour to save the crops in the agricultural disasters of the early 1960s. It could be argued that the Great Leap Forward was an economic failure, but that the communes achieved a great deal in terms of social welfare, health, education and the eradication of antiquated and harmful customs. In so far as it accustomed the local peasantry to cooperation and self-sufficiency, it could well have paved the way for future progress.

▷ **Question 2(a)**   *Tutor answer*

Source A was published in *Pravda*, the official Soviet Communist Party newspaper, after the split between the Soviet and Chinese communists. As *Pravda* was noted for its propagandist reporting, it is unlikely that this report would make any attempt to be impartial, so its reliability must be in doubt. Moreover, what *Pravda* reports is not first hand. It gleaned its information from 'materials posted around the city', and the second part of the text is a commentary on events rather than a reporting of events. The attitude of Moscow is clear in its rejection of the Chinese attempt to explain away the killings. Source B is obviously an eyewitness account. Its author may well be prejudiced by her experience, but despite its emotional overtones, there is no need to query the basic account of the ill-treatment of teachers by the Red Guards. Eyewitness accounts are not necessarily more reliable than other versions, but unless their authenticity is in doubt, they are the basic sources from which to reconstruct an account of historical events.

▷ **Question 2(b)**   *Tutor answer*

Source A talks of the extreme actions of the Red Guards, and this is confirmed in Source B where the action of the Guards against the teachers appears to be extreme in its use of humiliation and intimidation. Source A talks of the actions arousing discontent among the people, and although Source B does not specifically state this, the author's own attitude towards the events described is one of 'horror' and disapproval. The 'beatings and killings' referred to in Source A are not confirmed in Source B, but the Red Guard referred to there certainly appears brutal and unfeeling. Nor does Source B refer to the cadres and foreigners mentioned in Source A. The implication in Source A that the Red Guard activities are anything but 'legal' and 'revolutionary' seems to be borne out by the specific instance reported in Source B. Thus although *Pravda* has its own axe to grind in commenting unfavourably on the Cultural Revolution, such accounts as that of Source B serve to confirm its overall contention.

▷ **Question 2(c)**   *Student answer with examiner's comments*

'Try to give his full name, Liu Shaoqi.'

'Why not? You need to develop and explain this assertion.'

After the Great Leap Forward its critics came to the fore in Chinese politics, and Mao retired from the Presidency. By 1965 moderate leaders were in command, and Liu was often given equal precedence with Mao in official documents. Mao was probably not happy with a less commanding role, especially as the new leaders seemed to Mao to be consolidating bureaucracy and making the same sort of mistakes as Khrushchev in Russia. The impetus for the Cultural Revolution can hardly have been spontaneous. It follows that there must have been some sort of driving force to set it in motion. If Mao was alarmed that the Revolution was running out of steam and that he needed to do something about it before he was side-lined altogether, then it was more than merely making his position stronger. He wanted to give new energy to the Revolution, and he could only do that by resuming his leading role in Chinese politics. So he proved he was intellectually the best leader by his little Red Book, and that he was physically up to it by his much publicised swims in the Yangze. At the end of it bureaucracy and the moderates were routed and Mao was back in command.

Examiner's making scheme for 2(c)
Level 1: simplistic and/or generalized agreement/disagreement   (1–3 marks)
Level 2: narrative answers which describe events leading to the Cultural Revolution, or describe the Cultural Revolution itself   (4–6 marks)
Level 3: answers offer several reasons for the Cultural Revolution and relate them to Mao   (7–9 marks)

Level 4: answers focus sharply on the question, offering several factors for the Cultural Revolution and relating them to the contention in the question.   (10–12 marks)

Examiner's decision on the student answer

A sharply focused and well-argued answer which must be Level 4. But it is a little thin in offering substantiating evidence, so it would probably score 10/12.

▷ Question 2(d)   *Student answer with examiner's comments*

> *Ran out of time*

Examiner's decision on the student answer

This is inexcusable. After a good attempt at (c), 10 marks have been thrown away. It is essential to plan carefully the use of examination time.

SUMMARY

In this chapter, you have learned about:

▷   the early political, economic and social policies of Mao Zedong;

▷   the 'Great Leap Forward' and the Cultural Revolution;

▷   social reforms and the changing role of women;

▷   Chinese foreign policy under Mao;

▷   political and social changes after the death of Mao.

Further information on the Vietnam War and on the Sino-Soviet split is to be found in chapter 18.

The end of the Cold War

GETTING STARTED

Until the 1960s, the Cold War was a straightforward affair between the communist East and what its opponents in the West liked to call the 'Free World', i.e. the capitalist United States and its numerous allies in western Europe and elsewhere. The scales were unfairly weighted: the United States was vastly rich and could subsidize its allies when it needed; and it could always command massive support in the United Nations, where it took pains for many years to exclude communist China. But then the international balance subtly began to change.

MEG	NEAB	NICCEA	SEG	LONDON	WJEC	TOPIC	STUDY	REVISION 1	REVISION 2
✓	✓	✓	✓	✓	✓	**The Sino-Soviet split**			
✓	✓	✓	✓	✓	✓	Sino-Soviet relations after 1945			
✓	✓	✓	✓	✓	✓	The crisis in Sino-Soviet relations in the 1950s			
✓	✓	✓	✓	✓	✓	The Cold War triangle in the 1960s			
✓		✓	✓	✓	✓	**The war in Vietnam, 1963–73**			
✓		✓	✓	✓	✓	The end of French rule			
✓		✓	✓	✓	✓	The beginnings of US intervention			
✓		✓	✓	✓	✓	The United States and the war in Vietnam			
✓		✓	✓	✓	✓	**The arms race and disarmament**			
✓	✓	✓	✓	✓	✓	The build-up of the arms race			
✓		✓	✓	✓	✓	The beginnings of international agreement			
✓		✓	✓	✓	✓	**The end of the Cold War**			

WHAT YOU NEED TO KNOW

The Sino-Soviet split

▷ **Sino-Soviet relations after 1945**

Originally Stalin underestimated the Chinese communists, preferring to link himself with nationalist movements as part of his struggle against western colonialism. Thus he allied himself with Jiang Jie Shi and paid little attention to Mao's efforts to set up an alternative government. After 1950, however, he sent Soviet troops into Manchuria against the Japanese and began to see the advantages of cooperating with Mao to build communist power there.

Stalin's alliance with Mao

After the People's Republic of China was set up, Stalin in 1950 signed a 30-year *Treaty of Friendship and Alliance* with Mao, and soon began to agitate for the admission of communist China into the United Nations in place of the nationalist Jiang, who in effect now ruled only Taiwan.

There began about fifteen years of close and cordial cooperation between the USSR and China:

(a) Stalin supplied technical and scientific expertise in the development of new Chinese industries, sending Soviet advisers and providing the Chinese with substantial rouble credits. It was only after the death of Stalin that Mao began to question the highly centralized planning which his ally seemed to prefer.
(b) It seems unlikely that Kim Il Sung consulted extensively with either Mao or Stalin before launching the invasion of South Korea in 1950; both of them seem to have taken his word that his invasion would be short and easy.
(c) Indeed, Stalin was so ill-informed about the progress of the war that he allowed Soviet representatives to absent themselves from the Security Council, where as a major power they had a veto, in protest at the exclusion of communist China from membership – thus allowing the USA to rush through a resolution involving UNO in the Korean War.
(d) Stalin sent limited help, including a number of MIG fighters, to Korea; but generally he seems to have regarded the war as Mao's affair rather than his own.
(e) Stalin did, however, agree to withdraw Soviet forces from Manchuria – he had better uses for them in Europe – and afterwards handed over the Liaotung Peninsula and Port Arthur to Mao. (The USSR first acquired Port Arthur from China in 1898, but lost it to Japan in 1905; it was recovered from Japan only in 1945.)

Cooling relations between China and the Soviet Union

Communist China, however, was much larger and stronger than the Soviet Union's satellites in eastern Europe, and soon showed itself to be less than submissive to Stalin's efforts at control. Indeed, Stalin often had to defer to Mao's wishes rather than the other way round.

This was partly due to the fact that Mao did not fully sympathize with Stalin's aim of westernization: this for him was a long way off, if he wanted it at all.

It was only after Stalin's death in 1953 that Mao emerged as one of his champions, comparing the new leadership very unfavourably with him.

▷ **The crisis in Sino-Soviet relations in the 1950s**

The breakdown came in the course of domestic changes in the USSR brought about as a result of the death of Stalin.

Khrushchev and the twentieth party congress, 1956

At this congress, Khrushchev caused considerable surprise by attacking Stalin's character as leader of the Soviet Communist Party. He listed a number of criticisms of Stalin:

(a) He denounced him as authoritarian, egoistic and brutal, and guilty of glorifying himself by a 'cult of the personality'.
(b) He thought his thinking was rigid and old-fashioned, and that he was too much concerned with conflict and obsessed by the 'inevitable revolution'.
(c) Khrushchev himself rejected the inevitability of war. He thought that there was more than one 'road to socialism' and that 'co-existence' with the capitalist West was possible. In any case, he believed that the Soviet Union in a fair fight could beat the West at its own game ('We will bury you!')

All this was unwelcome in China. Mao was of the same generation as Stalin and cast in much the same mould. He levelled against Khrushchev the same kind of charge of 'deviationism' as Stalin had levelled against his opponents. Furthermore, he thought that by hobnobbing with western leaders and pandering to consumerism in the USSR, he was behaving altogether too much like the people whom it should have been his duty to denounce.

Mao even complained that Khrushchev was altering the character of Soviet state power and changing the state back into an instrument whereby 'a handful of privileged bourgeois elements exercise dictatorship over the mass of Soviet workers and peasants'. This was clearly an echo of Mao's fear of technocrats.

The break with the Soviet Union

Mao's criticisms of Khrushchev steadily mounted. When Khrushchev was crushing resistance movements in Poland and Hungary in the mid-1950s, Mao told him that his troubles were of his own making, and that his repression of socialist countries smacked more of imperialist than of communist motives.

In particular, Mao was doubtful about the idea of co-existence. He feared that the only way to come to terms with capitalism was to sell out to it, and this is what he thought Khrushchev was doing. He fumed when Khrushchev in his earthy peasant style made fun of him; he believed that Khrushchev stood condemned out of his own mouth when he criticized the simple notion of equality with the words: 'If a people walks in rope sandals and eats watery soup out of a common bowl, that is Communism, but if a working man lives well and hopes to live even better tomorrow, that's almost as much as restoring capitalism!'

Khrushchev vigorously defended co-existence, too, pointing out the need to avoid a 'doomsday' conflict and observing dryly: 'As for US imperialism being a "paper tiger", those who employ the phrase know quite well that the paper tiger is equipped with atomic teeth.'

Mao also resented Khrushchev's scepticism about the success of the Great Leap Forward, and believed that his decision to withdraw Soviet advisers from China in 1960 was pretty vindictive – even though he himself had been singularly ungracious about accepting help and was frequently critical of Soviet planning methods.

The Bucharest Conference, 1960, and its results

The problem came into the open at an international conference of communist parties held in Bucharest in 1960, when Khrushchev made no secret of his conversion to co-existence. He spelt out how East–West relations were changing, and explained how the communist powers ought to react to the new situation.

The Chinese delegates, on the other hand, emphasized the continuing danger from the capitalist powers. They said they believed that 'the competition between the United States and the Soviet Union had subsided because of the intrusion of China'.

As a result, Mao agreed with the 'hardliners' in the USSR in welcoming the fall of Khrushchev in October 1964.

Sino-Soviet relations under Brezhnev

The accession to power of Kosygin and Brezhnev did not make much difference to Soviet policies, and negotiations between Moscow and Washington were soon resumed. The Soviet press began once more to criticize China, while the Chinese complained bitterly of 'the anti-China atrocities of the new Tsars ... their Fascist heel tramples the motherland'.

Differences showed themselves in skirmishes along the border with China in Manchuria, the most serious clashes being along the Yussuri River, and on the borders of Kazakhstan, where Chinese defences were strengthened (see chapter 17).

Ill-will was also revealed in 1968, with the Czechoslovak crisis.

▷ **The Cold War triangle in the 1960s**

While he was quarrelling with the USSR, Mao was keeping up his campaign of propaganda against the western powers, so that what had been a two-way confrontation between East and West now developed into a triangular dispute.

The Czechoslovak crisis, 1968

After the rule of Czechoslovakia's strong man, Antonin Novotny, from 1957 to 1968, an attempt was made to distribute his powers more widely. General Svoboda became President, Alexander Dubcek Party Secretary and Oldrich Cernik Prime Minister.

Dubcek sought to produce what he called 'socialism with a human face' in Czechoslovakia, with more contacts with the West, a more liberal regime and less centralized planning.

This was popular with the Czechs, but aroused sharp criticism from the country's Warsaw Pact allies.

In August 1968 they ordered their troops into Czechoslovakia, and there was a brief, bloodless confrontation on the streets of Prague between puzzled tank captains and gesticulating unarmed mobs of Czech protesters.

Eventually, in an agreement signed in Moscow, Dubcek was obliged to renounce the dollar loans he had been offered by the USA, and to reverse his recent policy trends towards neutrality in foreign affairs and less rigid economic planning.

He was replaced by Gustav Husak as Party Secretary and steadily downgraded, first as Czech Ambassador to Turkey, and finally as a clerk in a woodyard. It was not a complete victory for the hardliners, however, since Svoboda and Husak still continued to introduce reforms, but this time more stealthily.

During the crisis, Brezhnev introduced what came to be called the *Brezhnev Doctrine*, claiming the right to intervene in neighbouring states in order to preserve communism. Mao took the strongest objection to such interference in sovereign states.

Mao's reconciliation with the USA

It was perhaps surprising that, at the time of the Vietnam War, President Nixon and Chairman Mao should come diplomatically closer than ever before.

Nixon was essentially a pragmatist who wanted to come to terms with China's real rulers rather than with Jiang Jie Shi in Taiwan. He wanted to pre-empt any possible help for North Vietnam from Beijing; in any case, he realized that the USA could no longer hope to 'contain' China as it had tried to do in Truman's day.

Mao simultaneously concluded that his quarrel with the USSR had left him isolated, and a deal with the USA would put an end to that, and at the same time allow his entry into the United Nations. He too placed pragmatism before ideology.

Restrictions on trade and travel were relaxed in 1971, and an American table-tennis team visited China in April, where they were promptly trounced by the Chinese. Shortly afterwards:

(a) This so-called *ping-pong diplomacy* was followed in July by the visit of Henry Kissinger, US Secretary of State, to Beijing, and in 1972 by the visit of Nixon himself, beginning the slow repair of relations between the two countries.
(b) The USA agreed to admit communist China to the UN, with a permanent seat on the Security Council; at the same time Taiwan was removed.

Mao had always insisted that US support must be withdrawn from the nationalists if relations were to improve. In 1975 Jiang Jie Shi died, followed by Mao himself in 1976. Quite suddenly, in 1978, the two powers reached agreement, and full diplomatic relations were resumed.

Deng Xaioping visited Washington in 1979, and American businessmen went off to China in search of promising new markets.

The Soviets showed some uncertainty over this. They applauded the admission of China to the UN – they had been pressing for it for 20 years! – but Brezhnev saw the USA–China grouping as a potential threat to the Soviet Union, or at least an attempt to disrupt more friendly relations between the USA and the USSR.

The war in Vietnam, 1963–73

After 1945, the French Empire in Indochina soon came to an end: encouraged by the Japanese, the local inhabitants of the French colony of Cochin China and various nearby protectorates aimed to create an independent state of Vietnam.

▷ **The end of French rule**

The attempt to recreate French control

Around Hanoi, the French had to contend with the nationalist leader Ho Chi Minh and and his followers, known as the Viet Minh. In 1945, Ho wanted to unite Cochin China with neighbouring territories as a new state of Vietnam, and at first the French seemed willing to go along with this.

France desired continuing links with the area, but Ho would not accept this, and in 1946 fighting began.

In 1950 France agreed to grant independence to Vietnam, Laos and Cambodia, provided they were willing to remain in the *French Union*, which was the new name given by the Fourth Republic to the former colonial possessions. The French proposed to make their former puppet in Annam, Bao Dai, Emperor of this independent Vietnam.

Ho rejected this solution as well, and fighting continued around Hanoi.

The end of French rule in Vietnam, 1954

A seasoned and well-equipped French army continued to fight for four years against a wily and elusive group of guerrillas. In May 1954 this army was penned up in Dien Bien Phu, supplied only by drops from the air after the loss of its air-strip, and forced to surrender with all its arms and equipment.

A conference had already met in Geneva to discuss the future of Vietnam, and France now had to accept the independence of the area:

(a) Cambodia was under Prince Sihanouk, and was still a member of the French Union.
(b) Laos was also independent, though here there was a power struggle between the nationalists and the communists, which the nationalists temporarily won.
(c) Vietnam was divided at the 17th parallel between communist North Vietnam under Ho Chi Minh and the south under Bao Dai. Later elections, under UN supervision, were suggested to bring about reunification. In the meantime about 900,000 people from the north (chiefly Catholics) moved to the south, and about 100,000 from south to north.

▷ The beginnings of US intervention

US aid under President Eisenhower

In 1955, the USA undertook the protection of South Vietnam and began to provide help. Shortly afterwards Bao Dai, whose corrupt and inefficient dictatorship had become an embarrassment, was deposed as the result of a referendum, and a new republic was proclaimed with Ngo Dinh Diem as President.

Diem's government, however, did not please everybody; in particular, it failed to build up popular resistance to communist propaganda or ease the burdens of the poverty-stricken South Vietnamese peasantry.

Diem's opponents formed the *National Liberation Front* in 1960, with support from the north. The NLF was not exclusively communist. It aimed to end US interference in Vietnamese affairs; its military wing was known as the *Vietcong*.

In particular, Diem failed to win over the Buddhist voters who formed the majority of the country. When he forbade the flying of Buddhist flags, a Buddhist monk publicly burned himself to death in protest, soon to be followed by others.

By 1963, Diem had lost even the confidence of his US supporters, and he was deposed in a coup and later murdered. There followed a swift succession of eight different governments between 1963 and 1965.

Increasing US involvement under President Kennedy

During this period of anarchy, the United States found itself increasingly sucked into Vietnamese affairs. Kennedy sent about 17,000 'advisers' to the country, followed by military equipment and then large numbers of helicopters.

Even so, by 1965, the Vietcong controlled about 40 per cent of South Vietnam, and the decision was taken to commit US troops to the struggle.

By the early days of the Johnson presidency, the USA found itself responsible for the defence of the country. It successfully sought the support of its ANZUS allies (Australia and New Zealand), which sent military contingents, but Britain declined to become involved. Anticipating a Soviet veto in the Security Council, the USA did not refer the problem to the UN and blocked the efforts of other powers to do so.

President Johnson and the Vietnam War

Gradually Johnson increased the numbers of US servicemen in South Vietnam until by the end of the 1960s there were well over half a million, together with 50,000 troops contributed by his allies.

Johnson felt sure that such a massive force of men and armour would speedily stamp out resistance and restore what he regarded as the 'rightful' government of the country. What he failed to recognize was that this was a war entirely different from the wars that the American army was good at fighting.

▷ **The United States and the war in Vietnam**

Increasing US involvement in the Vietnam War under President Johnson

Johnson, on military advice, tried to establish heavily defended fortresses with US garrisons from which the surrounding countryside could be kept under control.

But these were not conventional enemies fighting with conventional tactics; the forces of the Vietcong were as difficult to recognize as they were to defeat. After an engagement they simply melted into the countryside and disappeared.

Johnson also embarked on a systematic bombing of targets in North Vietnam, assuming that Ho Chi Minh was the main mover behind the Vietcong, and that after aerial punishment he would simply call off the war.

Considerable damage was done to Hanoi and Haiphong, the north accusing the USAAF of indiscriminate terror bombing; but it soon became clear that air attack was a strategy not likely to succeed. The Vietcong, on the other hand, had no air support, but fought only in small guerrilla groups, avoiding direct confrontation with US armour and artillery.

After 1965, South Vietnam was under the control of a new President, General Nguyen Van Thieu and a *National Leadership Committee*. But the committee's leadership was totally inadequate, and soon the USA found itself fighting the war on its own.

Johnson went for what he called 'a quick kill' against what the GIs called 'a bunch of Asian guerrillas in black pyjamas', but victory proved to be elusive. In the course of the struggle, over 70 tons of bombs were dropped for every square mile in the country, defoliants were employed on a devastating scale and 'search and destroy' missions produced enormous casualties (sometimes of innocent civilians, as in the case of the My Lai massacre, March 1968).

Nevertheless, in 1968 the Vietcong launched a dramatic counterattack called the *Tet offensive*, when they surged into the South Vietnamese cities and for a time actually captured the US Embassy in Saigon. However, the switch to open warfare caused the Vietcong heavy casualties. The American General Westmorland insisted that 'the enemy is on the ropes', and said that 200,000 more GIs would finish him off, but Johnson was so sickened by the opposition he faced at home that he agreed to stop the bombing in return for Ho's promise to open peace talks in Paris, and later decided not to run for re-election as President that year.

President Nixon and the end of the Vietnam War

Nixon, who had made numerous promises to end the war, now found himself unable to deliver. The peace talks dragged on and even the death of Ho Chi Minh in 1970 did not break the deadlock.

Nixon had already been driven to find another solution: one in which he tried to make the South Vietnamese take responsibility for their own war, a policy which he called *Vietnamization*. By 1970 the number of US troops in Vietnam had been cut by 50 per cent, but South Vietnamese efforts were quite unavailing, and the Vietcong were well on the way to completing their conquest.

Nixon was therefore compelled to redouble his efforts:

(a) He renewed his bombing campaign of the north in the hope of 'bombing the communists to the conference table'.
(b) He launched air attacks against Cambodia, through which ran the *Ho Chi Minh Trail*, the supply route along which support came for the Vietcong.
(c) He blockaded the north, dropping mines from the air to mine their ports.
(d) He increased his own supply of aid to the south.

Fig. 18.1 'If this boy of yours is real, how come we gotta wind him up all the time?' Cartoon from the *Guardian*, 3 May 1972

Eventually a ceasefire was arranged for January 1973, and the USA withdrew its troops and advisers. One of the last helicopters to lift off from the US Embassy in Saigon took with it the South Vietnamese gold reserves, and the city was left to the tender mercies of the incoming Vietcong. Order, however, was soon restored, and by 1975 North and South Vietnam were reunited under communist control, and a flow of refugees from the south (the 'boat people') departed often in unseaworthy craft for Hong Kong, where they were promptly interned.

The 'domino effect', by which an irresistible slide towards communism was predicted by US observers if the Vietnam War was lost, was anxiously awaited, but never in fact developed.

The arms race and disarmament

The arms race was a good deal easier to start than it was to stop. It began at the end of the Second World War, when the USA used the first atomic bombs against Japan. After that, nuclear destruction threatened the world for nearly half a century.

▷ **The build-up of the arms race**

The development of new bombs

Truman did not intend to share atomic secrets with Stalin, but hoped to use his scientific expertise to consolidate America's world position. When Stalin discovered Truman's feelings about him, his suspicions of the western world hardened, and relations between them gradually developed into a Cold War.

In 1949, the Soviets, exploiting pro-Soviet sympathies on the part of a handful of western scientists, gained atomic secrets, and developed and tested their own A-bomb, thus cancelling out the tactical advantage previously possessed by the West.

Things grew worse in 1953 when both the USA and the USSR tested the hydrogen bomb (H-bomb), many times more destructive than its predecessor. The USA, which had been stockpiling nuclear devices for a longer time than the USSR, still held the advantage; on balance, however, there was a kind of parity between them, since Soviet conventional weaponry – troops, tanks and aircraft – had a clear lead.

There was some relaxation on the death of Stalin, but competition soon asserted itself once more with the Soviet repression of the Hungarian revolt in 1956.

Rocket technology

In 1958 the USSR scored two significant triumphs:

(a) The testing of an *inter-continental ballistic missile* (ICBM), designed to carry an atomic warhead several thousand kilometres, threatened the USA with direct attack on its territories for the first time.
(b) The launching of Sputnik I put the Soviet Union ahead in the space race. Although as yet it had no military significance, it enabled the Soviet Union to put the first man, Yuri Gagarin, into space in 1961.

Under pressure, the Americans began to develop the *intermediate-range ballistic missile* (IRBM), and soon a number of NATO allies agreed to have such weapons stationed on their soil.

They also began to develop 'second-strike' weapons to make possible retaliation against a Soviet first attack. Retaliatory missies were hidden deep in massive concrete 'silos'; some were even sent to sea in Polaris submarines, where the Soviet authorities would be unable to locate them.

Soon there was a furious competition between the two blocs, and a nuclear 'stand-off' ensued, i.e. a situation in which both sides hesitated to attack the other for fear of the consequences. This came to be known as 'mutual assured destruction', or MAD for short. This stalemate meant, fortunately, that both sides drew back from the 'doomsday scenario' at the last moment rather than risk a conflict, as was seen at the time of the Cuban missile crisis in 1962.

▷ **The beginnings of international agreement**

Consequences of the Cuban missile crisis

When Kennedy and Khrushchev clashed over the siting of ICBMs in Cuba, world disaster threatened, but the two turned to negotiation instead of annihilation and the affair was settled peacefully. The crisis resulted in:

(a) the setting up in July 1963 of a Washington–Moscow telephone 'hot-line', so that the two sides could avert the possibility of a nuclear war by accident;
(b) a *Nuclear Test Ban Treaty* in 1963, ending all forms of testing except those carried out underground, where there was less chance of nuclear 'fallout';
(c) a *Non-Proliferation Treaty* in 1968, designed to prevent nuclear weapons falling into the hands of the smaller powers, which might be tempted to use them with less restraint. Such a motive continues to exist at the present time.

In fact a number of lesser powers, such as India, Israel and South Africa, later 'joined the nuclear club', though both China and France refused to do so. With France, the question was one mainly of prestige and of wishing to be in the forefront of nuclear research; with China there was the underlying feeling that China was so vast that it could survive the doomsday conflict longer than the West.

Later arms limitation agreements

In 1969 Johnson and Brezhnev renewed their negotiations, embarking at Helsinki on *Strategic Arms Limitation Talks* (or SALT) to place upper limits on the number of weapons they deployed. They eventually initialled an agreement on the subject.

As it became clear that such agreements could work, and as the budgetary costs of arms programmes mounted, agreements between East and West were taken further:

(a) President Nixon extended the scope of SALT talks with Brezhnev in his state visit to Moscow in 1972.
(b) President Ford reduced the permitted numbers of such weapons further in talks with the Soviet leadership in Vladivostok in 1975.
(c) President Carter reduced the numbers further in a more comprehensive agreement in Vienna in 1979, in the form of what became known as SALT 2.

The Reagan–Gorbachev negotiations, 1986–87

After the Soviets had invaded Afghanistan in 1980, however, cooperation between the major powers was halted. The new Republican President of the USA, Ronald Reagan, refused to ratify the suggested treaty, and the two sides squared up to each other once again.

All the same there were increasingly serious problems over the arms race:

(a) The heavy cost of rearmament problems was a grave burden, especially for the Soviet Union, whose whole financial stability was threatened by an increase in the military budget from $45 billion per year to over $70 billion.
(b) US technology developed with frightening speed: in the 1970s there was the *Multiple Independently-targeted Re-entry Vehicle* (MIRV) which threatened to shower a wide spread of targets with separately guided warheads from the same missile; and in the 1980s there was the so-called *Strategic Defense Initiative* (SDI, often referred to by reference to a popular current movie as 'Star Wars'), embodying a science-fiction plan to intercept incoming missiles and destroy them before they arrived.

In 1982, talks were resumed, this time under the name of *Strategic Arms Reduction Talks* (or START). The results at the first round in Geneva were slight, but in 1986, in meetings between Reagan and the new Soviet leader, Mikhail Gorbachev, at Reykjavik, the Soviets put forward proposals so radical that Reagan found them impossible to accept.

However, in Washington in 1987, talks were renewed and wide cuts were agreed, though still less than those demanded by Gorbachev; and agreements were initialled to come into operation at once.

It was, however, only the complete collapse of the Soviet Union in 1991 that really heralded any permanent improvement in East–West relations.

The end of the Cold War

▷ **Reform in the USSR and eastern Europe**

There were slight signs of change in the Soviet Union during the 1980s, though it would have taken more cunning than most western observers possessed to make any predictions about it. In 1982, the moribund Brezhnev eventually passed away, and the rule of the Soviet 'hardliners' continued with two brief spells of power, the first of Yuri Andropov (1982–84) and the second of Constantin Chernenko (1984–85). Then in 1985 Mikhail Gorbachev succeeded as Party Chairman at the comparatively youthful age of 54, and a new spirit of reform swept through the Kremlin.

Political changes at the accession of Gorbachev

Quite suddenly the USSR opened up to new styles of thinking. The catchwords were:

(a) *glasnost*, or openness – the Soviet Union was not so utterly dedicated to secrecy as previously;
(b) *perestroika*, or restructuring – the 'jobs for the boys' style of the former privileged *nomenklatura* (the party big-wigs) was changed, and party appointments were now made on grounds of ability and efficiency.

The state was opened up to debate and criticism. The dead wood in the political and economic planning systems was swept away, and there was new attention to results.

The warnings of the 'conservatives' in the Politburo that Gorbachev was sawing off the branch he was sitting on were ignored, and at first his changes worked.

Soviet 'liberals' began to trust Gorbachev and to believe that he could deliver results. At Reykjavik the charismatic Chairman Gorbachev (soon to be President) outshone the former film-star Ronald Reagan, and embarked on the task of lightening the burden of Soviet nuclear armaments.

Soon the powers of the secret police, the endless red tape and the obsessive secrecy of the Soviet system were lessened, and Gorbachev was beginning to explain himself and his policies in terms that were unusually honest.

Suddenly the USA and the USSR, bitter enemies for two generations, found themselves on a common path. No one was watching, but Stalin and Mao, so long prophets of conflict and destruction, may have turned over in their graves.

Changes in the eastern European bloc

Simultaneously, trouble developed in the states of eastern Europe, where discontent had simmered below the surface for many years. From time to time it showed itself, and was usually ruthlessly supressed as it had been during the Prague Spring in 1968. Communist leaders like Erich Honecker in East Germany reacted in the only way they knew by clamping down on any protest.

Gorbachev's attitude, when he visited these countries, was one of mild encouragement to the reform process. Two results followed: the eastern European peoples were encouraged to become bolder in their demands, and their leadership began to feel that the Soviet leader had pulled the rug out from under them and was denying them the support they felt they deserved.

Cracks soon began to appear in the eastern European monolith:

(a) Restrictions between East and West Germany were relaxed in 1989; the Berlin Wall was breached and then dismantled altogether.
(b) Poland moved towards democratic elections in 1990, and the communist leader was replaced by a genuinely elected figure, Lech Walesa, formerly a worker and trade union representative in the Gdansk shipyard.
(c) Popular governments replaced the old communist leaders in Czechoslovakia and Hungary, and were endorsed in free elections.
(d) In Romania, one of the most repressive communist regimes was overthrown, and the dictator Nicolae Ceauşescu and his wife were tried and summarily executed, and their bodies were exultantly displayed on TV. Even in Albania the forces of change were seen at work.

In 1991, the Warsaw Pact, for so long the cement holding eastern Europe together, was finally wound up, its partners concurring in Gorbachev's request for 'the liquidation of the Warsaw Pact military structures by 1 April'.

In place of the *Brezhnev Doctrine*, which prescribed intervention for the better preservation of communist regimes, it now appeared that the states of eastern Europe were moving towards the Sinatra Doctrine ('I did it my way').

As the fog of communism lifted, the outline of a new eastern Europe began to emerge, with nationalistic forces replacing those of communism. For the first time, people in the West saw communism as a force for stability – even tranquillity – in eastern Europe. Only time would tell whether the new forces of nationalism would prove themselves in the long run to be aiming at harmony or conflict.

Changes in the Soviet Union

The Soviet Union was not immune to the nationalist virus. Outlying states like the Baltic republics and Moldova, never entirely happy with their shotgun marriage with the Soviet Union, clamoured for freedom, soon to be followed by others like the Ukraine and Belorussia.

Half-hearted attempts were made by Gorbachev to allay discontent. He hovered between concession and repression, as in the military crackdown in Lithuania in January 1991. But for the most part, seeing the need for radical change, he was already more than halfway to recognizing the justice of nationalist claims.

The KGB, the Soviet army and the conservatives in the Kremlin were alarmed, their pride and self-esteem (not to mention their jobs) threatened by the sudden disintegration of the Soviet system. They blustered and threatened the breakaway states with violence and repression.

In 1991 there was an attempted coup against Gorbachev. This failed, not so much because of his own strength as because of the stout resistance put up against the communist hardliners responsible for the coup by Boris Yeltsin, now the elected President of the Russian Republic.

In the wake of the coup, the Soviet Union faded away altogether: the Hammer-and-Sickle flag was hauled down for the last time, and the constituent states went on to try to work out new relationships between themselves and the newly established *Commonwealth of Independent States* (CIS) which replaced it.

These relations were not always harmonious. Breakaway efforts by formerly federated states continued and were a grave headache for Boris Yeltsin, as could be seen from the long and bloody separatist war in the southern state of Chechnya in the Caucasus in 1995–96.

 GLOSSARY

Co-existence The possibility that, instead of resorting to conflict, opposing ideologies or states can come to a compromise together and learn to live in relative harmony side by side; a way of accepting differences without going to the lengths of war.

Deviationism A variation from the normally accepted ideas of a policy or political doctrine (usually communism). Where, as in communism, strict adherence to every detail of political teaching is important, deviationism is regarded as a serious political crime.

Domino theory The view that the knocking over of one domino (country) to the communists would in turn lead to the knocking over of neighbouring dominoes (countries), so that in the end the whole area would become communist. Resistance to such possibilities in the 1960s and 1970s was a favourite way of 'containing' the growth of communism. Domino theorists believed it was vitally important to prevent the first domino from being knocked over, as in the case of Korea or Vietnam.

Hardliners and revisionists Those who interpret a policy or a political doctrine strictly and do not allow the smallest deviation from it are said to be 'hardliners'; those who adopt a more flexible approach, and permit such things to be revised, updated and adjusted, are said to be 'revisionists'.

Hawks and doves 'Hawks' are usually regarded as fierce birds of prey showing little inclination to spare their victims, while 'doves' are more placid and peaceful, and prefer a quieter life. Hawks are full of warlike words and gestures even if they stop short of war; doves prefer conciliatory language and talk of peace.

Multilateral/unilateral For a policy (such as disarmament) to be carried out multilaterally, it is carried out in accordance with the terms of an agreement between a number of powers; for it to be carried out unilaterally, it is carried out on its own by a single power. A country which disarms unilaterally disarms regardless of whether other powers disarm or not. Most countries are unwilling to disarm unilaterally because they believe it would deprive them of bargaining counters in the event of negotiations for multilateral disarmament.

Pragmatism The pursuit of what is possible rather than what is ideally desirable. Thus capitalist countries may think it ideally and ideologically desirable to overthrow the political systems of communist states, but in practice overthrow might be impossible, and it might be more practical to learn to co-exist with them even to the point of signing trade and disarmament agreements with them.

 EXAMINATION QUESTIONS

▷ **Question 1** (a) 'It is vital that the USA gives full military assistance to Vietnam.' 'American troops should be withdrawn at once from Vietnam.' These two views were widely held in the USA in 1968. Explain the reasons for such opposing views.   (15 marks)

(b) 'Afghanistan was the Soviet Union's Vietnam.' This assertion has frequently been made. How similar were the Soviet Union's difficulties in Afghanistan to American difficulties in Vietnam?   (15 marks)

▷ **Question 2** Was it only fear of nuclear destruction which caused the Soviet Union and the USA to discuss and negotiate arms limitation during the years 1963 to 1987? Explain your answer.

(12 marks)

Question 3 'The Brezhnev Doctrine did the Soviet Union more harm than good.' Do you agree? Explain your answer. (12 marks)

EXAMINATION ANSWERS

Question 1 *Outline answer*

(a) Those who felt that the USA must defend South Vietnam felt that the USA had some obligation. From technical advisers to economic assistance and military hardware, the USA had become increasingly involved. Political involvement had led to American connivance at the removal and murder of Diem, and many Americans and politicians saw withdrawal as betrayal. It was incomprehensible to many Americans that superior arms would not eventually succeed. The notion that the USA could lose its first war in nearly two centuries was unthinkable. Those who accepted the postwar international role of the USA tended to support Vietnam involvement at least until 1968. Above all, memories of Korea were recent, and the domino theory suggested that without American involvement the whole of south-east Asia would rapidly fall to the communists.

Opponents of US involvement in Vietnam had various motives. Some were simply isolationists. A few were communist sympathizers. As casualties mounted, students, in particular, opposed US policies partly as student protest, but partly to avoid the 'draft'. Blacks had some sympathy with the Vietnamese underdog and resented the high proportion of black soldiers in the drafts being sent to Vietnam. Isolationists opposed intervention in south-east Asia as a matter of principle; a few Republicans used Vietnam as a stick with which to beat the Democratic President Johnson, and the heavy casualties of the 1968 Tet offensive caused widespread alarm. Humanitarian instincts were roused by the uncensored and on-the-spot reporting of the horrors that were taking place in Vietnam (murder of suspects, defoliation, napalm, indiscriminate bombings of North Vietnamese cities). The ceaseless demonstration of the vociferous minority against intervention gathered its own momentum.

(b) You might point out that Soviet involvement in Afghanistan was immediate and direct, while US involvement in Vietnam escalated from small beginnings. The one was deliberate, the other, at least initially, inadvertent. In Afghanistan the country tended to unite against the invader, with the communists drawing little popular support. In Vietnam there was, certainly in the early years, a good deal of support for an anti-communist South Vietnam. In Vietnam the north got little outside support, mainly some material assistance from the USSR. In Afghanistan the guerrillas were supported from Pakistan and received considerable material help from other countries. The number of troops involved also differed: there were far fewer Soviet troops in Afghanistan than there were American troops in Vietnam. Both Americans and Soviets suffered heavy casualties, but those of the USSR were proportionately higher. Failure in Vietnam was a blow to American prestige and power from which the USA was soon to recover; failure in Afghanistan was a Soviet disaster which contributed significantly to the collapse of the Soviet economy and the fall of the Soviet Union.

Nevertheless there are major and obvious similarities. Both superpowers were engaged in unwinnable conflicts in Third World states. Both poured in ever-increasing amounts of men, arms and equipment. Both ventures resulted in considerable increases in national expenditure. Both powers became increasingly bogged down, while slow to appreciate that the war could not be won by vast increases in military commitment. Both powers expected to win, and both powers eventually had to admit to failure.

Question 2 *Tutor answer*

The urgency which led to the disarmament discussions in 1963 arose from the Cuban missile crisis. Not only did the USA and Soviet Union establish a 'hot-line', but the world disaster so narrowly averted in October 1962 led to the first attempt to limit nuclear testing in 1963. The fear of nuclear annihilation prompted a determination to settle disputes by negotiation, but the fear of long-term nuclear destruction by atomic fallout prompted the Nuclear Test Ban Treaty. Similarly, the Non-Proliferation Treaty of 1968 attempted to reduce the danger of the spread of nuclear weapons and their use by irresponsible smaller states. During the 1970s progress was made through the Strategic Arms Limitation Talks in reducing the number of nuclear weapons held by each superpower bloc. This would not prevent world destruction should a nuclear war begin, but there was a powerful motive in it to reduce the growing cost of arms budgets. Moreover, there was, and had been even before the missile crisis, a genuine commitment to strive for and maintain peace on both sides. By the late 1970s, the superpowers were still stockpiling nuclear weapons. Neither side intended to use them, but each was wary of the other and felt that the stockpiles were necessary in case of attack. The Soviet invasion of Afghanistan heightened tension again, and the American search for a method of intercepting incoming nuclear missiles caused alarm in Moscow. If the Americans successfully developed such a method (Star Wars), the USA would be impregnable against a Soviet attack while the Soviet Union would be defenceless against an American attack. Now cost, from being an important factor, became a prime factor. Although Star Wars was a threat rather than a reality, any Soviet attempt to match it would have a devastating effect on the crumbling Soviet economy. Gorbachev genuinely wanted peace, and he certainly feared nuclear attack, but the immediate urgency was to cancel Star Wars and thus enable the Soviet defence budget to be brought under control. By 1987 the Soviet Union was making far-reaching proposals for defence cuts to save itself from financial collapse, rather than to save the world from nuclear destruction.

▷ **Question 3**   *Student answer with examiner's comments*

'Errors.'

'It is doubtful if Gorbachev was really trying to enforce the Brezhnev Doctrine at this stage.'

> *The Brezhnev Doctrine had its first success in Czechoslovakia. The Russians invaded, brought in Dubcek to replace Novotny and ended the Czechoslovak spring. But the success was only short-term. The invasion turned Czechoslovakia from a country that was mildly pro-Soviet to one that was smoulderingly anti-Soviet. It revealed cracks in the Warsaw Pact when Bulgaria refused to take part in the invasion, and it alarmed Czechoslovakia's neighbours like Poland, whose people, if not its rulers, were beginning to resent Soviet dominance. Throughout the 1970s the Brezhnev Doctrine kept Russia's satellites in check. Then in the early 1980s Andropov ordered the Russian invasion of Afghanistan, as the communist government there was under threat and had appealed to Moscow for assistance. The Russian invasion was universally condemned, and by Mao even more strongly than he had condemned the invasion of Czechoslovakia. While the Czechoslovak venture had been a short-term success, the Afghan venture was little short of a disaster. It ended détente, and almost made the Soviet Union an international outcast. It added enormously to the Soviet Union's spiralling defence costs, and contributed greatly to the economic burden which helped bring about the Soviet Union's end. Even so, Gorbachev tried to invoke the Brezhnev doctrine against the Balts in 1991; all it did was to confirm their desire for independence. So the Brezhnev Doctrine was expensive in terms of money and men, and politically it was counter-productive.*

Examiner's marking scheme
Level 1: generalized and unsupported statements   (1–2 marks)
Level 2: narrative treatment, especially of Czechoslovakia and Afghanistan or an answer offering several undeveloped factors   (3–6 marks)
Level 3: an answer which develops and substantiates several factors   (7–9 marks)
Level 4: an integrated argument which examines both short-term and long-term effects and arrives at a sharply focused judgement.   (10–12 marks)

Examiner's decision on the student answer

This answer is very promising, but its argument is undermined by several errors of substance, not all of which can be slips of the pen. If placed in Level 4, it could only be awarded the lowest mark of the Level, i.e. 10, but there would be a case for saying that the errors so undermine the argument that it could only be awarded a high Level 3.

SUMMARY

In this chapter you have learned about the following:

▷ the Sino-Soviet split and its consequences;

▷ the war in Vietnam, and its outcome;

▷ the arms race and the progress of nuclear disarmament;

▷ the ending of the Cold War and the Warsaw Pact;

▷ the formation of the Commonwealth of Independent States.

Chapter 19 deals with the Arab–Israel problem, which has sometimes had importance for the powers involved in the Cold War.

The Palestine Question

The collapse of Turkey during the First World War left confusion in the Middle East, much of which had been under Turkish government. During the war, Britain had offered to help the Arab countries of the area to free themselves and set up a state of their own. T.E. Lawrence (Lawrence of Arabia) helped to organize the *Arab Revolt*, and their forces, together with Britain's own troops under General Allenby, defeated the Turks and liberated Syria and Palestine.

MEG	NEAB	NICCEA	SEG	LONDON	WJEC	TOPIC	STUDY	REVISION 1	REVISION 2
✓*	✓*			✓	✓	**Palestine under the mandate**			
✓*	✓*			✓	✓	Establishment of the mandate system			
✓*	✓*			✓	✓	Palestine under the mandate			
✓*	✓*			✓	✓	The end of the mandate			
✓*	✓*			✓	✓	**The Arab–Israeli Wars**			
✓*	✓*			✓	✓	The First Arab–Israeli War, 1948–49			
✓*	✓*			✓	✓	The Second Arab–Israeli War, 1956			
✓*	✓*			✓	✓	The Third Arab–Israeli War, 1967			
✓*	✓*			✓	✓	The Fourth Arab–Israeli War, 1973			
✓*	✓*			✓	✓	Peacemaking, 1978			
✓*	✓*			✓	✓	**Some unresolved problems in the Middle East**			
✓*	✓*			✓	✓	The war in the Lebanon			
✓*	✓*			✓	✓	The completion of the peace accord in Israel			

* Coursework only

Palestine under the mandate

At about the same time, however, the British government gave its backing to a Zionist scheme to create a 'Jewish national home' in Palestine, which was the historic 'promised land' of the Jews.

▷ **Establishment of the mandate system**

British promises to the Jews

These promises took the form of the *Balfour Declaration*, sent by the British Foreign Secretary, Earl Balfour, in a letter to Lord Rothschild, the leader of the Jewish community in Britain. It said: 'His Majesty's government view with favour the establishment of a national home for the Jewish people, and will use their best endeavours to facilitate the achievement of this object, it being clearly understood that nothing will be done which may prejudice the civil or religious rights of the existing non-Jewish communities in Palestine.'

As far as Britain's attitude went, this really meant that nothing at all would be done, since Britain was already heavily committed to helping the Palestinian people living in the area, and anything done for the Jews would undermine this help.

British promises to the Arabs

In 1915, Macmahon, British High Commissioner in Egypt, had negotiated with Arab representatives of Sheikh Hussein for the establishment of independent Arab kingdoms in Arabia, Palestine, Iraq and Syria, in return for Arab support against the Turks.

The British government afterwards refused to be bound by these promises, on the grounds that Hussein was not entitled to speak for Arab opinion.

Thus the *Macmahon Correspondence* was later repudiated in an effort by Britain to leave its hands free to reach a Middle Eastern settlement to suit its own interests.

The Sykes–Picot Agreement, 1916

In fact, neither of these arrangements was put into effect at the end of the war. Instead, in 1916, British and French diplomats made an agreement – the Sykes–Picot Agreement – to carve up the whole area between them, awarding Syria and the Lebanon to France, and Iraq, Jordan and Palestine to Britain, as mandated territories.

Though the affairs of the other areas were fairly speedily settled, Palestine remained a thorn in Britain's side throughout the whole interwar period.

▷ **Palestine under the mandate**

The mandate lasted from 1920 to 1947, but Britain found itself involved in conflict between Jews and Arabs for the whole of nearly 30 years.

Immigration and racial conflict in Palestine between the wars

The chief problem here was the increasing conflict between the Arab inhabitants of Palestine and the increasing flow of Jewish immigrants.

The earliest Jewish settlements had been farm colonies conducted along communal lines and known as *kibbutzim*. The first had been set up in 1879 in the area of what is today Tel Aviv. By 1914 there were over 40 kibbutzim, and there was a sizeable Jewish minority in Jerusalem and other towns.

The Arabs, whose customs, language and religion were quite different, resented this influx, and in particular resented the money which the immigrants used to buy up the farmland which the Palestinian Arabs considered to be rightfully theirs.

It became increasingly clear that Britain's declared aims of permitting the creation of an Arab state and of simultaneously providing a Jewish 'national home' were contradictory.

There were riots in Jaffa in 1921, and British forces in trying to maintain order seemed to be fighting a losing battle. The British Colonial Secretary, Winston Churchill, in a government White Paper tried to reassure Palestinian opinion by declaring that a 'national home' for the Jews did not necessarily mean a 'national state'. But this was little more than a quibble, since Britain took no serious steps towards limiting Jewish immigration, which by 1925 was running at over 10,000 a year, mainly from Bolshevik Russia and Poland.

The 1929 riots and their results

Renewed rioting took place in 1929, sparked off when a Jewish boy kicked his football on to an Arab's land. Before the riots were quelled there had been about 50 Jewish and over 100 Arab deaths.

The British government issued a second White Paper, reaffirming British promises to the Palestinians; but this document aroused such furious criticism from the Jewish community that Ramsay MacDonald back-tracked in the face of their accusations of anti-Semitism, and issued instead what the Arabs referred to as a 'black paper', in which he declared he had no intention either of checking Jewish immigration into the country or of limiting Jewish purchases of Arab land.

Such a situation was obviously unsatisfactory. In fact it got worse after 1933, when anti-Semitic policies began to operate in Nazi Germany. Jewish immigration went up from 4,000 in 1931 to 30,000 in 1933 and over 50,000 in 1935. By 1936 there were about 400,000 Jewish inhabitants of Palestine, as against 850,000 Arabs.

The 1936 general strike and the Peel Commission

Communal trouble broke out again in 1936. The Palestinians organized a general strike, and armed bands of Palestinian volunteers roamed the countryside, attacking Jewish farms and terrorizing their workers. Britain increased its garrison in the country to about 20,000 troops, but failed to quell the disturbances.

In 1937 a Royal Commission under Lord Peel was set up to find a solution. The plan it put forward was to create three small states, one for the Arabs, one for the Jews and the third (including Jaffa and Jerusalem) as an international zone under the authority of the League of Nations. This solution pleased nobody, and was quietly dropped.

Demonstrations and violence continued. In 1939 the British government produced yet another plan: Jewish immigration was to be strictly limited and was to stop altogether after five years, while further transfers of Palestinian land to Jews were to be strictly controlled.

Later in 1939, however, the Second World War broke out and the whole question was put on ice.

▷ **The end of the mandate**

By 1945 the situation seemed to have gone on too long for any compromise solution to work, and Britain was despairing of finding a peaceful settlement.

The increase of violence in Palestine

The Palestinians were bitterly hostile to the continuation of violence and division in their land, and persuaded their Arab neighbours to use diplomatic and military pressure to resist it. In 1945 the *Arab League* was founded to support the Palestinian people.

Demonstrations took place against the British in the towns; in the desert, oil pipelines supplying oil to the West were blown up so as to harass the British as much as possible.

The Jewish settlers too were pushed in the direction of extremism. During the war, the Jewish Agency in Palestine created a defence force known as the *Haganah*, which was recognized by the British in the struggle against the Axis powers (Hitler had recently produced his 'Final Solution' of the Jewish problem). The Haganah was officered by men who had volunteered to fight against Hitler's Germany, and who in many cases were British trained and used British arms and equipment. While this body was operating, there were also terrorist groups:

(a) The *Irgun Zwei Leumi*, a National Military Organization formed first in 1937, directed its activities first against the Arabs and then against the British. From 1944 it was led by Menachem Begin, later Prime Minister of Israel.

(b) The *Stern Gang* was named after Abraham Stern, a Polish Jew who hated the British as much as the Nazis. He left the Irgun to form his own band of terrorists, only to be captured and shot by the British in 1942.

Britain fails to find a solution

During the war, Jewish leaders such as David Ben Gurion and Chaim Weizmann denounced terrorism, hoping to get a better deal by cooperating with the British.

Their claims were reinforced by the so-called *Biltmore programme*, issued by 600 influential Zionists from the Biltmore Hotel in New York in 1942, which said: 'Conference calls for the fulfilment of the original purpose of the Balfour Declaration and the Mandate, which recognized the historical connection of the Jewish people with Palestine and was to afford them the opportunity to found there a Jewish Commonwealth.'

Weizmann asked Churchill to relax immigration restrictions in favour of the masses of Jews trying to reach Palestine, but Churchill gave him a polite brush-off and shortly afterwards was defeated in the 1945 British general election.

The incoming Attlee government declined to permit wider immigration, and resisted
the pressure of the new US President, Truman, to change his mind. Ben Gurion therefore came out in open opposition to the British. Jewish extremists launched a terrorist
war, blowing up roads and bridges, and finally planting a bomb in the King David Hotel
in Jerusalem in 1946, killing over 90 British personnel.

Meantime, illegal Jewish immigration went on. Overloaded ships foundered, and the
Exodus, carrying over 4,500 refugees, was forced to turn round and take its unhappy
human cargo back to the 'displaced persons' camps in Germany whence they had come.
Others, however, like the *Smyrna*, the *San Demetrio* and the *Holgana*, brought several
thousands more successfully to ports such as Haifa.

The British pull out

In 1947 the British Foreign Secretary, Ernest Bevin, announced that his government was
going to hand over the whole Palestine question to the newly established United Nations
Organization.

The UN General Assembly sent a Special Commission on Palestine (UNSCOP) to Tel
Aviv, and it eventually reported in favour of a plan for the partition of the country similar to the one previously outlined by the British in 1937. The scheme, somewhat more
generous to the Jews than the British plan, since it awarded them most of the Negev
down to the Red Sea, was adopted by the United Nations, but was furiously rejected by
the Palestinians, who saw themselves becoming foreigners in their own land.

Nevertheless the British made it clear that they intended to withdraw from Palestine
whether there had been a settlement or not, and they began to make preparations for
their departure.

On the day the British left, 14 May 1948, Ben Gurion proclaimed the independence
of his country under the name of Israel, and this was recognized with remarkable alacrity
by the Truman administration. On the following day, Israel was invaded from all sides
by its Arab neighbours.

The Arab–Israeli Wars

The period after independence was a most troubled one for the infant Israeli state, and
the period between 1948 and 1978 has sometimes been referred to as the second 'Thirty
Years War'. This was because of the entrenched attitudes of both sides, and their stubborn refusal to make peace with each other.

▷ **The First Arab–Israeli War, 1948–49**

Israel's Arab neighbours in 1948 welcomed the opportunity of wiping the new state off
the map while it was still in its infancy:

(a) Egyptian forces moved along the coast of the Mediterranean towards Gaza, and from
there struck northwards in the direction of the Israeli capital, Tel Aviv.
(b) From the opposite direction, Syrian troops pushed across the Jordan and into northern Palestine.
(c) From the east, Jordan's crack Arab Legion – a force trained by Brig.-Gen. John Glubb
and equipped by the British – occupied the West Bank of the Jordan and seized
Jerusalem. Israel seemed on the verge of extinction.

At this stage, in July 1948, the UN succeeded in imposing a truce, with about a third of
Israel's territories in Arab hands. But fighting broke out again in July, and after a tough
campaign the Israelis enjoyed greater success:

(a) They succeeded in driving their Egyptian enemies from their soil, and clearing the
whole of the Negev in October as far as the port of Eilat.
(b) They cleared the whole of Galilee of Syrian forces as far as the Lebanese frontier and
the Golan Heights.
(c) They also negotiated a settlement with Jordan whereby they partitioned the West
Bank and even the city of Jerusalem between them. The result of these victories was
that Israel not only survived the invasion, but actually increased its share of Palestine.

There followed another UN truce, and the remaining Arab states followed Egypt's example of signing ceasefires with their Jewish neighbours. Unfortunately, the first UN mediator, the Swedish Count Bernadotte, was murdered by Jewish extremists, his job being taken over by his deputy, Ralph Bunche.

By February 1949 the war was over, but the Arab states refused to accept the finality of the outcome and indicated their intention of eliminating the Jewish presence at the first opportunity.

Results of the war

(a) The UN Truce Supervisory Commission in the meantime established the frontiers of the new state, and in 1950 Britain, France and the USA joined together to make a tripartite declaration that they would protect Israel against any future renewal of hostilities.

(b) About a million Palestinian refugees fled from the country to nearby Arab states: about 25 per cent northwards to Lebanon and Syria, about 35 per cent into the Gaza Strip – still held by Egypt – and about 40 per cent into the West Bank territory and into Jordan.

(c) In these places the refugees lived in conditions of poverty and squalor. The large number of these displaced persons only intensified Arab resentment and hardened their determination for revenge.

▷ The Second Arab–Israeli War, 1956

Colonel Gamal Abdul Nasser of Egypt, coming to power in 1954 after the overthrow of King Farouk, was bent on pursuing schemes not only for strengthening and modernizing his country, but for assuming the leadership of the whole Arab world and spearheading the drive to exterminate Israel. This was seen when:

(a) Nasser denounced western interference in Middle Eastern affairs, in particular the US-supported *Baghdad Pact*, set up in 1955 ostensibly to check the growth of communism in that area.

(b) He began to import arms from Czechoslovakia, and in July 1956 nationalized the Suez Canal, a move guaranteed to infuriate Britain and France, previously its owners.

(c) He mounted a sustained propaganda offensive against Israel, signalling clearly his hostility towards the Jews.

Incursions into Israeli territory by the *fedayeen* – devoted fighting men from the refugee camps – and endless raiding and counter-raiding across the frontier by armed bands produced a mounting sense of danger, until Nasser finally closed both the Suez Canal and the Straits of Tiran (Gulf of Aqaba) to Israeli shipping.

All these things led to something like a siege mentality in Tel Aviv, and the Israeli government decided to act.

At the end of October 1956, having earlier taken the precaution of concluding a secret agreement with Britain and France that if they invaded Egypt they would have Anglo-French support, the Israelis suddenly seized the Gaza Strip and invaded Sinai, reaching the left bank of the Suez Canal within hours of launching their invasion.

The USA proposed a resolution in the Security Council (unusually with the backing of the Soviet Union) demanding a ceasefire, but Britain and France vetoed it. Declaring that their sole intention was to prevent possible damage to the canal, Britain and France sent both sides an ultimatum demanding immediate withdrawal from the vicinity of the canal, and moved strongly to the support of their ally Israel.

An Anglo-French force, after a somewhat leisurely journey from their bases in Cyprus, landed at Port Said on 5 November, occupied it after devastating attacks on Egyptian air force machines on the ground, and began to advance along the canal towards Suez on the Red Sea.

Nasser appealed to the UN to intervene, and meanwhile blocked the canal by sinking ships in it. With the USA and the USSR for once acting together, and with overwhelming support from most Third World countries, the UN stepped in. Israel was ordered to leave the Sinai Peninsula, and reluctantly did so. Britain and France, neither of them willing to continue to defy such a clear expression of world disapproval, agreed to withdraw their forces, and the last troops left Egypt by the end of November.

Fig. 19.1 Israel versus Egypt, 1948–56

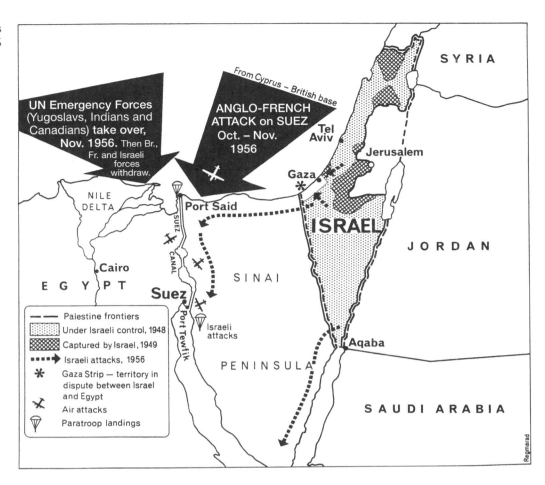

Results of the war

(a) Britain and France lost considerable international face, accused of piracy by most of the powers of the world, except a few Commonwealth countries. The British felt very bitter to have been let down by their customary ally, the USA; though most of their ill-feeling was vented on the interference of the United Nations.

(b) Israel found it difficult to present the war as a great success: the country gained no territory, remained exposed to the hostility of its Arab neighbours and was branded together with Britain and France as an aggressor. But at least for a time it had gained a respite from Egyptian frontier raids, and the Gulf of Aqaba – though not the Suez Canal – was opened to Israeli ships once again. Furthermore, Israel had proved once again that it could defend itself very effectively, and that it was determined not to be caught napping.

(c) Egypt, on the other hand, came out of the war in a stronger, more confident mood, with Arab ambitions unabated and Nasser's prestige strengthened.

(d) A solution to the question of the Palestinian refugees was as far off as ever, and the Arab states stubbornly refused even to acknowledge Israel's existence. In 1960 border incidents started up again with raids into Israel by Arab guerrillas and reprisal raids by Israeli forces. It was only a question of time before another spark set fire to the powder-barrel.

▷ The Third Arab–Israeli War, 1967

In the 1960s, the Arab states adopted an ever more threatening tone towards Israel. In 1964 Nasser said, 'Future prospects are for war against Israel, for which we shall set the time and place.' In 1966 the Syrian Defence Minister, Hafiz Hasad, took up the theme:

> We say we shall never call for or accept peace. We shall only accept war and the restoration of the usurped land. We have resolved to drench this land with your blood; to oust you, aggressors, and throw you into the sea for good. We must meet as soon a possible and fight a single liberation war against Israel, imperialism and all the enemies of the people.

Syria became more closely linked with Egypt in what was rather grandly called a *United Arab Republic* in 1963, and a Palestine Liberation Movement, known as *Al Fatah*, came into being. The PLM began guerrilla raids into less securely defended places in Israel, wrecking buildings and killing the inhabitants. The Israelis retaliated by striking into Lebanon and Syria to destroy PLM bases, and began attacking the Golan Heights from which Syrian artillery had been intermittently shelling Israeli targets.

Nasser persuaded UN Secretary-General U Thant to withdraw peacekeeping forces from Sinai, and began moving his troops into forward positions there.

Once again he sealed off the Gulf of Aqaba, and moved artillery and troops to Sharm-el-Sheikh at the tip of the Sinai Peninsula. Soon he had over 100,000 men in the Sinai Peninsula, with 1,300 tanks and 500 aircraft ready for action; while on the West Bank Jordanian troops were moving into position, accompanied by the Iraqi forces in alliance with them.

Once again the Arabs had made the mistake of giving Israel advance notice of their intentions. In fact since 1956 the Israelis had prepared themselves well. They had reduced the number of men in infantry detachments, and had given greater importance to armoured tank divisions and the air force.

Israelis realized that when the time came there would not be a minute to lose if the country was to survive. Hence the government committed itself to speed, mobility and attack. On 5 June 1967, Moshe Dayan, the tough Israeli Minister of Defence, decided on a pre-emptive strike.

In the early hours, Israeli troops poured into the Sinai Desert, while within two hours Israeli fighter-bombers had wiped out the Egyptian air force on the ground. With their air superiority immediately established, the Israelis had little difficulty in harassing and destroying Egyptian forces wherever they encountered them. Advancing along the Mediterranean coastline, the Israelis reached El Arish within a day, within two days Sharm-el-Sheikh on the Red Sea, and within three days the Suez Canal once again, in several places. The main Egyptian body at El Nakhl, more or less cut off in the middle of the Sinai Peninsula, was swiftly surrounded and pounded into submission.

Meanwhile, in the first few hours of the war, the Israelis occupied Jerusalem and over-ran the entire West Bank of the Jordan. Hussein swallowed his pride and asked for an armistice.

Against Syria, Israeli armour advanced into the Golan Heights, a hazardous undertaking considering that they were attacking the Syrian defence system at its very strongest point; but though the Syrians fought tooth and nail, they were no match for the opposing heavy armour, and the Israelis broke through to within 30 kilometres of Damascus. By 10 June the Syrians too asked for a ceasefire.

In the course of what became known as the *Six Days War*, Israel had doubled itself in size, and was left in secure possession of the Golan Heights, the West Bank and the whole area of the Sinai Peninsula as far as the Suez Canal, now its frontier with Egypt. The Egyptians once again blocked the canal, imprisoning a number of ships in it, most of which had virtually rotted away by the time the canal was reopened over ten years later.

Results of the war

(a) The UN once again sent a mission to determine and to protect the frontiers, but the peace was an uneasy one, constantly interrupted by new conflicts.

(b) A new truce had to be arranged in 1970, but both the Arabs and the Jews looked askance at the UN proposal for both parties to withdraw from the territories they had occupied; the US-sponsored *Rogers Plan*, UN *Resolution 272* and all the diplomacy of the UN emissary Dr Gunnar Jarring failed to persuade them to do this.

(c) Eventually Israel's Prime Minister, Mrs Golda Meir, rejected all the peace efforts completely, flatly refusing to budge an inch from the position that had been won until Israel had some guarantee for its future security.

(d) In desperation the Arabs turned to terrorism instead of negotiation and Arab governments started to turn the screw of increased oil prices through the *Organization of Petroleum Exporting Countries* (OPEC) in order to blackmail the western powers into taking a more pro-Arab line.

(e) The early 1970s saw a number of extremist Arab terrorist organizations spring into being to secure the acceptance of Palestinian demands.

▷ The Fourth Arab–Israeli War, 1973

One of these organizations, the *Popular Front for the Liberation of Palestine* (PFLP), began to hijack aircraft, seizing four of them, one a British VC10 which they flew to Jordan and blew up. They were also responsible for an outrage at Lydda airport in June 1972, where there were about a hundred casualties in a running battle between an Arab suicide squad and airport security. Another organization was called *Black September* (so called because of the violent crushing of an earlier Palestinian movement, this time by the Jordanians, in this month in 1970); this organization attacked Israeli athletes later in 1972 after they had competed in the Munich Olympics, murdering eleven of them before being gunned down themselves. The Israelis, following an 'eye-for-an-eye' policy, retaliated savagely in each case.

Then suddenly in 1973, this time without any preliminary warning, Egyptian and Syrian forces once more attacked Israel. This time they were unsupported by Jordan, whose king had recently quarrelled with the *Palestine Liberation Organization* (PLO), the leader of which had brought thousands of his supporters to Jordan and at one point seemed to be about to overturn Hussein's government. All the same, the Egyptian and Syrian invaders at first had good success. They enjoyed the diplomatic approval of the communist bloc, which supported them as native nationalist movements against Israeli imperialism, and they had been well equipped with Soviet arms. Furthermore, the day chosen for the Arab attack was Yom Kippur, the Jewish Day of Atonement, when many Jews were worshipping in their synagogues.

Nearly 1,200 Syrian tanks set about the reconquest of the Golan Heights, while Egyptian troops thrust across the Suez Canal and hurled themselves against the Israeli defence line there – the Bar Lev Line. Numbers of Israeli aircraft were shot down by heat-seeking Soviet-built SAM missiles.

But Israel itself was well supplied with US weapons and expertise, and within a fortnight was able to turn the tide. The Israeli air force began to recover the initiative, and eventually was able to knock out over 1,000 Syrian tanks. Israeli ground forces went on the offensive in Sinai and expelled the Egyptians. They crossed the canal and swung in behind Suez from the west, cutting off the entire Egyptian Third Army in a huge pocket on the west side of the canal.

The USA and the USSR joined to arrange a ceasefire, expressing the hope that this time a permanent settlement could be reached; but the position continued to be one of deadlock, with the Israelis refusing to give up anything they had won, and the Arabs stubbornly rejecting any agreement that involved recognizing the Israeli state.

Results of the war

(a) Israel retained all its conquests. Menachem Begin, who succeeded Golda Meir as Prime Minister, the Israeli Likud Party having recently ousted the Labour Party from office, refused to surrender territories until security arrangements were positively agreed with Israel's enemies.

(b) Palestinian terrorist organizations resumed their activities. The main sufferers were the Palestinian Arabs, who were not only driven from their homes to be herded into overcrowded refugee camps, but when at liberty were grimly brutalized by the Jewish police, suspected of all kinds of ill-doings.

▷ Peacemaking, 1978

Moving towards a settlement

As long as President Nasser lived, hostility towards Israel was as strong as ever, but when he died suddenly of a heart attack in 1970, and was succeeded by Anwar Sadat, Egyptian policies began to moderate. Nixon, as part of his 'shuttle diplomacy', had visited the Middle East, and his visit was returned by Sadat in 1975. Two years later Sadat took a further bold step towards resolving the dispute with Israel.

He visited Jerusalem, and in a speech to the Knesset (the Israeli parliament) made a personal appeal for a better understanding between the two countries. Though he exposed himself to the possibility of a rebuff at the hands of Israeli extremists, in fact he was given a cautious welcome by Menachem Begin. Some time later, Begin visited Cairo and indicated his country's willingness to look for a settlement.

Events in Lebanon caused these negotiations to falter in 1978, but President Carter breathed new life into them by inviting both men to Camp David, where they closeted themselves together and hammered out the framework for a settlement. Their agreement was eventually signed in March 1979. Begin and Sadat regarded the problem from quite different angles, and it was difficult to reconcile their viewpoints.

Fig. 19.2 Prime Minister Begin of Israel and President Sadat of Egypt have differing viewpoints over the Middle East peace talks

Source: Daily Mirror

The Camp David Peace Accord, 1978

(a) Sadat offered Israel a peace treaty and final diplomatic recognition.
(b) In return, Israel undertook to withdraw from Sinai in three stages, restoring the whole area to Egypt in spite of there being numerous Jewish settlements planted there in the interval; simultaneously, Begin promised he would set about the task of providing full autonomy (i.e. political independence) for the Arab communities living under Israeli rule in the Gaza Strip and on the West Bank – though both sides agreed that this would take some little time to bring about.
(c) The peace process was to be completed in the 1980s.

The conclusion of this agreement created a sensation, not least in the USA and the western nations. But extremist Arabs regarded Sadat's actions in breaking ranks with his allies as a gross betrayal, and the headquarters of the Arab League was abruptly moved from Cairo to Tunis. Moammur Ghaddafi of Libya (Colonel Ghaddafi) began to emerge as the new leader of the Arab national movement instead of the Egyptian President.

Prospects for lasting peace

Yet it was the Jews whose actions seemed most likely to wreck the agreement. Israel, after much heart searching and many protests from right-wingers, eventually completed the handing back of Sinai, but failed conspicuously to halt the planting of Jewish settlements on the West Bank.

Israel went on in 1980 to pass the *Jerusalem Law*, which transferred the capital from Tel Aviv to the Holy City, declaring it 'entire and united'. Then in 1981 Israel went on formally to annex the Golan Heights from Syria. Arab leaders, particularly Yasser Arafat, leader of the PLO, grew ever more disenchanted with these developments.

Sadat did not increase his popularity with Arab radicals when he offered sanctuary to the Shah of Iran, toppled in a coup by the Muslim Ayatollah Khomeini in 1979. The malcontents vented their displeasure in 1981 when they shot down their President in a hail of small arms fire at a military parade in Cairo. His successor was his Vice-President, Hosni Mubarak, though in practice he was a moderate, too, and made no effort to renew the war.

Some unresolved problems in the Middle East

▷ **The war in the Lebanon**

During the 1970s, the condition of the Lebanon became ever more disturbed. There were many Palestinian refugees in the country, and these frequently clashed with the Lebanese authorities. Another conflict was between a national movement of left-wing Muslims and conservative Christian groups supported by a Phalangist militia. Trouble first flared up in 1975–76, and there were more than 50 attempts to impose ceasefires on the warring factions.

Syrian intervention in the Lebanon, 1976–78

In 1976, in their efforts to restore order in the country, Syrian forces came into conflict with the Palestinians. As the result of a ceasefire in October, a more effective Arab Deterrent Force (ADF), consisting of 30,000 men from Syria and various other Arab countries, took up their positions there.

All this was very disturbing to the Israelis, who looked upon the Lebanon as a hotbed of Palestinian unrest and greatly feared the extension of Syrian authority there. Guerrilla raids into Israel by Palestinian bands provoked numerous incursions into Lebanon, but in 1978 *Al Fatah* staged a serious invasion and caused in turn a full-scale Israeli invasion of Lebanon. Their troops advanced along the coast as far as the Litani River, occupying Sidon and dispersing refugee camps as they reached them.

The UN intervened to send an interim force (UN Interim Force in Lebanon, UNIFIL) and eventually persuaded Israel to withdraw, and hand over to the right-wing, chiefly Christian, militia.

Internal strife in the Lebanon, 1979–85

Unfortunately, peace was not so easily restored. In 1979 Israel encouraged a right-wing Lebanese army officer to set up his own Independent Free Lebanon in the south, next to the northern frontier of Israel, policing it with his South Lebanese Army (SLA).

The Syrians retaliated by taking control of much of the north-east of the country, including the strategically important Beqa'a Valley, and this gave the Israelis the excuse they had been awaiting to renew their invasion. The war soon escalated into one to crush the PLO once and for all.

By August the Palestinians were in a desperate position, with more than 6,000 of them trapped in the capital Beirut. UN intervention arranged a ceasefire, under which a multinational peace force from France, Italy, Britain and the USA aimed to bring about the withdrawal of foreign troops from Lebanese soil.

Eventually the Israelis withdrew from the vicinity of Beirut, concentrating 30,000 of their troops in a security zone in the south where, with the support of the SLA, they continued to police the country. By the end of 1983, the UN force was able to agree the withdrawal from Beirut of Yasser Arafat and the PLO, under which he shifted his organization to Tunis while they were dispersed among a number of Middle Eastern countries.

Stalemate in Lebanon after 1985

Throughout 1984 and 1985 bitter fighting took place in Beirut to create a stable government, but without success. Fighting continued across the 'green line' separating Christian East Beirut from Muslim West Beirut. There was sometimes even fighting between the rival militias of the Muslims themselves – the Shi'ites and the Sunnis.

By the time the multinational force withdrew in 1985, Lebanon was effectively divided into three: the north and east of the country, under the Syrians; the south, still controlled by the Israelis; and the area around Beirut, under the shaky control of the Lebanese government.

The head of this government, General Aoun, attempted to remove the Syrians in 1989, but was ousted and a new Government of National Reconciliation formed. This had to allow the Beqa'a Valley to remain in Syrian control and the Israelis to remain in their Security Zone in the south, but succeeded in disarming all the militias apart from the left-wing Hezbollah and the right-wing SLA.

The country was still in a disturbed condition in the 1990s, with more than 200,000 refugees still on Lebanese soil. Elections were held and a new government under Rafiq Hariri was formed in 1992, but the Syrian and the Israeli presences prevented more permanent solutions. Lebanon did, however, take part in discussions on the Middle East peace accord from 1992 onwards.

▷ **The completion of the peace accord in Israel**

Palestinians had begun to fear that the promises made at Camp David about the withdrawal of Israeli garrisons and the grant of internal self-government to the disputed areas within Israel would never happen, but internal pressures and the pressure of world opinion began to yield results in the 1990s.

Steps to a settlement

The peace process once more got under way with multiparty talks in Madrid in 1991. Though the talks stalled, they led on to later agreements signed in October 1993 with the PLO under Yasser Arafat, and with Jordan.

These settlements were supported by the new Labour government of Israel under Yitzhak Rabin which came to office in May 1993.

The settlement with Jordan

The peace treaty with Jordan was signed in 1994, establishing:

(a) the return of all land taken from Jordan since 1967 – not the West Bank, which was to have self-government under the Palestinians, but areas such as the southern Araba Valley;
(b) full diplomatic and economic relations between the two, and the banning of terrorist raids on each other;
(c) the full sharing of the Jordan and Yarmouk rivers, the opening of border crossings and the establishment of telephone links.

Since 1994 relations between the two states have been more open and cordial.

The settlement of Palestinian differences

After the Six Days War, Israel held the Gaza Strip, the West Bank and east as well as west Jerusalem. In 1987, despairing of progress towards a settlement, the PLO launched a campaign of sustained unrest (the *intifada*) in the Occupied Territories, in the course of which 1,400 Palestinians and 250 Jews perished.

But in 1993 a *Declaration of Principles* was agreed between the two sides by which the PLO renounced terrorism and recognized Israel's right to live within secure boundaries, while Israel recognized the right of the Palestinians to govern themselves. The declaration set up a timetable for progress:

(a) the Israelis to withdraw from the Gaza Strip and Jericho in 1994;
(b) political power to be transferred to a nominated Palestinian National Authority (PNA) to organize elections to a new Palestinian Council;
(c) Israeli military authority to be replaced by a Palestinian police force;
(d) agreement to be reached over Jewish settlements on Palestinian land;
(e) a full peace settlement to be concluded by 1999.

Last-minute hitches

From the beginning, the timetable was subject to slippage; though about 9,000 Palestinian police became responsible for order in Gaza and Jericho, the Israeli military authorities remained in real control.

Difficulties resulted from Israeli retention of several thousand Palestinian prisoners convicted of terrorist offences, from continuing expansion of Jewish settlements on the West Bank, and from the revival of extremist violence which Yasser Arafat proved unable to check.

In November 1995 the Israeli Prime Minister, Yitzhak Rabin, was assassinated by a Jewish extremist. His successor, Shimon Peres, narrowly lost a general election in May 1996, and the new Prime Minister was Binyamin Netanyahu of the Likud party. He was able with the support of the minority parties to form a new right-wing government. Many observers believed this hardened Israeli attitudes and reduced the chances of the completion of a peaceful settlement in Palestine.

 ## GLOSSARY

Anti-Semitism Collective prejudice against the Jews. The prejudice can sometimes be confined to non-violent dislike, but in Hitler's Germany it took more sinister and violent forms, culminating in the horror of the Holocaust. In Palestine the vast majority of the Arab population had become in varying degrees anti-Semitic by the time Israel became independent in 1948.

Displaced persons These are often the victims of war or civil unrest. Moved from their homes, they may lose all their belongings and become refugees. If they have no papers, they may lose their civil rights, and if they are unable to find a country willing to accept their entry, they may become stateless. Many Arabs fled from Jewish territory in 1948, whether from Israeli intimidation or fear of it, and thus became the nucleus of the Palestinian refugee problem of later years.

Phalangist The word is similar in origin to that of the Spanish Falange. It refers to the neo-fascist Christian militia of the Lebanon.

Third World The First and Second Worlds are those of the East and West, sometimes known as the 'communist bloc' and the 'free world', i.e. the states supporting the former Soviet Union and those supporting the USA. The Third World consists of the politically non-aligned countries, many of them the developing countries of the Afro-Asian bloc, e.g. India.

White Paper A British government publication dealing with a particular problem and often advancing a solution to it recommended by the experts who have been investigating the problem. It is similar to the reports of Royal Commissions, which are produced as Command Papers or Blue Books (so called because of the colour of their covers).

Zionism This was a movement for the return of the Jews to Palestine, which for 2,000 years the dispersed Jews had regarded as their homeland. It was a reaction against the policies of anti-Semitism commonly practised in Europe in the nineteenth and twentieth centuries. It was launched by Theodore Herzl, under whose inspiration the first Zionist Congress was held in Basle in 1897. During the First World War, one of its leaders, Chaim Weizmann, won British support for the movement at the time of the Balfour Declaration. He remained a friend of Britain throughout his career, unlike David Ben Gurion, who turned against Britain in 1945 because he felt that the British had let him down.

 ## EXAMINATION QUESTIONS

▷ **Question 1** (a) Why did Britain decide, in 1947, to abandon the Palestine mandate? (10 marks)
(b) (i) superior weapons
(ii) Arab disunity
(iii) the element of surprise

Which of these was most important in explaining why Israel was so successful against her Arab neighbours during the years 1948–1973? Refer to each of (i), (ii) and (iii) in your answer. (15 marks)

▷ **Question 2**

Fig. 19.3 British newspaper cartoon of 1956, showing President Nasser of Egypt

'This is a British cartoon, and therefore it is of little use to historians.' Do you agree with this statement? Use the cartoon **and your own knowledge** to explain your answer. (10 marks)

▷ **Question 3** Did the involvement of the USA and the Soviet Union in the Middle East, 1945–1979, improve the situation there or make it worse? Explain your answer. (15 marks)

 EXAMINATION ANSWERS

▷ **Question 1** *Outline answer*

(a) A reference to British difficulties before the war, culminating with the Peel Commission, would be relevant. Continue with showing that irreconcilable differences between Arab and Jew made Britain's position even more difficult, especially when the Jews resorted to terrorism against the British, culminating in the blowing up of the King David Hotel. World sympathy immediately after the war was on the side of the Jews, in view of their sufferings at Nazi hands, and the sizeable Jewish vote in the USA meant that Britain came under considerable pressure from the USA to allow unlimited Jewish immigration into Palestine when to do so would alienate the Palestinian Arabs. Britain got a bad press from the rest of the world for trying to turn back refugee ships such as the *Exodus*. Impatient of finding a solution and irritated by worldwide pro-Jewish pressure, the British Foreign Secretary, Ernest Bevin, persuaded the British Labour cabinet to transfer the problem to the UN. It should be remembered that the British mandate was due to end in May 1948 anyway.

(b) The question suggests that you tackle each in turn and then come to an overall conclusion. Certainly the Israelis were better equipped at the outset than were the Arabs, whose forces, apart from those of Glubb Pasha, were poorly led and poorly trained, and had outdated equipment. After the USA and the USSR became seriously involved in supplying arms and equipment, especially after 1956, the superiority of western weapons to those of the Soviet bloc was soon apparent, particularly with regard to the air forces. Only the SAM missiles posed any real threat.

Arab disunity was a constant factor in Israeli success. Expectation of victory was so great in 1948 that the Arabs did not bother to coordinate their attacks, and there was no combined command structure. In 1956 it was Egypt which bore the brunt of the war for the Arabs, and although Egypt and Syria formed a United Arab Republic in 1963, it was subject to internal political strains which weakened the Arabs in the 1967 War. These two states attacked Israel in 1973 without the support of Jordan, which had quarrelled with the PLO. So although the Arab states breathed fire and brimstone against the Israelis, in none of the four wars of 1948–73 did they ever effectively combine against them.

In the one situation when Israel appeared in most danger, in 1967, the Israelis countered Arab threats by a surprise attack. Surprise was not an element in Israeli strategy in 1948 or 1973 when Israel was attacked by its Arab neighbours, and its use by the Israelis in 1956 did not produce, for them, a satisfactory result. The surprise factor seems hardly to have been the most important. Had the Arabs united more effectively against Israel, it seems likely that they could have overcome their military inferiority, especially in 1973. But it could be argued equally convincingly the other way.

▷ Question 2   *Tutor answer*

It would be useful to know whether this cartoon was published before the 1956 war began or during it. Either way there is no doubt that this is a hostile cartoon, and thus its historical accuracy is in question. The cartoon shows Nasser, his face, and presumably his voice, full of hate, surrounded by his broadcast texts which refer to broken treaties, embargoes on Israeli shipping, and anti-British broadcasts and lies. If the cartoon is before the 1956 war, it is certainly preparing British public opinion for it; if it is during the war, it is certainly trying to justify it. As such its value to historians lies not in the accuracy or otherwise of its representation, but in the way the cartoon illustrates British propaganda of 1956. Cartoons not only create opinion, they also reflect it. So to the historian this cartoon is valuable, partly to show a typical British press view at the time of the Suez War, but also to demonstrate what a sizeable proportion of the British public thought about Nasser at that time.

▷ Question 3   *Student answer with examiner's comments*

'Rather a distorted view, presumably of the Cuban missile crisis of 1962.'

'The Soviets were not specifically anti-Semitic, they were a closed society which did not normally allow any of its citizens to emigrate.'

'Vague. Be more precise.'

The USA and the USSR were important superpowers, and their rivalry during this period led to brinkmanship and the danger of war. Khrushchev had threatened the USA with nuclear destruction and both countries wanted strong influence in the Middle East which was important for its oil reserves. Many Jews lived in the USA which made the USA pro-Israeli, and the Russians were anti-Semitic and would not allow Soviet citizens to emigrate to Israel. The Soviet Union and the USA were both important members of the United Nations, and the problem of the Middle East was often discussed there. Usually the two superpowers were on opposite sides in these discussions but sometimes a United Nations resolution would be passed about the Middle East, but if it was everyone usually ignored it. The Jews had suffered a lot at the hands of the Nazis so there was much world-wide support for their hopes of

'A rather coloured view of 1956. There was no collusion between the USA and the USSR to remove British influence from the Middle East.'

'A dubious factor. At this time the Soviet Union was not seeking to placate its Muslim population as implied here.'

'This needs to be demonstrated.'

'A bit hard on the Soviets here.'

creating an Israeli state in Palestine. The problem after 1948 was how to defend it against its Arab enemies. One thing both the USSR and the USA agreed on was to keep the British out of the Middle East, so the two countries co-operated against Britain in 1956 to force Britain out of Egypt. The Russians became friends of the Arabs because the Arabs were of the Muslim religion and there were many Muslims in the Soviet Union. The Soviet Union wanted to stir up trouble in the Middle East because this would keep the USA busy while the USSR stamped out opposition elsewhere, as in Hungary in 1956. On the whole superpower intervention prolonged and worsened the problems of the Middle East, but President Carter deserves some credit for persuading the Israelis and the Egyptians to resolve their problems. The Russians don't deserve any credit at all. They merely sold inferior equipment to the Arabs at inflated prices, knowing that the Arabs would always get beaten by the superior American arms and planes which the Israelis had been buying. So, as I said before, the Russians were only interested in causing trouble in the Middle East. They did not really want to see either Israel or its Arab enemies successful; they just wanted to keep the 'Middle East cauldron' on the boil.

Examiner's decision on the student answer

This is lengthy and well-written. But it fails to answer the question. It is full of peripheral material and generalizations, but shows no depth of knowledge about the interrelationship of the superpowers in specific dealings with the various crises in the Middle East. The reference to arms sales and to the Camp David initiative towards the end redeem it somewhat. Even so, it is unlikely to score more than half marks.

SUMMARY

In this chapter you have traced the development of the Arab–Israeli confrontation in Palestine, including:

▷ the settlement at the end of the First World War;

▷ Palestine under the mandate;

▷ the Arab–Israeli Wars, 1948–78;

▷ the problem of the Lebanon;

▷ efforts to reach agreement over the 'occupied areas' of Palestine.

Chapter 20

Race relations in South Africa since 1945

GETTING STARTED

South Africa is the richest and most developed country on the continent of Africa. It is a major supplier of minerals, especially gold, diamonds and uranium. Its main economic weakness is its lack of oil, though with its plentiful supply of coal it is the world's main producer of oil from coal.

In the past, the country has combined white European capital with an abundant supply of cheap black labour to form an advanced economy which is the envy of most African states. It is the relationship between white and black there that has always been the dominant question in South African history, especially since 1945.

MEG	NEAB	NICCEA	SEG	LONDON	WJEC	TOPIC	STUDY	REVISION 1	REVISION 2
✓*	✓*		✓*	✓	✓	**The Nationalist Party in power**			
✓*	✓*		✓*	✓	✓	The growth of the Nationalist Party			
✓*	✓*		✓*	✓	✓	The policy of apartheid			
✓*	✓*		✓*	✓	✓	**Reactions to the policy of apartheid**			
✓*	✓*		✓*	✓	✓	Reactions within South Africa			
✓*	✓*		✓*	✓	✓	External pressures on South Africa			
✓*	✓*		✓*	✓	✓	**The end of apartheid**			
✓*	✓*		✓*	✓	✓	The role of Nelson Mandela			
✓*	✓*		✓*	✓	✓	Steps towards a new government			

* Coursework only

WHAT YOU NEED TO KNOW

The Nationalist Party in power

Political power in South Africa was at first monopolized by people of white European stock who constituted rather less than 20 per cent of the population; the others, of African and Indian origin, had no say at all.

▷ **The growth of the Nationalist Party**

After the Boer War, the two white races of South Africa, the Afrikaaners of Dutch origin and the British, shared power between them. The *Union of South Africa*, set up as a dominion in 1910, was ruled by Louis Botha and Jan Christiaan Smuts, themselves Boers, at the head of the South Africa Party. Dominion status was confirmed by the *Statute of Westminster* (1931) and by the *Status of the Union Act* (1934).

Origins of the Afrikaaner Nationalist Party

The moderate Nationalist Party came to power under James Hertzog in 1924, but made no effort to sever the Commonwealth connection. Neither the South Africa Party nor the moderate Nationalist Party believed in racial equality, but when Hertzog and Smuts joined forces in the United Party in 1933, they were both accused of being 'soft on the Kaffirs'

279

('Kaffirs' was an insulting name for blacks), and a new right-wing group, the Afrikaaner Nationalist Party, was formed by Dr Daniel Malan.

At the start of the Second World War, Hertzog resigned and was replaced as Prime Minister by Smuts, who narrowly carried South Africa into the war on the side of the Allies. He remained in power until 1948.

The idea of racial equality after 1945 seemed threatening to South Africans, and Malan conjured up visions for the voters of the 'black menace', holding out the lifeline of a policy of racial separation (*apartheid*) as a means of preserving white supremacy. On this programme he narrowly won the election.

The Nationalists in office

Malan used every means to build up his support in the South African parliament, pushing through changes such as the addition of new MPs from south-west Africa, all of them his own supporters. He ignored protests from the Natives Representative Council, calling this a 'toy telephone' that no one needed to answer.

By 1953, the Afrikaaner Nationalists had increased their hold on power, continuing to ignore opposition from bodies such as the newly formed Liberal Party. In 1954, Malan retired in favour of Johannes Strijdom, who died in 1958. He was succeeded by Dr Hendrik Verwoerd, who was shot by a supposedly deranged Boer farmer in 1960, but recovered, only to be stabbed to death by another attacker in 1966.

A referendum among white voters in 1960 decided by a narrow majority to leave the Commonwealth, and the country became the independent Republic of South Africa.

Verwoerd's successor was Johannes Vorster, who proceeded to consolidate racial policies, winning a landslide election victory on the issue in 1978. Ill-health forced him to retire in this year, but he went on to become President until his death in 1979. He was followed by P.W. (Pieter Willem) Botha, who was Prime Minister until 1989, when he was succeeded by F.W. (Frederik Willem) de Klerk. Both these last two Premiers attempted a modification of apartheid, though this was resisted by nationalist right-wingers.

▷ **The policy of apartheid**

This proved to be the main policy of the Nationalist Party in the later twentieth century until it was dismantled in the 1990s.

Racial composition of South Africa

Apartheid was based partly on an instinctive white feeling of superiority over the uneducated masses of the Bantu and the Indians, and partly on a wish to build up capital investment in the country and preserve white European control, which was exercised only by a small minority of the population.

Table 20.1 Population of South Africa by race

	1904		1946		1980	
	millions	%	millions	%	millions	%
Asians	0.1	2.6	0.3	2.5	0.8	2.8
Coloureds	0.5	8.4	1.0	8.1	2.6	9.0
Whites	1.1	21.6	2.4	20.8	4.5	15.7
Bantu	3.5	67.4	7.8	68.6	20.6	72.5

The *Asians* had been brought in originally in the colonial days as cheap mining labour or to help construct the railways. They were industrious and later frequently prospered commercially, but they were always denied civil rights and were treated no better than the 'Kaffirs'.

The *Coloureds* were those of mixed race, say with a European father but a native mother. Sometimes racial recategorizations meant that even though these people had originally been regarded as whites, they were liable to be suddenly downgraded.

The *Whites* were the privileged in society, with the most land, the best places to live, the best education and a monopoly of civil rights such as voting.

The *Bantu* were the native African people of the area. Though they were exploited and treated with contempt, they increased in numbers steadily and found conditions in South Africa good enough to want to continue to live there.

Attitudes towards racial segregation in South Africa

White attitudes

White attitudes were a compound of self-confidence and pride in their own achievement together with a determination to preserve what had been built up. They were also parochial attitudes, not much concerned with the approval of the rest of the world. They reflected what is sometimes called the *laager* mentality, dating from nineteenth-century pioneering days, when Boer pioneers found themselves cut off among hostile natives and surrounded themselves with a circle of laagers or wagons.

Originally, it had been hoped that the presence of British settlers among the Boers would transform their views, making them more enlightened; what in fact happened was that the British came to agree with the Boers that firmness, even harshness, with native peoples was the only answer.

There was some selfishness here, too: for example, a European mine employee, apart from having servants and a much pleasanter lifestyle, could often earn in a day what a native worker earned in a month. His success justified his privileges.

His excuse was that he had built up his homeland and brought in capital and know-how; left to native control, the country would soon be in ruins. Such a view was most stoutly defended by extra-parliamentary pressure groups such as the semi-fascist *Afrikaaner Broederbund*, many of whom thought their native opponents were inspired by communism.

Fig. 20.1 'Apartheid is better described as a policy of good neighbourliness' (Dr Verwoerd). This cartoon, which appeared in the *Daily Mirror* on 6 March 1961, is a not-untypical external comment on the system of apartheid.

Native attitudes

Native attitudes recognized the unfairness of apartheid: the European minority had the best jobs, the best salaries, the best houses and the best education, and they buttressed this basic injustice by excluding all but themselves from any share in political power.

They took the view that the actions and attitudes of the Europeans, degrading the natives to be no more than 'hewers of wood and drawers of water', contradicted the basic Christian principles which the Europeans professed.

They also believed that without native labour the whole economic system would collapse; if some were communists, it was because they saw the way the capitalist class was exploiting them as a coloured proletariat.

In the last analysis, apartheid was not even honest, since the real separation of the races would deprive the whites of their factory- and mine-workers and their domestic servants.

Their views were expressed by the *African National Congress* (ANC), founded originally in 1912, a body first established to enfranchise blacks. In 1926, at a conference in Kimberley, it formed a common front with representatives of the Asian community for the same purpose. It was headed by the Natal chieftain Albert Luthuli from 1952 until his death in 1967, but, together with its militant wing *Umkhonto we Sizwe* (Spear of the Nation), was banned by the Nationalist government between 1960 and 1990.

Development of apartheid

There was already evidence of racial discrimination in the country long before it was graced with the new name of apartheid:

(a) The first *Colour Bar Act* went back to 1926 in the interests of protecting the wages and working conditions of the whites. There was also an *Immorality Act* in 1927 forbidding sexual relations between people of different races.

(b) The Boers carried over *pass laws* from the nineteenth century and used them widely between the wars to regulate the movement of natives.

(c) The first curtailment of native voting rights in Cape Colony and Natal – no other provinces had any – which were supposedly safeguarded in the South Africa Act of 1909, came with the *Representation of Natives Act* in 1936, which removed their names from the common electoral roll and gave them only a tiny representation, provided that they elected whites (just three in number!).

(d) The South African judicial system already operated against blacks: there was colour prejudice among magistrates, excessive police powers, brutality and spying, and there were many technical offences for which white men would never go to court.

After 1948, this was elaborated into a system of government:

(a) *1948, Mixed Marriages Act* tried to regulate intermarriage between races (like the earlier immorality laws).

(b) *1950, Population Registration Act* required people to be classified as European, Coloured or Bantu, often with tragic consequences.

(c) *1950 and 1957, Group Areas Acts* provided that ownership and occupation of land should be confined to one racial group in any given area, most of the best land being reserved for Europeans.

(d) *1953, Separate Representation of Voters Act* (1953) removed coloured voters (like natives earlier) from the roll, but allowed them to vote for just four further whites.

(e) *1952, Abolition of Passes Act* abolished the former passes, but substituted for them new 'Reference Books' which controlled the movement and employment of non-whites, recording the owner's racial group. African women were included in these rules after 1961.

(f) *1956, Industrial Conciliation Act* gave the authorities power to reserve jobs for any specified race, and forbade non-whites to enrol in trade unions.

(g) *1960, Suppression of Communism Act* (1950) was tightened up when the ANC was banned, and South Africa was in effect forced out of the Commonwealth in 1961.

These and other laws led to the ruthless segregation of the races in South Africa after 1950:

(a) Jobs were reserved for whites, especially those jobs which carried responsibility.
(b) Africans were forced to live in unhygienic and overcrowded conditions in shanty towns, from where they took buses or trains to work; the best houses and the roomiest suburbs were reserved for whites.
(c) African children were educated separately from whites in inferior schools; their chances of university education were very limited.
(d) There was also *petty apartheid* for Africans: they were treated separately in shops and post offices; they had accommodation reserved for them in buses and trains; they were not allowed to bathe on 'white' beaches, etc.

All this created deep resentment on the part of Africans, and built up world opinion in the Commonwealth and elsewhere against their treatment.

Bantu homelands

Apartheid thinking regards each black tribe as a separate nation with a right to its own culture and homeland. Of these tribes five – Xhosa, Zulu, Sepedi, Tswana and Seshoeshoe – number between 1 and 5 million people, some of them more numerous than the smaller independent African states.

The *Promotion of Self-Government Act* (1959) extended the *Bantu Authorities Act* (1951) by excluding all Africans from the South African parliament on the grounds that they were now to have homelands of their own, and about 13 per cent of the country's area was set aside for the purpose, in spite of the fact that the areas were among the poorest and most eroded areas of the country.

Fig. 20.2 Bantu homelands in South Africa

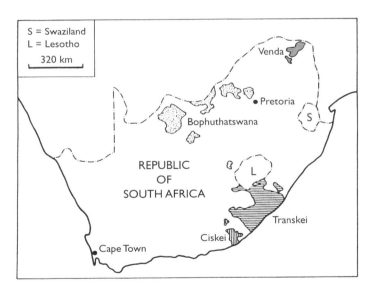

Transkei, the first to be granted independence in 1976 under a traditional leader, Chief Kaiser Matanzima, was home for about 3 million Xhosa.

Bophuthatswana (which is in seven separate pieces), *Venda* and *Ciskei* were also given independence in 1976, though this went unrecognized abroad.

KwaZulu (Natal) was even more fragmented, in over 40 pieces.

All the inhabitants of these places had to have permits to stay and work in South Africa, though efforts were made to set up 'border industries' within commuting distance, especially for Transkei.

Some, like the Zulu, refused to accept independent status; others, in spite of their poverty, made the effort to create genuine multiracial states.

The treatment of Bantu women

It remains very unusual for African women to advance far beyond poverty and ignorance, although a small minority of better-off women is now emerging.

A number managed to accompany their menfolk into the shanty towns, where they kept house and raised their numerous families, but they were often cleared out as these areas were demolished for 'development'.

Those who secured employment generally went into the following occupations:

(a) Domestic service, where, if they had a good 'boss', they might have a decent if not a very secure life. They received little or no protection, however, from Bantu Commissioners who were supposed to safeguard their interests.
(b) Unskilled manufacturing jobs, but here, like their menfolk, they were under Wage Boards and Industrial Councils, their trade unions being illegal and strikes an offence under the criminal law.
(c) Farm work in jobs considered suitable for them, often for wages of about £6 per month. They often preferred to accept the jurisdiction of their employer and spend time in 'farm gaols' rather than go for official trial.

The authorities persisted in regarding the African workforce as 'migrant', and spent as little on it as they could. But urban, domestic and industrial conditions served a useful purpose in breaking down the barriers of tribalism.

Reactions to the policy of apartheid

▷ **Reactions within South Africa**

Resistance organizations

Native organizations struggled to maintain their existence in the middle years of the century:

(a) The *African National Congress* proved powerless against the Nationalist Party. When Chief Luthuli, its leader, tried to organize resistance to apartheid in 1952, he was stripped of his chieftaincy and laws were passed to impose whipping on protesters.
    The ANC adopted a Freedom Charter in 1955, but was finally banned altogether in 1960. Its leader, Nelson Mandela, was gaoled in 1963, and he and his associates Walter Sisulu, Govan Mbedki and five others were given life sentences in 1964.
(b) The *Pan-African Congress* (PAC) was founded in 1958 by Robert Sobukwe on 'Africanist' lines because ANC policies were too moderate. It also agitated against apartheid, and shared the ban imposed in 1960. The society had a more militant wing, maintaining contacts with the African Liberation Committee of the *Organization of African Unity* (OAU), which trained it in methods of terrorism and guerrilla warfare.
(c) There were a number of other smaller allied bodies, such as the *South African Indian Congress*, the *Coloured People's Congress* and the *South African Congress of Trade Unions*.

Resistance efforts

In 1960, several thousand African protesters, organized by the PAC, assembled at *Sharpeville* near Vereeniging to protest against the pass laws. The authorities tried to frighten them by low-flying jets, and eventually the police opened fire, killing 67 protesters and wounding a further 200. There was widespread protest and a state of emergency was proclaimed in South Africa.

In the *Western Deep Levels* in the Transvaal in 1973, eleven miners were shot by police in the course of violent protest against working conditions.

At *Soweto* near Johannesburg in 1976, students demonstrated against a government order that part of their education should be in the Afrikaans language. Arrests and imprisonments followed, including that of Steve Biko, who died in police custody.

In the years following, there were a series of uncoordinated terrorist outrages by extremists against industrial plants and electricity installations.

Support for the campaign from the whites

Father Trevor Huddleston, a missionary worker and a leading campaigner for native rights, was forced to leave his work in Sophiatown in 1956, but continued his campaign from exile in Britain.

South African writer Alan Paton expressed the same theme in his novels such as *Cry, the Beloved Country*. He was also chairman of the South African Liberal Party, disbanded in 1968 when multiracial organizations became illegal.

Mrs Helen Suzman became leader of the Progressive Party, standing for equal voting rights for all peoples. At the 1976 election, she captured 26 parliamentary seats, six of them from the Nationalists.

Limited successes in the struggle

P.W. Botha, who became Prime Minister for the Nationalists in 1978, favoured some relaxation in petty apartheid: for example, some theatres, hotels and sporting events were now to be open to all races. This was as far as he could go at this time because of the fierce resistance of Nationalist right-wingers such as Eugene Terreblanche and his extremist followers.

Under Botha in 1981, the Fifth Constitutional Amendment was passed agreeing to the principle of some non-white participation in government, a decision followed by a referendum in 1983 which agreed on three separate assemblies for Whites, Coloureds and Asians, and an executive president chosen by the whites (see p. 287).

This was partly due to outside pressures on South Africa, but it did not prevent a new state of emergency being proclaimed in 1985.

▷ External pressures on South Africa

The development of protests

In February 1960 the British Prime Minister, Harold Macmillan, visited South Africa and made in Cape Town a speech mentioning the 'wind of change' blowing through Africa which made racist policies ever less welcome. But in condemning apartheid, Macmillan only increased Verwoerd's determination to continue with it.

Apartheid was roundly denounced by Commonwealth countries, especially India and countries in Africa like Ghana. Australia and New Zealand were less critical, as was Malawi under Hastings Banda, who was well aware of his country's economic dependence on South African trade links.

These condemnations helped to force South Africa to resign from the Commonwealth in May 1961 after a plebiscite among white voters. It then became a republic.

South Africa was also condemned by the OAU and by the UN for its continuing occupation of Namibia, originally, as South-West Africa, a mandate under the League, but annexed by South Africa instead of being surrendered to the United Nations in 1945. The OAU, as well as giving support to the PAC and the ANC, supported the African movement for independence in Namibia.

In 1962 the UN severed diplomatic relations with South Africa and imposed an economic boycott, but this was not very effective:

(a) Portugal, with colonies in Angola and Mozambique, had a vested interest in white supremacy, and refused to enforce the boycott.
(b) The Rhodesian Front regime to the north under Ian Smith looked to South Africa for support and encouragement in his bid to extend white supremacy there.
(c) Britain, France and the USA condemned apartheid verbally, but took no further action. They saw that the country was well situated in the fight against world communism, and went on selling arms to it for that reason. They believed it to be economically useful, with its important deposits of gold, diamonds and uranium. They also believed that its apartheid policies would eventually be modified.

The Wilson government in Britain suspended arms sales to South Africa and closed the British base at Simonstown, but this was not enough for some British people, who sabotaged a number of cricket fixtures in Britain and secured South Africa's exclusion from the Olympic Games in 1976.

The question of Namibia

South Africa resisted UN pressure to hand over Namibia after 1945, and fought a long case in the International Court over its possession. The court eventually condemned South Africa in 1971, but South Africa ignored its verdict and would promise no more than 'separate development' for the country in the future.

During the 1970s, the *South-West Africa People's Organization* (SWAPO) took to guerrilla warfare. Ignoring UN objections, South Africa set up a government of whites and black collaborators – the so-called 'Turnhalle Alliance' – and proscribed SWAPO, arresting and deporting its supporters.

After a false start in 1978, peace talks between the interested parties agreed on full independence for Namibia in 1988, and at the elections of 1989 SWAPO emerged as the dominant party.

In 1990 an independence constitution was adopted, and Sam Nujoma was elected President. In 1992, the disputed port of Walvis Bay, previously retained for defence purposes by South Africa, was placed under joint administration.

The war in Angola

In 1975 Portugal announced its willingness to hand over control of its former colony of Angola to a common front of Angolan liberation movements: the Republican Movement for the Liberation of Angola (MPLA), the National Front for the Liberation of Angola (FNLA) and National Front for the Total Independence of Angola (UNITA).

The MPLA secured the backing of the USSR and Cuba – Fidel Castro sent 15,000 troops to the country to enable the New World to bring 'freedom' to the Old – while the FNLA and UNITA secured the backing of the USA and of South Africa; thus international involvement produced a civil war which dragged on until 1979.

The MPLA won in 1979, and its leader, Dr Agostinho Neto, visited Moscow and Havana to thank his allies. Shortly after, however, he died, and UNITA took up a guerrilla campaign again, with South African backing. In 1984 South Africa promised to withdraw its forces if the Luanda government agreed not to accept help from Cuba or the Soviet Union, and in 1985 South Africa did withdraw.

A peace treaty was signed in 1988 agreeing the withdrawal of all foreign troops, but the struggle between the MPLA and UNITA went on into the 1990s, though South Africa was no longer directly involved.

The war in Rhodesia

Ian Smith of the National Front of Rhodesia (formerly a British colony) issued a *Unilateral Declaration of Independence* (UDI) in 1965. For fourteen years he refused to give a share of power to the black majority, though he tried in 1979 to put a puppet government in power under Bishop Abel Muzorewa as Prime Minister.

During this time he relied on South Africa for support and supplies, though his position was steadily getting more difficult. He was condemned by the United Nations, blockaded by Britain and increasingly in conflict with the *Front-Line Presidents* – those of Angola, Botswana, Mozambique, Tanzania and Zambia – who built up guerrilla bases on neighbouring 'neutral' territory and gave military backing to the *Patriotic Front* (an alliance of the *Zimbabwe African People's Union* (ZAPU) under Joshua Nkomo and the *Zimbabwe African National Union* (ZANU) under Robert Mugabe).

The British Prime Minister, Margaret Thatcher, accepted Commonwealth advice and called a conference at Lancaster House in London in 1979, granting independence to the country under the leadership of Mugabe and ZANU, in alliance with Nkomo.

This sent a clear message to South Africa that white minority government could not be expected to continue for ever in view of world opinion, and this made P.W. Botha and his successor in 1989, F.W. de Klerk, more inclined to be reasonable.

The end of apartheid

▷ **The role of Nelson Mandela**

Earlier career

Nelson Mandela was born in Umtata, Transkei, in 1918, and educated at mission schools before going to university at Fort Hare, from which he was expelled for his part in a student strike in 1940.

He worked as a clerk in a legal firm in Johannesburg, and studied law externally at Witwatersrand University before going into partnership with Oliver Tambo, with whom he set up a joint legal practice in 1952.

He joined the ANC in his early days, but was subject to a banning order, 1953–58, which prevented him from holding office or taking part in its activities. Mandela was arrested and sentenced to life imprisonment in the Rivonia Sabotage Trial, 1963, and imprisoned on Robben Island in 1964. He was later transferred to Pollsmoor Prison, Cape Town, in 1982.

Emerging importance

Mandela held various offices in the ANC, founding the *National Youth League*, of which he became National Secretary in 1950, and being co-founder and leader of the military wing *Umkhonto we Sizwe* in 1961, among other offices. Nevertheless he came to be even more important after his imprisonment in 1963 than before.

He was showered with international awards and honorary degrees while in prison, and was frequently honoured by left-wing councils in Britain who named play parks and tower blocks after him.

Released by President de Klerk in 1990, when the ban on the ANC was lifted, he became President of the ANC in 1991. In 1992 Mandela and President de Klerk agreed on the formation of an interim government under which reforms could take place in the direction of a multiracial South Africa.

He was married to the civil rights activist Winnie Mandela from 1955 to 1992.

▷ **Steps towards a new government**

The first efforts to reform apartheid came in 1984 when a new constitution extended the franchise to the coloured and Indian populations. Coloured and Indian voters elected members to a three-house parliament, adding to the already existing white parliament. However, whites still held the whip hand and the majority of over 75 per cent blacks were still excluded.

The work of CODESA

In 1989, F.W. de Klerk became President of South Africa and began the reform process. He relaxed restrictions on the ANC and released Mandela. In 1991 most of the laws implementing apartheid were abolished, and in 1992 a referendum among the whites approved of continuing reform measures by a majority of nearly 70 per cent.

Negotiations led to the opening in December 1991 in Johannesburg of the *Convention on a Democratic South Africa* (CODESA) between the government, the ANC under its President Nelson Mandela, and the *Inkatha Freedom Party*, which spoke for the Zulu community. After disturbances by PAC supporters, white extremists and ill-disciplined police, the ANC withdrew in June 1992, but violence escalated, culminating in a massacre at Bisho (Ciskei) in September 1992.

Talks were resumed with the ANC, and in February 1993 agreement was reached on setting up an interim multiracial administration, and on the formation of a five-year coalition government after multiracial elections.

In June 1993 a *Transitional Executive Council* (TEC) was set up, but neither the government nor the ANC would concede any real degree of regional autonomy, and the TEC and the interim constitution agreed in November were boycotted by the powerful *Freedom Alliance* (FA), composed of Inkatha, various homeland governments such as Ciskei and Boputhatswana, and even various small right-wing Boer organizations.

The strength and authority shown by Mandela averted the chance of civil war, although some elements, such as Inkatha, remained unhappy with the final arrangements because they had not played a part in making them.

The 1994 constitution

This provides for an executive *President*, elected by parliament, and Deputy Presidents, each one nominated by parties gaining at least 20 per cent of votes cast. There is a *Constitutional Court*, similar to the US Supreme Court and with similar powers to test the validity of legislation, and a two-chamber parliament:

(a) A *National Assembly* of 400 members directly elected for five years, 200 from national lists and 200 from provincial lists in an agreed proportion. Any party getting 5 per cent of the votes cast is entitled to a seat in the cabinet. Nine provincial parliaments are to be elected at the same time.

(b) A *Senate* of 90 members (10 from each province), indirectly elected by provincial parliaments on a system of proportional representation.

Laws may be introduced into either House, but must be passed by both to become law. If rejected, they must be referred to a joint committee of both Houses and then submitted again.

The ANC comes to power

Parliamentary elections were held on 26–29 April 1994 throughout South Africa; the electorate was 23 million and the turnout was 86 per cent. On 2 May, with fewer than half the votes counted, de Klerk conceded defeat.

Table 20.2 Election results, April 1994

Party	Votes (million)	% vote	Assembly seats
African National Congress	12.25	62.6	252
Nationalists	4.0	20.4	82
Inkatha	2.1	10.5	43
Pan-African Congress	0.25	1.2	5
Other parties	1.0	5.3	18
Spoilt papers	0.2	–	–
Total	19.8	100.0	400

At the same time, in the Senate, the ANC was awarded 60 seats, there were 17 Nationalists and 5 Inkatha, and the rest came from the small parties.

An independent commission received large numbers of allegations of fraud, especially on the part of Inkatha, but complaints were not pursued too far because of the threat to public order.

On 9 May, Nelson Mandela was elected as President, and he was installed on 10 May. The new President opened parliament on 24 May, outlining his party's plans. He aimed to reduce the government deficit without any increase in general taxation, and promised improved conditions for African people: 300,000 houses were to be built each year for five years, electricity was to be supplied to 2.5 million people by the year 2000, 30 per cent of farmland was to be transferred back to Africans, and ten years' free education were promised to African youngsters.

Shortly afterwards, South Africa was readmitted to the Commonwealth.

GLOSSARY

Economic boycott An economic sanction used against countries which in some way have fallen foul of the international community of nations. It generally means the barring of the offending country from international trade. Thus countries guilty of aggression against their neighbours, or of encouraging international terrorism, have been subjected to economic boycott. In South Africa's case it was universal detestation of apartheid which led to a worldwide trade ban. Usually some trade goods are exempt for humanitarian reasons, e.g. medicines. But an economic boycott is difficult to enforce, and it often causes severe hardship to the offending country's neighbours. Thus the economies of several of South Africa's neighbours depended so heavily upon South Africa's prosperity that they continued to trade with South Africa in defiance of world opinion.

Executive president   Most presidents, like constitutional monarchs, are little more than figureheads. A few countries, such as the USA, have an executive president, i.e. one who is head of the executive (the government). When countries have changed their constitutions in recent times, they have often replaced a ceremonial president by an executive one (e.g. France and Russia). And so did South Africa by its new constitution of 1994. An executive president, therefore, acts as head of the government, and is assisted by subordinate ministers whom he or she can usually appoint or dismiss at will.

Plebiscite/referendum   Both a plebiscite and a referendum mean the referring of some important decision to a vote of the people. The two words are often used interchangeably, but the plebiscite is more often concerned with the maintenance or transfer of political power, and the referendum with a decision on some important political issue. Thus dictators often confirm themselves in power by plebiscites, and plebiscites to decide sovereignty are often held in disputed territories. A referendum is often required in Switzerland when a new law is under consideration, and one was held in Britain in 1975 to decide whether Britain should remain in the EEC.

State of emergency   When civil disturbance gets out of control and governments cannot control it by ordinary force of law, governments often resort to a state of emergency. This usually means that normal civil liberties are suspended, that people may be imprisoned indefinitely without trial, and that areas, or even the whole country, may be placed under the direct control of the military, with ordinary law suspended and military (i.e. martial) law enforced.

▷ EXAMINATION QUESTIONS

▷ **Question 1**   (a) What arguments were used by its supporters to justify apartheid?   (10 marks)
(b) Did **all** whites support apartheid?   (8 marks)
(c) Why was apartheid eventually abandoned?   (12 marks)

▷ **Question 2**   Study the British newspaper cartoon on page 281, and then use your own knowledge to explain the content and purpose of the cartoon.   (10 marks)

▷ EXAMINATION ANSWERS

▷ **Question 1(a)**   *Outline answer*

The main argument was that of racial superiority, supported by the Dutch Reformed Church, and the fear that white supremacy would be swamped if the majority native peoples were enfranchised. The economic argument contended that the whites provided the educated and moneyed sections of the community, and that the future prosperity of the country demanded that political control stayed in the hands of the whites. As whites were generally much better paid than blacks, apartheid seemed the only way to preserve the financial privileges of the whites. Some attempt was made to suggest that separate development would benefit the native population, its languages, customs and way of life. The fear that South Africa's prosperity was under threat was supported by the assertion that the political leaders of the native population were communist in sympathy. Overall the arguments were simply and nakedly for the preservation of white political and economic supremacy.

▷ **Question 1(b)**   *Outline answer*

In the 1950s and 1960s, the Nationalist Party won landslide elections, but that does not mean that apartheid had universal white backing. The United Party still won a number of seats, and while it supported white supremacy it opposed the more repugnant features of apartheid. But there were individual whites who opposed apartheid for religious reasons (e.g. Trevor Huddleston) or for general humanitarian reasons. Some saw the end of white supremacy as inevitable and feared that apartheid would make the transition more bitter than it need be. Liberals such as Helen Suzman had enough following to win several seats in the white parliament. Intellectuals and writers voiced their objections, often in enforced exile. But it is true that fear and a hostile world united most Afrikaans and English-speaking South Africans in support of apartheid, and its white opponents remained a small but significant minority.

▷ **Question 1(c)**   *Tutor answer*

Apartheid did not end because the Nationalist Party recognized its systematic racialism and injustice. It ended because to continue it would bring about the very chaos and economic collapse that the supporters of apartheid so much feared. In the first place, the native populations refused to accept meekly the lot allocated to them by apartheid. The African National Congress (ANC) was banned, but fought on. Its dislike for violence contrasted with the government's use of it at Sharpeville and elsewhere, but in the end the ANC found a powerful weapon in economic sabotage – the attacks on petrol depots, power lines and railways. Repeated states of emergency and continued violence created a longing for peace and compromise, so that many of apartheid's most hardened supporters began to have doubts about its permanence. The show-cases of apartheid, the Bantustans, were widely recognized, even in South Africa, as mere window dressing.

At first, world opinion was ignored as white South Africans took refuge in their 'laager mentality' and tried to become self-sufficient. But one by one South Africa's dependent neighbours took independent paths: Rhodesia turned from white ally to black enemy, Mozambique succumbed to the communists, and Namibia became an expensive burden. It became much more difficult for South Africa to import much needed goods through its extensive land frontiers. South Africa might tolerate its exclusion from Commonwealth and Olympic Games, and from virtually all international sport, but voluntary boycotts of South African goods and trade embargoes were more threatening. These were having a serious effect on the South African economy by the end of the 1980s, and UN efforts to tighten these sanctions threatenened the stability of the currency and accelerated the number of bankruptcies and unemployed. At first the Nationalist government under Botha hoped to deflect world sanctions by tinkering with apartheid. But this merely encouraged its opponents both inside and outside South Africa to step up the pressure to win more concessions. And once the government had set out on the road to change, it became impossible to turn back and the only way was forward.

▷ **Question 2**   *Student answer with examiner's comments*

'It gives a bad impression to misspell names taken from the question!'

'The opening description of the cartoon is not really necessary.'

'It also probably reflects a considerable body of British public opinion.'

The cartoon shows the South African Prime Minister, Dr Verword, sitting comfortably in a deck chair surrounded by apples which had come from a tree grown by the two black South Africans. They live in a shanty hut with corrugated roof, while Verwerd looks contented and well fed. The apples represent the riches of South Africa and the cartoon suggests that the blacks are not getting their fair share of the wealth that they largely produce. It was certainly true that the standard of living of the blacks at this time was way below that of the whites. The cartoon is making a sarcastic comment about the apartheid policy of 'good neighbourliness'. Is it good neighbourliness for the whites to exploit their black neighbours as is suggested here? So the cartoon shows that apartheid is nothing more than economic exploitation. The purpose of the cartoon is to influence British public opinion against the apartheid policies of South Africa.

Examiner's decision on the student answer

Quite a good answer, but you could have used your own knowledge to back up the cartoonist's intent with the specific situation in 1961, with South Africa about to declare a republic and leave the Commonwealth. The British newspaper could well have wanted to extinguish any sympathy for South Africa in these circumstances. You might have noticed the uniform and the gun; their prominence makes the cartoon even more hostile.

SUMMARY

In this chapter you have studied the following topics:

▷ the Nationalist Party and the nature of its rule;

▷ attitudes of the South African peoples towards apartheid;

▷ the establishment, practice and development of apartheid in South Africa;

▷ Commonwealth and world reactions to apartheid;

▷ the modification and ending of apartheid;

▷ the roles of de Klerk and Mandela;

▷ the establishment of the new South African government in 1994.

Comparisons may usefully be drawn between racial policies in South Africa and those in the United States previously explained in chapter 14.

INDEX

Daily Book Cutting Log

datamation

Name: __Mariangel__   Date: __08/11/25__

BIN #	BOOKS COMPLETED	BIN #	BOOKS COMPLETED
Bin 1	50	Bin 41	
Bin 2	50	Bin 42	
Bin 3	30	Bin 43	
Bin 4	22	Bin 44	
Bin 5	25	Bin 45	
Bin 6	22	Bin 46	
Bin 7	22	Bin 47	
Bin 8	23	Bin 48	
Bin 9	22	Bin 49	
Bin 10	25	Bin 50	
Bin 11	25	Bin 51	
Bin 12	21	Bin 52	
Bin 13	21	Bin 53	
Bin 14	20	Bin 54	
Bin 15	20	Bin 55	
Bin 16	20	Bin 56	
Bin 17	33	Bin 57	
Bin 18	20	Bin 58	
Bin 19	28	Bin 59	
Bin 20	20	Bin 60	
Bin 21	22	Bin 61	
Bin 22	25	Bin 62	
Bin 23		Bin 63	
Bin 24		Bin 64	
Bin 25		Bin 65	
Bin 26		Bin 66	
Bin 27		Bin 67	
Bin 28		Bin 68	
Bin 29		Bin 69	
Bin 30		Bin 70	
Bin 31		Bin 71	
Bin 32		Bin 72	
Bin 33		Bin 73	
Bin 34		Bin 74	
Bin 35		Bin 75	
Bin 36		Bin 76	
Bin 37		Bin 77	
Bin 38		Bin 78	
Bin 39		Bin 79	
Bin 40		Bin 80	

TOTAL: _____ / 600

SHIFT: _____   STATION #: _____